Ashley,

With appreciation and best wishes!

Jere Merchuel
President, USA
November 4, 2019

Seeking Eden

SEEKING EDEN

A Collection of Georgia's Historic Gardens

STACI L. CATRON AND MARY ANN EADDY

PHOTOGRAPHY BY JAMES R. LOCKHART

The University of Georgia Press *Athens*

Designed by Erin Kirk New
Set in Adobe Caslon Pro
Printed and bound by Pacom
The paper in this book meets the guidelines for
permanence and durability of the Committee on
Production Guidelines for Book Longevity of the
Council on Library Resources.

Most University of Georgia Press titles are
available from popular e-book vendors.

Printed in Korea

22 21 20 19 18 C 5 4 3 2 1

Library of Congress Cataloging-in-Publication Data
Names: Catron-Sullivan, Staci, author. | Eaddy, Mary Ann, author.
Title: Seeking Eden : a collection of Georgia's historic gardens / Staci L. Catron
    and Mary Ann Eaddy ; photography by James R. Lockhart.
Description: Athens, Georgia : University of Georgia Press, [2018] | Includes
    bibliographical references and index.
Identifiers: LCCN 2017037409 | ISBN 9780820353005 (hardcover : alk. paper)
Subjects: LCSH: Historic gardens—Georgia.
Classification: LCC SB466.U62 G42 2018 | DDC 635.09758—dc23 LC record available
    at https://lccn.loc.gov/2017037409

page ii: Columns, urns, and a stone eagle, slightly raised on a terraced stage in the formal boxwood garden, Swan House

page vi: Walkway leading to the demonstration garden, Bulloch Hall

page viii: Lush tropical plants filling the atrium, Millpond Plantation

page x: Meadow with a stone lantern, Ashland Farm

page xvi: View of the cutwork and spring bloom, Battersby-Hartridge Garden

Publication of this book was supported in part by the following organizations:

THE MILDRED FORT FOUNDATION

For Mabel R. Milner and Lee C. Dunn,

and in memory of James R. Cothran and Brencie Werner

CONTENTS

ACKNOWLEDGMENTS

The genesis of this book was twofold: *Garden History of Georgia, 1733–1933*, published by the Peachtree Garden Club of Atlanta in 1933, and the Georgia Historic Landscape Initiative, established by the Garden Club of Georgia, Inc., in 2002 in collaboration with the Cherokee Garden Library of the Atlanta History Center, the Historic Preservation Division of the Georgia Department of Natural Resources, and the National Park Service–Southeast Regional Office. The Georgia Historic Landscape Initiative identifies, records, and promotes the state's garden heritage. Using *Garden History of Georgia, 1733–1933* as its foundation, the initiative set a goal of determining which gardens featured in the publication remain more or less the same, which have been changed, and which are lost. *Seeking Eden: A Collection of Georgia's Historic Gardens* chronicles each of those gardens.

The writing of this book would not have been possible without the encouragement, support, and contributions of many people who have a passion for and commitment to our state's rich garden heritage.

We extend our deepest gratitude to Mabel Milner and Lee Dunn of the Garden Club of Georgia for their support of this project, their encouragement, and their lifelong dedication to Georgia's historic gardens and their preservation. We also thank the Georgia Chapter of the American Society of Landscape Architects, the Georgia Department of Economic Development, and the Mildred Fort Foundation for their financial support of this volume. Our appreciation extends to the Garden Club of Georgia and its members for approving and supporting this project. We are grateful to Caroline Silcox (president, 2011–13), Suzanne Wheeler (president, 2013–15), Martha Price (president, 2015–17), Jane Hersey (president, 2017–19), and the members of the GCG Historic Preservation of Gardens and Sites Committee (now known as the Historic Landscape Preservation Advisory Committee), past and present.

We acknowledge with deep gratitude the founding members of the GCG Historic Landscape Initiative Committee: garden club representatives Mabel Milner, Brencie Werner, and Lee Dunn; James R. Cothran, FASLA, planner and garden historian; and Susan Hitchcock, historical landscape architect for the National Park Service–Southeast Regional Office. We were privileged to be among the founding members of this committee, Staci serving as the representative for the Cherokee Garden Library, a Library of the Kenan Research Center at the Atlanta History Center, and Mary Ann as the representative of the Historic Preservation Division of the Georgia Department of Natural Resources.

We extend our thanks to the Peachtree Garden Club of Atlanta for approving the use of the original photographs and drawings published in *Garden History of Georgia, 1733–1933* and for supporting this project.

We extend our gratitude to the Atlanta History Center for its support. For their unwavering support, we are particularly grateful to Sheffield Hale, the center's president and CEO; Michael Rose, executive vice president; the Goizueta Gardens staff; and the Kenan Research Center staff. A special thank-you goes to Jennie Oldfield, Cherokee Garden Library cataloguer and archivist, for her excellent copyediting of many components of the book and her assistance with research.

We also thank the members of the Cherokee Garden Library Advisory Board for their belief in our efforts. For their encouragement, special thanks go to Libby Prickett, Cherokee Garden Library Board president, 2011–2013; Claire Schwahn, Cherokee Garden Library Board president, 2013–15; Kinsey Harper, Cherokee Garden Library Board president, 2015–17; and Jane Whitaker, Cherokee Garden Library Advisory Board chair 2017–19. We also extend our thanks to the Cherokee Garden Club for supporting this project.

This project would not have been possible without the following people, who opened their gardens to us and shared their knowledge about their gardens' histories: Diana and Craig Barrow; Jennifer and Roger Bigham of Dunaway Gardens Foundation, Inc.; Michelle and Will Goodman; Cornelia McIntire Hartridge; Mary and Bill Land; Mary and Bob Norton; Kathy and Bryan Patten; Irene Briedis, Ellery Sedgwick, Tod Sedgwick, and Walter Sedgwick; Barbara and Charles Slick; and Karon and Don Williamson. We also thank Mike Crozier, property manager for Millpond Plantation.

We thank the following institutions, agencies, companies, their staffs, other scholars, and community volunteers for sharing their knowledge about the sites included in this book:

- Andrew Low House, Savannah: Stephen Bohlin, director, and The National Society of The Colonial Dames of America in the State of Georgia
- Barnsley Resort, Adairsville: Sandy Sanders, site horticulturist, and Clent Coker, Barnsley historian and museum curator
- Barrington Hall, Roswell: Robert Winebarger, historic site coordinator, and Janet S. Rigsby, site horticulturist
- Beech Haven, Athens: Andrew Saunders, environmental coordinator, Unified Government of Athens–Clarke County; Helen Kuykendall; Nat Kuykendall; Alice Rowland; and Lucy Minogue Rowland

- Berry College, Mount Berry: Timothy D. Brown, former director, Oak Hill and the Martha Berry Museum
- Bradley Olmsted Garden, Columbus Museum: Rebecca Bush, curator of history, and Kristin Miller Zohn, director of collections and exhibitions
- Bulloch Hall, Roswell: Pam Billingsley, historic site coordinator; Gwen Koehler, education director; and Connie Huddleston
- Cator Woolford Gardens, Frazer Center, Atlanta: Kimberly Hays de Muga, director of development; Paige Kubik, executive director; Mary Norwood, former board member; Cooper Sanchez, consulting gardener; and Cator Sparks, family historian
- Coffin-Reynolds Mansion, Sapelo Island: James Maund, manager, Reynolds Mansion; Merryl Alber, director, University of Georgia Marine Institute on Sapelo Island; Beth Richardson, Friends of the University of Georgia Marine Institute; June Thomas, Odum Garden Club
- Dunaway Gardens, near Newnan: Josh Bigham, director of operations
- Governor's Mansion, Atlanta: Joy Forth, director, and Kirk Talgo, grounds manager
- Hills and Dales Estate, LaGrange: Carleton B. Wood, executive director, and Jo Phillips, horticultural manager
- Lullwater Conservation Garden, Atlanta: Kim Storbeck, Jennifer J. Richardson, and Darlene Mashman, past presidents of the Lullwater Garden Club
- Rock City Garden, Lookout Mountain: George Schimpf, retired director of horticulture for See Rock City, Inc.
- Swan House, Atlanta History Center: Michael Rose, executive vice president; Don Rooney, director of exhibitions; Sarah Roberts, vice president of Goizueta Gardens and Living Collections; Jessica VanLanduyt, director of 20th Century Historic Houses; and Valerie VanSweden, curator of Goizueta Gardens
- University of Georgia North Campus, President's House and Garden, and Founders Memorial Garden, Athens: Janine L. Duncan, preservation planner; Brett Ganas, RLA, director,

Grounds Department, Facilities Management Division; David B. Nichols, associate professor and director of Founders Memorial Garden, College of Environment and Design; Maureen O'Brien, horticulturist and manager of Founders Memorial Garden, College of Environment and Design; and Anne M. Thompson, administrative specialist, Office of the President
- Wormsloe and Wormsloe State Historic Site, near Savannah: Sarah Ross, director, Center for Research and Education, University of Georgia, and the staff of the Wormsloe State Historic Site

A broad range of archival repositories were used in the creation of this book, and we are grateful to the knowledgeable staffs of these institutions for their assistance.

Thank you to the following Cherokee Garden Library research fellows, garden club members, graduate students, master gardeners, and other volunteers of the Georgia Historic Landscape Initiative for completing the surveys from which we gleaned significant information for the chapters in this book: Winette Almon, Janet Barrickman, Jean Berry, Jennifer Rae Bigham, Rebecca Born, Jennifer Britton, Kathrine S. Clark, Janet Coleman, Erica Danylchak, Nancy S. Gadberry, Will Goodman, Monica D. Hayden, Paula Henderson, Michelle Hendrickson, Susan L. Hitchcock, Carolyn A. Humphries, Molly McLamb, Nicole Mullen, Mary and Bob Norton, Kathleen Posey, Jennifer J. Richardson, Tod Segwick, Dee Smith, and Caroline Turlington.

An essay regarding Millpond Plantation (the Jeptha Homer Wade estate), written by Staci L. Catron, appears in the volume *Warren H. Manning: Landscape Architect and Environmental Planner* (2017), edited by Robin Karson, Jane Roy Brown, and Sarah Allaback. Thank you to the staff of the Library of American Landscape History and the University of Georgia Press for allowing portions of this research to appear in both publications.

We extend our gratitude to the following people for sharing their expertise and time: Edward L. Daugherty, FASLA; Kenneth H. Thomas Jr., historian; Susan L. Hitchcock, historical landscape architect; Andrew D. Kohr, ASLA; William T. Smith, ASLA; Lynn Speno, National Register specialist, Historic Preservation Division of the Georgia Department of Natural Resources; Julie Groce, preservationist; Spencer Tunnell II, ASLA, of Tunnell & Tunnell Landscape Architecture; Sara L. Van Beck, author and scholar; Holly Witchey, Ph.D., adjunct professor and director of the Wade Project, Western Reserve Historical Society; Cari L. Goetcheus, associate professor and director of the Cultural Landscape Laboratory, College of Environment and Design, University of Georgia; Elaine DeNiro, archivist, Roswell Historical Society / City of Roswell Research Library and Archives; Michael W. Miller, AIA; Ced Dolder, preservationist; Mary Lee Lockhart; Melanie White, Media Center director, First Baptist Church Decatur; Barbara Linder, English teacher and editor; and Sharon Maier, attorney.

The project would have been untenable without the extraordinary efforts of our developmental editor, Jennifer Yankopolus. Throughout the long and sometimes overwhelming process of creating this book, she remained an invaluable anchor, guiding us with wisdom, skill, and grace.

We extend our thanks to the knowledgeable and dedicated staff of the University of Georgia Press.

We owe our families and friends much gratitude for their steadfast support and encouragement. Thank you for still loving us even though we were frequently absent during the two years spent writing this book and for understanding our obsession with this project. Special thanks go to Gladys Hite, Dorothy Aiken, Mary Ann Williams, and Lynn Cothran. Thank you to Anne Catron, Sara Catron Cox, Erica Danylchak, the late Ryan Gainey, Louise Gunn, Elissa Gydish, Randy Jones, Fred Mobley, Carter Morris, Gloria Palmer, Jimmy Roberson, and Angie Tacker for their steadfast support and encouragement. Finally, to Carol Lee Eaddy, who was with us from the beginning, read our draft chapters, and lifted our spirits. Your grace, kindness, and unfaltering faith in us made this journey far less difficult.

Countless people have helped us throughout this project. If we have inadvertently failed to include anyone, please know that it was an unintentional omission. We are deeply grateful for everyone's support and assistance.

Seeking Eden

Introduction

IN GARDENS, nature, art, and beauty converge. Countless poets and writers have extolled their value for centuries. In *Utopia*, Thomas More writes, "The many great gardens of the world, of literature and poetry, of painting and music, of religion and architecture, all make the point as clear as possible: The soul cannot thrive in the absence of a garden." In the hurried, crowded, changing, concrete-coated twenty-first century, gardens remain essential. Gardens nourish us aesthetically, intellectually, and spiritually, and historic gardens provide a direct link with the past, helping us understand who we are today.

Georgia has a rich gardening history, from its colonial origins in Savannah and the coast in the early eighteenth century to the eclectic styles found in its burgeoning cities of the early twentieth century. The state's garden history is as vast as the state itself, from Savannah and the sea islands to the fall-line cities of Augusta on the Savannah River and Columbus on the Chattahoochee, and from the Red Hills region of southwestern Georgia to the foothills of northern Georgia. The stories of gardens past are captivating and inspiring, lending insight into their creators and the diversity of their histories. They are also vital to the state's heritage, essential not only for understanding Georgia's past but also for contributing to the health of its communities today.

One facet in the journey of understanding Georgia's complex history is the study and appreciation of our state's cultural landscapes, which can range from thousands of acres of agricultural land to an ornamental garden on a half-acre residential lot. The National Park Service defines a cultural landscape as "a geographic area, including both cultural and natural resources and the wildlife or domestic animals therein, associated with a historic event, activity, or person or exhibiting other cultural or

To have a small share in recording the gardens that were, and are, and will be, has been a pleasure, and this volume, a Georgia product, is dedicated to gardeners of all climes, with the hope of a wider appreciation of Georgia gardens.
—Loraine Meeks Cooney,
Garden History of Georgia, 1733–1933

aesthetic values."[1] Regarding the value of cultural landscapes, the Cultural Landscape Foundation notes, "Cultural landscapes are a legacy for everyone. These special sites reveal aspects of our country's origins and development as well as our evolving relationships with the natural world. They provide scenic, economic, ecological, social, recreational, and educational opportunities helping communities to better understand themselves."[2] The National Park Service identifies four general types of cultural landscapes: historic sites, historic vernacular landscapes, ethnographic landscapes, and historic designed landscapes. Within the last category, the breadth is broad, including parks, cemeteries, battlefields, campuses, estates, scenic highways, residential gardens, rural communities, and more. A historic designed landscape is one that was intentionally created by a landscape architect, architect, horticulturist, or amateur gardener in keeping with design principles. The historical importance of a historic designed landscape is based on its association with an important person or persons, trend, or event in landscape architecture. Its significance may also exemplify a pivotal development in the theory and practice of landscape architecture.[3] *Seeking Eden: A Collection of Georgia's Historic Gardens* is focused on historic designed landscapes in Georgia.

An in-depth history of gardening and garden design in Georgia has yet to be written, but a brief overview of the topic is essential to the understanding of the chapters ahead. In recent decades, we have been fortunate to have the benefit of scholarship by James R. Cothran, Susan L. Hitchcock, Catherine M. Howett, Jeff Lewis, William R. Mitchell, Richard Westmacott, and others regarding our state's garden history. Yet many aspects of Georgia's landscapes have yet to be explored. One of the challenges is that the history of garden styles, unlike architectural styles, transcends strict definitions; landscape styles were often slow to change and often merged into one another. Gardens are also much more fluid than buildings, constantly changing through the seasons and evolving with the life cycles of plants. This fluidity often makes the study and preservation of gardens difficult, which partially explains why Georgia's gardens have been studied less than its architecture.

Georgia was the last of the original thirteen colonies to be settled. The colonial period in Georgia essentially began with James Oglethorpe's town plan for Savannah. Started in 1733 and completed in the mid-nineteenth century, this seminal colonial town plan contained twenty-four wards with an open square at the center of each, surrounded by four trust blocks for public and religious buildings and four tithing blocks, each subdivided into ten residential building lots. The new colonists strove to control nature by carving out a formal system in a world they viewed as wild and untamed. Oglethorpe and the new colonists quickly established the Trustees' Garden, a ten-acre experimental garden to determine what kinds of plants might be grown commercially in Georgia. Although the primary purpose of the garden was scientific, it was also designed to be beautiful, its walks lined with orange trees and organized beds filled with fruit trees, herbs, and vegetables.[4] The Trustees engaged several plant explorers to investigate the flora in parts of Mexico, Central America, and the West Indies for specimens that might be commercially viable in the new colony.[5] Some of these plants were sent to England to be tested by Philip Miller, the head gardener of the Chelsea Physic Garden in London and author of the influential work *The Gardeners Dictionary*, first published in 1733.

Before Georgia's founding, the English had expressed great interest in the area's natural history. From 1722 to 1725, England sponsored the botanist and illustrator Mark Catesby to explore the Lowcountry of South Carolina, then referred to as "Carolina." His journey included areas that later became part of Georgia. Catesby shipped collections of seeds and dried plants to England, resulting in the introduction of several native American species to gardens there and beyond.[6] In 1765, John Bartram of Philadelphia was appointed the king's botanist in North America. From July 1765 to April 1766, he and his son, William, explored the newly acquired colony of East Florida, which led them on a journey through parts of the Carolinas and Georgia. John's published diary of this adventure provided a glimpse of the flora of coastal Georgia. William Bartram, a naturalist and artist, made an epic trek through the American Southeast from 1773 to 1777. An account of his trip, published in 1791 as *Travels through North and South Carolina, Georgia, East and West Florida*, became one of the most significant works on the area's plants, animals, and people, including those in colonial Georgia.

From the founding of the colony until the American Revolution, Georgians molded the landscape by establishing towns such as Brunswick, Darien, Ebenezer, Hardwick, and Wrightsborough. As in Savannah, gardens for sustenance and beauty were an integral part of town design. Agriculture has played a vital role in Georgia's economy for over 250 years.[7] Colonists learned agricultural practices from the Native Americans and successfully cultivated corn for export to England. They experimented with other field crops, finding rice and indigo to be most profitable. Other early enterprises included the production of silk and wine.[8] From the Revolutionary War to the early antebellum period, more towns were founded, including Augusta, Columbus, Macon, and Milledgeville. They generally followed a grid plan containing a central square with broad avenues and land set aside for parks, public buildings, and cemeteries.[9] Tobacco and cotton were the major crops, and cotton quickly became the state's primary commodity.[10] In the 1820s and 1830s, the removal of the Cherokee and a series of land lotteries ushered settlers into western and northern Georgia, further expanding the development of towns and agriculture.

From 1733 to 1820, designed ornamental gardens followed the age-old practice of creating parterres, decorative geometric patterns using boxwood, dwarf yaupon, or low-growing herbs as edging material. Private pleasure gardens in Savannah and other colonial towns generally contained symmetrical plans, which were simplified versions of seventeenth- and eighteenth-century formal designs from Continental Europe. These early Georgia gardens were frequently surrounded by picket fences or enclosed by walls made of brick or tabby, and the formal beds were subdivided by prominent walkways made of crushed oyster shells, packed soil or sand, or brick. The parterres were planted with flowers and ornamental plants, bulbs, and herbs—specimens from Europe mixed in with native flora from nearby forests.[11]

From 1820 to 1860, Georgians, like other southerners, primarily retained the formality and geometry of the garden designs that had prevailed in the colonial era. These plans complemented the formality of the Greek Revival and Federal-style architecture popular among the planter aristocracy. Frequently laid out in front of the main residence in order to be viewed from the second floor or veranda, and enclosed by fences or walls, these formal patterned gardens constituted one component of a town or larger plantation landscape.

Outbuildings like the kitchen, dairy, smokehouse, and well were constructed near the owner's residence to create a work yard. There, domestic slaves performed most of their household duties: preparing and preserving food, cooking, and washing dishes and clothing. In both town and rural settings, the work yard was generally placed behind the main house; kitchen gardens for fruits, vegetables, and herbs were frequently nearby. Surviving antebellum examples include the "sun and moon" parterre garden and work yard of Valley View, near Cartersville; the cutwork parterre garden at the Battersby-Hartridge Garden, in Savannah; and the double parterre garden at Kolb-Pou-Newton Place, known as Boxwood, in Madison. Garden design in Georgia was influenced to a much lesser degree by the naturalistic style of gardening prominent in Europe during the period and advocated in North America by the New York horticulturist and tastemaker Andrew Jackson Downing. One example in Georgia is the landscape developed by Godfrey Barnsley in Adairsville, from the 1840s to the 1860s, based on the picturesque ideals championed by Downing. Historic designed gardens in antebellum Georgia rarely contained grass or lawns; clay or swept yards were the main component of the work yard.

The variety of ornamental plants grown in Georgia's gardens increased because of the establishment of nurseries such as Fruitland, in Augusta, in the 1850s. The distinguished horticulturist Louis Edouard Mathieu Berckmans and his son, Prosper Jules Alphonse, moved to Augusta to run a nursery on a property known as Pearmont, which they purchased in 1857. The following year, they purchased the adjacent Fruitland Nursery from the horticulturist Dennis Redmond. The Berckmans combined the two operations under the Fruitland Nurseries name. One of the first commercial nurseries in the South, Fruitland was a world-class experimental station and botanical garden, growing numerous varieties of fruit trees and ornamentals and disseminating them throughout the United States and abroad.

In 1931 the property on which Fruitland Nurseries was located was sold; it later became the site of the Augusta National Golf Club, the home of the Masters Golf Tournament. Other important horticulturists in antebellum Georgia included Stephen Elliott, the first bishop of the Episcopal Church in Georgia; Joseph and John LeConte of Liberty County; Robert Nelson, who established Troup Hill Nursery in Macon and later helped manage Fruitland Nurseries in Augusta; and Dennis Redmond of Augusta, who, besides being a nurseryman, was an early editor of the agricultural journal the *Southern Cultivator*, begun in 1843. Also influential were Jarvis Van Buren, who established Gloaming Nursery in Clarksville and wrote prolifically for agricultural and horticultural journals; and William N. White of Athens, who wrote *Gardening for the South* (first published in 1856), which became the standard gardening book in the southern states, and who later served as editor of the *Southern Cultivator*, a publication that never missed an issue during the chaotic years of the Civil War.

During the Civil War, Georgia became a battleground that saw physical devastation of the landscape and the collapse of the political, economic, and social structure of plantation society, which was based on cotton culture and slavery. From 1866 until the close of the century, many large plantations were divided into smaller farms, and agriculture shifted to tenant farming and the sharecropping system. Cotton remained a primary crop, although some reformers called for more diversified agricultural practices. Significant changes to the landscape occurred as exploitation of the state's natural resources led to the promotion of lumbering, mining, quarrying, and turpentine production.[12] Many cities and towns in Georgia recovered economically in the decades after the Civil War, while the countryside continued to languish. Atlanta, ideally situated for business and trade, embodied the prosperity of the New South.[13]

Postbellum designed gardens in Georgia represented both continuity and progress. Some garden owners tried to maintain or simplify their existing formal gardens by using fewer resources and less labor. Others created new gardens based on prewar traditions, harking back to the Old South. Still others embraced Victorian-era gardening trends popular in the North that emphasized flora over design. Victorian-period gardens often included the elaborate bedding out of exotic, showy, and colorful plants and the extensive use of ornamental fountains, benches, and urns.[14] Beginning in the mid-nineteenth century, Georgia gardeners could obtain exotic plants from all over the world because of plant explorations in China, Japan, South America, and beyond. In the later decades of the nineteenth century, the number of residential landscapes increased statewide. Lawns gained in popularity; improved types of grass were introduced, as was the lawn mower in the late 1860s.[15]

The early decades of the twentieth century brought myriad changes to Georgia's landscape. Boll weevils infested the state's cotton farms in 1915, decimating thousands of acres. This decimation, coupled with low cotton prices after World War I and the extreme topsoil erosion caused by cotton farming, made crop diversification imperative.[16] Georgia's plantations underwent change as well. Between 1880 and 1930, many of the old plantations in southwestern Georgia were merged, replaced, or expanded as wealthy northerners, enticed by the area's temperate climate and natural resources, transformed them into winter homes and quail-hunting estates. The urban landscape was affected as farmland around city cores was transformed into planned suburban neighborhoods for affluent city dwellers. This development was fueled by the prosperity of many of Georgia's cities, coupled with the expansion of streetcar lines and the rise of the automobile. The neighborhoods were laid out in park-like settings. Curving streets were lined with trees, broad sidewalks, large lawns with informal plantings of trees and ornamental shrubs, uniform setbacks, and sophisticated homes and gardens, frequently designed by leading architects and landscape architects. Examples include Druid Hills and Peachtree Heights in Atlanta, Summerville in Augusta, and Wynnton in Columbus.

Georgia's designed gardens during the early twentieth century were largely defined by eclecticism. Owners adapted a range of historical garden styles, anything from Italian Renaissance designs to those of the colonial period.[17] Less popular gardening trends in the South, such as the Arts and Crafts style, were occasionally found in Georgia, too. The period's embrace of multiple garden traditions is most evident in the Country Place era, a movement in landscape architecture between 1880 and 1940 in which wealthy Georgians, like their peers across the country, hired professional designers to create grand houses and extensive gardens for their estates. This new affluent class, including northern business magnates who established residential retreats in Georgia, sought to emulate the grand European gardens they had seen on their travels. Many of these large estates were in the new suburban neighborhoods of Atlanta, Columbus, and Macon. Georgians followed the national trend of creating "country houses" based on classical styles: Italian Renaissance, French Renaissance, English Palladian, English Tudor, and American Colonial designs.[18] The Country Place–era landscape is characterized by the use of formal garden styles, with an emphasis on formality and symmetry, and prominent architectural elements such as elaborate walls, stairs, fountains, and a range of garden structures. Sites often featured allées, formal geometric gardens, and terraces. Examples highlighted in this book include the Cator Woolford Gardens and the Swan House Gardens in Atlanta, Salubrity Hall in Augusta, and Millpond Plantation in Thomasville.

The Colonial Revival movement, also popular in the late nineteenth century and the early decades of the twentieth, was propelled by Americans' desire to escape industrialization, their interest in the country's colonial-era history, and a longing for simpler times.[19] Colonial Revival gardens, which were most popular in the eastern United States and prevalent in Georgia, were influenced by early efforts to restore gardens like those at Colonial Williamsburg.[20] Compared with the designed landscapes of the Country Place era, Colonial Revival gardens had a broader appeal, because they could be executed on a smaller scale, and unlike Victorian-period gardens, they eschewed complicated bedding-out schemes. Some Colonial Revival gardens were created by professionals, and others by the residential owners. They contained formal elements such as a parterre or sunken garden next to the home, and informal aspects such as groups of canopy trees and flowering shrubs placed farther away. Other common elements include arbors, clipped boxwood hedges, heirloom perennials and roses, fountains, pergolas, stone walls, sundials, and brick walkways, as well as antiques to add a sense of days past.[21] This book features the Founders Memorial Garden, a Colonial Revival–style garden in Athens.

Concurrent with the Country Place era and the Colonial Revival vogue was American's interest in the Arts and Crafts movement, which was seen in the popularity of the wild or naturalistic garden. Born in late nineteenth-century England, the Arts and Crafts movement opposed industrial mass production and favored nature as the key to inspiring artistic expression. Like the gardens of the Colonial Revival movement, Arts and Crafts gardens were relatively small in scale and affordable by middle-class and upper-middle-class homeowners. Some were designed by professionals, others by home gardeners. Arts and Crafts gardens emphasized the integration of formal and informal components: formal gardens were placed next to the residence, and wild gardens in surrounding meadows and forests. Instead of the finicky exotics used in the Victorian period, Arts and Crafts–style gardens featured hardy plants, particularly native or traditional plants from the region. They also employed native or traditional stone or other materials for hardscape features, and color schemes inspired by nature.[22] Beech Haven in Athens, discussed in this book, is a noteworthy example of an Arts and Crafts garden.

The early decades of the twentieth century saw a renaissance in gardening in the South and the rest of the nation. According to the historian Davyd Foard Hood, the underpinning of this renewal in the Southeast was based on factors including the range of plants suitable for the southern climate, inspiration from many surviving gardens from the Colonial era through the Victorian period, and a plethora of books and guides containing photographs and descriptions of these earlier gardens and contemporary examples.[23] One of the earliest twentieth-century volumes on southern gardening was *The Blossom Circle of the Year in Southern Gardens* (1922), which documented the gardens designed by Julia Lester Dillon, a native Augustan.

The resurgence of gardening saw the growth of garden clubs, which was propelled by suburbanization, a growing middle class, and a desire of people with means to live in planned neighborhoods with fashionable homes and gardens. Georgia has played a vital role in the garden club movement since its birth. The first garden club founded in the United States with a constitution and bylaws was the Ladies' Garden Club, established in Athens, in 1891. In the South, that was followed by the formation of several garden clubs in Virginia from 1913 to 1919. Statewide garden clubs were established across the United States in the 1910s through the 1930s. In Georgia, the Garden Club of Georgia, Inc., was founded in 1928. Nationally, the Garden Club of America was formed in 1913 when eleven garden clubs from northern and southern states met in Philadelphia, Pennsylvania. In Georgia, five clubs currently belong to the Garden Club of America: the Junior Ladies Garden Club in Athens, the Sand Hills Garden Club in Augusta, the Trustees' Garden Club in Savannah, and two in Atlanta, the Cherokee Garden Club and the Peachtree Garden Club. Today, approximately four hundred clubs belong to the Garden Club of Georgia, Inc. National Garden Clubs, Inc., was established in 1929 when thirteen states, including Georgia, became charter members at an organizational meeting in Washington, D.C. Through individual clubs, state organizations, and the two national organizations, garden clubs have, for over one hundred years, made an invaluable impact on beautifying their communities and educating the public regarding the value of gardening and conserving nature.

Southern garden clubs, including those in Georgia, have also played a key role in documenting their state's garden histories. The James River Garden Club's *Historic Gardens of Virginia* (1923) was the first of a landmark series of books produced by American garden clubs in the 1920s and 1930s that profiled aspects of the country's garden history. In 1931, the Garden Club of America published *Gardens of Colony and State*, a survey of northern gardens. Three years later a second volume under the same title was released on southern gardens. *Garden History of Georgia, 1733–1933* (1933) was published as part of the state's bicentennial celebration.

Garden History of Georgia was compiled and published by the Peachtree Garden Club of Atlanta. Loraine Meeks Cooney, the club's president, served as chair of the project, and Hattie C. Rainwater, the Atlanta public schools supervisor for gardening and nature study, was the editor. The goal was to compile "a most comprehensive record of gardening in Georgia from Oglethorpe's day, 1733, to the most

modern garden of 1933."[24] The book opens with "A Genealogy of Georgia Gardens," an extensive essay on Georgia's garden history from 1566 to 1865, written by Florence Marye, a Savannah-born leader in the Garden Club of Georgia who established the Planters Garden Club in Atlanta in 1931. The bulk of the book consists of a survey of over 160 historic and contemporary gardens and landscapes. The first section profiles Georgia's early high-style gardens, dating to 1865, including Barnsley Gardens, the Andrew Low House and Garden, Ferrell Gardens (later Hills and Dales Estate), Oakton, and Valley View. It contains exquisite drawings by Florence Marye's husband, the architect and preservationist P. Thornton Marye, and documents numerous lost gardens, such as The Terraces in Atlanta and the Stevens Thomas Place in Athens. Early twentieth-century gardens, labeled "modern gardens," are discussed in the second section. Examples include the sunken bowl garden at Woodhaven in Atlanta, the parterre gardens at Sandy Acres in Augusta, and the extensive formal gardens and grounds at Green Island Ranch in Columbus. The third portion features garden club projects, institutional gardens, and school gardens and campuses from the early twentieth century. Projects such as the Lullwater Garden Club's conservation garden in Atlanta, the Cherokee Garden Club's Dolly Blalock Black Memorial Garden at the Henrietta Egleston Hospital for Children in Atlanta, and the Transylvania Garden Club's Sandersville Library Garden in Sandersville showcase these clubs' involvement in their communities. The involvement of garden clubs in the gardening programs in public schools in Atlanta and Savannah is highlighted, along with gardens at high schools and universities, such as those at Berry College and the University of Georgia.

The book's many illustrations, photographs, landscape drawings, and plans enhance the descriptions of the gardens. In the first section, Marye's illustrations help place the surviving gardens from the early period of Georgia's history in the broader context of their environs: the main house, outbuildings, and larger landscape. Part one includes contemporary photographs and a discussion of plants found in these old gardens, too. The last two sections provide an invaluable record of Georgia's early twentieth-century estate gardens and public landscapes, including the clients who created them, the professional designers with whom they worked, and the plants used at each site. Like other books of the period, *Garden History of Georgia* is a product of its time, with limitations and challenges reflecting its creation in the Jim Crow South. Yet it is nonetheless a valuable document and the only extensive record of historic designed landscapes in Georgia covering a two-hundred-year period.

A renewed interest in America's cultural landscapes, including historic designed gardens in the South, began in the 1970s and 1980s. The Garden Club of Georgia reprinted *Garden History of Georgia* in 1976 (it is now out of print). The Garden Club of Virginia published *Historic Virginia Gardens* in 1975. To promote southern gardening, document southern garden history, and preserve books, papers, drawings, photographs, and other records of southern horticultural heritage for study by the public, Anne Coppedge Carr and fellow Cherokee Garden Club members started the Cherokee Garden Library in Atlanta on the campus of the Atlanta Historical Society in 1975. The Southern Garden History Society was formed in 1982 under the direction of three North Carolinians—Flora Ann Bynum of Winston-Salem, William Lanier Hunt of Chapel Hill, and John Baxton Flowers III of Hendersonville—as an outgrowth of the series of conferences titled "Restoring Southern Gardens and Landscapes," held biennially in Winston-Salem beginning in 1979. The society, the first U.S. regional garden history organization, was established "to stimulate interest in Southern garden and landscape history, in historical horticulture, and in the preservation and restoration of historic gardens and landscapes in the South." In the 1980s and 1990s, the preservation movement in the United States evolved to recognize that cultural landscapes, including historic designed gardens, provide valuable insight into the nation's history. One manifestation of this is the Historic American Landscapes Survey (HALS), a program established by the National Park Service in 2000 to systematically document America's historic landscapes.

In the 1990s, the Garden Club of Georgia focused on promoting appreciation of the state's landscape heritage. The group initiated the annual Historic House and Garden Pilgrimage and the Historic Landscape and Garden Grant program. Between 1937 and the advent of World War II, the group had held annual garden pilgrimages to highlight the state's rich garden heritage. During the presidency of Peggy White (1989–91), the Atlanta landscape architect James R. Cothran suggested to her that the club should begin a garden tour that would be like Garden Week in Virginia (established in 1929) and reminiscent of the earlier pilgrimages sponsored by the club. In 1995, a partnership between the Garden Club of Georgia and the Historic Preservation Division of the Georgia Department of Natural Resources initiated an annual Historic House and Garden Pilgrimage to raise awareness about the state's historic gardens and to encourage preservation. The first pilgrimage took place in the following year. After two pilgrimages, enough funds had been raised to establish the Historic Landscape and Garden Grant Program, which assists in funding landscape restoration projects for nonprofit historic gardens in Georgia that are open to the public. In addition to the Georgia Historic Preservation Division, the Garden Club of Georgia works with the Southeast Regional Office of the National Park Service, the Cherokee Garden Library of the Atlanta History Center, and the Georgia Department of Economic Development to administer this grant. From the program's inception to 2016, over one hundred landscapes have received matching grants totaling more than $200,000. More recently, tours and lectures have also raised money to fund the matching grant program. The Garden Club of Georgia's Historic House and Garden Pilgrimage (now known as the Historic Preservation Fundraiser) and the Historic Landscape and Garden Grant (now known as the Historic Landscape Preservation Grants) programs are still active.

In recognition of the need for a statewide inventory of historic landscapes, in 2002 the Garden Club of Georgia formed the Historic Landscape Initiative Committee. Founding members were Mabel Milner, Brencie Werner, and Lee Dunn, garden club representatives; James R. Cothran, planner and garden historian; Staci Catron, director of the Cherokee Garden Library; Mary Ann Eaddy of the Historic Preservation Division; and Susan Hitchcock, historical landscape architect for the National Park Service–Southeast Regional Office. The purpose of the committee was to oversee the compiling of a statewide inventory. The result of the committee's work was the Georgia Historic Landscape Initiative, a project to identify, record, and promote the state's garden heritage. Using *Garden History of Georgia* as its foundation, the project's goal was to determine which gardens featured in the publication are extant, which have been changed, and which are lost. Hitchcock oversaw the development of a survey form to establish a consistent baseline of information for each site. In March 2002, Cothran, Eaddy, and Hitchcock participated in the National Park Service's HALS Documentation Guidelines Symposium in New Orleans. The symposium helped ensure that the information collected for the Georgia Historic Landscape Initiative was, as much as possible, consistent with HALS documentation requirements and standards.

To accomplish an undertaking such as the Georgia Historic Landscape Initiative, volunteer support from garden club membership was crucial, as was adequate training. The first in a series of workshops held over the years began in Macon in August 2002. These provided a foundation for garden clubs that took on survey responsibilities. In addition, the Cherokee Garden Library was selected as the repository for all materials related to the initiative, and the Cherokee Garden Library Research Fellowship was expanded to involve graduate students in the documentation effort, particularly compiling and cataloguing information as well as undertaking survey work. Beverly Taylor of Columbus, a leader of the Garden Club of Georgia, subsidized the fellowship program for many years; later support came from the Garden Club of Georgia and the Cherokee Garden Library.

Between 2002 and 2016, approximately 190 surveys were completed through the Georgia Historic Landscape Initiative. For each garden, the survey documented its type and features, significant characteristics that warranted preservation, a general description, overall condition, any potential threats, design history (including its development chronology), historical significance, integrity, and inclusion in the National Register of Historic Places (if applicable). The records include additional articles and publications about the garden, historic photographs and plans (if available), and contemporary photographs and rough sketches of each site.

In the first phase of the Georgia Historic Landscape Initiative, documentation was completed on all the gardens described in *Garden History of Georgia*. About one-third of those sites have been lost, another third contain only remnants of the original garden, and, fortunately, about one-third survive today. The Historic Landscape Preservation Committee of the Garden Club of Georgia is currently discussing the next phase of the program. It hopes to survey a broader range of cultural landscapes, including cemeteries, parks, and rural communities as well as historic vernacular landscapes.

The best way to bring this body of research and documentation to the public's attention and to acknowledge the efforts of countless contributors is through this book. *Seeking Eden: A Collection of Georgia's Historic Gardens*, unlike the 1933 volume, is not a "most comprehensive record of gardening in Georgia" but rather a glimpse at one aspect of the state's garden history. Inspired by the findings of the Georgia Historic Landscape Initiative survey, it showcases thirty of the extant gardens profiled in *Garden History of Georgia*. The book also includes a brief update on all the gardens contained in the original *Garden History of Georgia*.

The gardens were chosen for this volume according to several criteria. They came from a range of geographic locations, to show the variety of gardens throughout the state. All but ten are public gardens, so readers can visit many of the sites in person. The private gardens included relied on the willingness of the owners to participate in the project. Historic gardens were chosen to show design types across an almost two-hundred-year period. The gardens needed to display a sufficient degree of integrity and be visually appealing. Space constraints rather than the supply of candidates, it should be noted, limited how many gardens could be included. Ultimately, this volume is a record of each historic garden: how it looks in the early twenty-first century, how it has evolved over time, and what the garden means to the people who care for it. (Note: The spelling of botanical names or common plant names in quoted material has been left as it appears in the original source.)

Just as the photography in *Garden History of Georgia* serves as an invaluable record for garden historians and preservationists today, Jim Lockhart's photography here, undertaken in 2014–16, will serve as a resource for the ongoing study and care of these sites. This point was sadly highlighted after Hurricane Matthew hit Georgia in the fall of 2016. Hundreds of trees were lost in the Savannah Squares, forever changing their appearance. Damage also occurred to other sites, including the Coffin-Reynolds Mansion landscape on Sapelo Island.

Historic gardens belong to many generations of Georgians and reflect many aspects of Georgia's history and culture. Their impressive variety includes the squares of Savannah, a late nineteenth-century kitchen garden in Cobb County, and a major geological formation turned tourist attraction near Lookout Mountain. In a state where the devastation of the Civil War changed much of the landscape, it is remarkable that formal antebellum boxwood gardens survive, as do the ruins of a rare A. J. Downing–influenced Georgia estate. Landscapes representative of early twentieth-century Country Place–era design in Atlanta's Buckhead neighborhood and a winter estate near Thomasville illustrate a period of enormous wealth. The names of professional designers such as J. Neel Reid, Philip Trammell Shutze, William C. Pauley, Robert B. Cridland, the Olmsted brothers, and Hubert Bond Owens are associated with some of the most striking landscapes. Exquisite gardens were created also by talented and knowledgeable owners, including Frieda and Garnet Carter, Sarah Coleman Ferrell, Effie and Charles Rowland, and Loyer Lawton Zahner. The role of women in the life of many of these gardens cannot be overstated. Martha Berry's vision saw the development of one of Georgia's most beautiful campuses, and the stewardship of three generations of strong southern women ensured the future of the spectacular Hills and Dales in LaGrange. The landscape architect Clermont Lee was closely involved with the documentation and preservation of Savannah's early parterre gardens and world-renowned squares. This book tells their stories.

In *American Eden: From Monticello to Central Park to Our Backyards*, the historian Wade Green gets to the heart of why gardens of the past matter today: "Every good garden is a window—into the individual mind or minds of its makers, owners, inheritors, or inhabitants, and through their stories layered on top of one another, a window to the collective mind, our common experience."[25] Just like Georgia's historic buildings, its historic designed landscapes provide glimpses into the past, and like so many historic places, they are not static. They have evolved to reflect changing times and tastes. Many are stunningly beautiful. They are, as the expression goes, a feast for the eyes. They provide places for enjoyment, rest, and rejuvenation, but they also provide windows into the intricacies of Georgia's history.

It is hoped that this publication will increase public awareness of Georgia's historic designed landscapes and their role in the state's history, encourage the preservation community to become more attuned to historic landscapes when evaluating historic resources, and promote ongoing scholarship and research into Georgia's historic landscape and garden heritage. Proceeds from this publication will be directed to the Garden Club of Georgia's Historic Landscape Preservation Grants Program, which supports the preservation and restoration of historic properties across the state.

View of the Andrew Low front parterre garden and house

Andrew Low House and Garden

SAVANNAH'S ANDREW LOW HOUSE is one of the city's most architecturally and culturally interesting properties. Its formal front garden is one of the area's oldest and most identifiable, and its rear courtyard provides insight into the twentieth-century work of one of Georgia's first female landscape architects, Clermont Lee. The house offers visitors a glimpse into the rarefied world of affluent mid-nineteenth-century Savannah made possible by powerful men such as the wealthy cotton merchant Andrew Low. This was also the home of Juliette Gordon Low, Low's daughter-in-law, when she brought scouting to the girls of the United States in 1912. In 1928 the National Society of the Colonial Dames of America in the State of Georgia acquired the property for its state headquarters. Today, the Low House, which opened as a museum in 1952, contains the furnishings, art, and other material culture collections of the state's Colonial Dames. Included within both the Savannah and the Juliette Gordon Low National Historic Landmark Districts, the Andrew Low House possesses one of only a handful of the city's surviving antebellum gardens, and the only one open to the public.

In 1829, the young Scotsman Andrew Low traveled to Savannah with the promise of a position in his uncle's thriving mercantile business, Andrew Low & Company, which had lucrative contacts in England. Low proved hardworking and dependable, and by 1836 he had become a partner in the enterprise.[1] In January 1844, Andrew Low married Sarah Cecil Hunter of Savannah, and soon after they had a son and two daughters. When his uncle died in 1849, Low inherited the business, and under his leadership, Andrew Low & Company continued to prosper. A savvy businessman, Low held positions of influence with the Central Railroad and Banking Company of Georgia and the Merchants' National Bank of Savannah.[2] He became one of the wealthiest cotton factors, or brokers, in the city, accumulating an immense fortune.

The big square building, with its gardens and carriage house, occupied a whole city block. Two lions, at the [bottom] of the steps, guarded the entrance, a touch of elegance with a particular appeal for Daisy.—Gladys Denny Shultz and Daisy Gordon Lawrence, *Lady from Savannah*

As the family grew, the Lows decided to build a new house. In 1847, Andrew Low purchased a trust lot across from Lafayette Square. When James Oglethorpe conceived the plan for Savannah in 1733, he designated what were called trust lots on the east and west sides of each square, which were to be locations for public buildings. After the Trustees in England, who had guided the early colonial settlement of Georgia, relinquished their charter to the king in 1752, the trust lots eventually became available for private use. Their prominent location and size attracted wealthy citizens seeking a desirable setting for a house.[3] Although Low's property had an inauspicious beginning as part of "the yard attached to the city jail," the site soon became one of Savannah's most prestigious addresses.[4]

Low selected the New York architect John Norris to design his family's residence. Norris had come to Savannah in 1846 to work on the U.S. Custom House building, a project that led to other commissions in the city. Until the Civil War neared, Norris was sought after to plan many of Savannah's public structures and private houses. Although Greek Revival architecture was still quite popular in the South, Norris was also interested in new styles found in other parts of the country, especially Italianate and Gothic Revival. For Low's business partner, Charles Green, Norris designed the Gothic Revival Green-Meldrim House. For Andrew Low, he was inspired by Greek and Italianate architecture.

In *Architecture of the Old South* (1986), Mills Lane describes the Low House as combining "a Greek Revival entrance and interior with Italianate bracketed eaves and mock-casement windows."[5] Completed in 1849, the imposing two-story stuccoed brick residence, which faces east toward Lafayette Square, sits on a raised basement. Its five bays are punctuated by a classically pedimented, recessed front entry with fluted columns and pilasters. A cast-iron balcony extends beneath the double-hung first-floor windows on either side of the front entrance. A decorative cast-iron balcony with "pagoda-type roof" is a striking component of the south façade.[6] The architect John Linley, in *The Georgia Catalog* (1982), describes the Andrew Low House as "an outstanding design, expressive of its time, locale, and climate."[7]

For a man of Andrew Low's standing, a formal garden would have been essential. While many Savannah houses were built up to the property line and had either rear or side gardens, residences constructed on a trust lot had additional space. Laura Palmer Bell, in her study of late nineteenth-century Savannah gardens, describes these rare front landscapes: "On the street front, most of them were protected by a low wall or coping, surmounted with a wrought or cast iron fence of appropriate height, and these walls invited inspection through the openings of their sometimes intricate designs."[8] The Andrew Low House follows this model with a decorative cast-iron fence enclosing its front garden. Inside the entry gate, a central flagstone path divides the nearly symmetrical parterre garden and leads to the front steps, where two cast-iron lions guard the house and welcome guests.

The parterre garden is said to have been laid out concurrent with the construction of the house, but its designer is unknown. One theory is that Norris was involved in its planning, along with Sarah Hunter Low.[9] Parterres were popular in Savannah and in the South during the antebellum years, and the Lows' hourglass-shaped flower beds edged with tile would probably have been quite stunning. No records, however, have been found describing what was planted here during this period.[10] The garden was designed to be seen and enjoyed by people looking down on the landscape from the house or strolling through the grounds. A recessed moat designed to provide drainage ran along both sides of the house, leaving little room for plantings. The rear yard contained the carriage house, stable, and, possibly, slave housing.

Before the Lows could move in, tragedy struck. Andrew Low's young son and his wife, Sarah, died within months of each other in 1848 and 1849. Soon after, Low sailed with his two daughters to England, where the girls would remain and attend school.[11] In 1854, Andrew Low remarried. His bride, Mary Cowper Stiles, was a well-connected and well-liked young Georgian. When Martha "Mittie" Bulloch, a close friend, married Theodore Roosevelt in 1853, Mary Stiles was a bridesmaid in their wedding at Bulloch Hall in Roswell, Georgia.[12] After the Lows' wedding, they settled into the house on Lafayette Square. Their new life involved entertaining such

Symmetrical front parterre garden

notable guests as the British author William Makepeace Thackeray and traveling to England. There is speculation that Mary may have been involved in refining the formal garden, although no documentation for that claim has been found.[13] Andrew and Mary had four children who survived, including their only son, William Mackay Low, born in the summer of 1860. In the upheaval of the Civil War, Andrew Low was arrested in the fall of 1861 for activity sympathetic to the Confederacy and was not reunited with his family until the following spring.[14] Mary died unexpectedly in their home on Lafayette Square in 1863. The next several years were difficult as Low tried to take care of his family and his business while the war ended and an uncertain recovery began. He settled his children in England while managing his financial affairs in both America and Great Britain. Low's life in Savannah focused on work. One especially noteworthy social event, however, was a visit by the family friend Robert E. Lee in 1870, during which numerous Savannahians came to the Low House to pay their respects to the former Confederate general. Andrew Low began reorganizing his business interests in 1872, and by 1877 he was fully retired and living in England.[15] His health gradually deteriorated, and in 1886 he died.

In that same year, his son, William "Willy" Mackay Low, married Juliette Magill Kinzie Gordon, or "Daisy," as she was known to those closest to her, a member of one of Savannah's leading families. Willy Low inherited most of his father's extensive fortune, including the house on Lafayette Square, which became the young couple's Savannah home. They refurbished the residence, but soon left for England, where they would spend much of their married lives. Daisy continued to deal with a severe hearing disability that plagued her throughout her adulthood. Over the years, Daisy and Willy's marriage disintegrated. After Willy's death in 1905 and the settling of legal problems resulting from their estrangement, Daisy took sole possession of the Savannah property. She rented out the Low house, continued to spend a good deal of time in Great Britain, and traveled extensively, but she felt that her life lacked purpose. In 1911, Daisy met Sir Robert Baden-Powell, founder of the Boy Scouts, a life-changing encounter. Through her friendship with Baden-Powell, Daisy became involved in the Girl Guides in England,

and she decided that American girls would benefit from such an organization. On March 12, 1912, in Savannah, Juliette Gordon "Daisy" Low founded the Girl Scouts of the USA.

After the death of her father in 1912 and her mother in 1917, Daisy made the Low House her permanent residence. She turned the carriage house into the headquarters of her scouting organization and a place for troop meetings. Upon Daisy's death, in her Lafayette Square home in 1927, the Savannah Area Girl Scout Council inherited the carriage house. The building continues to serve the scouting community as the Girl Scout First Headquarters museum, housing a program center, archives, and a gift shop. Daisy Low's impressive legacy is seen in the nearly three million young girls and women associated with scouting today and the millions of women who proudly call themselves former scouts.

After Daisy Low's death, the National Society of the Colonial Dames of America in the State of Georgia acquired the Low House for its state headquarters. Founded in 1891, the national society is dedicated to the promotion of the country's heritage "through historic preservation, patriotic service, and educational projects."[16] In 1893 Daisy Low's mother, Eleanor "Nellie" Kinzie Gordon, had been instrumental in the formation of the Georgia Society of the NSCDA. Initially, the organization used the house primarily to host meetings and out-of-town members. It was later converted into a museum, which still operates today.

From the earliest years of the Colonial Dames' ownership, the grounds and their care were important components of the overall management of the property. When the Low House was acquired, the front garden was said to still contain "its form and a portion of the original planting," although no records describe these plants.[17] In 1933 there were "foundation plantings of cycads (*Cycas revolta*), camellias, and large magnolias in the street."[18] Pole-like structures, apparently used for roses or wisteria to climb, lined both sides of the central walk, although they are no longer in the garden.[19]

Advised by an official Garden Committee, the Colonial Dames worked to restore the front garden "as nearly as possible to the original Victorian pattern, with suitable flowers and shrubs."[20] Because an original planting plan for the garden has not been

Elevation view of the front of the Andrew Low House and Garden

View of the parterre garden looking toward Lafayette Square, showing the manicured boxwoods and border plantings

found, decisions about what to plant were based on what seemed appropriate. In 1946, the landscape architect Clermont Lee was asked to prepare a plan that identified historically accurate plant material of the period.[21] While Lee's recommendations were not implemented at the time, over the years the document has provided guidance for plant selections.

Accounts found in Garden Committee reports illustrate the care that members have taken over the years to keep the landscape healthy and attractive. One fall they planted 603 pansies "in front of the house on each side of the walkway and around the perimeter."[22] Summer maintenance in 2006 required "trimming the small boxwood, watering the containers, cleaning out beds and putting down mulch."[23] In addition, plant material in the parterres has changed over time. In the late 1950s, following Clermont Lee's advice, the committee planted the center beds

with roses and used violets and spice pinks as borders.[24] In 1975, the hourglass beds were planted with "4 ilex Fostoria standards ... and 50 hedra helix."[25] In 2001, the two outer parterres contained "Foster holly standards under planted with Asian jasmine."[26] One plant that continues to bring pleasure to visitors is the Juliette Gordon Low camellia found in the garden's northeast corner.

To provide the impression of an antebellum garden, it was important that a specific time frame be established for the front garden's interpretation. A historic landscape master plan, prepared by the Atlanta firm of Robert and Company in December 2009, recommended that the 1860 time period be the point of reference for any work undertaken in the garden and that appropriate plants from that era be used.[27] The team, led by James R. Cothran, recommended removing three Foster hollies within the boxwood edging and replacing them with sago palms (*Cycas revoluta*), which historically were a "prized ornamental."[28] For years the garden's historic terra-cotta edging tiles were prominent features, but most were stolen in the mid-1990s. Concrete reproductions have replaced them. The master plan encouraged raising their visibility by decreasing the level of the gravel paths.

While the structure of the front garden has remained largely unchanged, the rear yard has undergone a number of alterations over the years. By 1933, a few years after the Colonial Dames purchased the Low House, the rear yard contained an open lawn with trees and shrubs and a planting bed adjacent

to the carriage house. A pathway of flagstone pavers extended across the rear of the house and the northern side of the yard. The old carriage house on the west and the brick walls on the north and south sides provided privacy.[29] A wooden fence ran along the carriage house, but in 1929 the Colonial Dames' Garden Committee reported that it was in bad repair and needed to be replaced with a brick wall.[30] In the late 1930s, this brick wall became the boundary line between the Low House and the former carriage house, by then owned by the Girl Scouts.[31] The wall contained a fountain and served as a backdrop for plantings of yuccas.[32] By 1941, wrought-iron gates opening into the rear yard had replaced

Fountain in the rear garden

Rear garden from the second-floor enclosed porch with a view of the former carriage house

Rear courtyard garden, originally designed by Clermont Lee

wooden ones.[33] With the advent of World War II, projects throughout the property were delayed. By 1945, when plant material was available once again, delighted Garden Committee members planted 150 daffodil bulbs in the rear yard. The results were noteworthy: "They are blooming beautifully and look very gay against the old wall."[34]

In preparation for the opening of the Low House as a museum, the Dames turned their attention to the rear yard. In 1951, Clermont Lee prepared construction plans for the space, and the project was completed the following year.[35] Lee, an authority on period landscapes, was the first woman to be registered as a landscape architect in Georgia.[36] A proponent of preserving Savannah's historic public squares, she was responsible for the renovation of five of them.[37] For the Low House's rear garden, Lee needed to design a landscape that would accommodate numerous visitors, require minimal maintenance, and provide a place of beauty and serenity. Lee is credited with the

Rear courtyard in
spring bloom

garden's courtyard concept of a paved, open space enclosed by a wall and bordered by plants.[38] The landscape historian Susan Hitchcock described Lee's work in the rear garden as evidence of her "talents at designing small spaces."[39] To provide a visual contrast to the pedestrian surfaces, Lee had two large brick panels, surrounded by flagstones, installed on the north and south sides of the yard.[40] The courtyard's brick walls were repaired, and raised planting beds edged with Savannah gray brick were used to line the north and south walls.[41] Hitchcock mentioned Lee's "finely tuned sense of scale and color harmony," and found "equally impressive . . . her respect for the sense of place that precedes her work."[42] While Lee may have made

plant recommendations, the 1952 planting beds were planned by the Colonial Dames.[43] For many years after this work was completed, Lee continued to provide consulting services for both the front and rear gardens. After a long and successful career, she died in 2006.

In 2009, Robert and Company's *Historic Landscape Plan* recommended rehabilitating the rear courtyard, focusing mainly on irrigation, maintenance, and guests' safety and enjoyment. It advised installing a fountain on the west wall where, years earlier, a piece that Juliette Low sculpted had been located. This sculpture has been placed in storage to protect it from exposure and deterioration. Surrounded by a metal arbor and seasonal flowers, a cast-iron lion's

View of the
Andrew Low
House and Garden
from Lafayette
Square

Landscape plan of the Andrew Low House and Garden by P. Thornton Marye from the *Garden History of Georgia*

head fountain is now a focal point. The garden courtyard, sometimes a site for special events, is the area used primarily by visitors as they wait to enter the Low House. The landscape is now filled with azaleas, camellias, Confederate jasmine, tea olive, gloriosa lilies, dwarf boxwood, and four Natchez crape myrtles. This peaceful setting has evolved somewhat since originally designed by Lee but still retains the essence of her work.[44]

Although the mostly volunteer-run Andrew Low House and Garden hired its first director in 2006, the Garden Committee still plays an important role in decisions related to the landscape. It oversees plant selection, determines what needs to be removed, and hires the gardener. Some committee members spend time working on the grounds. The Albany and Athens Town Committees financially underwrite spring and fall plantings.[45]

Care of the landscape sometimes requires difficult decisions that must be made for practical reasons. While every attempt is made to include historically accurate plant material, a number of period-appropriate plants were found to be quite labor intensive; others did not adapt well to the changing twenty-first-century climate.[46] A recommendation to use oyster shell paths backfired when white dust from

visitors' shoes was brought into the historic house, requiring extra maintenance.[47] There is a constant striving to respect the integrity of this historic place while managing its daily care, preserving it, and enhancing visitors' experiences. Although the plantings may have changed over time, the parterre garden's basic form has remained intact for nearly 170 years.

For nearly ninety years, the Andrew Low House and its gardens have been under the watchful care of the National Society of the Colonial Dames of America in the State of Georgia. The society has been recognized for its restoration of the house by the Georgia Trust for Historic Preservation and the Historic Savannah Foundation. A popular tourist destination that hosts nearly forty thousand visitors annually, the Low House reveals fascinating stories important to America's cultural history. The site's authenticity is enhanced by its antebellum parterre garden. The Colonial Dames' commitment to the preservation and public use of this important historic site is clearly articulated in their 2013 mission statement: "By preserving a distinguished example of domestic and landscape architecture and exhibiting furnishings and decorative arts of the period, we further promote the understanding of historic preservation and the history of Savannah."[48]

Ashland Farm's stone entrance

Ashland Farm

SITUATED IN THE FOOTHILLS of Lookout Mountain, Ashland Farm embodies the vision of Zeboim Cartter Patten and his wife, Sarah Key Patten, to create a refined country estate in rural Walker County in the early twentieth century. The Pattens, in collaboration with the Biltmore Nursery, swathed the property's pasturelands and woodlands in thousands of native and exotic trees, shrubs, perennials, and bulbs, as well as a million wildflowers, creating an otherworldliness evocative of the grandeur of eighteenth-century English landscapes. The landscape is both formal and naturalistic; although evolved, it maintains its ethereal character, which exhibits a grace and splendor rarely seen in the twenty-first century.

Ashland Farm is on the Cumberland Plateau in the area of northwestern Georgia bordering Tennessee. Known for its scenic beauty, Walker County is home to beautiful mountains, rolling hills, picturesque valleys, rock formations, caves, and natural creeks and springs. In the county's northwestern corner, Lookout Mountain and Pigeon Mountain form a V in which sits the Chattanooga Valley. The fertile Chattanooga Valley has long supported agriculture, first by the Native Americans and then by settlers who arrived because of the 1832 land lottery. The county saw several battles during the Civil War, including the Battle of Chickamauga in 1863, one of the conflict's bloodiest. After the war, Walker County lost half its population; many residents resettled west of the Mississippi River in search of new opportunities. Population levels did not recover until the 1890s.[1] Unlike plantations in southern Georgia, the farms in Walker County were small-scale operations, generally 300–400 acres, that included livestock (cattle and hogs), orchards with fruit trees (apples and peaches), crops of corn and hay, and vegetable gardens (primarily for home use). In the twentieth century, the textile industry and tourism, with attractions such as nearby Rock City, supplemented

Each season, in turn, brings to this woodland paradise fresh loveliness, yet it is perhaps nearest perfection when in April the spreading branches of countless flowering dogwoods whiten the landscape as though an untimely snow-storm had smothered hillside and deep ravine with dazzling white.

—*Garden History of Georgia*

Neoclassical Revival–style mansion designed by the Atlanta architect Walter T. Downing

farming as the main economic forces.[2] As neighboring Chattanooga, Tennessee, became a vibrant industrial center in the 1880s, many affluent families from the city were drawn to Lookout Mountain and its surrounding valleys, including Walker County, where they created tranquil and beautiful estates. Among those families were the Pattens. Untapped business opportunities brought one northerner, Zeboim Cartter Patten, to Chattanooga just after the Civil War, where he became a prominent industrialist, capitalist, and philanthropist. In the first decade of the twentieth century, he and his wife, Sarah Key Patten, built Ashland Farm, an idyllic estate in the Chattanooga Valley.

Hailing from Wilma, New York, Zeboim Cartter Patten served in the Union army with the 115th Illinois and the 149th New York Infantries and was wounded in the Battles of Chickamauga and Resaca in northwestern Georgia.[3] After the war, he and another veteran, Thomas H. Payne, returned to Chattanooga and founded Patten and Payne, a book and stationery store.[4] After a few years, Patten sold the store and invested in the *Chattanooga Times*. In 1879, he and several partners established

the Chattanooga Medicine Company, now known as Chattem, to produce patent medicines.[5] The company prospered, and Patten later developed or worked with other successful companies, including the Stone Fort Land Company, which built the Hotel Patten, Chattanooga's first high-rise building, in 1908. In 1903, Patten and other partners established the Volunteer State Life Insurance Company, a significant regional financial institution.[6] He was also a founding director of the American Trust and Banking Company (later American National and now SunTrust Bank), a founder of the First Trust and Savings Bank, and the developer of several other companies.[7] In 1870, he married Mary Miller Rawlings, and the couple had two children, Elizabeth Olive Patten in 1871 and Mary M. Rawlings Patten in 1875, who died the following year. Mary Patten died two weeks after the birth of their second child.[8]

Patten remained a widower until 1902, when he married Sarah Avery Key, the daughter of a distinguished Chattanooga family.[9] The Pattens had one son, Zeboim Cartter Patten Jr., who was referred to as Cartter, born in 1903. The family resided in downtown Chattanooga, but in 1904 began looking

View toward the pond

Wildflower meadow and flowering trees at Ashland Farm

Spring blooms and a stone lantern in a meadow

for a place in the country. They selected the old Crutchfield Farm, called Mimosa by the Crutchfield family, in the Chattanooga Valley between the small communities of St. Elmo and Flintstone, Georgia. Located about seven miles from downtown Chattanooga, the property comprised over three hundred acres of rich farmland and forest with scenic views of Lookout Mountain to the northwest. Z. C. named it Ashland Farm after fond memories he had of a picturesque farm of the same name in Lowville, New York.[10]

The Pattens transformed the property's farmland and woodlands into a picturesque landscape containing a balance of naturalistic and formal elements. The house was sited on a knoll with a large front lawn sloping away from it and eventually

giving way to woodlands. Anchoring the site's picturesque landscape is a stone mill that stands on the edge of a one-acre pond west of the main house that is also cradled by woodlands. A small meandering creek feeds the pond. Spatially, the pond serves as a transition between the formality of the house, with its adjacent structured garden rooms, and the naturalistic elements throughout the rest of the site, as well as the mountain in the background. Stonework is abundant throughout, creating an Old World feel. Miles of stone fences, varying in height from four to five feet, lined the property's edges until a highway expansion claimed the fencing. Circular stone columns, together with what remains of the stone fencing, mark the entrance to Ashland Farm, and a stone pathway follows part of the creek.

Stream in the lower meadow

Front portico

Historic photo from *Garden History of Georgia*

The thousands of native and exotic trees, shrubs, perennials, and bulbs planted over time have matured to produce a romantic and tranquil setting.

The Pattens hired the Atlanta architect Walter T. Downing to design the main residence.[11] Downing created a commanding two-story brick Neoclassical Revival–style house that features a portico with twelve white fluted Corinthian columns topped with a heavy entablature with dentils. Like the exterior, the interior is a masterpiece of the Neoclassical Revival style, although the large first-floor sunroom features art nouveau design elements, including the furniture.[12] The completion of this impressive structure was celebrated at a housewarming in May 1906.[13] Because few people owned automobiles, and a horse-drawn trip from Chattanooga took almost four hours, the Pattens had the Chattanooga Southern Railroad, whose passenger line between Chattanooga and Gadsden, Alabama, skirted the edge of Ashland Farm, run a special train for guests attending the big celebration.[14]

Several dependencies surround the main house. Downing designed two one-story brick servants' cottages, both with hip roofs and four-column front porches, situating them just behind the main house. A nearby barn was constructed of hand-pressed brick salvaged from the old Crutchfield house. There was also a small brick gashouse that produced acetylene gas used to light the main house and cottages until electricity reached the Chattanooga Valley around 1910.[15] The property featured several unique structures, including a mill and an open wooden shelter that housed a Conestoga wagon. The mill, which Sarah acquired in 1929, contains the interior of the old Peeler mill from Peavine Creek near Ringgold, Georgia. She then arranged for the architect Malcolm Chisolm to design the stone-sided gabled exterior.[16] A concrete dam was built to provide water for the mill.

In addition to serving as the country estate of the Pattens, Ashland Farm was a farming operation, which needed to be largely self-sufficient in its early years because of its distance from Chattanooga. Ashland Farm's primary field crops were corn and alfalfa hay. The site also had a large vegetable garden, a peach orchard, a strawberry patch, carriage horses, a Shetland pony named Daisy, a few milk cows, and chickens.[17] A German superintendent named Fritz Grindler managed the farming and gardening duties with a labor force that ranged from three to five men, depending on the time of year.[18] According to the family, Grindler was the caretaker until around 1924, followed by Melvin Campbell until 1944.

From the fall of 1906 until 1908, the Pattens worked with the Biltmore Nursery to create the ornamental gardens and grounds at Ashland Farm. Established in 1889 and guided by the vision and expertise of the American landscape architect Frederick Law Olmsted, the Biltmore Nursery was created to supply millions of plants for George W. Vanderbilt's resplendent Biltmore Estate near Asheville, North Carolina.[19] The nursery grew into a huge commercial enterprise that furnished plants to customers throughout the United States and abroad between 1889 and 1916. According to the landscape historian Bill Alexander: "As a commercial nursery, it produced and sold one of the broadest selections of hardy, temperate, ornamental plants available anywhere."[20]

Letters between the Pattens and the Biltmore Nursery lend insight into the nursery's involvement

Cypress bog

Rhododendron next
to a stream

Sunken garden

Hillside path

at Ashland Farm. A November 1906 letter from the nursery to Sarah indicates that it provided design and planting plans, although the plans have not been located: "We are sending a tracing and two solar prints showing the planting scheme and arrangement which we propose for your beautiful residence site near Chattanooga, Tennessee.... We trust that the arrangement will appeal to you as satisfactory and artistic. The kinds of plants that we are now planning in the arrangement of the groups will be well adapted to a colonial home such as you have and in harmony with the natural surroundings, not omitting, however, the pleasure that may be derived from evergreen effects in winter and floral effects in summer."[21] A letter later the same month contains a list of over 100 varieties of bulbs, flowers, vines, shrubs, and trees—6,011 plants in all—that the nursery recommended, such as boxwood, forsythia, honeysuckle, hydrangea, iris, kalmia, leucothoe, magnolia, narcissus, privet, redbud, rhododendron, spirea, viburnum, tulips, and yucca.[22] White pines were selected to line the entrance road to the

mansion. It is likely that the stone columns that denote the lower entry drive as well as the miles of stone and rock fences found throughout the site were added during this period.

The nursery created a plan for the formal boxwood garden southwest of the mansion, according to a letter dated November 27, 1906, which suggested that the Pattens' gardener, Fritz Grindler, could oversee most of the work with two employees from the nursery (Mr. Swope and Mr. Shuford) handling the staking out of the lines and right angles of the formal garden.[23] The family describes the original boxwood garden as "a series of brick walks forming some nine triangular flower beds, bordered by small clipped boxwood hedges. Tulips, peonies, geraniums, and the like were grown in the various triangular beds."[24] A small greenhouse anchored the far end. The Biltmore Nursery's plant list for the formal garden included 3,066 dwarf English boxwood, 4 umbrella trees (*Catalpa bungei*), candytuft, dianthus, phlox, purple foxglove, English daisy, lemon daylily, blackberry lily, oriental and Iceland poppy, lavender,

Boxwoods in the formal garden

peonies, juniper, salvia, and German, Japanese, and Siberian iris.[25] An April 1907 letter confirms that the nursery sent the plants for the formal garden.[26] Other correspondence details the shipping of kalmias, hemlocks, rhododendrons, white pines, and large specimen boxwood to be planted throughout the property, as well as "50 of our best roses" for the rose garden adjacent to the pathway leading to the mill.[27] The Biltmore Nursery's plans addressed drainage challenges on the property and additional plantings of kalmias and azaleas along a streambed.

The woodlands near the mansion, according to *Garden History of Georgia*, were blanketed with thousands of wildflowers, including delicate Quaker Lady bluets, birdfoot violets, foam flower, pink wood sorrel, Solomon's seal, trillium, wild delphinium, and wild geranium.[28] Around the pond and stone mill were "great patches of the delicate blue and pink of mertensias (Virginia bluebells) and along the winding pathways wood anemones."[29] Beneath the oaks and pines, native azalea, dogwood, rhododendron, and honeysuckle were planted.

Naturally, changes were made to the landscape over time. In the 1920s, the formal garden was altered: most of the brick walks were removed, as were most of the plantings except boxwood.[30] The greenhouse on the southern edge of the formal boxwood garden was converted to a sunken garden in the late 1930s. An iron arbor supported by stone columns marks the entrance to this garden, which is enclosed with large boxwood and other evergreen shrubs. One end of the garden is anchored by an arched-back stone bench and the other by a stone arched structure with a central niche enclosed by an iron gate. The niche contains a religious sculpture. The sunken garden features a small pond encased in stones. Also in the 1930s, evergreen shrubs and trees were added, open walkways were created, and more natives were planted—likely a result of Cartter Jr.'s influence, since he had studied agriculture at Cornell University.

Other important features were added to the woodlands beginning in the late 1930s through the 1950s, including a large path encircling the pond, a

A historic photo from
Garden History of Georgia

large stone bridge traversing the stream, a wildflower meadow, a large planting of rhododendrons near the wooden shelter for the Conestoga wagon, and a new woodland area planted with magnolias (many varieties), crape myrtles, dogwood, yellow wood, water oak, and table pine.[31] Longleaf pines planted in the 1940s today have become a lovely stand that encompasses five acres just south of the pond and mill. Cartter Jr. planted a grove of bald cypress where a portion of the pond became silted in during the early 1950s—a perfect habitat for cypress—and a fully mature grove now graces the western edge of the pond. Some of the pastures were converted to orchards in the 1950s.

The Pattens divided their time between Ashland Farm and their homes in Florida and Maine.[32] Following the death of Z.C., at Ashland Farm in 1925, Sarah began acquiring residential properties, "many houses scattered from Maine through Tennessee and Georgia to Florida."[33] She and her sister, Margaret Key, moved among the more than twenty properties throughout the year until the late 1940s, when the holdings were reduced to eight.[34] Even with all of Sarah's traveling, her love of Ashland and its gardens and grounds was evident. During a journey to Japan before her marriage, she became a

great admirer of Japanese gardens, which is reflected at Ashland Farm in the numerous stone lanterns placed along the trails and the Yoshino cherry trees planted around the pond. She also added thousands of naturalized daffodils throughout the property. In 1944, she commissioned the Chattanooga sculptor Harold Cash to create a bronze sculpture of her twin grandsons, Zeboim Cartter Patten III (Cartter) and W. A. Bryan Patten (Bryan). The sculpture sits at the edge of a large open lawn on the south side of the mansion and is encased on three sides by dwarf boxwood.

After Sarah died in July 1958 at the age of ninety-three, Cartter and Elizabeth Patten inherited Ashland Farm. Cartter had married Elizabeth Bryan of Nashville in 1931. Besides twin sons, the couple had two daughters, Sarah Key Patten and Emma Berry Patten.[35] Cartter, like his father, was a successful businessman and philanthropist in the Chattanooga community; he served one term in the Tennessee House of Representatives and three terms in the Tennessee State Senate. Elizabeth, also a philanthropist and civic leader, started the Tennessee Conference on Historic Preservation and was elected to the board of the National Trust for Historic Preservation in 1967.[36]

Over the next three decades, the Pattens maintained Ashland Farm as a country retreat. Both Cartter and Elizabeth held great respect for the history of the site as well as its extraordinary landscape. They made improvements to the mansion and numerous outbuildings, restored parts of the structures when needed, and added to the flora, particularly evergreens and natives. Following the death of Cartter in 1982 and Elizabeth in 1990, the property went into a family trust. Today, Bryan Patten—the grandson of Sarah Key Patten and Zeboim Cartter Patten—and his wife, Kathy, own Ashland Farm, free from the trust. Together with their two daughters, Kathleen and Sarah, both of whom now live in Asheville, North Carolina, they guide and care for this unexpected Eden. Its grand mansion; formal and naturalistic gardens, which benefit from ideal conditions of soil, sun, and shade; its magnificent spring, which supplies the pond and historic mill; and the loving care of four generations of Patten gardeners make Ashland Farm an enchanting treasure among the gardens of Georgia.

Mill

Servants' quarters
behind the main
house

Stone wall and
mansion

Stone wall and scenic vista

Mill pond and
flowering cherry trees

View from the foyer at Barnsley Gardens

Barnsley Gardens

LOCATED IN THE FOOTHILLS of northwestern Georgia near the towns of Adairsville and Kingston, Barnsley Gardens is an antebellum estate with a compelling history filled with stories of love, war, tragedy, and rebirth. Once known as Woodlands, it was the home of Godfrey Barnsley, a wealthy English cotton broker living in Savannah, and his family. For three decades, Barnsley worked to realize his grand vision, which, unlike that of his southern peers, followed national rather than regional trends.[1] He built an Italianate manor house within a picturesque landscape—quite a departure from the prevailing southern tradition of a Classical-style building set among formal geometric gardens. Barnsley was clearly influenced by the British American architect and landscape designer Calvert Vaux, who later designed Central Park with Frederick Law Olmsted, and Andrew Jackson Downing, the renowned nineteenth-century American landscape gardener and arbiter of taste. Today, the grounds of Barnsley Resort hold the remnants of Barnsley's efforts—the ruins of the Italianate manor house and the only significant surviving example in the state of an antebellum landscape based on Downing's ideals.

Barnsley arrived in Savannah from England in 1824 and later established a successful business as a cotton factor, marketing and selling cotton to clients in the North and abroad. He became part of the Scarborough family when on Christmas Eve 1828 he married Julia Henrietta Scarborough, the daughter of William Scarborough, a wealthy Savannah merchant who was instrumental in building the first steamship to cross the Atlantic Ocean.[2] The need for a healthier climate for Barnsley's sickly wife and their children, along with the desire to escape the Scarborough family turmoil following the death of his father-in-law in 1838,

The roses were blooming which is unusually early and there was a promise of an abundance of fruit— the tulips were also blooming— during the War, I counted 2,200 in bloom at one time—a gorgeous sight—when I returned from England in '65, the gardens at Woodlands appeared to me more beautiful than I had seen.
—Godfrey Barnsley, April 23, 1871

brought him to Cass County (now Bartow County) in 1840 in search of land. In 1841 he purchased 3,680 acres there, which provided him a central location from which to travel to port cities in the South for business.[3] Soon after, he moved his family to the property, which he dubbed "Woodlands," and began work.

Barnsley was eager to build a showplace to signify his wealth and status. To do that, he looked outside the South for inspiration. During the antebellum period, Greek Revival, Classical Revival, and Federal homes were in vogue in the South. These imposing structures had a symmetrical shape, central entrances flanked by stately columns, pediment gables, and a heavy cornice. To complement this formality, which harked back to the proportioned architecture of classical Greece and Rome, the preferred design of high-style antebellum gardens of the southern elite was geometric. Barnsley, however, built his mansion in the romantic Italianate style, characterized by almost flat roofs, massive brackets, and wide eaves, a style adapted from the romantic villas of Renaissance Italy. The Italianate style became popular in America in the 1840s through widely published pattern books by Alexander Jackson Davis, Calvert Vaux, and Andrew Jackson Downing. Barnsley's letters from the period confirm he used as his guide Vaux's pattern book *Villas and Cottages* (1857), which he owned.[4] The resulting design suggests Vaux's influence. The illustrations of an Italian villa in Vaux's book are very similar to the manor house Barnsley built, the most prominent features being the square tower and the piazza.[5]

For the grounds and gardens, Barnsley followed the romantic picturesque style, which complemented the Italianate mansion, using the garden design patterns and planting suggestions promoted by Andrew Jackson Downing. Downing was heavily influenced by the English style of naturalistic landscape gardening developed during the eighteenth century, which grew out of dissatisfaction with the formality of French gardens and a rekindled fascination with nature. Led by the English landscape designer Lancelot "Capability" Brown and continued by his successor, Humphry Repton, and later John Claudius Loudon, the English style of landscape gardening moved toward picturesque design, an effort to emulate uncultivated nature. Barnsley was familiar with Downing's ideas through his books *Treatise on the Theory and Practice of Landscape Gardening* (1841), published in the same year that Barnsley established Woodlands, and *Cottage Residences* (1844). Barnsley made numerous references to Downing in his correspondence. His right-hand man and manager, John Connolly, mentioned Downing in letters to Barnsley.[6] Although there is no evidence that Downing and Barnsley ever met, scholars speculate that Barnsley learned about Downing through his business connections in Philadelphia and New York or through Bishop Stephen Elliott Jr., a disciple of Downing's teaching, a passionate gardener, and a founder of the Montpelier Institute near Macon, which Barnsley's daughter Julia attended.[7]

In his books, Downing promoted the idea of creating harmony between the buildings and grounds, and that architectural and landscape styles should conform to the character of the site.[8] He differentiated between the two kinds of beauty shaped by the art of "modern" landscape gardening: formal beauty, based on symmetry, proportion, and unity; and picturesque, or naturalistic, beauty, based on asymmetry and the irregularities found in nature.[9]

Barnsley drew upon the general principles in Downing's *Treatise* and likely found the idea for the general layout of the grounds from Downing's pattern book *Cottage Residences*. The book mixes romantic architecture with a landscape design that recalled the pastoral nature of the English countryside and that capitalized on topographic features and favored asymmetrical design compositions. Among the design ideas presented in *Cottage Residences* is an illustration of an Italianate villa placed on a plateau above a river with a gently curving drive that terminates in an oval directly in front of the house. It specifies areas near the house for a front lawn, curved walks, flower plantings, an orchard, and a kitchen garden.[10] When comparing Downing's illustration with a map of Barnsley's estate, as well as with a drawing that John Connolly made of Woodlands in 1843, the connection between the two is evident. The house at Woodlands is sited on a knoll overlooking a spring and creek with an oval drive that terminates directly in front of the main house. The orchard and kitchen garden are sited similarly to those in Downing's illustration.[11]

OPPOSITE: View into the formal front garden showing the grand fountain

Oval parterre radiating from the centrally placed fountain

The creation of Woodlands was ambitious. When Barnsley and his family moved to the estate in 1841, he had a log house constructed to serve as a temporary home while the Italianate mansion was being built. Since Barnsley had to be away on business throughout the year, his wife, Julia, was in charge of the daily supervision. Barnsley hired caretakers to supervise workers doing the timbering operations on the property, planting crops, erecting buildings, and laying out and tending the gardens; the workforce consisted of eight enslaved African Americans and dozens of day laborers.[12] Barnsley hired Irishman John Connolly soon after arriving at Woodlands, and he became indispensable for enacting Barnsley's vision and caring for Woodlands.[13] A local farmer named Edward Villiers oversaw the clearing of the land, the planting of the first corn crop, and later the construction of the manor house.[14]

Construction of the house and outbuildings occurred simultaneously with work on the grounds and gardens. Bradley Nestor and William Mann's groundbreaking 1998 study of Barnsley Gardens describes the garden elements installed around what later became the main house: "A dwelling house for the family was built on a sculptured knoll overlooking a stream. Shortly thereafter, a large oval parterre garden was fashioned in front of what would become the manor house. The oval was separated into symmetrically positioned beds bordered by English boxwood and lined with crushed granite walks. Another boxwood garden consisting of irregularly shaped beds was constructed on the terrace in front of the dwelling house."[15]

A drawing of Barnsley Gardens by P. Thornton Marye in *Garden History of Georgia* depicts the intricate oval parterre garden, which followed the regional gardening style of placing a formal garden near the house. Even though Downing was an advocate of the naturalistic style, he tolerated formal gardens deemed appropriate for a site. He explains in *Cottage Residences*: "We are not admirers of geometric or formal flower gardens like this, considered by themselves, and merely as flower gardens, because we think a natural arrangement is more replete with grace and beauty, and is capable of affording a much higher kind of pleasure. But this kind of architectural flower garden, so common in Italy, and so appropriate an accompaniment to residences of this kind,

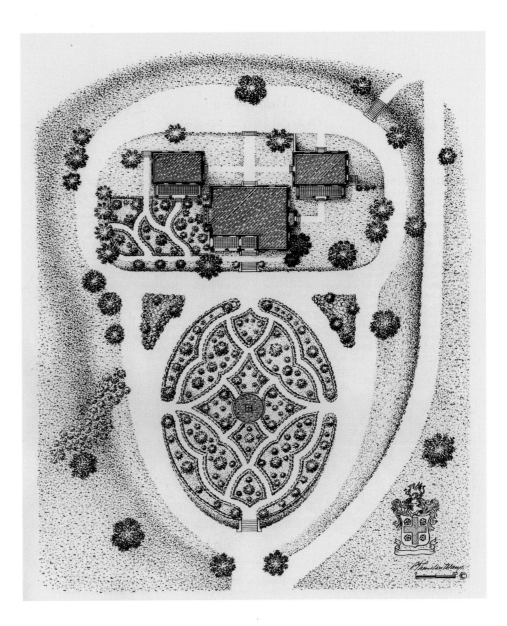

requires to be regarded in another light. It is not only a garden for the display of plants, but it is a garden of architectural and floral beauty combined."[16]

The inclusion of an oval parterre was the only departure from Downing's naturalistic style, although it was planted following the method Downing advocated in *Treatise*, as confirmed by correspondence between Barnsley and Connolly. They arranged a large variety of plants in a logical fashion to provide the family with pleasure throughout the year, with a consistency and duration of blooms, color, and fragrance. They planted trees and taller shrubs in the background, medium-sized plants in the middle ground, and the smallest plants near the edge of the planting beds, providing a balanced arrangement allowing all the plants to be viewed. A photograph from around 1870 clearly shows this planting scheme in the oval parterre garden.[17] Barnsley added an irregularly shaped

Landscape plan of Barnsley Gardens by P. Thornton Marye from *Garden History of Georgia*

Central fountain

Cutwork path

boxwood garden on the south side of the house, which is depicted in the Marye drawing.

The Marye drawing shows the parterre garden paired with two irregular rock gardens in front of Barnsley's house.[18] Barnsley and Connolly followed Downing's advice by adding two triangular rock mounds—one type of embellishment that Downing discusses in *Treatise*—emulating those occurring in nature.[19] Yet they placed this rock work, which still exists, directly in front of the house, in a departure from Downing's recommendation to place such a feature in a remote and wild area away from the residence.

Downing's books provided lists of plants his readers could use. Correspondence and receipts from nurseries indicate that Barnsley planted species of plants identical or similar to those included in *Treatise* and *Cottage Residences*.[20] This documentation confirms Barnsley's passion for, even obsession

with, gathering native and exotic plants and amassing a vast collection of specimens commercially available in the United States in the mid-nineteenth century. He purchased plants from two sources, Buist Nurseries in Philadelphia, between 1842 and 1852, and Fruitland Nurseries in Augusta, between 1860 and 1864.[21] By studying Barnsley's letters and receipts, Nestor and Mann created a list of approximately 550 trees, fruit trees, shrubs, grasses, flowers, and roses. Of particular note was their discovery of about 130 varieties of roses.[22] The plethora of roses remaining in the garden in 1933 was described in detail in *Garden History of Georgia*: "Roses abound: daily and moss roses in red, pink and white, green roses, purple roses, Picayune roses, Malmaisons, Louis Phillippes, gold of Ophirs, musk clusters, little seven sisters, Jane Hachettes, red and white tree roses from Germany, General Jaquimenots, cloth of gold, Marechal Niel and Devoniensis. There are many more varieties, their names now forgotten. A veritable Niagara of Cherokee roses, pink, white and double, tumbles down the south fall of the hill."[23] Appropriately, the Barnsley family motto was "Ut rosa sic vita," or "Life is like the rose."

Much was achieved with the gardens in the first few years of Barnsley's ownership. Ledger records show that in the first two years on the property, 18 percent of the money that Barnsley spent on the buildings and grounds went to the terrace and gardens, an indication of their importance.[24] In April 1842, Julia wrote to Barnsley: "We have azaleas, fringe trees, and a most beautiful tulip tree just down at the bottom of the hill near the spring. . . . John has planted the dahlias this afternoon. He seems delighted."[25] Besides showing the location of the oval parterre garden, the front lawn, drive, and the orchard, Connolly's 1843 map includes the site of a number of springs, the use of a fence around the property, and a farmyard southeast of the house. In the farmyard, the daily work for the estate was carried out by enslaved African Americans, whose housing was "completely out of the view of the dwelling house."[26]

Just as great strides were being made, tragedy occurred. In the summer of 1843, one-year-old

Rose-lined drive leading to the main house

Osage orange trees bordering
the lower meadow

Parterre on the south side of
the house

Godfrey Jr., the couple's eighth child, died of fever.[27] The remainder of 1843 and 1844 brought brief periods of improvements in Julia's health, but ultimately pain and decline. Frustrated that his business kept him away from his family for long periods, Barnsley voiced deep regret in his letters for his absences, along with love and affection for his wife and children. Julia died on February 16, 1845, and Barnsley returned to Woodlands to arrange for the care and education of their six surviving children and to plan the continued development of Woodlands under Connolly's astute management.[28]

In 1845, work started on the large brick Italianate manor house, the corn crop was successful, and the gardens and orchards were thriving. In February 1847, Connolly wrote to Barnsley regarding improvements in the gardens: "I am preparing beds for the new plants which you ordered from Philadelphia on the bank in front and south of the new house. I intend having them in groups of beds of different shapes. They will look better in this way and having the spare ground underneath it will have a fine effect. This mode is most adapted in the flower gardens of G. Britain."[29]

By the close of the 1850s, the Italianate manor house was complete. It featured modern plumbing, imported marble, and luxurious furnishings. The gardens were flourishing as well. An 1858 drawing by Barnsley's son George beautifully depicts their elegance, which was soon to be overshadowed by more adversity.[30] Barnsley's relations with his son Harold became strained, and his newly married daughter, Adelaide Barnsley Reid, returned to Woodlands; she died in 1858 while giving birth to her son, Godfrey. Barnsley's reliable and knowledgeable manager, John Connolly, left the estate in 1857 after being accused of mismanaging funds.[31]

When the Civil War began, Barnsley remained at Woodlands and when able, ordered plants from Fruitland Nurseries. But the estate was not immune from the ravages of war. In May 1864, Union troops under the command of General James B. McPherson camped on the property, pillaging the site and stealing many of Barnsley's possessions. By the war's end, his time away from his business had led Barnsley into financial ruin.

Following the war, Barnsley's daughter Julia and her husband, James P. Baltzelle, assumed management of the estate. Correspondence shows that Baltzelle hired an English gardener, Mr. Packer, to help with the management.[32] Baltzelle died in an accident in 1868, leaving Julia and their young daughter, Addie, with Barnsley, who was in poor health and depressed. On July 3, 1869, Barnsley wrote of his state of mind: "I want to get away from this place unless fortunate to make it a permanent resting place. This place is a mess, little crops and many weeds & I am considering letting it, and myself go to the dogs. I am heartily tired of it and everything else."[33] After several unsuccessful attempts to return to the cotton trading business, he died on June 7, 1873, in New Orleans. He was brought back to Woodlands to rest beside his beloved Julia and other family members.

At the time of Barnsley's death, four of his children had died and three lived abroad, leaving the estate in the care of his daughter Julia.[34] As part of her effort to maintain "Barnsley Gardens," as it was known locally, in the early 1870s she established a sharecropping system to generate income.[35] She married Charles Henry Von Schwartz in the summer of 1872, and the couple hired Jake Sherman to manage the estate. Under his leadership, Woodlands recovered. Von Schwartz's business success enabled him to expand the farming and timber operations and to refurbish the gardens and grounds. Julia was also able to thwart her brother George's desire to sell the estate and divide the proceeds among the family by granting him a portion of the property for his house and medical practice.[36]

When Julia died in 1899, the Woodlands estate passed to Adelaide "Addie" Barnsley Saylor (the daughter of Julia Barnsley and James Baltzelle) and her husband, B. F. A. Saylor. They established new sawmills, expanded the peach orchards, and worked with George Sherman, an agricultural manager and the son of Jake Sherman, to develop improved methods for farming the land. Amid these accomplishments, though, they faced mounting challenges, as Addie expressed it: "While my husband lived, he managed to keep affairs at Barnsley running in somewhat the grand old fashion. He made a sincere effort to keep the great house in repair, even though this was a gigantic task. The years had already brought about a certain amount of deterioration, and the huge arched windows were targets for vandals who would throw rocks through them just

View of the main house through one of the symmetrically placed triangular rock gardens

for the fun of seeing them break."[37] In 1906, a year after Addie's husband died, a tornado tore the roof from the manor house. With no funds to replace the roof, Addie and her children moved into the estate's kitchen and dining room wing. Exposed to the elements, the manor house fell into ruin.[38]

The endless struggles and tragedies that followed the Barnsley family in the nineteenth century continued into the twentieth. Without money for upkeep, Barnsley Gardens continued to disintegrate. More misfortune came to the estate on November 5, 1935, when Godfrey Barnsley's great-grandson Preston Saylor murdered his brother, Harry, in front of their mother, Addie.[39] After Addie Barnsley Saylor died in June 1942, the property was sold. Two successive owners raised cattle on the 1,200 acres and tried to protect the remaining historic elements from vandals. A continued lack of funds meant that the historic manor house and gardens fell further into disrepair.[40] By the 1980s, invasive vines and undergrowth had overtaken the house, oval parterre garden, and rock-work gardens.[41]

The fate of Barnsley Gardens changed in 1988 when Prince Hubertus Fugger Babenhausen pur-

chased the property and developed a plan for the adaptive reuse of the estate. From 1988 to 1994, staff members, some of whom were local devotees of the site, uncovered and restored the majority of the architectural and garden features.[42] Drawing upon a Rome Area Heritage Foundation report entitled *A Plan for Barnsley Gardens* (1977), extensive historical research conducted by the local historian Clent Coker, and archival records in numerous repositories, workers stabilized the ruins of the manor house and restored several buildings. The original right wing of the manor house was turned into a museum. Professional horticulturists supervised the replanting and expansion of the gardens.[43] In the late 1980s, a replica of the Tullie Smith House at the Atlanta History Center was constructed northeast of the mansion ruins and placed next to the Rice House (built around 1856), which had been moved from Rome. They were used as a restaurant, gift shop, and visitor center.[44]

Most of the original plant material had long disappeared from the site by the 1980s, and the antebellum garden design based on Downing's pattern books was obscured. Restoration work was carried out on the garden elements that survived near the mansion ruins, including the original drives, the large oval boxwood parterre garden (including a replica of the original fountain), and the irregular rock gardens. During this period, new elements were also folded into the historic landscape. Southwest of the ruins of the manor house, a grand lawn was added and enclosed with a long perennial border punctuated on one end by a redwood and brass arbor overlooking the lower garden. This lower garden features several ponds, a waterfall, and a bog garden, all part of the original nineteenth-century design. The hillside leading to the ponds was planted with thousands of daffodils, and a nearby slope contains native and exotic rhododendrons and camellias, Japanese andromeda, maples, and sourwoods. Winding paths in the woodlands lead past the pond and over a flagstone sluice. Other additions include rows of cherry trees planted along the old stagecoach route that runs the length of the estate, an orchard with heirloom fruit trees, and an extensive collection of antique roses. To guide the restoration of the gardens and grounds, a team of horticulturists and landscape architects in 1996 used the extensive research of Nestor and Mann, including a time line of the conception and construction of the gardens and a comprehensive list of trees, shrubs, flowers, and roses that Godfrey Barnsley had planted.[45] In 1990, the site was included in the National Register of Historic Places as part of the Etowah Valley Historic District.

The adaptive reuse plans called for building an upscale village-style resort with thirty-three buildings housing seventy guest suites around a common green, an eighteen-hole golf course, a spa, restaurants, and other amenities. The resort opened to the public in 1999. Andrew Jackson Downing's influence at Barnsley Gardens was still at work 150 years later, seen in the decision to build the new structures in the Gothic Revival style, which Downing advocated as part of his interest in the picturesque. The Barnsley Gardens Resort was sold to Julian Saul, a former president of Shaw Industries, and his partner, Mike Meadows, in 2004, and they expanded the site by acquiring an additional 1,700 acres.[46] They have focused their efforts on general maintenance, redecorating many buildings on the property, and developing additional recreational activities,

including biking, hiking, horseback riding, kayaking, fly-fishing, clay shooting, and hunting. Future plans include developing the site into an anchor for residential and commercial development in northwestern Georgia.[47] A professional horticulturist on staff manages a crew of gardeners who oversee the historic garden areas and the vast plant collection as well as new additions such as an extensive vegetable garden.

Today, the Barnsley Resort blends the past with the present. Besides earning a reputation for its luxury and charm, it is a sought-after destination for garden and history enthusiasts. Visitors can enjoy the restored elements of Barnsley's vision, including the ruins of the Italianate manor house and the only significant surviving example of an antebellum Downing-esque landscape in the state of Georgia while experiencing twenty-first-century amenities and recreational activities tucked away in the middle of northwestern Georgia.

View from the ponds and bogs on the lower hillside to the south of the main house

Barrington Hall's classic Greek Revival–style north façade

Barrington Hall and Bulloch Hall

IT IS NOT OFTEN that communities are able to provide visitors the opportunity to experience the homes of their founding families, but travelers to Roswell, Georgia, can have that privilege. Barrington Hall and Bulloch Hall, two historic sites that date from the city's earliest days, have been preserved and are open to the public.[1]

Constructed when Georgia's last frontier was rapidly being settled, these properties were designed in the Greek Revival style then quite popular in America. This style, inspired by the world's oldest democracy, reflected the new nation's optimism during a time of growth and progress. Barrington Hall and Bulloch Hall, two symbols of the country's promise, tell the story not only of Roswell's origins and the families that called these houses home but also of the preservation challenges facing historic sites.

The similarities between Barrington Hall and Bulloch Hall are striking. Both were part of the original town of Roswell, and both were owned by founding citizens. Both feature temple-form Greek Revival architecture, and both are believed to have been constructed by the same New England carpenter-builder. Both survived the Civil War as well as difficult economic circumstances afterward. Both had benefactors who understood their intrinsic value and invested generously in their rehabilitation. Both are now house museums with landscapes that retain components of their antebellum heritage. The City of Roswell had the foresight to acquire both properties, ensuring their availability for future generations to study and enjoy. Yet despite their similarities, each has its own story to tell.

Roswell owes its beginning to an ambitious man named Roswell King. While traveling through Georgia's Piedmont region on a business trip for the Bank of Darien around 1830, King saw property that intrigued him. The Connecticut native, who, as a young man, had moved to coastal Georgia to make his fortune, had become a successful businessman. What he discovered in the hills near the banks of the Chattahoochee River sparked his entrepreneurial spirit. An abundance of trees for timber, a source of waterpower (in what today is called Vickery Creek), and fertile soil on which to live and farm were the raw materials needed to build a new town and a new enterprise.[2] He began acquiring land and preparing for the hard work to follow.

King returned to the coast and persuaded his son Barrington to join him in establishing what was eventually to become a thriving manufacturing center. The two invited friends and family to take part in this promising undertaking. They offered them incentives that included land for homes and an opportunity to buy stock in the cotton mill that was to be the economic heart of the community. The Kings would then sell them additional land for plantations or farms.[3] The families who linked their futures with Roswell and Barrington King called themselves the "Colony" and included names such as Bulloch, Dunwody, Smith, Lewis, Hand, and Pratt.

The Kings envisioned not just a manufacturing center but also a carefully planned settlement to be located on a bluff above the creek. Preparation of the site began with the cutting down of trees and clearing of land. The town square, or park, reminiscent of a New England village green, became a focal point. A commissary located east of the square was the first of several commercial buildings.[4] To the north was the village's religious center, a Presbyterian church, organized in 1839. Services were held the following year in the newly constructed Greek Revival–style house of worship.[5] Next to the church sat the academy, or school.[6] The mill was constructed within a short walking distance southeast of the square on the bank of the creek. Housing for mill workers was erected on higher ground nearby. Impressive houses for the colonists were built not far from the square; they included Barrington King's residence, situated directly south of the park and completed by 1842, and James Stephens Bulloch's house, west of the square, completed by 1839.[7]

Roswell King died in 1844 at age seventy-eight. Ten years later, when the town was officially incorporated, it was named "Roswell" in his honor. The Roswell Manufacturing Company, incorporated in 1839, was as successful as Roswell King had imagined. By the 1850s, additional mills had been built and were, along with other businesses, employing more workers. The Presbyterian church had grown from 15 charter members to over 100 congregants—white and black—by 1857.[8] The academy, managed by the church, provided local children with an opportunity for a basic education.[9] The original settlers committed to building their homes, raising their families, and supporting this new enterprise in northern Georgia, and their efforts proved fruitful. The colony was prospering.

BARRINGTON HALL

Oh! Beautiful place of my childhood,
With its boxwood walks and its trees,
With their tangled growth of wildwood,
And the cheerful hum of the bees—
—F. K. Pratt, "The Old Garden"

When Barrington King moved his family to northern Georgia in 1838, he was intent on a new challenge—cotton manufacturing. Through his marriage to Catharine Nephew King, sixteen years earlier, King had acquired South Hampton plantation in Liberty County, which flourished under his direction. When the offer came to start a business with his father, King sold the property to his brother Roswell and invested in the new venture.[10]

Barrington King, who one day would be named president of the Roswell Manufacturing Company, wanted to provide a comfortable, fashionable home for his wife and children. Willis Ball, a carpenter-builder from Connecticut, constructed a two-story Greek Revival white clapboard residence. Its most prominent feature was a series of fourteen fluted Doric columns supporting the roof, which sheltered a wide porch encircling the front and sides of the house. In the center of the low-pitched gable roof with side pediments stood a small lookout, or widow's walk, perhaps a nod to King's New England roots. The stately design of the house reflected King's position in the community as well as the anticipated success of the new settlement.

King chose the highest ground overlooking the town as the site for his house. Standing in the front hall, a person could see directly to the town square. Visitors to the estate first passed through a decorative tripartite picket gate. Its side sections consisted of two swinging gates for the use of carriages and riders on horseback; one side was used to enter the property, and the other to leave. The central section was framed by two columns capped by finials and a fanned arch with a sun design. Between these columns was a rather unusual pedestrian gate that pivoted on a central post.[11] Upon entering the grounds, guests were met by an expansive front lawn with "post oaks . . . pines, hickory, and chestnut trees."[12] An oval carriage drive lined with cedars guided guests to the house.[13] Those on foot walked up the long central path leading directly from the entry gate to the front steps.

Barrington Hall's formal garden, located on the east side of the house, featured three terraces. The upper, most elaborate level contained rings of boxwood arranged in concentric circles.[14] The design of the lower levels included two squares, each divided by a walkway. There has been much speculation about who was responsible for this space. A marker on the edge of the property attributes the grounds to an unnamed English landscape gardener. *Gardens of Colony and State* (1934; edited by Alice Lockwood) credits Catharine King.[15] The current theory is that Catharine King developed the design with Francis Minhinnett, a stonemason who worked on the mill and other colony projects.[16] On the garden's southern edge, a plant pit was constructed. Made of "brick and mortar, topped by wooden sashes containing glass panes," this small greenhouse offered protection for "new plants and exotics" in cold weather.[17] Sources provide information about the types of plants historically found throughout the garden, but relatively little is known about what was used in the upper terrace.[18]

King modestly referred to his home as the Cobb farm.[19] The property was being called Barrington Hall by 1923; however, it is unclear when that name was first used.[20] The "farm" covered approximately 1,500 acres and provided sustenance for King's family and the enslaved African Americans who lived and

Barrington Hall's east garden, with a large cluster of oakleaf hydrangea in bloom

East parterre entrance

worked there. The Kings had twelve children, nine of whom lived to adulthood. In such a large household, there was always work to be done. Lucretia Merrell Camp, who, along with her husband, George Hull Camp, boarded with the Kings, wrote to her mother-in-law in 1843: "The house and familys arrangements are upon a large scale. Mrs. King has no less than 12 servants about the house & kitchen, beside gardeners & carriage driver. Of the number upon the plantation, I would not attempt an estimate."[21] In the rear yard, or work yard, were outbuildings that supported the daily routine of the household: a detached kitchen, a brick icehouse and dairy, a smokehouse, two wells, a barn, stables, and slave quarters.[22] A kitchen garden was located approximately 1,200 feet south of the residence near a freshwater spring.[23] In later years, the garden was planted closer to the house. George Hull Camp described the thriving fruit orchards in a letter to his mother in 1846: "We have peaches, apples,

pears, and other fruit in great abundance. Dont you envy us."[24]

With the coming of the Civil War, life in Roswell, as it did all over the South, dramatically changed. Two of Barrington and Catharine King's sons were killed in battle, and two others were critically injured. The town of Roswell was directly in the path of General William Tecumseh Sherman's march to Atlanta in the summer of 1864. The mills, along with a bridge that crossed the Chattahoochee River, were strategic targets. Anticipating that Union troops would descend on Roswell, the Kings, along with a number of town residents, fled to safety. Union occupation resulted in the destruction of the mills, but Barrington Hall and most of the town's other houses were spared.

At the war's end, Barrington King made plans to rebuild his business, only to die in January 1866 in a riding accident.[25] Catharine continued to live

East parterre, containing historic and new plantings of boxwood

Looking through the scuppernong arbor toward
the nineteenth-century cast-iron urn

Oakleaf hydrangea, one of Barrington King's favorite plants, in the east garden landscape

Trellis of wisteria at an entrance to the east garden

at Barrington Hall; she was later joined by her daughter Eva, who had returned to Roswell with her husband, William Baker, to look after her mother. After Catharine's death in 1887, the Bakers remained at Barrington Hall and made it their home. The Reverend Baker served as the acting pastor of Roswell Presbyterian Church throughout the 1890s.[26]

Eva Baker, a gardener, is credited with adding an informal rose garden on the west side of the house. A family story recalls Katharine Simpson, one of Eva's grandchildren, remembering early summer mornings when her grandmother, while "gathering roses for the dining room table . . . would always pleasantly comment to the children how beautiful a particular rose was, calling it by name."[27] Eva also enjoyed house plants, which in the summer were carefully

placed "on the front porch and steps." The young members of the family made themselves useful: "The grandchildren would run around with watering cans and she would brag on how smart they were."[28] On at least one occasion, Eva used vines as porch decoration, winding them around a number of the fluted columns that graced Barrington Hall.[29] The lawn's central path appears to have been widened before 1900, probably under Eva's direction.[30] One way for the children to please their grandmother was "to rake down this long front walk." Lois Carson Simpson, Katharine's adopted daughter, added, "We never rake it now but we think of how happy Grandmother would be if she were here—and small wonder for it's even longer than it looks."[31]

Many admired Barrington Hall and its garden. Eva's niece, Frances K. Pratt, wrote a poem in 1918 describing the "wonderful place of my childhood."[32] She mentioned several plants and landscape features, including boxwood walks, crape myrtle, a smoke tree "by the old-gate," mimosa, the juniper bush, and a Spanish bayonet.[33] Of special interest was the hydrangea, said to be a favorite of Barrington King, "planted by fingers, long since in silence are hushed."[34] In an article for the *Atlanta Journal* in 1923, Peggy Mitchell, later known as Margaret Mitchell of *Gone with the Wind* fame, described Barrington Hall as standing "at the end of a long walk, bordered by old-fashioned flowers," and she noted "the tall white columns, glimpsed through the dark green of cedar foliage, the white veranda encircling the house, the stately silence engendered by the century-old oaks."[35]

The Reverend Baker had died in 1906, and Eva in 1923. She left Barrington Hall to their seven children and their granddaughter Evelyn Simpson. The heirs put the property up for sale, but funds were then raised that enabled the home to stay in the family, with Evelyn as the legal owner. Finances continued to be a concern throughout the rest of the twentieth century. Maintaining such a property on a tight budget was a challenge, although Evelyn and her younger sister, Katharine Simpson, remained committed to its preservation. They decided to open the property to visitors for a small fee. It was included in *A Guide to Early American Homes South* (1956), which listed "private homes whose owners . . . have generously agreed to let their homes be visited."[36] The entry on Barrington Hall remarked on "its fluted columns" and called it "handsome indeed, with a beautiful gate and fine boxwood."[37]

Katharine, a former schoolteacher, took on sole responsibility for Barrington Hall when Evelyn passed away in 1960. Katharine was interested in the preservation of Roswell's heritage, as well as Barrington Hall's, and became a charter member of the Roswell Historical Society.[38] She supported the nomination of Barrington Hall to the National Register of Historic Places in 1971 and sought out ways to ensure the property's long-term protection.[39] In this endeavor she was joined by her friend Lois Carson, who in the 1970s moved into Barrington Hall to assist Katharine; Katharine eventually adopted her. Both struggled to care for the house and grounds.

Among the many challenges Katharine and Lois faced was the widening of Marietta Road (State Highway 120) adjacent to Barrington Hall in the mid-1980s. The work required lowering the grade of the road along the front of the property. The entrance was moved to the lawn's northeast corner, and a stone wall was constructed along the front and eastern sides of the site, to provide privacy from the busy roadway.[40] A more daunting event occurred on November 4, 1987, when a fire destroyed the roof and attic. The Roswell Fire Department succeeded in preventing the flames from spreading. Police officers, firefighters, and local citizens, including members of the Roswell Historic Preservation Commission and the Roswell Historical Society, worked both during and after the fire to save family papers, furniture, and mementos.[41] The roof and attic were eventually rebuilt; however, the lookout was not reconstructed.

When Katharine Simpson died in 1995, Lois inherited Barrington Hall. A chance meeting with Sara Winner, who was interested in seeing the house, led to a close friendship between the two women and a momentous change for Barrington Hall. Winner purchased Barrington Hall in 2002. The terms of purchase included a living trust that allowed Lois to remain in the house for the rest of her life. Winner, sensitive to the property's historic significance, used her financial resources, and great personal effort, to begin a major rehabilitation. The Atlanta architect Eugene Surber, who is known for his skill in working with historic buildings, directed the project. Unfortunately, Lois, who died in 2003, did not live to see the restored Barrington Hall. Anticipating a promising future for this historic site, over three hundred people gathered on the grounds in 2004 for a reunion, organized by Winner, of King's descendants. The following year, Barrington Hall received an Award for Excellence in Restoration from the Georgia Trust for Historic Preservation.

Sara Winner and her husband, Les Hunter, briefly lived at Barrington Hall before transferring it to the City of Roswell in November 2004. Barrington Hall officially opened to the public on Labor Day weekend 2005.

Over the years, most of Barrington Hall's land was sold, leaving only the main house and immediate grounds. The City of Roswell owns approximately

7 of the original 1,500 acres belonging to the estate. The city's annual budget includes appropriations for the site, and ticket sales support special projects. In addition the estate is used as a venue for events such as weddings and the summer's increasingly popular Roswell Lavender Festival. The nonprofit Friends of Barrington Hall raises funds to provide for the property's ongoing care.

In Barrington Hall's transition from a privately owned to a publicly owned property, it was necessary to determine what was critical to the estate's role as a historic site. Decisions had to be made about the significance and interpretation of the main house and the landscape. A site manager with a strong background in historic preservation was hired in 2005. A master plan addressing the house's cultural landscape was prepared in 2006, and a plan to assist in interpreting each of the city's three historic sites—Barrington Hall, Bulloch Hall, and the Smith plantation—was produced two years later.[42] Today, Barrington Hall's interpretation spans 1842 to 2004, that is, from its completion until its sale by Sara Winner.[43] Over 160 years of private ownership, the changing fortunes of the King descendants, and their commitment and struggle to preserve Barrington Hall are all part of the narrative.

Making decisions related to the landscape's restoration and interpretation is sometimes complex.

West garden and historic icehouse and dairy

Oval drive on the north side of Barrington Hall facing downtown Roswell

Former owners' lack of resources resulted in years of neglect in the formal east garden. When the city took over the property, the lower two terraces were virtually nonexistent. The upper terrace retained its outer ring of boxwood; the other circles were missing, and in their place were two ellipses.[44] Staff members needed to uncover as much historical information as possible before undertaking the garden's reconstruction and rehabilitation, although questions remain. Written records, family memories, and early photographs were studied.[45] Of primary importance was the plan of Barrington Hall's "formal, circular" garden found in *Gardens of Colony and State*.[46] Descriptions such as the one in *Garden History of Georgia* provided clues to its historic appearance: "On the east a little circular box maze is nested in bridal wreath spirea, crape myrtle, Spanish bayonet

and tiger lilies."[47] Evidence found in the landscape itself was extremely significant. Robert Winebarger, the site manager, recalls removing vegetation from the lower terraces and uncovering the outlines of the squares.[48]

The interpretation of the east garden recognizes its changes over time as well as the women who cared for this landscape. When restoration of the upper terrace began, the outer circle of English boxwood was fairly intact, although there were gaps where plants had died. American boxwood was selected to fill in these spaces, illustrating the "old versus new" sensibility and making clear which plants were replacements. English boxwood, however, was used in the reconstruction of the two inner rings. A few of the historic English boxwood were salvaged and incorporated into the revived circles.

To ensure future healthy replacements, a "boxwood hospital" of cuttings from the garden's historic plants is located on site.[49]

The three terraces pay tribute to the women who nurtured them; this can be seen especially in the progression of plant material on each level.[50] The boxwood parterre nearest the house illustrates Catharine King's original vision, but may include plant material introduced before 1866, the year of Barrington King's death. This level contains the pride of the east garden—the breathtaking oakleaf hydrangea (*Hydrangea quercifolia*). The middle terrace reflects Eva Baker's interests, containing plants available from the late nineteenth century until her death in 1923.[51] Here the reconstructed scuppernong arbor, the main component of this level, separates two squares filled with plants. A white cast-iron urn, said to have been a gift to Barrington and Catharine King from their son James, can be seen through the arbor and adds visual interest to the lower terrace.[52] This level reflects the stewardship of the Simpson sisters, Evelyn and Katharine, as well as of Lois, with plants found through the 1960s and 1970s.[53] In addition, the terrace contains two planted squares divided by a walk. At its eastern edge is a modern wooden swing. The inclusion of reconstructed cedar benches throughout the garden is based on a photograph from around 1905.[54] In *Daffodils in American Gardens* (2015), Sara Van Beck refers to jonquils in Barrington Hall's 1854 landscape; they are also present today.[55] Leyland cypress planted by Sara Winner line the garden's eastern wall, reflecting twenty-first-century additions. Hedges of bridal spirea on the north and English dogwood on the south form the garden's borders.

With assistance from the Garden Club of Georgia's Historic Landscape and Garden Grant Program, the small west garden next to the house was brought back to life in 2012. Historical references and photographs, along with the discovery of remnant bulbs, guided its planning. When determining what kind of plants to introduce into Barrington Hall's landscape, the staff first selected those that could be documented as having been there previously. If the historical record was unclear, heirloom and period-appropriate plants, with some new cultivars, might be used.[56] For example, the reimagining of Eva's garden contains a bed of sweet lavender and an informal rose garden, along with laurels and lilacs, all mentioned in *Garden History of Georgia*.[57] Also found are cape jasmine (gardenias), snowball viburnums, *Camellia sasanqua* 'Yuletide', and daffodils. Eva's granddaughter Evelyn Simpson enjoyed lavender, and this space is a tribute to her as well.

Although changes have occurred to Barrington Hall's setting, it still provides important context for the historic site. After purchasing the property, the city tore down the portion of the stone wall located at what had been the original entrance. This reopened the view from the house down the front lawn's central walk toward the town square. The historic gate is gone; a remnant of a replica exists in storage. Although a storm in 2013 resulted in the loss of a number of the main canopy's oaks and hickories, trees will be replanted.[58] A stone marker identifying Barrington Hall as the home of Roswell's cofounder was placed on the front lawn in 1937 by the James Edward Oglethorpe Chapter of the Daughters of the American Colonists. Although most of the outbuildings in the rear yard no longer exist, the brick icehouse and dairy, the smokehouse, and the well still stand. The rehabilitated barn is used for meeting space and administrative offices.

The care of such a historic property, especially its landscape, requires continual attention. In the early years of Barrington Hall's ownership by the city, the Roswell Garden Club volunteered to provide much-needed assistance. Members worked throughout the grounds, identifying and clearing out beds and helping solve some of the landscape's puzzles.[59] The property's staff is committed to making the gardens as visually appealing and as authentic as possible. Barrington Hall Garden Guild members volunteer weekly to ensure that the gardens are well tended. A part-time horticulturist employed by the city continues to seek out historical information to guide and enhance the site's interpretation. There is still much to be learned.

Sarah sends this jasmine to you, how much more romantic she is than I am, you know who I mean, the little girl about the house, she came to me and said, "please Miss Mittie, send this to Mr Roosevelt, and tell him it came off of our vine."—Mittie Bulloch to Theodore Roosevelt, September 14, 1853

James Stephens Bulloch was one of the men who joined Roswell and Barrington King in making a home in the Georgia Piedmont as well as serving as a stockholder in the Roswell Manufacturing Company. Both Bulloch and his wife, Martha Stewart Elliott Bulloch, were members of prominent Georgia families, descendants of men who had distinguished themselves in the fight for independence from England. Archibald Bulloch, James Stephens Bulloch's grandfather, was president of Georgia's provincial congress and commander in chief of the Georgia militia. Martha's father, Daniel Stewart, a brigadier general in the militia, fought in the Revolutionary War and the War of 1812.[60]

Like Barrington Hall, the Bullochs' Greek Revival home in the colony is believed to have been constructed by Willis Ball. Located at the end of what is today Mimosa Boulevard, it was sited atop a gently rising slope reached by a heart-shaped drive. The front portico of the two-story clapboard house is distinguished by four large unfluted Doric columns supporting a gable-end pediment. Like Barrington Hall, Bulloch Hall had a view directly to the town square. The land at the rear or west side of the house dropped away, providing an open vista to the valley below and the surrounding hills. In a biography of Theodore Roosevelt, the historian David McCullough noted that Mittie, the Bullochs' youngest daughter, found "the view of the valley to the west . . . especially lovely in the late-afternoon light."[61] In her recollections of a childhood visit in 1839, Mittie's cousin Catherine Elliott Sever described looking, "night after night," at the "distant hills" covered in springtime with "wonderful flowers, azaleas . . . [of] every hue and shade of scarlet, crimson, orange, pale yellow and white, and every variation of these until on one hill we counted forty varieties."[62]

Regarding the landscape at Bulloch Hall, *Garden History of Georgia* mentions "a scuppernong arbor and an informal planting of flowering shrubs and fruit trees," but asserts that a garden never existed there.[63] A more recent theory, however, is that some type of garden may have been planted near a summerhouse, although not to the scale of that found at Barrington Hall.[64] Like its much larger neighbor, the Bulloch Hall estate was self-sufficient. There was a vegetable garden and a fruit orchard, although their exact locations are unclear. Outbuildings necessary to support day-to-day activities were located mainly in the service yard north of the house. Catherine Elliott Sever remembered that "near my aunt's house were the slave quarters, two nice little houses each divided into two parts, though several of the servants always slept in the house near their mistress."[65]

Unfortunately, James Stephens Bulloch did not have many years to enjoy either his new home or his new life in Roswell, since he died unexpectedly in February 1849. A family friend, Major Archibald Howell, purchased Bulloch Hall in 1850, but Martha and her children remained there.[66]

Mittie's youth at Bulloch Hall was described by David McCullough as filled with "picnics and riding parties, a life spent almost constantly in the out of doors, in all seasons, in unspoiled open country, with sweet-smelling trees and flowers in bloom."[67] Life for young residents of the colony was filled with social activities, and close relationships formed. In fact, when Mittie married Theodore Roosevelt, Sr., a young man from a wealthy, established New York family, at Bulloch Hall on December 22, 1853, three of the King siblings (including Eva as a bridesmaid and Tom as a groomsman) from Barrington Hall were part of the wedding party.

After her wedding, Mittie left Roswell to live with her husband in New York. Mittie's mother, Martha, and her sister Anna eventually moved north as well, and by 1856 they were part of the Roosevelt household. Martha became "grandmamma" to Mittie's four children: Anna, Theodore Jr., Elliott, and Corinne.[68] The Civil War brought great emotional strain to Martha and Mittie, since family and friends from home supported and fought for the Confederacy, while Roosevelt sympathies lay with the Union.

Martha had left Bulloch Hall in the hands of Tom King, who, along with his wife, rented the property.

Bulloch Hall's stately Greek Revival–style façade

View through the historic osage orange grove toward the front of the house

Tom joined the Confederate forces and was killed in battle in 1863. His wife remained at Bulloch Hall until the occupation of Roswell during Sherman's Atlanta Campaign. The house is said to have been used as quarters for Federal troops.

With the close of the Civil War, the Bullochs' connection with Roswell faded further. Martha Bulloch died in New York six months before the war's end. Mittie and her husband both died in their forties—he in 1878, she in 1884. They did not live to see their son Theodore Jr. become the twenty-sixth president of the United States. Nor did they know that their son Elliott had a daughter, Eleanor, who would marry Franklin Delano Roosevelt and become one of the country's most respected first ladies. Both of these national figures, though, made pilgrimages to Roswell. In 1905, President Theodore Roosevelt stopped in the town to see his mother's childhood home. While there, he paid a visit to his mother's friend Eva King Baker at nearby Barrington Hall. First Lady Eleanor Roosevelt visited her grandmother's former home some years later during a trip to Warm Springs.[69]

Before her death, Martha had regained control of Bulloch Hall from Archibald Howell.[70] Her executor sold the house to Jason Wood in 1872, and in the ensuing decades it changed hands several times. Wood's son Eugene became its owner in 1888. Then it was sold to the Laurel Mills Manufacturing Company in 1892 and to Isaac Roberts in 1898. J. Bartow Wing, Eugene Wood's brother-in-law, purchased the house and grounds in 1907, having lived there with his sister and her husband for a while when he was younger.[71]

Bulloch Hall became home to the Wing family: Bartow; his wife, Mary Virginia "Hattie" Suddath Wing; their daughter, Virginia "Ginnie"; and their son, J. B. Jr. In 1917, when Ginnie was eleven, her father was killed in a car accident. Her remembrance of that sad day includes seeking refuge in her special hiding place, the mimosa tree next to the front porch.[72] Hattie and her children remained at Bulloch Hall, and although Ginnie eventually settled in Chattanooga after marrying George Power, she retained vivid memories of her old home. When asked about Bulloch Hall many years later, she described "where the avenue of cedars was, the specially fine walnut tree in front of the house, the ivy tree from which decorations were taken for Mittie Bulloch's wedding, the old fashioned garden down near the big white oak."[73] As Hattie grew older, the family became unable to care for Bulloch Hall. Ginnie closed the house, and it stood vacant.[74] The property remained in the Wing family until 1971, the year Hattie died. When listed in the National Register of Historic Places that same year, Bulloch Hall was characterized as being "unoccupied, deteriorating, and threatened with destruction."[75]

Bulloch Hall's time as a home came to a close when the businessman Richard S. Myrick saw the property. He understood its significance to Roswell's history. Realizing that it would amount to an irreparable loss if Bulloch Hall were allowed to fall into ruin, Myrick purchased and restored the building, opening it as a house museum in 1972. Unfortunately, the venture did not meet financial expectations, and within two years, Myrick closed the museum.[76]

The City of Roswell purchased Bulloch Hall in 1978. Financial support came from a citywide bond referendum, a grant from the Georgia Department of Natural Resources, and funds from the Roswell

Heart-shaped drive leading to the front entrance of the house

Reconstructed slave cabins viewed through the stand of osage orange trees

Historical Society. For a time, the society was based on the grounds of Bulloch Hall and provided on-site assistance. Gradually the city, represented by the Roswell Preservation Commission, expanded its leadership role, which continues today.[77] The city increased Bulloch Hall's acreage from ten to sixteen. Staff positions were created, and funding for the property was included in the city's annual budget. The nonprofit Friends of Bulloch Hall is an active and important component of the site's success. The group's fund-raising events, such as the long-standing Magnolia Ball, have made possible numerous projects, including archaeological investigations and a reconstruction of the carriage house.

When Bulloch Hall became public property, the need for site planning took on greater significance. Over time, master plans, archaeological surveys, and an interpretive plan were prepared. The latest document, a master plan update focusing on the preservation of the historic grounds as well as future expansion, was produced in 2009.[78] The site's interpretation focuses on the period 1843 to 1853, the years leading up to the wedding of the future parents of a U.S. president and the grandparents of a first

lady—the most significant event associated with Bulloch Hall.[79] This time frame guides all decisions affecting the house and its cultural landscape.

Finding clear-cut answers to questions concerning the interpretation of the landscape has not always been possible. Bulloch Hall's historic core consists of the house, the site's entrance (with the heart-shaped drive and lawn), the old well, and a grove of osage orange trees next to the house. Wooden fences separate this area from other parts of the site. There has been debate about whether the front lawn contained a central walk during the Bullochs' ownership. When the city purchased Bulloch Hall, there was a flagstone walk, laid in the early twentieth century, but its path was considered "probably not original except as a 'cut-through'" and was subsequently removed.[80] The origin and evolution of this central walk remain unclear, and there is still speculation that it was an antebellum feature. Site staff has not discounted the possible reconstruction of the walkway.[81]

Although Bulloch Hall may not have had a garden on the scale of the one at Barrington Hall, research has uncovered mention of a rose garden, shrubbery, and a gazebo or summerhouse, all believed to have been in the southeast corner of the front yard.[82] The landscape historian Catherine Howett determined that a simple garden with a "boxwood-bordered 'parterre' with flowers and shrubs planted within the box patterns" would have been historically appropriate in the Georgia landscape during this period.[83] This was the style selected when a small boxwood parterre garden was constructed in the corner of the front lawn in the 1980s.[84]

A demonstration garden maintained by the North Fulton Master Gardeners is located south of the house. It was established in 1995 to highlight gardening techniques appropriate for the Georgia Piedmont; a 2005 renovation refocused its purpose. It now emphasizes heirloom plants and those that adapt well to the region. Wooden pergolas and a picket fence frame the garden. Its geometric design, consisting of four quadrants, reflects the layout of ornamental antebellum gardens. The quadrants contain a children's garden, an area showcasing plants that attract butterflies and hummingbirds, an herb garden, and a section for roses and perennials. The area southeast of the house also contains visitor parking and a gift shop.

North Fulton Master Gardeners' demonstration garden

A critical part of the site's narrative acknowledges the lives of the enslaved people who were integral to the construction and operation of Bulloch Hall's world. Two slave cabins have been reconstructed in the former service yard north of the house. One, which contains an exhibition on slave life, is used for educational purposes; the other houses staff offices and the Bulloch Hall archives. In a nearby vegetable garden grow plants that the slaves would have raised for food. This area also includes the reconstructed carriage house and privy. Farther north are modern additions: a parking lot, an open-air pavilion, and a nature trail.

Trees have always been an important element of Bulloch Hall's landscape. Virginia "Ginnie" Wing Power wrote: "Large logs for heating were no problem in the old days in Roswell. Everywhere was forest primeval. On the long sweep of hill behind Bulloch Hall grew oaks, tulip poplars, chestnut and hickory trees. There were also huge, straight pines of the type from which some of the sixty-foot beams of the house had been hewed by hand."[85] A 1994 tree inventory identified thirty-three varieties of trees on the site.[86] In that same year, the Georgia Urban Forest Council listed the "Trees of Bulloch Hall" in the state's Landmark and Historic Trees Register.

While the architecturally and historically significant main house continues as the centerpiece of the site, there has been recognition for a long time that the surrounding landscape is an integral part of Bulloch Hall's story. Over the years, those in charge of the site have supported ongoing research to gain additional insights into how the grounds were used and how they might have looked. The goal is to better understand Bulloch Hall's overall historic context—the house and the families who once resided there, the enslaved African Americans who lived and worked on the property, and the land itself.

With a current population of over 90,000, the city of Roswell is far different from Roswell King's frontier colony. When Barrington and Bulloch Halls were first constructed, land was cleared for buildings, pastures, and fields, creating open vistas to neighboring houses and the town square. Today's urban environment has dramatically changed this landscape, and both Barrington Hall and Bulloch Hall have evolved as well. These historically significant sites, however,

Gazebo and boxwood parterre reminiscent of an antebellum garden

can still help visitors experience the sensation of being in a time and place quite different from an early twenty-first-century city. They provide a glimpse into Roswell's early days and offer insights into two of the town's founding families and the people with whom they shared their lives. Seeing the houses and walking the grounds provide experiences that written texts alone cannot offer.

In recognition of Roswell's commitment to preserving its historic properties, including Barrington and Bulloch Halls, the city received an Excellence in Stewardship award from the Georgia Trust for Historic Preservation in 2008. The city was cited for its "remarkable commitment to the citizens and historic resources of Roswell."[87] The decision made years earlier that the public benefit of preservation was worth the concomitant challenges, including a long-term financial investment, has made an immeasurable difference in the community's ongoing understanding and appreciation of its heritage as well as its place in state and national history.

Expansive lawn and border plantings highlighting the landscape

Statue of St. Francis in the Battersby-Hartridge fern garden

Battersby-Hartridge Garden

IN HER DESCRIPTION of late nineteenth-century Savannah, the local historian Laura Palmer Bell evokes a picturesque image: "All over town at that time there were big sprawling walled gardens, flower filled back yards completely hidden from the street, a few front gardens, and many side gardens planted in orderly parterres. These side gardens were nearly always overlooked by a porch or narrow veranda, where the owners would sit during the late afternoon of the long summertime to enjoy the coolness of their gardens."[1] Bell, writing in the 1940s, especially lamented the loss of many of the city's nineteenth-century parterres. Today, most of the sites that she and the landscape architect Clermont Lee identified in their 1940 study of the city's existing nineteenth-century gardens have been lost. One that has not only survived but also flourished is known as the Battersby-Hartridge Garden.[2]

Established in 1733, Savannah owes much of its twenty-first-century charm to its eighteenth-century town plan, introduced by James Oglethorpe. Designated a National Historic Landmark in 1966, Savannah's historic district is highly regarded for its green space, tree-bordered streets, architecturally interesting private and public buildings, and walkable neighborhoods. Critical to Oglethorpe's plan were the city's visually distinctive public squares, which today number twenty-two. Particularly appealing is Lafayette Square, named for the marquis de Lafayette, who visited Savannah in 1825. The French aristocrat had befriended George Washington and fought with the colonists against the British during the American Revolution. From this peaceful square, with its oak trees and palms, its benches and brick walks, and its flowing fountain, the twin spires of the Cathedral of St. John the Baptist are visible, as is the childhood home of the writer Flannery O'Connor. Also close by are two notable houses, both built by cotton merchants in the years before the Civil War:

This is a family home and garden, not a museum.—Cornelia McIntire Hartridge, March 19, 2015

Fern garden

ambitious newcomers as well as local entrepreneurs. Personal financial success was often reflected in the design of the city's houses and gardens.

William Battersby, a wealthy cotton merchant, was one such entrepreneur. After the creation of Lafayette Square in 1837, the surrounding land eventually became available for purchase. Andrew Low, a successful Scottish-born merchant with offices in Savannah and Liverpool, England, acquired property on the square for his residence. He sold another lot to his business associate William Battersby, who constructed his house a short walk across the street from Low's residence.[3] Born in England around 1820, Battersby came to Savannah as a young man. He and his brother Joseph were partners in William Battersby & Co., a trading business with offices in Savannah and Manchester, England.[4] He married a Savannah native named Sarah E. Hartridge and built her an elegant house with an elaborate parterre garden.

For the house, Battersby selected a design that was unusual for Savannah. It resembled structures found on the Caribbean island of Barbados or in the coastal city of Charleston, South Carolina. The rectangular three-story brick residence sits on a stuccoed, raised basement. Steps from the sidewalk lead to a side bay with a solid paneled door and a large transom highlighted by a decorative stone lintel. Next to the doorway is an "unusually handsome wrought-iron bracket light."[5] The Charlestonian or Barbadian influence is seen in this front entrance, which opens onto a large two-story piazza. The wide piazza, or porch, with its high ceilings, extends along the east side of the house and wraps around to the southern exposure, offering views of the side garden and rear patio, where the carriage house is located. A doorway from the piazza provides access to the interior of the residence.

There has been speculation about who designed Battersby's house. The architects John Norris and Charles Cluskey have both been mentioned, but no definitive record has been found. The building's year of construction is also not known, although 1852 is most often cited. The designer of the formal garden is also unknown. According to oral tradition, it was laid out while the house was being constructed.[6] Clermont Lee, who studied Savannah's gardens from this period, believed that some were probably designed by the architects of the houses.[7] The

the Andrew Low House, now a museum; and the Battersby-Hartridge House, still a private residence, which, behind its high brick walls, boasts one of the city's last remaining antebellum town gardens.

Savannah played a prominent role in the growth of the state's pre–Civil War economy. The port city was a major exporter of goods, especially cotton and lumber, to foreign markets. The Central of Georgia Railway, based in Savannah, opened access to the state's interior and to new trade opportunities. As agricultural production boomed throughout the state, the city served as a key distribution center. Savannah had strong ties with England, and many young men from the United Kingdom came to Georgia to build businesses and encourage international trade. Savannah's economic development meant opportunity for

current owner believes that Battersby's wife, Sarah, influenced the garden's final appearance.[8]

The Battersby garden, located on the east side of the residence, extended from the front of the property to the rear. According to Laura Palmer Bell, "In the older parts of town, practically every house, with the exception of those on the trust lots, was built up to the property line of the sidewalk."[9] The garden's design was in keeping with many of the characteristics common to gardens from the period. In *Gardens and Historic Plants of the Antebellum South* (2003), James R. Cothran states that in antebellum gardens, "with few exceptions, southerners remained wedded

to formality and the principles of geometric garden design that had prevailed throughout the colonial era."[10] Parterres were quite popular. Cutwork parterres featured a "combination of geometric shapes, including squares, triangles, rectangles, and circles," and by 1850, "ovals, curves, and flowing lines" were regularly seen.[11] Garden paths could be of sand or brick, and beds and walks were delineated with edging tiles or bricks.[12]

Enclosed by a high brick wall, the Battersby cutwork parterre garden featured beds of circles and ovals as well as ones formed by both curved and straight lines and decorative shapes. Interesting

Moss-draped oaks framing the walled garden and house

Cutwork parterre and house inside the brick wall

patterns and colorful flowers were designed to be seen easily and appreciated by family and friends as they looked down from the piazza. According to *Garden History of Georgia*, numerous camellias were planted, along with roses and tea olive. The flower beds, which were lined with "violets and snowdrops," were edged with terra-cotta tiles, which still exist.[13] Steps leading from the side of the piazza provided a convenient entrance into the garden. The carriage house and the area directly behind the residence and adjacent to the garden were used as a stable and service yard.

Over the years, the property was owned by many families involved in Savannah's civic, social, and business communities. When William and Sarah Battersby left Savannah after the Civil War to make their home in England, Sarah's brother Julian Hartridge and his wife, Mary Charlton Hartridge, acquired the house. A lawyer active in state and national politics, Hartridge served in Georgia's House of Representatives as well as nearly two terms in the U.S. Congress from 1875 until his death in 1879. The businessman Joseph John "J. J." Wilder purchased the house and its grounds in the 1880s. Alterations made in 1887 included increasing the size of the dining room—thus cutting into the rear porch—and moving the kitchen from the basement into an addition. This addition also connected the residence to the carriage house.[14] It is easy to speculate that work may have occurred in the garden at the same time. According to *Garden History of Georgia*, Wilder's wife, Georgia Page King, is credited with preserving the property's walled garden.[15] The Wilders also owned Oakton, a summer home with a formal kitchen garden, in Marietta, Georgia. By 1914, after both J. J. and Georgia Wilder had passed away, their daughter, Anne Page, who was married to J. Randolph Anderson, a lawyer and state legislator, took possession of the two properties. When *Garden History of Georgia* was published in 1933, the Savannah garden was described as "now cherished" by Anne Page Wilder Anderson.[16]

While today's garden is known for the cutwork parterres' boxwood, the landscape that Anderson tended contained numerous varieties of plants and was filled with color. Noteworthy was its "original planting of camellias," which included "Don Kaleare, Camellia reticulata, Lady Hume's blush, the Ella

Drayton, Legeman, Abby Wilder, alba plena, and a large, bold red and white variegated, catalogued as 'unnamed.'"[17] Also identified were "Pyrus japonica, tea olive, Devoniensis and Gen. Jacqueminot roses, and the lilac begonia which completely covers the walls."[18] The tile-lined beds were edged with ivy, and a decorative fountain reflected a Victorian influence.[19] In 1933, Anderson's garden was said to have "the distinction of being the oldest surviving Savannah garden retaining its original plan and planting."[20]

In 1971, Donald Livingston and his wife, owners of the property, renovated the residence and installed a garage in the carriage house.[21] They hired Clermont Lee, a well-known consultant in Savannah, to prepare a tree-planting plan for the garden and to make recommendations for new beds in the rear courtyard.[22] Lee advised adding dogwoods, loquat, podocarpus, white redbud, American holly, and Chinese star jasmine, among others.[23] It is unclear how closely the Livingstons followed her guidance. Lee's expertise was in re-creating formal antebellum landscapes and in recommending period-appropriate plantings, as she had done for the parterre garden at the nearby Low House. When Lee studied the Livingstons' garden, she found that few older plantings remained, with the exception of "one camellia, a tea olive, the [white] Lady Banks Rose, a Cherokee

Photograph of the parterre, circa 1933, from *Garden History of Georgia*

Rose, big leaf periwinkle, snowflakes, dwarf English ivy, the American Plane tree, and a crab apple."[24] When Lee prepared her plan in March 1971, the steps leading into the garden from the eastern side of the piazza had been removed, and a new bed was to be installed in their place.[25] At some point during the Livingstons' ownership, this bed evolved into a full oval parterre, resulting in paired ovals at the garden's northern end.[26] In their overall planning, the Livingstons maintained the geometric patterns of the parterres, keeping the basic form of the garden intact.

In 1978, Walter C. Hartridge II and his wife, Cornelia "Connie" McIntire Hartridge, purchased the residence. They were part of a growing group of young married couples who wanted to live and raise their families in Savannah's historic neighborhoods.[27]

This preference, part of a national trend in the preservation movement, grew in popularity and influence over the next several decades. People appreciated the craftsmanship and architectural detail often found in historic places. They enjoyed the mature landscapes found in older neighborhoods and valued the character of the inner city and its sense of community. In Savannah, as in many cities, people had long been leaving downtown for the suburbs. The "urban pioneers" who stayed often confronted increased crime, buildings in need of rehabilitation, and a belief that tearing down older buildings was necessary for progress to occur. The Historic Savannah Foundation had been formed in 1955 to combat such tendencies. One of the women instrumental in the organization's founding was Lucy Barrow McIntire, the grandmother of Cornelia McIntire Hartridge.

Spring bloom in the garden

The Hartridges became active members of Historic Savannah; Walter Hartridge was one of the early presidents of the foundation, and Connie Hartridge served several terms on its board.

An avid genealogist and student of history as well as a corporate and maritime lawyer, Walter Hartridge found that he had a personal connection with the Battersby House, since he was related to Sarah Hartridge Battersby, wife of the property's first owner, and her brother Julian. For Connie Hartridge, the house fulfilled her desire for a home in the historic district and a garden. She was immediately confronted by the practical consideration of maintaining such a space. Her husband was building his law practice, and she was an interior decorator. They were also rearing a family. Although she enjoyed working in the garden, she found many of the recommended antebellum plants to be quite labor intensive and

Rear courtyard garden with its specimen plane tree

View of the courtyard garden with stairway leading to the fern garden

Before the Hartridges purchased the property, the former service area at the rear of the residence had been converted into a brick courtyard; a low brick wall separates it from the main garden. A large American plane tree, identified as one of the garden's oldest plantings, remains the focal point of this space. Curved steps from the courtyard lead to the fern garden. Ferns and aspidistra line both sides of the walkway, and American holly trees stand next to the rear wall. At the east end of the walk, a decorative cast-iron bench provides a peaceful spot for reflection next to a brick prayer niche containing a statue of St. Francis of Assisi. A gate opens onto the parterres from the courtyard.

The landscape offers a variety of seasonal color. Hartridge's garden includes wisteria, white Cherokee rose (*Rosa laevigata*), virgin's bower (*Clematis virginiana*), Confederate jasmine (*Trachelospermum jasminoides*), and notably, one of its oldest and largest plants, the Lady Banksia rose (*Rosa banksiae* 'Lutea'), which drapes over the brick walls. A pair of Japanese maples (*Acer japonicum*) and a flowering peach tree (*Prunus persica*) are vivid against the green landscape. Hartridge also tries to maintain the historic nature of the space. When the last of the early camellias died a few years ago, she replaced them with a row of heirloom camellias in the fern garden.

One of Clermont Lee's recommendations to the Livingstons was to increase the use of boxwood, a suggestion that Hartridge has enthusiastically followed.[30] She has bordered the beds with these shrubs and filled the oval parterres with boxwood planted in a "hugs-and-kisses" pattern (*X*s and *O*s).[31] Boxwoods shaped into "knots" are also found throughout the garden's geometric parterres. This use of boxwood reflects an English influence and reduces the amount of labor needed to maintain the garden. The majority of the plants are Japanese boxwood (*Buxus microphylla* var. *japonica*), although Hartridge has planted other varieties as well. With the help of a gardener, she prunes the plants twice a year. When any shrub needs to be replaced, her method of acquiring a new one is simply to collect from the gardens of others. While a few plants have come from a family garden in South Carolina, most were discovered on her travels with her husband. Whenever they saw healthy boxwood, they stopped and asked whether the owner was willing to part

somewhat impractical when dealing with the realities of caring for a family garden in the late twentieth century. Apprehensive about taking on such a historic landscape, Connie Hartridge sought the guidance of a close friend, who told her, "You are going to make your own mistakes."[28] This advice has given her confidence to experiment over the years.

Careful to respect the antebellum garden's historic form, Connie Hartridge realized that she had flexibility in selecting the plant materials. A master gardener, she prefers green parterres and uses different shades of green plants, such as chartreuse coleus, throughout the beds. The Livingstons had paved the paths with exposed aggregate, a treatment that Hartridge decided to maintain.[29] The garden is divided into three distinctive "rooms"—the historic parterre garden, with its geometric shapes and boxwood; a fern or shade garden along the south brick wall; and the courtyard, or brick patio, area.

Formally clipped boxwood parterre with its geometric pattern and infill

View of the parterre garden from the shuttered porch

Cutwork parterre flowing into the fern garden

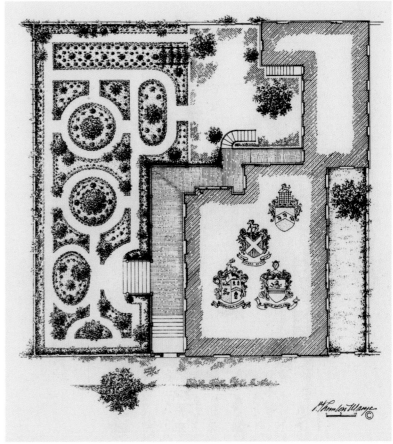

Landscape plan of the Battersby-Hartridge Garden by
P. Thornton Marye from *Garden History of Georgia*

Geometric cutwork

with a plant. Most people kindly obliged.[32] Over the years, Hartridge family members, especially the children, have enjoyed the garden. They have spent countless hours playing hide-and-seek among the boxwood, whose varying shapes make an ideal maze in which to wander. In many ways, this landscape has been a secret garden.[33]

Although the Battersby-Hartridge House is a private residence, many people mistake it for a museum or tourist destination.[34] Strangers often stop by and ask to come inside. On many mornings, Hartridge has found people on her front steps waiting for the door to open.[35] The Hartridges have generously shared this historic place with the public. The property has been opened for tours, including one held during the 2014 annual meeting of the Southern

Garden History Society. The house and garden have been featured in numerous publications.

Although the garden's form remains largely true to its original design from more than 160 years ago, changes have occurred to accommodate the tastes and needs of succeeding generations. To safeguard the integrity of one of the city's last remaining antebellum parterre gardens as well as the exterior of the historic house, the Hartridges gave a preservation easement to the Historic Savannah Foundation, which ensures the property's long-term protection. Connie Hartridge continues to work daily in her garden and understands her responsibility to this special place: "The garden is either thriving or dying. It reminds me that I am only here for a short time. I do not own the garden; I am only a temporary occupant."[36]

Camel-back bridge at Beech Haven

Beech Haven

ANYONE CRUISING DOWN the congested Atlanta Highway in Athens, Georgia, past fast-food joints, car dealerships, and shopping malls, would find it hard to believe that a sanctuary filled with nature and history sits tucked away a few hundred feet from the road. Beech Haven is a rare Arts and Crafts landscape that was designed by its owners, the Rowland family, and built by local craftsmen in the first decade of the twentieth century. Preservationists and other concerned citizens have recently banded together to save this gem hidden in the middle of Athens beneath a dense forest canopy. Beech Haven is one of the most significant examples of a vernacular Arts and Crafts–style landscape in the southeastern United States.

The Arts and Crafts movement began in England and flourished in Europe and North America between 1880 and 1910. It was a reaction against the formality of the Victorian era and the uniform machine-made goods of the Industrial Revolution. The style embodied a holistic philosophy for living in which all elements of material culture were designed to complement one another: architecture, garden design, interior furnishings, and decorative objects. The style looked to nature for design inspiration. In contrast with Victorian norms, gardens were now considered an indispensable component of the house and an integral part of daily life. Arts and Crafts advocates believed that incorporating natural beauty into daily settings supported healthy, moral living and would ameliorate the societal troubles of the industrial age. The Arts and Crafts style was influenced by the Japanese architecture and gardens featured at the World's Columbian Exposition in Chicago in 1893 and at the California Midwinter International Exposition in San Francisco in 1894.

Arts and Crafts gardens varied widely in form, as the landscape historian Judith B. Tankard explains: "While certain features (pergolas, arbors, beautiful flower borders) may come to mind when thinking of an Arts & Crafts garden, by and large, they elude

From early spring, when the fruit trees and flowering Japanese cherries are in blossom, on through the seasons of wistaria, redbud and dogwood, laurel, rhododendron and iris, Beech Haven is a center of attraction to the nature-lovers of Athens and the surrounding communities.
—*Garden History of Georgia*

The bridge, deep in the woodland canopy, with a stone picnic table and bench nearby

Gravel approach road winding through the mature woods

definition. That's because there are no hard and fast rules: Arts & Crafts gardens are an approach to design rather than a style. But what they lack in common shape, size, or location, these gardens make up for in individuality, regionalism, craftsmanship, and, most important, a harmonious relationship with the house."[1] The Arts and Crafts period saw the popularity of the wild, or naturalistic, garden. Advocates promoted the cultivation of hardy plants rather than the fussy bedding plants favored during the Victorian period, as well as an integration of both formal and informal components.[2] Formal gardens were placed near the house, and wild gardens, filled with bulbs and wildflowers, were located in surrounding forests and meadows. Besides the use of nature as the primary source for artistic expression, other common characteristics included the use of traditional or native materials and plants, the use

of naturalistic color schemes, and a balanced appreciation of a plant's flowers and foliage.[3]

In the 1910s, the Arts and Crafts movement had a direct influence on one family in Athens: the Rowlands. Born and raised in Augusta, Georgia, Charles Alden Rowland II came from a dedicated Presbyterian family. He moved to Athens in 1887. In 1892, he married Effie Elizabeth Hampton, a native Athenian active in the Presbyterian Church. Two years later, they purchased a home on Dearing Street in the heart of the city. The Rowlands had five children: Hampton, Katharine Whitehead, Elizabeth Leonard, Alice Alden, and Charles Alden III.[4] Rowland operated several successful businesses and founded a thriving feed and seed company.[5]

Athens, the seat of Clarke County, sits in the Piedmont region of Georgia near the foothills of the southern Appalachian Mountains. The area is home to the upper, middle, and lower branches of the Oconee River. The area's native forests were once lush with hickories, oaks, and pines, which farmers in the nineteenth century timbered and turned into fields of corn, cotton, oats, and wheat. By 1887, only 10 percent of the county remained forested.[6] By 1900, Athens was a thriving urban hub with a population of over ten thousand. It boasted a streetcar system, a plethora of stores and banks, and the University of Georgia. Athens experienced rapid growth in the opening decades of the twentieth century; the population doubled between 1900 and 1940.[7] Seeking a sanctuary from their busy life in Athens, the Rowlands purchased land four miles from their city home. There they created a rustic retreat—Beech Haven—for the enjoyment of family, friends, and community groups. It served also as a center for Charles Rowland's wide-ranging Christian endeavors.

Rowland's early life experiences and his extensive travels as a missionary for the Presbyterian Church nourished a deep love of nature. When Rowland was a teenager, his family sent him to Tennessee to live with family friends to improve his health by working on a farm and drinking the local water.[8] At the same time, he became active in the YMCA, through which he met Weston Gales, a leader in the organization. Gales introduced him to an initiative to establish a rustic mountain retreat and Bible conference grounds in North Carolina as a sanctuary for Christians and a school for local children. In 1897, Gales, Rowland, and others purchased a four-thousand-acre site in a valley near Asheville for their spiritual refuge, which was later acquired by the Presbyterian Church and renamed Montreat. Rowland's involvement with the project showed him that a connection with nature was healthy for the soul as well as the body.[9] The retreat's bucolic character and examples of Asheville's Arts and Crafts architecture inspired Rowland in his development of Beech Haven.

Rowland's journeys abroad also shaped his design interests. Over time, he became an active religious leader locally, nationally, and globally as a result of his involvement in Presbyterian organizations. In 1910, he attended the World Missionary Conference in Edinburgh, Scotland, a city where the Arts and Crafts movement flourished.[10] He was exposed

Stone lanterns dotted throughout the property

to East Asian landscapes in 1914 when he and his daughter Katharine traveled to China, Korea, and Japan to do missionary work. This influence can be seen in a number of elements at Beech Haven, including the use of stone and water as focal points, stone lanterns and bridges, and, specifically, the Camelback Bridge.[11]

To create Beech Haven, the Rowlands amassed 230 acres a few miles from the heart of Athens between 1910 and 1918. The steep and rugged topography drew Effie and Charles Rowland to the site.[12] Three water sources traverse the property: the Middle Oconee River to the west; Boulder Creek, which divides the site east to west; and Owl Spring. Both the creek and the spring feed into the Middle Oconee. A forest of hickories, oaks, and pines covers much of the property; it is complemented by a pine forest, a holly forest, a pecan orchard, and some of the largest beech trees in Athens.[13]

The Rowlands spent many decades reshaping the land in the Arts and Crafts style, reflecting their individuality, regional tastes, local craftsmanship, and a unity between the structures and the landscape. They constructed myriad rustic buildings, including a log cabin, houses, and utilitarian structures, nestling them into clearings in the woods and flat areas where agricultural fields once stood. They

Boulder Creek winding alongside the approach road

added a formal garden, informal gardens, and recreational areas throughout the site. These spaces were filled with numerous man-made naturalistic features such as stone benches, bridges, lanterns, ponds, and even an outdoor kitchen, all made by local craftsmen using local materials. Beneath the native forest canopy, the landscape was bursting with hardy ornamental trees, shrubs, and bulbs. A dirt drive as well as dozens of woodland paths and horse-riding trails snaked through the site. In later decades, more houses and structures were added by family descendants.

The property is entered via the main drive, which descends through a natural forest of oaks, pines, sweet gums, and more; crosses a discontinuous stream; and passes through rustic stone entry piers, one bearing the word "Beech," and the other "Haven." The road is bordered on each side by an allée of southern magnolias (*Magnolia grandiflora*) and, for the last four hundred feet, parallel rows of historic bulbs: lily of the valley, narcissus (*Narcissus* 'Stella Superba' and *Narcissus* 'Telamonius Plenus'), and red spider lilies (*Lycoris radiata*), a favorite of Effie Rowland.[14]

Just past the allée of magnolias, the drive diverges. One fork leads to a section of the property that contains an assemblage of buildings and landscapes dating to Beech Haven's first three decades. One largely forested area with a few clearings contains a log cabin and a vernacular Arts and Crafts landscape created by Charles Rowland in the 1910s. The first building constructed at Beech Haven in 1910, the log cabin once served as a home for the property's caretaker and later was used as a residence by Charles's son Hampton.[15] Also in this area is a combination garage and workshop (circa 1911), where Charles built and repaired furniture. Naturalistic features of the landscape that remain include a stone walk encompassing the house, a grouping of three dry-stacked stone benches, woodland paths, white rock edging around the planting beds, and ornamental plantings near the woodland edges, including informal groupings of heirloom bulbs such as *Narcissus* 'Trevithian', *Narcissus* 'Emperor', *Narcissus* 'Empress', and *Narcissus pseudonarcissus*.[16]

Nearby, another wooded area, located north of the log cabin, is home to the Wildwood homesite and the Walnut Hill equestrian complex. At Wildwood,

Stone bridge with built-in benches

Stone bridge crossing Boulder Creek

Pair of stone pillars at the property entrance

Hampton Rowland built a one-room house in the 1930s, which his descendant Jack Rowland and his wife, Jeffie Pearl Landers Rowland, moved and expanded after World War II.[17] Effie and Charles Rowland developed the nearby Walnut Hill area for horses, including an eight-stall wooden horse barn, which was built around 1940, and a large paddock-fenced oval corral atop the hill.[18] Oral histories from descendants and historic photographs show the Rowland family's keen interest in horseback riding.

Returning to the main drive, the dirt and gravel road continues, lined with naturalistic rock work. As the road descends through dense forest and rugged terrain reminiscent of the mountains of northern Georgia, it immerses visitors in the majesty of nature. The road crosses over Boulder Creek on a large Arts and Crafts–style bridge, designed and constructed around 1910. Built with uncut stacked and mortared stones, the bridge features built-in stone benches at the center facing each other.

Along the roadway near the stone bridge, the Rowlands added three ponds. They are now dry and overgrown but still detectable through the extensive rock work around them. The shallow eastern pond is notable for its small island, which contains a stone bench and a fire pit. Two rounded stones at the roadside denote the place where three raised stepping-stones, once floating, gave access to the island. Mature cypress trees, their knees formerly poking out of the water's surface, stand along one edge of the pond; the other side contains a planting of hemlocks. Once a vibrant fishing pond filled with bream and bass, the southern pond has a large vernacular Arts and Crafts–style stone bench on its southern edge; the Rowland family and their guests could sit there and dip their feet into the cool water on a hot summer's day. Native azaleas fill the adjacent forest. Dubbed the Lotus Pond, the irregularly shaped western pond, the smallest of the three, was once filled with lotus flowers. It, too, has two rounded stones along the road that mark a series of raised stepping-stones that led over the pond to a stone lantern and a path to Boulder Creek.[19]

As the road continues, it trails the banks of Boulder Creek to the heart of Beech Haven: the Arts and Crafts–style Summer House and surrounding gardens and landscape. An article in the *Athens Banner* in 1913 describes the rustic beauty of the property: "The place has many natural advantages, and as a country seat it is the rival now of many places developed on a much more elaborate scale. The house is situated upon a high hill, overlooking a picturesque brook, which rushes madly between huge boulders on its way to the Oconee river. To drop into Beech Haven from Athens seems indeed like a drop into the mountains. The illusion is complete."[20]

Designed by Effie Rowland, with advice from the Athens city engineer, the Summer House, constructed around 1911, is an exceptional example of the vernacular Arts and Crafts style, inside and out. True to the style's principles, wood for the house came from trees on the land, rough-hewed and sawed on-site; local stone and other materials were likewise used. The house and other structures on the property were built by local artisans, including Jim Glenn (head carpenter) and Ike Osborne (rock mason).[21] The two-story rustic residence is made of wood clapboard siding, now painted deep green. It has a stone foundation, rustic stone pillars, two interior chimneys, and three open-air porches—one made of stone and two of wood. The east porch is noteworthy for its Arts and Crafts pillars made of local stone and grapevine jointing; an unusual multi-level stone fountain is embedded in one of the columns.[22] The double-story wooden porch on the west was constructed of loosely woven peeled logs.

The design of the Summer House brings the natural world inside. Two walls in the main living room contain extensive rows of pocket windows, which can be lowered into the wall for better air circulation. This room also has a rare and artfully engineered floating staircase. The most remarkable feature is the large stone fireplace. It incorporates deposits of rose quartz found on the property: inset below the mantel is a long course of quartz, and just above the mantel is a heart-shaped piece. The interior furnishings were locally sourced and locally made, in keeping with the Arts and Craft style. In her memoir, the Rowland's oldest daughter, Katharine, describes some of the furnishings: "Our dining room table was made from sections of trees as legs and rough boards for the top. This was covered with white oilcloth which was much used in summer homes at that

Stone bench on the edge
of a former pond

Rock steps leading to an island

Stone lantern

Broader view of the landscape
showing a stone bridge and
stone bench

time. Chairs were bought from a country wagon. These chairs had white oak, split bottom seats."[23]

Beech Haven was a true collaboration of spouses. While the house was the territory of Effie, Charles designed not only the landscape on the rest of the property but also a number of gardens, recreational areas, and other features that radiate from the house. Nestled within the curve of the entry drive, the formal garden was placed near the house, as was typical with Arts and Crafts gardens. The garden's naturalistic elements include irregularly shaped planting beds, rustic stone pathways, and informal plantings of bulbs in the surrounding woodlands. A photograph from about 1912 shows a circular stone fountain with water spraying from an ornate urn in the center and a long rustic bench nearby surrounded by planting beds. The stones were locally sourced, and the urn came from the Rowland's house on Dearing Street.[24] The urn was later replaced by a water pump. A stone path surrounding the fountain connects to additional stone pathways to the northeast and southwest.[25] The start of each path is marked by large round stones, which are commonplace throughout the site. Numerous amoeba-shaped planting beds scattered about the fountain garden area are filled with a mass of historic bulbs, including yellow and red spider lilies, grape hyacinth, *Narcissus pseudonarcissus*, *Narcissus* 'Mount Hood', *Narcissus* 'Sir Watkin', *Narcissus* 'Stella Superba', and *Narcissus* 'Sulphur Phoenix'.

Elsewhere around the house, Charles added a flight of twenty-eight stone steps that lead down the steep slope and connect the house with the banks of Boulder Creek. The stairs are "flanked by two rows of stone lanterns built of the natural rock set at intervals along the stairway."[26] Inspired by his trip to East Asia in 1914, he designed these unique stone lanterns, which have become iconic symbols of Beech Haven. The base of the stairs is punctuated by a large built-in stone bench known as the Bus Stop, because the family driver used to pick up family members at this spot.

Charles, with assistance from his daughter Katharine, placed a number of landscape features northeast of the Summer House. Near the middle of the drive roundabout in front of the house stands the remnant of a garden, designed by Katharine,

composed of three concentric triangular beds outlined in stone and planted with *Narcissus* 'Stella Superba', dogtooth violet, and vinca. Across from the roundabout, the outdoor kitchen north of the home was once used for "picnic suppers and barbecues."[27] A prominent Arts and Crafts–style element in the landscape, it has a stone grill in the middle, flanked by curved stone benches and stone stairs that lead to a flat area above. Local stone and grapevine jointing used in the structure is much like that seen on the east porch columns of the Summer House.[28] A nearby path leads to the site of a former clay tennis court dating from the 1920s, as described in *Garden History of Georgia*: "Opposite the rough-hewn stone porch of the main residence a long path cuts through the trees and irregularly paved with stepping stones mounts the hill to a tennis court and furnishes a vista somewhat like the pleached allees of more formal gardens."[29] The court was used regularly by the Rowland family and their guests. Today, only a few of the white granite stones that once lined the long pathway survive.

West of the house, Charles added more recreational and utilitarian features. An informal path west of the entry drive, which once held a long rustic arbor covered in scuppernong grapes, leads to stone piers, the only indication of the barn that used to stand there.[30] The path continues to the remnants of the rectangular vegetable gardens, the bounty from which was once enjoyed by the family and their many guests; today, a chain-link fence, concrete posts, and agricultural terraces denote the location. This forested area is home to woodland paths and hundreds of historic bulbs, including *Narcissus pseudonarcissus* and *Narcissus* 'Telamonius Plenus', which blanket the forest floor in early spring.

The path continues through the woods and down a steep hillside to Owl Spring, a forty-acre section at the western edge of Beech Haven bordered by the Middle Oconee River. The most prominent Arts and Crafts–style feature in the area is the Camelback Bridge, an Asian-inspired moon bridge that spans Owl Spring. Charles designed the bridge in the 1920s, and in 2014, the Athens-Clarke Heritage Foundation raised funds to stabilize it. Other design elements in the area include a concrete

Path lined with stone lanterns leading to the main house

cistern and the concrete foundation of a former pump house. Constructed in the 1930s, the cistern, which once had a hand-cranked engine above it, supplied freshwater to the Summer House.[31] A rectangular spring pool with built-in stone benches and stairs, constructed in the 1920s, is located on the west bank of Owl Spring. Set into the wall of the pool is a stone plaque containing a Bible verse, John 4:14: "Jesus said whosoever drinketh of this water shall thirst again; but whosoever shall drinketh of the water that I shall give him, shall never thirst," possibly indicating that the pool was used for baptisms.[32] Farther down the woodland path are several landscape features that were built in the 1920s from local stone, including a large table topped with a massive stone slab, a bench carved out of the hillside, and the remnants of two stone benches. A

woodland path leads over the hill to Silver Shoals. This recreation area on the Middle Oconee River was used by the Rowland family and their guests, as well as by numerous religious and civic groups, in the first half of the twentieth century.

Besides serving as a summer retreat for the Rowlands, and later as their permanent home and family estate, the naturalistic world of Beech Haven was an epicenter of religious outreach as part of Charles Rowland's contributions to Presbyterianism in America.[33] Beginning in the 1910s, Charles frequently hosted religious meetings at Beech Haven, often referred to as "little Montreat." A 1913 announcement in the *Athens Banner* shows Charles extending an invitation to the community: "I want to give you a most cordial invitation to attend the Bible Conference to be held at my summer place, . . .

Stone bench and a fire pit adjacent to the house

Remnants of a formal garden with a fountain, located near the house

[We hope] to make this informal, but at the same time we trust that the messages may prove a great spiritual uplift to all who attend."[34] Over time, an annual Beech Haven conference, featuring national Presbyterian leaders as speakers, was established for laypeople active in the church and in missionary work. The Rowlands frequently hosted local Bible conferences, church groups, student groups, and YMCA and YWCA members. A 1915 description of a weekend at Beech Haven gives a glimpse into how guests were entertained: "On Saturday afternoon the guests arrived at all hours, and found that Mrs. Rowland had already made everything beautiful and in readiness for them. After the jolly picnic supper all gathered around a huge fire in the living room and listened to music and stories. . . . On Sunday morning just after the Sabbath school lesson had been studied a party of Athens friends arrived, and all the glorious woods were explored."[35] The Rowlands' eldest daughter, Katharine, continued her father's religious work. She and her husband, William Crane, returned to Athens in 1960 and established the Pastoral Counseling Center on the property. They later constructed a one-story facility called Brookside on the southern slope of Boulder Creek across from the Summer House to house the center.[36]

Today, Beech Haven is in peril. Many key historic structures and landscape elements are deteriorating, and invasive exotic plants, such as bamboo and wisteria, are encroaching on the property. A coalition of groups, including Rowland family members, is working to preserve it. Just over ninety acres is now owned by the county and protected as part of the Athens–Clarke County greenway network. Beech Haven is not yet open to the public, but the hope is that a combination of public and private funds will enable it to serve as a vibrant greenspace and heritage site for the community. In June 2014, the Athens-Clarke Heritage Foundation entered into a contract with Athens–Clarke County to lease the Summer House and Camelback Bridge, and the group is currently raising money to stabilize and preserve them.[37] Additionally, the University of Georgia's Cultural Landscape Lab, led by Cari Goetcheus, has conducted extensive survey and documentation work in recent years, partially funded by the Watson-Brown Foundation. This effort has culminated in the draft nomination of the Beech Haven Historic District to the National Register of Historic Places. In recent years, a Friends of Beech Haven group was formed. Local advocates frequently lead private tours of the site to garner support for the preservation of the Arts and Crafts–style structures and the exquisite forests. Helen Kuykendall, past chair of the Athens–Clarke County Historic Preservation Commission, captured the feeling of this remarkable site: "When you first set foot across that gate at Beech Haven, you know you are in a special place. You are completely immersed in nature. Nature dominates that site everywhere you turn and is celebrated everywhere you look."[38] The early advocates of the Arts and Crafts movement believed that nature was crucial to people's health. With the preservation of Beech Haven, its beauty and vitality will be available to all Athenians.

Oaks on the terraced lawn of Oak Hill at Berry College

Berry College

Oak Hill and House o' Dreams

THE ORIGINS OF Berry College can be traced to a young woman's simple desire to teach Sunday-school classes to mountain children, a desire that evolved into the establishment of what the historian William F. Holmes describes as "the most distinctive private schools founded in Georgia during the early twentieth century."[1] The woman was Martha Berry. She realized that if rural mountain families were to break free from a cycle of poverty, education was crucial. As a result, she built a series of schools—day schools, residential boys and girls high schools, a junior college, and, by 1930, a four-year institution of higher learning— known collectively as the Berry Schools. Located in Mount Berry at the base of the hills and mountains on the outskirts of Rome in northwestern Georgia, the Berry Schools were founded on the tenets of academic achievement, hard work, and religious faith. Students were expected to work while completing their studies; as a result, they provided much of the physical labor on campus. No project seemed too difficult: constructing buildings, laying out roads, planting and moving trees, working in the gardens, and doing whatever was needed to make the Berry Schools both self-reliant and attractive. While providing educational opportunities for her students and helping shape their characters, Martha Berry created one of the most beautiful campuses in the country.

Born in 1866, Martha McChesney Berry was the second of Thomas and Frances Berry's eight children.[2] In 1860, Thomas Berry, a Tennessee native and entrepreneur, married Frances Rhea, the daughter of a wealthy Alabama family. The early years of their marriage coincided with the Civil War and Berry's service in the Confederate forces. After the war, Berry and several others founded Berrys and Company, a Rome-based business that specialized in the sale of cotton and the distribution of wholesale and retail groceries.[3] The town's postwar economy relied heavily on both cotton and industrial development, and Berrys and Company prospered. Thomas Berry bought property in Rome as early as 1866.

A garden for a lovely home; a campus that is a garden for America's largest school estate; and a garden to God, where stately branches of lofty poplars are lifted against the rugged rocks and tower of the Lavender Range; these are the three gardens created in Georgia for her schools by Martha Berry.—*Garden History of Georgia*

View of the formal garden looking toward the main house, which is now obscured by mature trees

In 1871 he purchased over one hundred acres for his family's new home, known as Oak Hill.[4] When Berry became ill in the early 1880s, Martha, who was close to her father, left finishing school to be with him and assist her mother. Thomas Berry died in 1887; he left Martha property across from Oak Hill on the other side of Summerville Road, now known as U.S. Highway 27 or Martha Berry Highway.

Berry's life took a dramatic turn around 1900. While the exact details of the story vary, its essence involves her deciding to teach Sunday school to some young boys from the area. She held class in a log cabin, a former playhouse, on the grounds of Oak Hill. Each Sunday the number of children, both boys and girls, grew, and soon their parents joined them. Known today as the Original Cabin, the structure is sometimes cited as the birthplace

of the Berry Schools.[5] As Berry grew to know the young people and their families, she became aware of the poverty in which they lived, but also of the children's potential. She became convinced of the urgent need to provide them with an education.

Berry's concern coincided with a time of political, social, and economic reform throughout the United States. In the later years of the nineteenth century and the first two decades of the twentieth century, Progressive-era activists worked to stamp out political corruption, enact child labor laws, encourage Prohibition, and ratify a constitutional amendment for women's suffrage. One area of interest, especially in the South, was the need to increase educational opportunities for children.[6] It was not uncommon for rural schools in the South to be limited to an elementary school curriculum and to be open for only

The formal garden at Oak Hill, from *Garden History of Georgia*

a few months a year.[7] Reforms in Georgia eventually sparked legislation that allocated funding for high schools, required mandatory school attendance for children between the ages of eight and fourteen, and ensured that public schools were open for at least four months a year.[8] The need was great, and Berry attacked the problem of access to education by establishing a series of private schools that targeted the children of the Georgia mountains.

Her endeavor quickly began to evolve when the Sunday-school class outgrew the small cabin. She constructed a one-room building on her land a short distance away. She also established a Sunday school at the abandoned Possum Trot Church, sometimes referred to as the "cradle of Berry College" and now a historic property included on the Berry College campus.[9] She expanded to other locations in the Rome area and was soon running day schools with some support from the county school board. In 1902 she founded the residential Boys Industrial School. The following year, her commitment to the education of mountain children was confirmed when she deeded to the school eighty-three acres her father had left her. On this site and on the thousands of acres she accumulated over time, she founded the

Martha Berry School for Girls (1909), Berry Junior College (1926), and Berry College (1930).

Especially in the schools' early years, there always seemed to be a need for money to fund day-to-day operations, scholarships for the growing number of students, new facilities, land acquisition, and eventually an endowment. Fortunately, Berry was a talented fund-raiser. Although financial support came from many small donations, she was able to connect with wealthy and powerful people such as Emily Vanderbilt Hammond, who became a close friend; First Lady Ellen Axson Wilson, a former resident of Rome and the first wife of President Woodrow Wilson; President Theodore Roosevelt; and Andrew Carnegie, the well-known industrialist and philanthropist. Berry's relationship with the automotive industrialist Henry Ford and his wife, Clara, generated funds that resulted in a significant expansion of the girls' school. The couple gave money for what eventually became known as the Ford Buildings, designed in the nationally popular Collegiate Gothic style of architecture by the Boston architectural firm of Coolidge and Carlson. The formal landscape around the buildings, with its reflecting ponds, stone walkways, boxwood borders,

Approaching Oak Hill via the winding drive

Gazebo overlooking the hillside garden

Central fountain and pool anchoring the formal garden

and transplanted trees, was designed by Robert B. Cridland. The Ford Complex remains one of Berry College's most visually impressive areas.

Martha Berry had a vision for the physical appearance of her schools. As a young man, Hubert Bond Owens, who later established, at the University of Georgia, one of the country's earliest landscape architecture programs, briefly taught at Berry. In his autobiographical *Personal History of Landscape Architecture in the Last Sixty Years, 1922–1982*, Owens states that his affinity for the "value of attractive natural surroundings" was strengthened during his stay on the Berry campus.[10] He described its landscape as

"more like the grounds of a magnificent, vast country estate than like an educational institution."[11] He noted the types of trees and the campus layout: "Its plantings included existing mature oak, maple, pine, and dogwood forests, as well as pastures and agricultural lands. Its buildings were grouped in various parts of 30,000 acres of campus according to certain eclectic styles of architecture."[12]

Although Berry had a clear idea of how she wanted her campus to appear, she knew when professional services were needed. One of her first advisers was the architect John Gibbs Barnwell, who helped turn her early plans into reality.[13] Over time, she used the services of a small number of architectural firms. For landscape design, she often relied on the expertise of Robert B. Cridland. His influence can still be seen across the campus.

A celebrated Philadelphia-based landscape architect, Robert Cridland was known for his work on the gardens of what is now the Vanderbilt Mansion National Historic Site in Hyde Park, New York.[14] Among his commissions in Georgia were the Cator Woolford residence in Atlanta's Druid Hills neighborhood and the nearby Avondale Estates development. Throughout the 1920s and 1930s, Cridland worked in northwestern Georgia with Martha Berry as she built the Berry Schools. Cridland, who specialized in designing suburban estate gardens, wrote of his design philosophy in *Practical Landscape Gardening* (1918). He appreciated the benefits of views, open lawns, terraces, formal gardens with separate garden rooms, architectural features, ponds and pools, and native plants. Since he believed that "there is beauty as well as convenience in order," he and Martha Berry were well suited.[15]

Bridal Walk

Boxwood-lined pathway of the sundial garden

The grounds of two properties at Berry—Oak Hill and House o' Dreams—still reflect Berry's personal taste and Cridland's design skills.

Berry became responsible for Oak Hill upon the death of her mother in 1926. Two years later, she deeded the property to the Berry Schools.[16] Oak Hill, impressively sited on a plateau overlooking the Oostanaula River valley, was an elegant venue where Martha could host guests visiting the Berry Schools. Kate Macy Ladd, a department store heiress and Martha's friend, provided funds to remodel and modernize the house and improve the landscape.[17] Visitors today are still greeted by the house's imposing two-story Greek Revival façade. Six Ionic columns support the striking embellished pediment, underneath which is a second-floor balcony enclosed by a decorative railing. Both the central entrance and the entrance onto the balcony contain elaborate entryways with double doors surrounded by a transom and sidelights. The rear façade contains elements found on the front, including six fluted Ionic columns supporting a pediment.

Major work on Oak Hill's landscape occurred between 1927 and approximately 1933. Berry and Cridland were concerned with the appearance of the overall property as well as of the formal garden. From the steps of Oak Hill, Berry could look out onto "a wide terrace and the great oak grove" in front of the house.[18] Guests riding through Cridland's planned entrance drive could appreciate the beauty of the house and its setting.[19]

Cridland, who believed that a garden's main entrance "should be from the house and on an axis with some important door or window," designed a stone path to lead from the corner of Oak Hill's front porch into the formal garden.[20] Here he planned various garden rooms, including a formal box garden, a walled (goldfish) garden, and a rose (sundial) garden.[21] A sunken garden was designed at Berry's request. Paths and walkways connect the gardens.

The boxwood garden features a rectangular pool containing a fountain surrounded by a lawn with boxwood at each corner of the pool. Today, a stand of crape myrtles behind a row of boxwood provides vibrant color during the summer months. Cridland designed a small horseshoe garden attached to this formal space. The goldfish garden is enclosed by a low

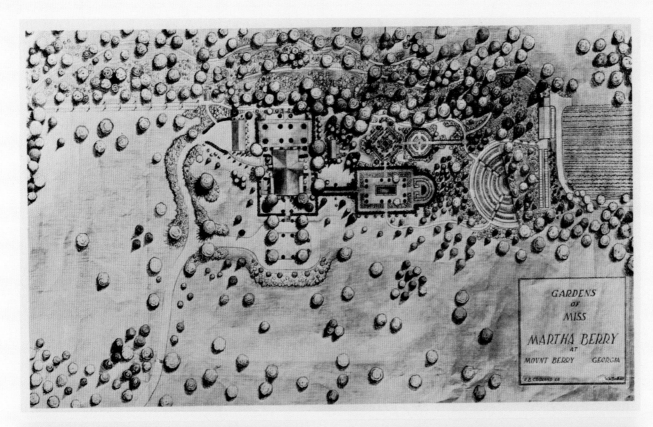

Landscape plan of
Oak Hill by Robert B.
Cridland, from *Garden
History of Georgia*

Sunken garden with
central fountain

Azalea-lined walking paths winding through the rear grounds

OPPOSITE: Historic entrance to the main campus

stone wall with a fountain inside a diamond-shaped pool at the garden's center; annuals and perennials are planted in surrounding flower beds. The sundial garden was originally a "circular rose garden, where several hundred rose bushes brighten the spring and summer air with fragrant blooms."[22] This space is now shaded by mature trees, and the roses have been replaced by annuals and perennials. At the garden's center is a granite sundial placed in the stone pathway. Of special interest to Berry was the sunken, or iris, garden, which she envisioned as a setting for entertainment.[23] *Garden History of Georgia* describes the space: "Where a natural semi-circle occurs in the bluff, an iris garden has been made in a series of terraces."[24] This amphitheater-style setting features brick walks and stone terracing. The garden's focal point is at its bottom level, where a low stone wall framed by a semicircular pool forms a curved niche that contains a fountain. In the 1980s, the plantings in this garden were enhanced by daylilies donated by

the Georgia Daylily Society.[25] Repair work on the rock walls and fountain was undertaken in 2007.[26] Perennials such as rudbeckia, coreopsis, and dianthus were introduced.[27] This lovely spot is enhanced by Japanese cherry trees, a long-ago gift to Martha Berry that continues to add a profusion of spring color to the landscape.[28]

Close attention was likewise given to the landscape at the back of the main house. At the northwest edge, Cridland planned "a golden rose-arched pathway" that led "to a summer house two hundred yards away, at the edge of the bluffs overlooking the Oostanaula river valley."[29] Berry designated this flowered path, now known as the Bridal Walk, a spot for engaged former students to stroll and make a wish. Reflecting his interest in views and vistas, Cridland designed a hillside garden overlooking the Oostanaula floodplain. *Garden History of Georgia* describes this natural setting: "A pine-needle path wanders on down the bluffs into the shadows of giant oak and pine trees where a gurgling spring whispers over a large worn rock, drips into a fern bank and scurries down the slope toward the waiting river. Azalea, laurel, dogwood, and flowering bulbs of various kinds lend color to this forest garden."[30]

Berry called Oak Hill home until her death, in 1942; she was buried on the grounds just south of Berry College Chapel. One of Georgia's most highly honored citizens of the early twentieth century, she was recognized in 1992 as one of Georgia's Women of Achievement. Among the many ways Berry College celebrates her legacy today is through Oak Hill, which has functioned as a house museum since 1972. A separate building that opened in 1974, the Martha Berry Museum, traces the evolution of Berry's vision.[31] The Martha Berry Walkway of Life, dedicated that same year, highlights the path Martha used to walk to the campus.

Attention has also been given to Oak Hill's landscape. Over the years, projects have been undertaken to refresh the garden and grounds. The hillside garden, neglected after Berry's death, became overgrown. A Historic Landscape and Garden Grant from the Garden Club of Georgia in 2012 assisted in the removal of invasive plants, and an additional project enabled the stone steps to be reset and a stone garden seat to be repaired. Ongoing attention to the

Martha Berry's grave, located on the main campus next to the Berry College Chapel

hillside garden is bringing back this special setting. Also in 2012, planting plans and blueprints prepared by Cridland were uncovered, providing information on Oak Hill's early twentieth-century landscape.[32] This exciting discovery provides the foundation for ongoing restoration and rehabilitation efforts.

Plants filling Oak Hill's gardens are grown in greenhouses on the property. A horticulturist cares for the site, and Berry students help in the garden.[33] A director is responsible for the overall management of the 170-acre site that includes Oak Hill and the Martha Berry Museum. In addition to those attractions, visitors can enjoy several historic outbuildings, nature trails, a catfish pond, and a wildflower meadow.

One of the loveliest and most secluded parts of the Berry campus is atop Lavender Mountain. On a clear day, in the quiet of the summit's solitude, it is possible to enjoy views of Georgia, Alabama, and Tennessee. It was on this site that Berry alumni and students gave Martha Berry a most special gift, a retreat and a place of contemplation called the House

o' Dreams. To reach this remote location, guests must travel on a steep, unpaved road that winds through woodlands and passes underneath a rustic gateway consisting of two stone towers supporting a pergola and a hand-carved sunburst-shaped gate. At the top of the mountain, a loop-shaped drive similar to one found in Cridland's *Practical Landscape Gardening* leads to the house.[34] An architecturally interesting cylindrical water and fire tower made of stone is sited nearby.

The Boston architectural firm of Coolidge and Carlson designed the one-and-a-half-story stone and board-and-batten Arts and Crafts–style cottage. Cridland was commissioned to design the landscape. The Berry Alumni Association, with the support of Berry's board of trustees, initiated a fund-raising campaign in 1921, and Berry students constructed the cottage.[35] Stone and wood from the mountain supplied materials for the house and garden. The house sits on the site's highest elevation; the land at the top of the mountain was leveled for its construction.[36]

In keeping with Cridland's belief that "a garden constructed on different levels may be made very interesting, as it affords an opportunity to introduce many architectural features and to vary greatly the planting on the different planes," the formal garden at House o' Dreams gradually descends into a series of terraces.[37] *Garden History of Georgia* notes that in 1933 "the various garden levels are held by thick rock walls, and flagstone paths connect the lawn (where a blue peacock spreads his brilliant fan) with the garden and the lily pool."[38] The garden begins a short distance from the house where the lawn leads into an enclosed garden with stone stacked walls on three sides; interior beds next to the walls are edged in stone. In the center of the garden, four beds are arranged in a geometric pattern, with two placed on each side of the central grass path. Steps lead down into the garden's oblong-shaped second level where a rectangular reflecting pool, originally called the lily pool, is prominently featured. At the base of this level is a pergola, anchored on both ends by stone garden pavilions. *Garden History*

of Georgia describes it as "a wistaria-covered arbor [that] offers shade from the bright sun and a frame for the panoramic view."[39] These two garden rooms contained "fragrant boxwood, lilacs and snowballs," along with "hollyhocks, delphinium, dahlias, chrysanthemums," and roses, as well as other flowering plants.[40] The third terrace remains a large tree-bordered lawn. Berry was especially interested in having a terraced orchard, inspired, it is said, by one that her sister Eugenia Ruspoli had at her home in Italy.[41] As a result, the lowest terrace was an orchard "given over to peach trees, strawberries and raspberries."[42] While a few fruit trees remain, the former orchard now consists primarily of grass panels.

The House o' Dreams remains a significant part of Berry College. It was rehabilitated as a result of a funding challenge in 1983 by a generous donor.[43] The House o' Dreams can now be visited by the public as part of scheduled tours of the historic campus, and Berry faculty and staff members use the site for meetings and retreats. The original furnishings are in storage at the Oak Hill Museum.[44] In their place

Ford complex

House o' Dreams, at the pinnacle of Lavender Mountain

House o' Dreams, from
Garden History of Georgia

are reproductions appropriate to the 1920s setting, although visitors may enjoy the historic tables and chairs that remain on the porches. While the gardens at the House o' Dreams were once filled with flowers, today the emphasis is more on drought-resistant native plants and annuals.

Over the last seventy-five years, many changes have occurred at Berry. Schools that Martha Berry founded closed over time, and the name "Berry Schools" was changed to "Berry College, Inc." In 1983, Berry College became the institutional focus. Today's Berry College, a private liberal arts school with an interdenominational Christian emphasis, represents the life work of Martha Berry.[45]

One of the most significant aspects of the Berry campus is the preservation and continued use of so many of the buildings and landscapes associated with the early years of the school and its founder. As a testament to the historic integrity of the campus, Berry College, which includes the

Oak Hill and House o' Dreams sites, was listed in the National Register of Historic Places in 1978. The school's efforts are aided, in part, by the *Berry College Campus Preservation Report* (2006), funded by a Campus Heritage Grant from the Getty Foundation. It identifies Berry's historic buildings and landscapes and makes recommendations for future preservation treatments. An awareness of the importance of this setting is also incorporated as part of the college's mission: "Berry emphasizes an educational program committed to high academic standards, values based on Christian principles, practical work experience and community service in a distinctive environment of natural beauty."[46] Although Berry College has continued to move forward and take its place as a center of twenty-first-century education, decisions over the years by school officials and alumni to retain as much as possible of the school's physical heritage have enriched the Berry experience.

Formal gardens extending from the front porch at House o' Dreams

Stone gazebo at the lower
corner of the garden

Stone water and fire tower
adjacent to House o' Dreams

Stone-and-wood
entrance gate

View of the surrounding landscape from the house and garden

Daffodils blooming on the hillside at House o' Dreams

Hillside with many
varieties of azaleas
in the Bradley
Olmsted Garden

Bradley Olmsted Garden

SUNSET TERRACE, the garden of William C. Bradley in Columbus, Georgia, was designed by the influential Olmsted Brothers landscape architecture firm of Brookline, Massachusetts. Of the fourteen residential commissions the firm designed in Georgia, the Bradley garden was its largest and most important. The property was also the only Olmsted Brothers–designed landscape included in *Garden History of Georgia*. Referred to today as the Bradley Olmsted Garden of the Columbus Museum, this Country Place–era garden was created by William Bell Marquis of the Olmsted Brothers firm between 1925 and 1928 for William C. Bradley, a leading industrialist, and his wife, Sarah Hall Bradley, in the upscale Columbus neighborhood of Wynnton.

Columbus, a city in the Georgia Piedmont, was established by the state legislature in 1828 as the seat of Muscogee County. Fashioned along the eastern banks of the Chattahoochee River near the Alabama state line, the city first served as a cotton-trading center and then quickly became one of the largest mill towns in the state.[1] In the second half of the nineteenth century and into the early twentieth century, Columbus thrived as a result of its booming textile industry. Wynnton, one of the most prestigious residential areas of Columbus, became home to many of the city's industrialists and other wealthy citizens. Located east of the city center atop Wynn's Hill, which marks the beginning of the Piedmont plateau, Wynnton in the mid-nineteenth century was the site of large antebellum estates. At the opening of the twentieth century, the city's prosperity, its expanding streetcar lines, and the rise of the automobile set into motion the subdividing of these estates into planned suburban neighborhoods for the city's affluent citizens. The neighborhoods featured a parklike setting with curving streets lined with trees, generous sidewalks, circular medians at street intersections, large lawns with informal plantings of trees and ornamental shrubs, uniform setbacks, and elaborate homes and gardens,

By the time of its completion in 1928, the landscape design at the Bradley home would be the most significant residential design installation the Olmsted firm completed in the state.—Lucy Lawliss, "Residential Work of the Olmsted Firm in Georgia"

Stone fountain in the garden

often designed by leading architects and landscape architects in Georgia.[2] This area, which included William C. Bradley's house and garden, was listed in the National Register of Historic Places in 2005.[3]

The Olmsted Brothers firm was founded by the sons of Frederick Law Olmsted, who is known as the father of American landscape design and its most significant practitioner. Olmsted died in 1903, over two decades before the Bradley garden was begun, yet his design principles still exerted a strong influence on the firm. The Olmsted Brothers firm worked on myriad projects, including the design of residential grounds—thousands of them.[4] For private estates, the firm's work largely incorporated Frederick Law Olmsted's main design criteria. As explained by the landscape historian Arleyn A. Levee: "The concern was to create tasteful domestic settings, artistically coherent, appropriate in scale and unblemished by extravagant materialistic displays. He sought to enhance natural site features to create a series of separate spaces, giving the home its distinctive character."[5] Yet the Olmsted Brothers

firm was sometimes asked to include purely decorative and formal elements, such as pools, pergolas, and teahouses.[6] Although the firm did many residential projects in the South, only fourteen were designed for sites in Georgia.[7] Of these, the firm produced plans for three residential properties in Atlanta and four in Columbus,[8] which, in addition to William C. Bradley's, included designs for Claude Scarborough, E. W. Swift, and D. Abbott Turner.[9]

The landscape design for the William C. Bradley residence was, according to the landscape architect and Olmsted scholar Lucy Lawliss, "the most significant residential design installation the Olmsted firm completed in the state."[10] It was also the firm's largest commission in Georgia. The property was initially developed by Brick Stonewall Miller and his wife, Mary. In 1911, they bought ten acres from the developer Lloyd Bowers, and the next year they built a grand two-story Mediterranean Revival–style home designed by the Atlanta architect A. Ten Eyck Brown. Miller hired the landscape architect William Bell Marquis to design a garden for the property. The design work was challenging, since the house sat atop a steep hillside overlooking a ravine. At the time, the Illinois-born, Harvard-educated Marquis was employed by the landscape design enterprise of the P. J. Berckmans Company in Augusta, Georgia.[11]

The house sat on a narrow flat plain at the crest of a steep hillside. It was called Sunset Terrace because of its expansive views of Columbus and the Alabama hills in the distance. A preliminary design by Marquis shows a rose and cut-flower garden on the east side of the house adjacent to the back drive, a formal expansive lawn north of the house, and a formal square garden surrounded by a balustrade with a small central ornamental pool west of the house. The proposal also shows pathways winding through the hillside and a spring covered by an arbor.[12] Other planned features included a pergola, a rose arbor, a swimming pool, and even limestone finials for the entry gateposts.[13] Lucy Lawliss hypothesizes that the construction of the landscape features was likely never accomplished; however, it is plausible that the Millers developed the formal square garden and a terrace filled with roses, according to *Garden History of Georgia*.[14] The square garden appears as an existing element on a 1925 plan showing the proposed arrangement for a swimming pool and a new rose garden.[15]

Ravine garden meandering downhill from the waterfall

Small pond at the foot of the ravine garden

Azaleas in the ravine garden

Ravine garden filled
with azaleas

William Bradley acquired the property in 1925 when he swapped his downtown home for Miller's Mediterranean house; Miller was Bradley's lawyer.[16] Bradley expanded the estate's boundaries by purchasing some adjoining properties, including a defunct trolley line and station, bringing the total acreage to thirteen. The trolley line previously operated on a loop from downtown Columbus to the outlying suburbs. Bradley was a highly successful businessman, serving as the president of the Columbus Bank and Trust Company and as chairman of the board of Coca-Cola, Eagle and Phenix Mills, the W. C. Bradley Company, the Columbus Manufacturing Company, the Columbus Iron Works, and the Bradley Realty and Investment Company.[17] Bradley and his wife, Sarah Matilda Hall Bradley, were leading philanthropists in Columbus, establishing the W. C. and Sarah H. Bradley Foundation in 1943. When the Bradleys moved to Wynnton, they were in their sixties, and both their daughters, Minnie Hall and Elizabeth Bradley, were married with their own households.[18]

Bradley asked William B. Marquis to resume work on the property. Marquis had moved to the Olmsted Brothers firm in 1920, and he brought the plans for the Miller estate with him. Bradley's letter to Marquis, dated June 4, 1925, lends insight into his intentions: "I have in mind the carrying out of some of your original plans regarding the development of this property. . . . I also have in mind the consolidation of the two springs located on the place, and the building of a modern swimming pool, which I am sure would give added pleasure to my family and friends."[19] By the close of June 1925, Olmsted Brothers, with Marquis as the project lead, agreed to proceed. Bradley also requested that a permanent superintendent be assigned to the site, and the firm engaged Percy Huxley, a gardener from Massachusetts. A man in his thirties, Huxley resided in a cottage, located on the north side of the property, originally constructed for servants or tenants.[20]

Bradley admitted his limited knowledge of landscape planning, writing to Marquis, "I know absolutely nothing about flowers, or anything pertaining to your work," but his business acumen played a pivotal role in the development of the property.[21] Correspondence between Bradley and Marquis indicates Bradley's influence, evident in compromises

Stone stairs along
the hillside

made on several design decisions. A significant concession involved the placement of the swimming pool. Marquis had sited the pool at the terminus of a long axis.[22] Because of the expense of Marquis's proposal, Bradley insisted that the old trolley station be converted into a pool house and that the pool be placed beside it, breaking the visual cohesion of Marquis's original plan. In addition, the Bradleys disputed the need for a parterre rose garden near the house. Other correspondence highlight compromises over budgets and other details.

Percy Huxley oversaw the implementation of Marquis and Bradley's joint landscape vision between 1925 and 1928. He managed half a dozen African American men, who helped install and maintain the gardens and grounds. Since the census records of the time do not show any African Americans living on Bradley's property, it is likely that the workers came from the Bottoms, a working-class African American neighborhood next to the property. People from the Bottoms walked up Wynn's Hill every day to work in the residential homes of the area's white elite. Marquis and Bradley

discussed the need to plant trees and shrubs to serve as a visual barrier between Bradley's estate and the adjacent houses of the Bottoms and nearby factories, selecting red cedars to screen the view.[23] Against the advice of Marquis, Bradley eventually installed a metal fence topped with barbed wire along the perimeter of his property to provide additional separation. When the gardens were completed, in the fall of 1928, Huxley left, and Bradley hired Azor Grantham, a Columbus resident, who served as head gardener for many years.[24]

Marquis's landscape plan took advantage of the site's topography by locating the formal gardens on the level area around the house and peppering the hillside with naturalistic landscape features, including a ravine garden containing waterfalls, winding paths, big rocks, and rock stairs, all of which terminated in a large fishpond. The P. J. Berckmans Company in Augusta supplied the majority of the plant material. More formal plantings were made near the house, and native trees and shrubs were put along the hillside. Marquis left the original automobile circulation plan intact: the main entrance off Wynnton Road

View from the
ravine garden toward
the open lawn

was marked by two large brick columns topped with limestone finials, and the drive stopped at a garage at the east end of the property. Where the drive forked into a broad turnaround south of the residence, the center oval was planted with ornamental shrubs. Foundation plantings of ornamental trees and shrubs, including clipped boxwood and red cedars, hugged the perimeter of the house.

The house featured many outdoor spaces from which to enjoy the distant views: a loggia to the north, a front porch to the south, and on the west, a narrow patio with a double staircase leading down to a square formal garden. This garden was composed of a lawn with a small ornamental pool and fountain at the center, surrounded by a balustrade; it was dotted with clipped hedges at its corners. A gravel pathway crossing the western edge of the formal garden had a sundial at its center on axis with the fountain. To the west of the pathway was a half-moon-shaped lawn with a low curved hedge over which one could view the naturalistic landscape below. A broad open lawn, which terminated at the gardener's cottage, filled the area north of the house and was connected to the formal

garden by a series of pathways. Somewhere near the formal garden and open lawn was the terraced rose garden dating to the Millers' ownership. Although plans do not show its exact location, a few written sources refer to it being near the house. Sarah Bradley was particularly fond of these roses. Other than the formal garden, the open lawn, and the terraced rose garden, the three major features in the landscape were the swimming pool, the ravine garden, and the fishpond, all located on the hillside, which took up a significant portion of the Bradley property.

Although located a good distance from the house, the rectangular swimming pool and its adjacent converted pool house continued the formality found atop the hill. The glade surrounding the pool was "bordered with hundreds of flowering shrubs and Japanese iris, and shaded by pine trees."[25] A long curved bench overlooked the pool on the west, while the east side led to a broad walk that curled among the towering pines and was skirted on either side by azaleas, camellias, dogwood, pittosporum, viburnum, and Japanese yew, with a ground cover of ivy. Several 1930-era photographs show the Bradleys luxuriating

Mr. William C. Bradley, Columbus, Ga., Sketch Plan Showing Arrangement of Rose Garden and Swimming Pool, Olmsted Brothers, Landscape Architects, Brookline, Mass, File No. 6797, Plan No. 25, November 18, 1925. Courtesy of the National Park Service, the Frederick Law Olmsted National Historic Site Archives, Brookline, Massachusetts

Historic entrance to the estate

amid this lush environment, just as William Bradley had intended. The glade and broad walk served to unify the overall design, functioning as transitional elements between the formal and naturalistic components.

On the rest of the hillside, Marquis created a naturalistic landscape, filling the space with winding dirt pathways, large rocks, rustic rock staircases, a stone grotto with a granite fountain, and a plethora of trees, shrubs, and bulbs. A central feature of this area was the ravine garden, in which water was a key element. One of the natural springs on the property fed into a fountain set in a stone grotto near the top of the hill. From the grotto, the water wound its way down the ravine, creating a sequence of ten cascades. A series of rock steps and dirt pathways snaked through the ravine to a stream that was "overhung by water oaks, sweet gum, sycamore, and dogwood trees, and in their shade grow camellias, euonymous, ligustrum, nandina, abelia and gallberry."[26] The stream's edges were planted with liriope, ferns, forget-me-nots, and an array of wildflowers. The waterfalls terminated in a sizable fishpond, which was crossed by a rustic wooden bridge. The pond was made of gunite—a concrete and sand mixture—sprayed over a rebar framework. This was the first gunite pond in Georgia.[27] *Garden History of Georgia* describes this idyllic setting: "Between the spring and the fish pond are ten little cascades twinkling over huge water-washed boulders brought from an old dam on the Chattahoochee river and each cascade empties into a pool set about with large rocks and surrounded by woodland flowers, ferns and shrubs."[28]

Following the death of William Bradley in 1947, his daughter Elizabeth and son-in-law donated the estate to the City of Columbus to be used as a center for culture and education. The city subdivided the estate's thirteen acres and converted the 1912 Mediterranean Revival–style house into the Columbus Museum of Arts and Crafts (now the Columbus Museum), which opened to the public in 1953. As a result of these changes, some aspects of the historic gardens were lost, while others endure, although in an altered context. In the late 1940s and early 1950s, the Bradley Memorial Library and the Muscogee County School District administrative building were constructed on the land below the swimming pool. What was once a grass drive

Early twentieth-century pool, recently converted to a boxwood parterre

Fishpond with
ornamental bridge

Fishpond and bridge,
from *Garden History
of Georgia*

leading to the swimming pool was paved. These changes broke the connection between the hillside cascades and the fishpond below.[29] Over time, the formal lawns and gardens near the house were lost to building additions and parking lots, and other components were lost to neglect.

In the 1980s, the original Bradley home was incorporated into a major expansion of the Columbus Museum. The institution began plans to improve access and parking. Sarah Turner Butler, the granddaughter of William and Sarah Bradley, requested that the Atlanta landscape designer Julia Orme Martin be hired to restore and redesign the landscape. Martin insisted that further research be conducted in order to understand the Olmsted Brothers' vision for the Bradley estate. Lucy Lawliss, a recent landscape architecture graduate of the University of Georgia, conducted in-depth research at the Library of Congress in Washington, D.C., and the Olmsted National Historic Site in Brookline, Massachusetts. Her work supported Martin's landscape design recommendations, which strove to preserve Olmsted Brothers' design intentions while accommodating the requirements of a twentieth-century museum.[30] After this work was completed, however, the garden fell into neglect for some years.

In the 1990s, the garden experienced a revival when a Columbus Museum volunteer group called the Guild Gardeners began to restore parts of the landscape. They also added markers highlighting important features of the historic garden. An endowment fund was established to ensure that the Bradley Olmsted Garden would remain a treasure for generations to come. In 2013, on the eve of the Columbus Museum's sixtieth anniversary, interest in the garden was renewed, resulting in new plantings of *Cryptomeria*, Encore azalea, Japanese maple, edgeworthia, aucuba, hellebores, *Farfugium*, mondo grass, creeping yew, peegee and oakleaf hydrangeas, *Viburnum tinus*, and autumn and southern shield ferns.[31] These efforts included building a viewing terrace, creating a series of Olmsted-inspired "walks and talks" in the gardens for the public, and conducting research to compile a list of period-appropriate plants to be added to the landscape over time.

Today, the Columbus Museum is one of the largest museums in the Southeast, recognized for its American art and regional history collections. It is

also home to the historic Bradley Olmsted Garden, which has served as a public green space for over sixty years. Some components of the late-1920s Olmsted Brothers–designed landscape survive, and are maintained by the Columbus Museum garden volunteers. With the exception of the pool house, all formal components have been lost. A number of the naturalistic design elements survive, including the ravine garden, the grotto with its original granite fountain tucked into the hillside, the rock-lined stream, the rock pathways and stairs, the fishpond, and mature native trees and ornamental shrubs, particularly azaleas (*Azalea indica*). The Columbus Museum's recognition of the importance of this historic garden is reflected in its 2015–19 strategic plan, which mandates that the Bradley Olmsted Garden be integrated as a key part of the museum experience.[32]

Contemporary bronze statue marking the former site of the historic overlook

Access to the lower gardens from the house and upper terrace
via a grand staircase in the Cator Woolford Gardens

Cator Woolford Gardens

THE CATOR WOOLFORD GARDENS, located in the Druid Hills Historic District of Atlanta, is a 1920s Country Place–era garden that has evolved from a private retreat for Cator Woolford and his family to the home of two nonprofit organizations, the Atlanta Hospital Hospitality House and the Frazer Center. One of the few surviving estate gardens from early twentieth-century Atlanta, it was designed for large-scale entertaining and the enjoyment of nature. Today, the site is a blend of woodlands, historic garden rooms, and original garden structures, with adaptations made in the late twentieth century to support its new public vocation and its role as a venue for outdoor entertaining. Much as it did in the 1920s and 1930s, the Cator Woolford Gardens today makes an aesthetic contribution to the city as a site for social gatherings year-round or as a place where Atlantans can find a respite from city life.

The Woolford estate got its start in the 1920s, three decades after the plans for the Druid Hills neighborhood were begun. In the early 1890s, the Atlanta entrepreneur Joel Hurt assembled a large tract of land, roughly 1,500 acres, a few miles northeast of downtown Atlanta, where he intended to create an ideal residential suburb. The gentle hills, formerly farmland, were home to several streams and springs, eroded fields, and woodlands filled with oaks, hickories, and pines. Hurt envisioned a luxury subdivision accessible by streetcar and automobile. He hired America's premier landscape architect, Frederick Law Olmsted, who set out a vision for Druid Hills in 1893. When the aging Olmsted retired in 1895, Hurt continued the project with his successor firm, Olmsted Brothers. The result was one of Atlanta's first, and one of the Southeast's most refined, residential suburbs. The landscaped residential community was developed with a series of linear parks as its central focus, and Ponce de Leon Avenue as the main parkway. The residences were set out on large lots facing the parks, and curving streets gracefully danced among the rolling, wooded terrain.

There are many important reasons for the careful planning of the home grounds and I would lay particular stress on these: The greater enjoyment of our surroundings; The expression of taste and personality; The enjoyment of others; The uplift of the community; The economy of execution.
—Robert B. Cridland, *Practical Landscape Gardening*

Border plantings, an expansive lawn, and a woodland setting highlighting the lower formal garden

Many of those who purchased property in Druid Hills hired notable architects and landscape architects to design fine homes and beautiful landscapes. Among them were the Atlanta architects Neel Reid, Philip Trammell Shutze, Ernest Ivey, Lewis Crook Jr., and W. T. Downing, and the landscape architects William C. Pauley, of Atlanta, and Robert B. Cridland, of Philadelphia.

Garden History of Georgia credits Robert Cridland as the designer of the Cator Woolford Gardens.[1] Cridland, like other northern landscape architects, journeyed to the Southeast in the winter months to expand his business and to design gardens for those of means. Dating to the 1920s and 1930s, his notable projects in Georgia included the suburban development of Avondale Estates, the gardens of Oak Hill and House o' Dreams for Martha Berry in Rome, the campus landscape at Berry College in Rome, and residential gardens in Atlanta for Arthur Harris, Mrs. Richard W. Johnson, and Governor John M. Slaton.[2] In his book *Practical Landscape Gardening*, first published in 1916, Cridland expressed his landscape design philosophy. The proper siting of a house was crucial and ideally should be on a high point of the

property. Walkways and roads were necessities that should not dominate the overall landscape design, and entrance drives should either be direct, using a straight line of approach, or follow a graceful curving line. An open lawn, which should be surrounded by ornamental trees and shrubs, was a vital element in landscape design. The entire landscape should be framed by a woodland background of hardwoods such as oaks, elms, and poplars. The "highest personal note" of any landscape was the formal flower garden, which should be on axis with the house. Formal gardens should be enclosed with walls or plants to create a feeling of seclusion. Wild or informal garden areas should work in harmony with the formal elements. Rock gardens were another desirable and distinct element. Architectural features and garden ornaments such as fountains, pools, benches, pergolas, and sundials completed the overall landscape picture. Careful planning of the plantings in each garden area was essential to a design's success. Many of Cridland's aesthetic principles are evident in the gardens he designed for Cator Woolford.

In 1916, the Atlanta businessman, civic leader, and philanthropist Cator Woolford purchased land in the

Curvilinear paths within
the lower garden

Mid-1990s
flagstone-paved
bridge

Large sunken formal garden at the home of Cator Woolford, circa 1930s. Courtesy of the Frazer Center Archives

Druid Hills neighborhood and continued acquiring adjacent property into the 1920s. Woolford, along with his brother Guy, had founded the Retail Credit Company in 1899, which eventually became Equifax, one of the top three credit-reporting agencies in the United States.[3] In 1917, before much work on the house and gardens had commenced, Woolford began hosting social gatherings at his Druid Hills property, which was first dubbed Camp Woolford and later renamed Jacqueland.[4] On January 1, 1920, Cator Woolford married Charlotte Louise Boyd of Griffin, Georgia.[5] After an extensive honeymoon in Europe, they returned to Atlanta to establish their new home and start a family. Their daughter Charlotte was born in 1922, and Isabelle in 1925. Woolford hired Cridland around 1921 to design an elaborate series of gardens amid the heavily wooded parcel for social gatherings, recreation, and the enjoyment of the family.[6] Woolford commissioned the Louisiana-born architect Owen James Southwell, who practiced in Atlanta from 1919 to 1931, to design the main house and to collaborate with Cridland.[7]

The Woolford property comprised two parcels of approximately twenty acres each. The eastern tract was home to the gardens and house. The two-story Neoclassical Revival–style mansion, with a dramatic front-façade portico, was built in 1926 atop a hill, in keeping with Cridland's design principles, to

overlook the formal and informal gardens as well as the recreational spaces. The western parcel was dominated by a canopy of mature hardwoods—oak, hickory, beech, pine, and poplar—with a winding stream at its lowest point.[8] Several outbuildings were constructed to support social and recreational activities.

The varied character of the hilly site, located at the confluence of two small tributaries of Lullwater Creek, gave Cridland the opportunity to create gardens of different types. There were two formal sunken gardens, vegetable gardens, orchards, a walled court garden, a rock garden, a keyhole garden, and wild gardens with bridle paths. Recreational areas on the estate included a tennis court, a swimming pool, a clubhouse with a dancing terrace, and even a miniature golf course. Fourteen gardeners maintained the elaborate gardens.[9]

The main entrance to the estate was defined by iron gates anchored by two prominent square columns topped with stone orbs. A long winding drive led through native and ornamental trees to the mansion. From the mansion, a large open lawn descended the hill to a grand Italian-inspired staircase with an elaborate balustrade. This long flight of steps led to a Neoclassical Revival–style clubhouse with a terrazzo dancing terrace and an adjacent small sunken formal garden.[10] The lawn around the clubhouse was enclosed by low privet hedges with narrow borders of spring bulbs that were "replaced by ageratum and petunias for summer."[11] Nearby, the tennis courts were "enclosed by a colonnade with pergola top over which pink and white Cherokee roses clamber"; "tall plantings of sweet bay trees" were near the columns.[12] Besides such formal structures as the pergola and the staircase, Cridland placed furnishings such as ornate benches, chairs, and urns among the formal gardens.

Beyond the tennis courts was the larger sunken formal garden, its distant edges encompassed by woodlands filled with pink and white dogwood, cherry laurel, and pine.[13] The entrance to the sunken garden was planted with wide curving beds of azaleas. A 1930s-era aerial photograph shows eleven additional curvilinear beds.[14] Each held a huge specimen of a clipped columnar conifer, *Juniperus communis* 'Ashfordii', at its center, "around which Madonna lilies, delphinium and varicolored peonies" were

Azaleas bordering
the lower garden

Azaleas lining the pathways

Perennials and annuals bordering the lawn of the lower garden

massed.[15] Winding around and between the eleven beds were wide gravel paths. The inner paths were bordered by dwarf boxwood. Other pathways were edged with German iris, hyacinth, and narcissus.[16] The shadier beds nearest the woods were filled with "Japanese and Siberian Iris, fragrant pink viburnum carlesi, lilies of the valley and violas."[17] Two 1930s-era photographs show a raised keyhole garden to the south of the larger sunken garden. Shaped like an antique keyhole, the garden sat atop a small flat mound, and was surrounded by a rustic stone retaining wall. Two rustic bridges, encompassed by flowering trees and shrubs, led to the garden. The garden itself contained a circular pathway and was planted with shrubs.[18]

Cridland designed a rock garden adjacent to the mansion. A flagstone walkway bordered by azaleas led from the house to the rock garden, which was surrounded by a figure-eight stepping-stone pathway and featured a cascading waterfall and two stone pools. A 1929 *Atlanta Journal Magazine* article described this unique landscape: "Fern fronds wave their lacy fingers above the rocks, while trilliums, heart leaves and trailing vines grow in riotous profusion. At a lower level there are two pools, one the form of a heart. In one of these pools an electrical device is being arranged, which when completed, through an effect of flood lighting will give the impression of a liquid rainbow—a sparkling galaxy of color."[19] Surrounding the rock pools was a rustic stone bench and a large variety of wildflowers, rhododendrons, laurels, and azaleas. The artificial rock pools—water was pumped from a stream below—were similar in design to those illustrated in Cridland's *Practical Landscape Gardening*.

In the wooded areas, Cridland laid out dozens of dirt paths, many of which crossed natural streams over stone and wooden bridges. The woodlands were "augmented by plantations of smoke tree, euonymous, viburnums and English laurels,"[20] with ivy draping the bridges and clematis climbing the trees.

In their elaborate gardens and recreational areas, the Woolfords hosted many social and community gatherings, which are highlighted in period photographs and publications such as the Garden Club of Georgia's *Garden Gateways*.[21] In the mid-1930s, the gardens were opened in the springtime to public tours; there was much interest in the masses of azaleas on the site.[22] The property's role as a private estate soon came to a close. The Woolfords relocated to Georgia's coast in the mid-1930s, and after their divorce, the estate was sold to Marjorie and William McRae in 1943. Cator Woolford died the following year. During the McRaes' ownership, the Southwell-designed mansion suffered a major fire. In 1949, the newly formed Cerebral Palsy School Clinic of Atlanta purchased the property, making its home there in 1951. In the second half of the twentieth century, the school made numerous changes to adapt the property and its buildings to their new role, including, in 1961, constructing the Lane Building and an adjacent parking lot on the northern end of the property accessed by Ridgewood Road.[23]

By the close of the 1950s, the gardens on the property had become overgrown from a lack of maintenance. In the early 1960s, the Atlanta landscape architects William L. Monroe Jr. and Isaac Williamson were brought in to oversee their rehabilitation.[24] They added the limestone colonnade and flagstone walkways to the sunken formal garden.[25] The original dancing terrace and tennis courts were removed to provide additional space for the garden. Photographs from the early 1960s show the sunken formal garden with its irregular beds reinvigorated with an evergreen shrub at the center of each bed surrounded by grass and edged with annuals.[26] The images show bordering beds filled with azaleas and tulips. Photos and articles from a 1960s-era scrapbook highlight children and teachers enjoying the beauty of the gardens.[27] Other efforts included a garden therapy program established by the Indian Creek Garden Club for the students of the Cerebral Palsy Center in 1962. One of the program's projects was the creation of a woodland path planted with wildflowers near the side entrance to the new Lane Building.[28]

In 1963, the Cator Woolford Memorial Garden was dedicated and opened to the public. From the 1970s to the 1990s, the gardens were partially maintained by high school students enrolled in a vocational training program at the site, led by Fernbank Science Center horticulturists, in conjunction with the Cator Woolford Memorial Garden Association. During these decades, more elements of the original Woolford-era gardens were lost, and invasive exotics grew uncontrolled on many sections of the property.

Activities on the site expanded in 1980 when the Cerebral Palsy School built additional facilities. The following year, the school leased the Woolford mansion to the Atlanta Hospital Hospitality House, which provides food and lodging to people who have family members convalescing in metro Atlanta hospitals. In 1988, the Cerebral Palsy School dedicated a new Adult Center building and changed the organization's name to Rehabilitation and Education for Adults and Children, Inc. (REACH).

In the 1990s, REACH raised approximately $1.5 million to revive the gardens and rehabilitate or restore a number of the site's structures, which would then be used to generate rental income by hosting special events. Most notable was the restoration of the Neoclassical Revival–style clubhouse to serve as an event pavilion, the conversion of the

Historic entrance to the estate

Rock garden in a woodland setting

Fountain and
stone bench in the
rock garden

Stone bench in the rock garden

Central fountain in the rock garden

Early-morning shafts of light penetrating the woodlands

New plantings in the restored rock garden

summer kitchen into a modern catering facility, and the addition of restrooms in the former greenhouse. This work was managed by the Atlanta architectural firm of Surber, Barber, Choate and Hertlein. In the mid-1990s, REACH hired the Atlanta landscape architect Edward L. Daugherty to create an adaptive reuse master plan for the gardens and woodlands. Daugherty drew upon Cridland's original garden design to create a series of garden rooms that could serve as event spaces. The first phase of the plan was implemented, including the addition of a circular stone court near the restored clubhouse to serve as a limited access point for event vehicles as well as an intimate space for events. Daugherty created a smaller event space by adding a small terrace in front of the historic pavilion; to connect the terrace to a small lawn across a creek, he designed a flagstone-paved bridge. Maintaining the scale and feel of Cridland's design, Daugherty transformed the space that was once home to the sunken garden into an area that could accommodate large groups. He created a formal flower garden with a small central lawn flanked by perennial beds in an *S* curve encompassed on the east and west sides by a colonnade and arbor. A much larger open lawn was added north of the flower garden.

Daugherty created meandering paths to connect the different parts of the landscape, although the extensive system of pathways he envisioned, along with an orchard, a wildflower glen, a bog garden, and grotto, were not fully implemented.[29] Other partly implemented components of Daugherty's plan included the establishment of new areas for plantings using plants characteristic of early twentieth-century Atlanta gardens and the much-needed removal of invasive plants throughout the site. In addition, Daugherty provided a maintenance plan for the care of the trees.[30] The Cator Woolford Gardens site was dedicated in 1998. The same year, the gardens received an outstanding achievement award from the Georgia Trust for Historic Preservation.

Recent work at the Cator Woolford Gardens has included the restoration of the historic rock garden in 2013 and 2014. The restoration was funded by the Sara Giles Moore Foundation of Atlanta and implemented by the Atlanta artist and gardener Cooper Sanchez, whose work was guided by old photographs, extant elements, and the chapter in Cridland's book entitled "Wild Garden and the Rock Garden."[31] The process involved the extensive removal of invasive plants, including English ivy, poison ivy, Japanese honeysuckle, privet, wisteria, and mahonia. The stone pathways and rock pools were resurrected from years of settling and debris from material dumped on the site.[32] Healthy existing native plants were saved, and woody ornamentals and shade-loving perennials were added. In 2016 and 2017, other elements of the landscape were revitalized by Cooper Sanchez, including the enhancement of the formal flower garden with a central lawn, which is used for events, and the removal of invasives in the woodlands along the entrance drive. In 2016, REACH, renamed the Frazer Center in 1999 in honor of one of the founders of the Cerebral Palsy School, established a three-year partnership with Trees Atlanta. Together, they launched a forest restoration project to protect and enhance the health of the city's urban forest.[33]

The transition of the Cator Woolford estate from a private residence to the home of two organizations dedicated to serving others parallels Cator Woolford's philanthropic efforts. Woolford supported a number of civic and social causes, including vocational guidance in the Atlanta public schools, community employment services, and the Georgia College Placement Bureau.[34] As a trustee of the Warm Springs Foundation, he was instrumental in raising funds for the construction of Georgia Hall at the renowned polio treatment center established by Franklin Delano Roosevelt in Warms Springs, Georgia. One of Woolford's last good works was the gift of 350 acres in Glynn County to the State of Georgia for use as a public park named Santo Domingo Park.[35]

Today, the Cator Woolford Gardens is home to the Frazer Center, where children and adults with a variety of abilities come together to learn and to flourish, and the Atlanta Hospital Hospitality House, a temporary retreat for outpatients and for caregivers of patients in Atlanta-area hospitals. The Frazer Center graciously keeps its gates open so that Atlantans can freely wander through the Cator Woolford Gardens and revel in its beauty and history.

Coffin-Reynolds Mansion situated near the southern end of Sapelo Island

Coffin-Reynolds Mansion

OFF THE COAST of Georgia lies Sapelo, a barrier island that buffers the mainland against storms and strong tides from the Atlantic. No road or bridge leads there. Tourists and residents must take a ferry that runs three times a day between the dock at the small community of Meridian and the landing on Sapelo. In the early twentieth century, the island's isolation, beauty, and abundance of historic and natural resources attracted the attention of two extremely wealthy but very different men, Howard E. Coffin and R. J. Reynolds Jr. Both made Sapelo their home and retreat, and both left their mark on its landscape. Sapelo is also the setting of Hog Hammock, "the last intact Gullah-Geechee community left on Georgia's sea islands."[1] Descendants of Africans who were forcibly brought to Sapelo continue to live there and preserve their unique culture. In the late twentieth century, the State of Georgia recognized the island's plentiful yet fragile resources and became its primary steward.

A road race brought Howard Coffin, a pioneer of the country's automotive industry—he was a founder of the Hudson Motor Car Company—to the Savannah area around 1910. He and his wife, Matilda, discovered the appeal of coastal life. On a return visit to the state the next year, Coffin traveled to Sapelo and viewed what remained of the once-prosperous antebellum plantation owned by Thomas Spalding.[2]

Known as "a statesman, a businessman, and a writer, as well as one of the leading agriculturists of his day," Spalding was one of the most respected planters in Georgia.[3] He purchased Sapelo's southern acreage in 1802, and by his death in 1851, most of the island was under his purview. The land supported the cultivation of sugar cane, indigo, and sea island cotton. Cattle grazed in the fields, and timber was abundant. All this was maintained by a large labor force of enslaved African Americans who lived in settlements throughout the island.

In dreams I see the live-oak groves;
In dreams I hear the curlews cry,
Or watch the little mourning doves
Speed softly by.
—Carlyle McKinley, "Sapelo"

East Side, from
*Garden History of
Georgia*

Spalding was especially interested in the use of tabby, a combination of oyster shells, lime, sand, and water. Structures throughout the island were constructed of this sturdy mixture, including his own house, which he designed.[4] Located on the southern end of Sapelo less than a mile from Nanny Goat Beach and the Atlantic Ocean, this residence was the center of Spalding's family life with his wife, Sarah Leake Spalding, and their children, as well as a setting for entertaining. It was known for "the perfection of its gardens, for the luxury of its Old World furnishings, for its library, and for the unusual beauty of its architecture."[5]

Spalding's death preceded major changes on Sapelo. Family members continued to live there, but with the outbreak of the Civil War, the island was abandoned and the slaves were sent inland.[6] Vandalism and the elements took their toll, and buildings and grounds fell into ruin.[7] Although Spalding's descendants continued to own island property after the war, financial need resulted in the land being sold, lost, or subdivided. When Coffin saw Sapelo, the landscape was overgrown and used primarily for hunting and fishing. New owners of the island's south end had constructed lodging for

sportsmen on the remains of Spalding's former home.[8] Despite the island's physical condition, Coffin was intrigued by its history and its seemingly endless possibilities. By the end of 1912, he had acquired nearly the entire island, with the exception of the land owned by former slaves who had returned after the war and purchased property.

Coffin's plan was to use Sapelo as a winter retreat. He and his wife would spend the remainder of the year at their home in Grosse Pointe Shores, Michigan.[9] Almost immediately, he made improvements to the property and renovations to the former hunters' lodge to make it more comfortable. He later added a cruciform pool in the front yard, which both guests and thirsty cattle were known to enjoy.[10] Business interests and Coffin's service to the government during World War I often kept the couple away, but by the early 1920s they had decided to make the island a more permanent residence.

The Coffins' interest in the Georgia coast was shared by other affluent northern families who built sea island estates. These included, among others, the Carnegies of Cumberland, the Lewises of St. Simons, and the Torreys of Ossabaw. The exclusive Jekyll Island Club, with its private "cottages," claimed well-heeled members with names such as Rockefeller, Morgan, and Vanderbilt.[11] This all coincided with the Country Place–era movement of the late nineteenth and early twentieth centuries. Wealthy industrialists built private estates removed from the noisy, polluted life of the city. Their romantic vision of country life included grand houses with complementary gardens and landscapes. The surrounding acreage often supported an idyllic farm setting. Life generally revolved around entertaining, and opportunities for games and sports were plentiful. Country houses and their elaborate landscapes signified status but also represented an attempt to lead an idealized, healthy, and natural life.[12]

Upon deciding to live primarily on the island, the Coffins rebuilt the main residence. Coffin undertook major work on the former lodge, where he and his wife had lived since they purchased Sapelo, and constructed their new house on the footprint of the former Spalding mansion. They salvaged some features and retained the old foundations and some exterior walls.[13] The plan for the new house was heavily influenced by Spalding's antebellum design. Albert Kahn,

East lawn, featuring a large cruciform
pool and a marble statue

Cruciform pool and the decoratively tiled east terrace

an architect well known in Detroit's automotive industry, prepared renderings; Arthur Wilson was the builder. Even when away from Georgia, Coffin remained closely involved in construction decisions. The house took several years to build, but appears to have been completed around 1927.[14]

The Coffin mansion consisted of a central building with flanking wings. Terraces on the front and rear opened onto the garden. Details concerning the planning for these formal grounds are unclear. Coffin, however, was interested in incorporating components of Spalding's garden design into the new landscape.[15]

The front (east) side of the house was distinguished by a recessed porch with four large tapered columns. The connecting, decoratively tiled terrace, with its "potted tropical plants and gay colored urns," provided a transition from the building's interior to the outdoor space.[16] *Garden History of Georgia* describes the landscape in front of the house:

> Broad steps descend to the level of the main garden which is rectangular in shape, extending the full length

of the house, and raised about two feet above the level of the surrounding woodland. The garden, in a grove of two hundred year old live oaks draped with Spanish moss, is simple in design, except for the ornate detail of the pool. On the main axis, the wide oyster shell walk terminates in a flight of steps leading to the path which winds through the woodland toward the green houses and pool garden, and at either end of the cross walk are pieces of Italian statuary.[17]

A "causeway" was "built from the front of the mansion to the sea."[18] From the terrace, there was "a flower-bordered vista of the Atlantic."[19] Plants bringing seasonal color to the front garden included azaleas, camellias, Carolina jessamine, Cherokee roses, and wisteria. The rear side of the house contained the "great lawn" and two "flat, circular lily pools."[20] The entire garden featured the "lush green of palms, ferns, and tropic shrubbery."[21]

The area beyond the rear lawn was woodland with "groupings of palms, camellias, orange trees, oleanders, and other semi-tropical shrubs."[22] A path led to Coffin's water garden, "an immense duck pond

dotted with islands masked in tropical growth."[23] Coffin added a tennis court within a short walk from the main house. Nearby was the administration building for the estate and a grouping of farm buildings that included a barn and stables.

Coffin's plans also included a greenhouse complex. He selected a modular design by one of the country's leading greenhouse manufacturers, the Wm. H. Lutton Company of New Jersey, known for its innovative use of "steel, steel reinforced glazing rafters and wide glass lites."[24] The main greenhouse contained "a palm room, a rose bay, water lily propagating pools and vegetable beds in addition to the usual flower benches."[25] There was a two-story gardener's residence, along with structures such as cold frames and a lath house to protect young plants. Nearby were "several acres of orchards and vegetable gardens which surround the fruit house where oranges, grapefruit, figs, pomegranates, and other fruits are grown."[26] The location and orientation of the complex, northeast of the Coffins' home, were probably carefully selected, since both were "ideal for proper

solar radiation."[27] A rock garden was located within sight of the greenhouse.[28]

Although Coffin employed a staff to manage the gardens, he enjoyed working with plants himself.[29] A reporter in a 1928 article in the *Macon Telegraph* described Coffin: "Shirt-sleeved and sun-helmeted, the man with the hoe grubs at the grass in his flower plots and loosens the earth about the roots of his favorite shrubs."[30]

The house and grounds were Coffin's showplace, but he wanted the estate to be sustainable and to provide work for island residents. At one point, he employed "some 200 gardeners, road builders, farmers, herdsmen, and house servants."[31] Coffin had "a scientific truck garden in which more than a dozen varieties of vegetables thrived."[32] He maintained a herd of Guernsey cattle for dairy farming and employed locals at his seafood cannery. The island had its own sawmill, carpenter's shop, and marine railway to handle boat repairs. Workmen drilled wells and cleared fields.[33] All this was done to ensure that Coffin's Sapelo prospered.

East lawn, with live oaks, large decorative urns, and low tabby walls

West side of the house

With island operations going smoothly, the Coffins, who enjoyed entertaining, made certain that their guest register was filled with the names of friends and business associates. President Calvin Coolidge and First Lady Grace Coolidge visited in December 1928.[34] Charles Lindbergh landed on the island in 1929 and stayed for lunch.[35] Hunting, fishing, boating, riding, playing tennis, swimming, walking on the beach, or strolling through the gardens—all these activities and more were part of the hospitality generously offered.

Howard Coffin was not one to be satisfied with leisurely pursuits. A 1914 biographical sketch described him: "Far from rich in the world's goods, he began life with an abounding energy—and a smile. He has believed . . . that rewards come only through hard work."[36] Coffin exhibited that philosophy when he built his Sapelo estate and undertook a new venture with a young cousin, Alfred W. "Bill" Jones. Jones visited Sapelo in 1923, stayed, and eventually helped Coffin manage the island. Over time, this young man became almost a son to Coffin.[37] Together they began creating a year-round resort that was to feature the popular Cloister hotel on Sea Island.[38]

As it turned out, hard work alone did not allow Coffin to see his dream for the resort come to fruition. His fortunes dramatically changed after the stock market crash of October 1929. Intense financial pressure and the death of his dear wife in 1932 devastated Coffin. It became clear that if there was any hope of saving the Sea Island project, Sapelo would have to be sold. Coffin's twenty-two-year ownership of the island ended in 1934, but his sacrifice enabled Bill Jones to salvage the dreamed-of resort. With an influx of funds and careful management, the Sea Island Company, the corporation established by Coffin, was out of debt by 1940.[39] Coffin died in 1937.

In a 1934 article, W. Robert Moore, a writer for *National Geographic* magazine, described the setting of the main house on Sapelo as R. J. "Dick" Reynolds Jr., the island's next steward, would first see it: "In the midst of a cathedral-like bower of live oaks, with hoary beards of Spanish moss depending from their outstretched limbs, stands the majestic colonial home. Projecting from the porticoed entrance is a cruciform formal pool which catches and tosses back the reflection of the mossy oaks and the vast white walls. In its center a kneeling woman of Florentine

marble, 'The Awakening,' had just caught in her upstretched hands a wisp of the live moss that had dropped from the overhanging boughs."[40]

When Reynolds acquired Sapelo in 1934, he was a young man of twenty-eight. His father had made an immense fortune as the founder of R. J. Reynolds Tobacco, and his mother, Katherine, had developed their Winston-Salem estate, Reynolda. Both had died by the time Reynolds turned eighteen. Reynolds was recently married when he purchased Sapelo, and he and his young wife, Elizabeth "Blitz" Dillard, were also building a rural estate called Devotion in the Blue Ridge Mountains of North Carolina. Over his lifetime, Reynolds was to call several places home, but Sapelo was a constant. He owned this island retreat for thirty years, until his death in 1964.

Shortly after purchasing the property, Reynolds hired the Atlanta architect Philip T. Shutze to update the main house.[41] The landscape architect William C. Pauley was asked to prepare a preliminary plan for redeveloping the grounds; however, it was never implemented.[42] Pauley completed a topographical survey of the area around the residence in May 1935. This document provides the best record of the landscape that Reynolds purchased from Coffin and

West side, from *Garden History of Georgia*

Small reflecting pool
on the west lawn

confirms that the basic form of the gardens remained unchanged over the years.[43] A 1998 landscape analysis surmised that any alterations made during Reynolds's ownership "appear to have been limited to maintaining and enhancing the plant materials."[44]

Like Coffin before him, Reynolds remained the main source of employment for island residents, using their services "in agriculture, the dairy operation, in machinery maintenance, as domestics, and in operating the boats that ran between Sapelo and the . . . mainland."[45] Reynolds updated Coffin's former farm complex with new buildings. The architect Augustus Constantine arranged them in a quadrangle, with a grass courtyard at its center.[46] The sculptor Fritz Zimmer added "a stone drinking trough . . . surmounted by a fountain and three sculptured wild turkeys."[47] As part of a plan to use the northern end of the island for hunting, Reynolds, in a controversial move, consolidated Sapelo's private holdings. Land ownership by black residents was transferred,

not always willingly, from several communities to one—Hog Hammock, located almost two miles northeast of the main house.[48]

Perhaps Reynolds's most important contribution to the island and to the citizens of Georgia occurred as a result of a chance meeting in 1948 with Eugene Odum, a zoologist who one day would be known as the father of modern ecology. Their encounter led to the establishment of a research facility on Sapelo's quadrangle that eventually became the University of Georgia Marine Institute.[49] Reynolds allowed the "marshes, maritime forest, and magnificent beach" on the south end of the island to become a living laboratory.[50] Studies carried out by scholars such as Odum, John Teal, and others led to the conclusion "that the marshes, estuaries, coastal ocean, and land interact as one great natural system."[51] Among its many benefits, the salt marsh, with its extraordinary smooth cordgrass (*Spartina alterniflora*), carries out a critical role in the food web.[52]

After Reynolds's death in 1964, Sapelo was sold to the State of Georgia in two transactions—the first in 1969, the second in 1976. Today, the island is home to the R. J. Reynolds Wildlife Management Area, the Reynolds Mansion, and the University of Georgia Marine Institute. As part of the National Estuarine Research Reserve System, Sapelo provides educational and research opportunities that support ongoing coastal stewardship. The Georgia Department of Natural Resources holds overall responsibility for Sapelo's management.

Residents of the privately held Hog Hammock remain intensely proud of their heritage. In 2006, Congress designated the coastal areas of Georgia and South Carolina, as well as portions of Florida and North Carolina, as the nation's Gullah Geechee Heritage Corridor. This includes Hog Hammock, where the culture's long-held traditions are valued and the melodic Geechee dialect is still spoken.[53] The area's population, however, is dwindling. Over the years, as opportunities for island employment grew more limited and educational options for the young vanished, people have moved away. An aging demographic now must deal with increased property taxes and pressure to sell their land. This culturally rich community faces an uncertain future.

Although Coffin and Reynolds would recognize Sapelo today, changes have occurred since their time.

Greenhouse complex

Greenhouse entrance

Sculpture, designed by Fritz Zimmer, featuring a stone
watering trough topped with stone turkeys

Alligator Pond

Alligator Pond pergola

Public tours now bring visitors to the historic south end. Small groups are able to rent the mansion, and weddings are held on the grounds. Live oaks and Spanish moss continue to dominate the landscape, and the basic structure of the formal garden is maintained. Palms add lushness, and two large clay urns at the edge of the front walkway provide visual interest. Azaleas and camellias still bloom near the house. The former swimming and lily pools are drained but remain intact. Upkeep of the garden is labor intensive, and help sometimes comes from unexpected sources. For years the Odum Garden Club, from the small community of Odum in Wayne County, has chosen this site as its special project. Members visit several times a year to weed, prune, and plant—in general, to do whatever is needed to help maintain this noteworthy landscape.[54]

The woodland behind the mansion contains live oaks and numerous shrubs. Coffin's former water pond between the main house and quadrangle is now aptly named the Alligator Pond. A prominent sign instructs visitors: "Do not feed, harass, or throw at alligators." A wooden walkway leads to one of the water pond's "islands," or small land formations, where a moss-draped concrete pergola stands as a reminder of another time. The tennis court and now-vacant administration building are in need of repair. The quadrangle of historic buildings continues

to be the center of activity for the Marine Institute, and the unusual turkey sculpture retains its prominence in the center of the courtyard. The greenhouse complex has long been abandoned, but the nonprofit group known as Friends of the University of Georgia Marine Institute has removed most of the structures' glass panes to protect them. Nearby remnants of the old rock garden are hidden in a wooded area. Little remains of the former orchards.

Sapelo is a unique blend of the natural and manmade. People committed to its preservation and protection work daily to ensure its future, but the landscape and structures associated with its twentieth-century history are especially vulnerable. Statewide priorities make competition for public dollars intense, and adequate funding is always a challenge, especially for an isolated, unique property like Sapelo.

For many visitors and residents, however, what the island offers is priceless. Howard Coffin, who found so much joy in this place, is said to have especially appreciated the following lines from Carlyle McKinley's poem "Sapelo":[55]

Here, care ebbs out with every tide,
And peace comes in upon the flood;
The heart looks out on life, clear-eyed,
And finds it good.[56]

View of the marsh along the road leading to the Atlantic Ocean

Sunken garden at Dunaway Gardens

Dunaway Gardens

FOR YEARS, drivers traveling south of the rural crossroads community of Roscoe, Georgia, probably barely glanced at what they passed along the side of the road: the remnants of an old stone gate guarding what appeared to be a densely overgrown woodland. What long ago were cleared fields and later a garden was merely a faint memory covered in kudzu and poison oak. Jennifer Bigham was different, though. When she saw the property, she realized the place was special. She had discovered the hidden remains of Dunaway Gardens. Located above Cedar Creek, a tributary of the Chattahoochee River, about six miles from Newnan, this former garden theater had been the dream of Hetty Jane Dunaway Sewell.[1] Developed in the 1920s and the early years of the Depression, the rock and floral garden was a popular destination until the mid-twentieth century. After many years of neglect, Dunaway Gardens nearly disappeared, but Bigham's perseverance and vision brought this remarkable landscape back to life.

Before marrying Wayne P. Sewell, a Georgia native, in 1916, Hetty Jane Dunaway was a successful actress who performed in circuit Chautauquas. An outgrowth of the Chautauqua movement, which originated in southwestern New York around 1874, the circuit Chautauquas provided education and entertainment for rural areas and small towns across the country. From the early twentieth century until around the Depression, Chautauquas made lectures, theatrical productions, music, and other programs accessible to numerous communities. Hetty Jane was especially known for her "living character readings in costume, with musical accompaniment."[2] One review described her work as "exceedingly clever and interesting," adding, "She has an excellent sense of humor and an equal capacity for expressing the more tender emotions."[3]

Wayne Sewell's roots were in Roscoe, where his family once had a cotton plantation. He, however, was interested in the theater and owned an agency in Atlanta, the

I never take the garden for granted.
—Jennifer Rae Bigham, September 26, 2014

New stone gazebo with an obelisk in the background

Office

Wayne P. Sewell Producing Company.[4] After his marriage to Hetty Jane, he decided to relocate the business to his family's land. It is said that his wife was reluctant to move to such a rural area; however, Sewell promised her that she could take on whatever projects she wanted.[5] She took him at his word and decided to develop a theatrical center on their property. Productions would be held, and actors, directors, and producers would have an opportunity to be trained in their craft. The backdrop for this venture would be a beautiful garden. Hetty Jane and her husband would work together to ensure its success.[6]

In designing the garden theater, Hetty Jane decided to develop a rock garden. This decision was appropriate, given the area's granite outcroppings, and also reflected the popularity of rock gardens at the time. In the 1920s and 1930s, rock gardens "were all the rage."[7] Generally low maintenance and visually interesting, these gardens could be found in many types of landscapes, from small yards to large estates. The landscape architect Robert B. Cridland prepared a section on alpine, or rock, gardens in his *Practical Landscape Gardening* (1918), providing tips for homeowners interested in creating these distinctive landscapes.[8]

Hetty Jane provided "the original idea and the individual planting details."[9] She relied on the advice of Mr. Cagle of Monroe's Landscaping and Nursery Company, known for its expertise in rock gardens.[10] The services of Ed Powers, a rock mason, proved invaluable in developing the garden's network of terraces and rock walls, which took him over ten years to complete.[11] Local African Americans supplied the labor force. Work began in the 1920s, and Dunaway Gardens officially opened in 1934.[12]

Hetty Jane's garden, consisting of approximately twenty acres, was filled with interesting sites, distinctive garden rooms, and a number of buildings that supported the operation. A period flyer advertising Dunaway Gardens emphasizes its scope and variety: "Said to be the largest Natural Rock Garden in the South. Terraced into 22 Levels, 12 Pools fed by Natural Springs[.] Flowers, Trees and Shrubbery placed in a Natural Setting through Expert Landscaping."[13] It also describes a "Dramatized Garden," which included "3 Theaters, Square Dance Pavillion [*sic*], Swimming Pool, Wishing Well,

Woodland path

Little Stone Mountain and surrounding landscape

Honeymoon House and the—Blue Bonnet Lodge Where Delicious Meals are served by Reservation."[14]

The Blue Bonnet Lodge, or Tea Room, was located in a repurposed older structure. From its porch, guests could step down into "the outdoor living room, paved with flagstones around the trunk of a huge oak which is said to be several hundred years old. This area is raised four feet above the garden proper, thus affording a view of the whole."[15] A guesthouse called Windy Hill was near the garden's entrance. The Honeymoon House, also known as Shangri-la, located in the seclusion of the terraced Hanging Garden, was popular with newly married couples.

Near the Blue Bonnet Lodge was the sunken garden: "Against a background of rugged beauty, . . . a cascade dances over mossy boulders. The stream winds its way through the garden and forms three lily pools farther on. . . . Centering the sunken garden is an old-fashioned 'wishing well.'"[16] A short walk led to Little Stone Mountain, over half an acre of granite outcropping. Nearby, waterfalls filled the Great Pool, formed by blasting holes in the granite. Among other sites to be enjoyed were a rose garden, a Japanese garden, and a hillside rock garden.

Of particular interest to theatergoers was the terraced amphitheater, designed to seat one thousand people. Located at the garden's highest level, this space was "planted with a back-ground of white and green, featuring native pines, red cedars, and magnolias."[17] Towering over the outdoor theater was a rather unusual object, a forty-five-foot-high totem pole designed by Hetty Jane and painted by Frances Goodman of California.[18] Made of native poplar, it depicted images related to the garden and was topped by the Dove of Peace.[19] Surrounding the large pole were four pools formed in the shape of arrowheads. Nearby, on the road to Roscoe was the Patchwork Barn, a theater that held 350

View into the
Japanese Garden

people. Productions were staged there, and barn dances were held on Saturday night by the Roscoe community.[20]

As for Hetty Jane's selection of plants throughout the landscape, they were numerous. An early brochure provides this description: "All varieties of Georgia flowers, trees, plants, and shrubs as well as many from other sections of the world that thrive in Georgia soil are planted here. Masses of wild azaleas, thousands of Paul Scarlet and American Pillar Roses, Dogwood, Honeysuckles, rare plants and old fashioned flowers all have their place."[21]

As a theatrical center, Dunaway Gardens proved successful. People who trained there were part of a network of professionals who traveled to small communities and assisted with local amateur productions. In the summers, nationally known theatrical groups performed at Dunaway.[22] A young Sarah Ophelia Colley worked a number of seasons as a drama coach while developing the character that evolved into the Grand Ole Opry's Minnie Pearl.[23]

Time brought change to Dunaway Gardens. Business fell off during World War II, and new developments in mass communication, specifically television, lessened the public's interest in local entertainment venues. Wayne Sewell sustained severe injuries in a car accident, and Hetty Jane turned her attention to looking after her husband, although the gardens remained open.[24] Before her death, in 1961, Hetty Jane described her devotion to Dunaway Gardens: "I have spent all my energy, my time, and our money on this undertaking. It seized me and has never let me go."[25] Sewell passed away in 1965. The site changed hands several times, and a number of plans for its future were discussed, but nothing materialized. Gradually, Dunaway Gardens fell into ruin. The neglected landscape was soon overrun with invasive plants. The once carefully maintained stonework,

Obelisk surrounded by
arrowhead-shaped pools

View of the Hanging Garden

garden paths, and pools became covered with vines and thick vegetation. Fire destroyed the once-popular Blue Bonnet Tea Room, and the Patchwork Barn was torn down as part of a road-widening project.[26] The result of years of work gradually faded, and the garden grew quiet.

Dunaway Gardens' fortune changed at the beginning of the twenty-first century when Jennifer and Roger Bigham first saw the overgrown site. Jennifer, a nurse and clinical instructor, and her husband, an anesthetist, wanted a place for a weekend getaway and family retreat. After being told about the site, they decided to investigate. What they found was a veritable jungle, but Jennifer was intrigued. She told her husband that it was the most incredible thing she had ever seen.[27] In June 2000, they purchased Dunaway.

Jennifer threw herself into finding out what was hidden in the landscape. She enjoyed gardening, but was no expert, although today she is a master gardener. She and a team of fifteen to twenty men that summer dealt with heat, snakes, ticks, poison oak, and almost impenetrable vines. The first task was to remove the undergrowth so that they could walk around and see what was beneath the kudzu and other invasive plants. Jennifer described the work as "not for the faint of heart," but also as the "most excellent adventure I have been on."[28] Within a few months, Jennifer realized that the bones of the historic garden were largely intact and that some of the early plant material had survived. Although the Bighams had originally intended to maintain the property for their personal use, she and Roger decided that the garden should be shared with others.

Bringing the garden back to life was a major undertaking. A hydrologist was hired to get water flowing in the garden once again, a process that took about a year. Stone paths, walls, pools, and other features were repaired. A new entrance to Dunaway was constructed, along with a drive. Setting up a public garden required a business license and a zoning variance. It took three years to make the garden ready for the public.

Jennifer had hoped to fully restore the garden, but soon discovered that many of the plants that Hetty Jane used thrive in sunlight. Trees planted in the early twentieth century had matured, casting shadows, which made shade plants more suitable for many parts of the garden.[29] To assist in identifying

View from the wetlands overlook

Sunken garden with the historic well and stone stage

Amphitheater, with seating for one thousand

Sunken garden and the historic wishing well

and rebuilding the garden rooms, some historic materials from the Newnan-Coweta Historical Society and interested community members were found and studied. As the site was cleared, crucial information unfolded about its physical layout, historic plant material, and architectural features.[30] To support early restoration efforts, Dunaway Gardens received a Historic Landscape and Garden Grant from the Garden Club of Georgia.

Danny Flanders, a reporter for the *Atlanta Journal-Constitution*, wrote an article entitled "Diamond in the Rough" about the rebirth of Dunaway Gardens. The Bighams hoped it might attract interest in the soon-to-be-opened site. Its publication on Father's Day, June 8, 2003, had an unexpected but exciting impact. That morning, cars lined up at the gate, their occupants eagerly waiting to be admitted. Although they had not expected guests, the Bighams "opened the doors and had a great time."[31]

Visitors to Dunaway Gardens may now experience the essence of Hetty Jane's garden while enjoying the changes Jennifer has made. After passing through the entry gate, bordered on both sides by new stone pillars, guests veer left, following the asphalt drive. On the immediate left are the remains of Windy Hill: two fireplaces with chimneys. Nearby is a recently constructed stone gazebo,

designed by the Bighams' son Josh Fisher and constructed from rock found at Dunaway.[32] Atop the hill is the main office, a building that was standing when the Bighams purchased the property and that originally served as a family retreat. Adjacent is the parking area for guests.

On the right of the entry drive is an open lawn. In its center is a large, forty-five-foot-high stacked stone obelisk topped with the figure of a bald eagle that was painted by the Bigham children.[33] Jennifer had the obelisk erected in place of the original totem pole, which had deteriorated long ago. 'Ballerina' roses bloom in the corner of each of the four surrounding arrowhead-shaped pools. This area signals the path to the heart of Dunaway Gardens.

The terraced amphitheater still seats one thousand people. Guests look down onto the lower level, the stage; a stone floor has replaced grass for safety reasons. This popular outdoor theater has been used for plays, fashion shows, weddings, and cooking events, as well as other public occasions.[34] Magnolias are found throughout this area. Nearby is the hanging garden. A small waterfall, a curved stone staircase, and lush ferns are prominent features of this shaded space. Of special interest to the Bighams is wetlands reclamation. During the years that the property was left untended, Cedar Creek changed dramatically.

Sunken garden

Garden pool

Beaver dams altered the water flow, and vegetation grew in what had been a gently flowing waterway. The Bighams hope to bring back the creek's original course and remove debris.[35] Highlighting this endeavor, a new feature next to the hanging garden was installed: a wetlands overlook with an impressive view.

The sunken garden retains the waterfalls, which flow into pools. This peaceful setting still contains the old wishing well. The granite outcropping that forms the garden's Little Stone Mountain remains an intriguing feature. Adjacent to it is the tranquil Japanese garden, with its torii gate, which symbolizes entry into a sacred space. A pathway leads to the Great Pool, once used for swimming. A new cedar deck and outdoor seating provide an opportunity for rest and reflection. Some other sites within Dunaway include the historic oak Wedding Tree, the location of many weddings over the years; a hillside rock garden; and a new rose garden.

Many varieties of trees and plants are found throughout Dunaway's landscape. Some were planted by Hetty Jane, and others have been added by Jennifer. Walking through the garden rooms, visitors can find azaleas, crape myrtles, hydrangeas, camellias, lilies, water hyacinths, rhododendron, elaeagnus, water oaks, holly trees, magnolias, roses, ferns, hosta, hemlock, gingko, and mountain laurel, to name only a few.

The gardens at Dunaway today consist of twenty-five acres. The Bighams purchased surrounding acreage to protect the site from encroachment by possible future development. Jennifer remains committed to Dunaway and is quick to credit her husband Roger as "her biggest supporter."[36] Their sons Josh Fisher, director of operations, and Zach Bigham are actively involved in the site's management.

Sources of revenue vary. The garden is open to the public, accommodating individuals and tours, for a small admission fee on specific days each month.

During the summer, the garden is generally closed for maintenance. The grounds are becoming a popular wedding venue and an interesting setting for professional photographers. Special events are also held there. In 2011 a new project was begun: the cultivation of tea. A number of plants that the garden designer Ryan Gainey described as "true tea," or *Camellia sinensis*, were discovered growing at Dunaway.[37] Josh, who has a business degree from the University of Georgia, hopes to develop and distribute this USDA-certified organic tea.[38] Dunaway now has several tea fields, and the resulting beverage is served at events.

In 1996, Dunaway Gardens was listed in the National Register of Historic Places as part of the Roscoe-Dunaway Gardens Historic District, a testament to Hetty Jane's original vision and a reminder that the passage of time does not always fully obscure the past. Recognizing the garden's significance, the Bighams established the Dunaway Gardens Foundation, Inc., "to support the preservation of the history and natural beauty of Dunaway Gardens, through educational programs, historical exhibitions, cultural events, research and environmental activities."[39]

In many ways, Dunaway Gardens still reflects Hetty Jane Dunaway's vision, although Jennifer Bigham has made it her own. The similarities between the two women are striking, and the serendipity that entwined their lives is noteworthy. Of no small consequence are the roles of the men in their lives. Just as Wayne Sewell supported Hetty Jane when she wanted to build her garden, Roger Bigham supported Jennifer in her desire to bring it back to life. Writing in 1961, Doris Lockerman might have foretold the garden's fate when she said that "someday a new incarnation of Hettie Jane" will arrive in the garden and exclaim, "this . . . is just the place for an outdoor theater! Why on earth hasn't anyone thought of this before?"[40]

Garden pool and stone steps

Terraced bowl garden at the Governor's Mansion

Governor's Mansion

THE GEORGIA GOVERNOR'S MANSION and gardens, located six miles northwest of downtown Atlanta in the prestigious Buckhead neighborhood, were once home to Woodhaven, the first great estate to be built along West Paces Ferry Road in the early twentieth century. The property was the residence of Robert Foster Maddox, a banker and mayor of Atlanta, and his wife, Laura Baxter Maddox. When the State of Georgia purchased a portion of the estate in the early 1960s as the site for a new governor's mansion, a Greek Revival–style house and new landscape features were added, and important aspects of the early twentieth-century gardens were preserved. Since 1968 it has been home to Georgia's first families while serving as an appropriate symbol of the office of governor.

When Robert Maddox purchased seventy-three acres along Paces Ferry Road (now West Paces Ferry Road) in 1904, the small crossroads community of Buckhead was composed largely of farms and woodlands. Paces Ferry Road served as a rural transportation route between Buckhead and Pace's Ferry on the Chattahoochee River to the west. At the time, the area was becoming a place where well-to-do Atlantans built summerhouses on extensive tracts of land ranging from seventy-five to over two hundred acres as retreats from the noise and pollution of the city. Woodhaven, Maddox's house, was among the area's first rural oases and later the epicenter of residential development for the next three decades. The extension of the Atlanta trolley to Buckhead by 1907 made the area more accessible, and the rise of the automobile further fueled development, affording civic leaders, bankers, businessmen, doctors, and lawyers a convenient way to travel to and from the heart of the city. Over time, permanent residential communities were established throughout Buckhead, where some of Atlanta's most esteemed citizens built grand estates.[1]

Visitors from around the world come here, and we consider it a great privilege to welcome everyone. We are thankful that our own pride and enjoyment can be shared with so many of you who love Georgia—its present and its past.
—Governor Jimmy Carter, 1973

Georgia Governor's
Mansion and Gardens

Maddox, a native Atlantan, was reared among affluence and influence. One of Georgia's leading bankers and civic leaders in the early twentieth century, he was known as "Mr. Atlanta," serving a two-year term as mayor beginning in 1909. In June 1895, Maddox had married Laura "Lollie" Baxter, who was raised in a prominent family in Nashville, Tennessee.[2] They resided in a fashionable home at Peachtree and Ellis Streets in downtown Atlanta with their three children, Robert Jr., Baxter, and Laura.

On their newly acquired land along West Paces Ferry Road, the Maddoxes built a house, a stable, servants' quarters, a hennery, and other outbuildings, dubbing the site "Woodhaven." The house they built was deemed "neither a show place nor an expensive bungalow, but that happy medium, a well-designed cottage in which there are no small economies and no lavish expenditures."[3] Woodhaven was designed to give them respite from the city. The cottage, with its many porches, was placed along the highest natural ridge in order to take advantage of the breezes, and the southern veranda was screened as a protection against mosquitoes. They made changes to the grounds, which were covered with woods and contained an eroded ravine. The Maddoxes served as designers and superintendents of the project and hired African American day laborers to carry out their vision. Lollie Maddox, a knowledgeable and passionate gardener, has been credited in

several articles and by family descendants as the lead designer of the gardens.[4]

The most significant feature that the Maddoxes added was the terraced bowl garden. Three hundred feet west of the house was a deep horseshoe-shaped ravine that offered picturesque prospects. Day laborers with teams of mules pulled scrapers to fashion it into ten semicircular terraces, each two hundred feet long and six feet wide, with a sunken garden at the bottom. Every other terrace was planted with grass and bisected by stone steps; the other five were planted with hundreds of roses and a variety of annuals. The rose selection included American Beauty, The Bride, Catherine Mermet, Duchesse de Brabant, Marie Van Houtte, Lady Mary Fitzwilliam, La France, Meteor, Paul Neyron, and Souvenir de la Malmaison.[5] The sunken garden had a sundial at its center encircled by geometric flower beds shaped into triangles, squares, and circles. A vegetable garden and a small orchard were added to the north.

In 1911, following his two-year term as mayor, Maddox and his family permanently moved to Woodhaven and began transforming it from a summer place into a Country Place–era estate worthy of their status in Atlanta society. They sold the eastern portion of their property, including the original summerhouse and a few outbuildings, to William H. Kiser and then hired the Atlanta architect Walter T. Downing to design them a proper mansion. By the time the Maddoxes engaged Downing, he was

Expansive front lawn of the Governor's Mansion

Formal garden west
of the mansion

a well-established designer of stylish private residences that were in keeping with popular trends in American architecture.

For the Maddoxes, Downing created an English Tudor–style mansion with every modern amenity. The Tudor Revival style, which was popular in early twentieth-century America, drew inspiration from the architecture of sixteenth-century England. The mansion was a large, rambling brick-and-half-timbered stucco structure with a steeply pitched roof, dormers, and multiple chimneys. It boasted four full floors, including a grand Gothic entrance hall, a living room with a Caen stone fireplace, a dining room that could host forty guests, and a library on the main floor; six bedrooms on the second floor; and a gymnasium, pool room, and additional bedrooms on the third floor.[6] A large kitchen, laundry, and other service spaces were located on the lowest level.

The Maddoxes made enhancements to the garden and grounds. In the sunken garden, they added a circular pool with a fountain surrounded by tall clipped golden biota (most likely *Thuja orientalis* 'Aurea Nana') and four seventeenth-century Italian marble statues representing the four seasons. Photographs

from the 1930s show each of the ten terraces more refined than they were in 1908. At the top of the steps in each of the five grass terraces, they added a pair of large square concrete containers containing golden biota, creating a visual link to the sunken garden. The other five terraces, once home to roses and annuals, were lined with dwarf boxwood and filled with an array of plants, including roses, peonies, irises, lilies, and larkspurs. A pergola that served as a teahouse, "swathed with roses and wistaria,"[7] was built on high ground to the north, where it offered a breathtaking view of the terraced bowl garden. Large trimmed *Retinospora plumosa*, a cultivated conifer, lined the path between the sunken garden and the pergola. In the wooded area north of the pergola were plantings of rhododendron and laurel, which descended to a stream bordered by bamboo and native ferns.

Other improvements to the landscape were the addition of a row of Deodar cedar behind an existing hedge of Amur privet (*Ligustrum amurense*) that the Maddoxes had earlier planted along West Paces Ferry Road. To the grand lawn in front of the new mansion they added hardwood and ornamental trees to the existing stand. The winding entrance drive

Pathways near
the mansion

leading to the house contained "heavy plantings of abelia, spireas, hardy hydrangeas and massed conifers tall enough to screen from view the vegetable gardens, cold frames, garage and servants' quarters."[8] Behind the mansion, a playhouse was built for the Maddoxes' daughter, Laura. A clay-floor tennis court surrounded by stucco-covered marble columns crowned with a half pergola draped with climbing roses was placed to the west of the terraced bowl garden.

In keeping with the Maddoxes' social status, Woodhaven was a lavish place for hosting parties and distinguished guests. During Maddox's term as Atlanta's mayor, Theodore Roosevelt was the celebrated guest at a white-tie-and-tails dinner held there. The *Atlanta Constitution* headline described the event as "World's First Citizen Dines with Atlanta's First Citizen."[9] Woodhaven's guest book contains the autographs from famous opera stars such as Enrico Caruso and Geraldine Farrar, and leading politicians and socialites in Atlanta.[10] The Maddoxes hosted many musical performances, including the Metropolitan Opera in 1910. The terraced bowl garden made an ideal amphitheater for such occasions. As an active member of the Peachtree Garden Club,

Lollie Maddox welcomed over four hundred women from all over the country in April 1932 for music and refreshments among the gardens for the Garden Club of America's annual convention, hosted by the Peachtree Garden Club.[11] Woodhaven was also a featured site on several of the Garden Club of Georgia's annual statewide garden pilgrimages, including its first one, in 1937. For decades, the social-minded Maddoxes generously opened the doors of their mansion and exquisite gardens for the benefit of charitable and cultural organizations.

Change came to Woodhaven following World War II. The Maddoxes subdivided the property, although they retained the majority of the acreage. Lollie Maddox died in 1955, and Robert Maddox continued to reside at Woodhaven until the close of 1962. In the late 1950s, political leaders had begun discussing the need for a new governor's mansion, and in 1961 a committee was formed to study the idea. After extensive debate in the Georgia Legislature, the Maddox property was selected, being the largest tract of undivided land available in a neighborhood befitting a governor's mansion. Buckhead had changed dramatically since the Maddoxes first purchased

View from formal garden overlooking the terraced bowl garden

modernism, which is evident in the many government commissions he later received.[13] In the 1950s, Bradbury and Associates designed the district of modern classical state office buildings that encompass the Georgia capitol in downtown Atlanta. In 1957, the firm was hired to make renovations to the capitol.[14]

In a striking departure from his modernist style, Bradbury's design for the new governor's mansion paid homage to Georgia's first governor's residence, a Greek Revival–style mansion built in Milledgeville in the 1830s.[15] The most prominent feature is the series of thirty two-story white Doric columns that support the verandas that encircle the structure. Bradbury faced the mansion in pink-toned Virginia brick and paved the verandas and walkways with St. Joe brick set in a herringbone pattern. Housed in the mansion's twenty-four thousand square feet is a grand ballroom on the ground level for hosting large gatherings. The main floor holds a state dining room and living room, a library, a kitchen, several bathrooms, and several smaller rooms for use by the first family. A circular staircase leads to quarters for the first family and their guests on the top floor, including six bedrooms, eight bathrooms, and offices for the governor and first lady.[16] After numerous construction bids were reviewed and debated during the administration of Governor Carl Sanders, the P. D. Christian Company was awarded the contract in July 1965, and the new Georgia Governor's Mansion was completed by the close of 1967.

Concurrent with the design and construction of the mansion, attention was given to the grounds. In 1964, the state hired the landscape architect Edward L. Daugherty to work with Bradbury to create a landscape that would accommodate the executive family, public tours, and special events. Daugherty, a native of Atlanta and one of the first and most significant post–World War II landscape architects in Atlanta and the Southeast, had studied architecture at the Georgia Institute of Technology and landscape architecture at the University of Georgia and the Harvard Graduate School of Design. He opened his practice in Atlanta in 1953, and since then has worked on a broad range of commercial, residential, and institutional landscapes, including projects for the Atlanta Botanical Garden, the Atlanta Historical Society, the Georgia Institute of Technology, and

the property. What was once a sparsely populated rural area had become filled with affluent residential neighborhoods, including Peachtree Heights Park, developed in the 1910s, and Brookwood Hills, developed in the 1920s. The 1930s and 1940s saw further expansion and more commercial and entertainment amenities added. In 1952, the City of Atlanta annexed Buckhead. By 1964, the State of Georgia purchased the Maddox property and began plans to adapt the site to its new role.[12]

The Maddox house designed by Walter Downing could not be retrofitted to serve the diverse needs of a governor's mansion, including a comfortable and private place for the first family to reside, offices for the governor and first lady, and space suited to hosting public events such as large formal dinners and even larger galas. The state hired A. Thomas Bradbury, a well-known midcentury architect of governmental buildings in Georgia, to design a new structure. According to the architectural historian Robert M. Craig, Bradbury's work in the 1940s demonstrates his interest in the progressive, functional style of

Terraces terminating on the north end at a pergola

View of the terraces looking southward from the pergola

All Saints Episcopal Church. Daugherty's love of Atlanta and respect for historic places helped guide his thoughtful design work for the governor's mansion. Daugherty's objectives for the project were to "enhance the setting of the new formal residence, adapt the original drives to new circulation needs, develop unobtrusive parking for visitors, save as many trees as possible, preserve the historic terraced bowl garden, and create new gardens to serve the governor's family and state visitors."[17]

To preserve as much of the historic landscape as feasible, Daugherty advocated that the new executive residence be constructed on the same natural ridgeline as the Maddox residence. Instead, Bradbury placed the large neoclassical structure parallel to West Paces Ferry Road so that it would have a more commanding presence when seen from the street. Daugherty did retain the original road system, however, which he enlarged and paved. He preserved the existing broad lawn in front of the residence, with its forest of hickory, oak, and dogwood, although some trees had to be removed in order to expand the roadways and other features. Additional parking lots were nestled among the large hickories, oaks, and magnolias on the east side of the property so that cars would not be viewable from the front porch of the mansion nor from West Paces Ferry Road. To provide space for vehicles to turn around, Daugherty designed an octagonal traffic circle in front of the mansion. In the middle, he placed the Fountain of Progress, a circular pool and fountain of white Georgia marble with the outer edge carved in the Greek key design. First Lady Betty Sanders had raised the funds for the fountain's construction through a statewide tour of artworks she created.

To serve the first family and state visitors, Daugherty designed three new gardens—the East Garden, West Garden, and Spring Flower Garden—to be an integral part of the executive mansion. Located near the State Dining Room, the East Garden was intended to host family gatherings and small groups. Designed by James Wiley of Daugherty's office, the East Garden was contemporary in design, with a blend of hardscape and grass, and enclosed by a brick wall. Traditional southern plants were selected for the space. The beds along the walls were bordered with boxwood and filled with flowering crabapple trees (*Malus coronaria*

Photo from *Garden History of Georgia*

'Charlottae'), hydrangeas, and a blended ground cover of pachysandra and ajuga, creating a sense of enclosure.[18] The West Garden, which was intended for large groups, was positioned to receive guests from the State Reception Room. It featured a center terrace enclosed by sixteen large containers planted with trees. From the garden's west side, guests had a spectacular view of the historic terraced bowl garden. Adjoining the West Garden to the south was the Spring Flower Garden. Guests descended on concentric stairs to a rectangular lawn surrounded by borders filled with blooming trees, evergreens, perennials, bulbs, and annuals. Daugherty chose Dan Franklin, one of his staff landscape architects, to prepare the planting plan, which had a seasonal rotation of blooms.[19]

Daugherty had designed the West Garden to give privacy to the grounds toward the north, where he added an area for the family with a play space for children and a designated space for a future swimming pool.[20] A double staircase connected this area to the rear veranda above. He also made general planting recommendations for the entire site, providing a consistent, elegant palette of trees and shrubs native to the Piedmont region of Georgia.

OPPOSITE: View of the terraced bowl garden looking toward the north

Large fountain surrounded by a circular boxwood parterre, providing a focal point

how to acquire furnishings for the mansion, since there was no allowance for them in the budget. In the summer of 1966, Governor Sanders issued an executive order establishing a seventy-five-member Fine Arts Committee, which was charged with overseeing the interior decoration and additional landscape work. The goal was to appropriately furnish the new million-dollar residence with beautiful antiques and to enhance the gardens and grounds to ensure that the site would be an impressive place for visiting dignitaries and tourists. Betty Sanders played a pivotal role in the selection of committee members. Sanders appointed the renowned antiques collector Henry D. Green as chairman. Green and the committee members acquired one of the finest collections of Federalist-period antiques—furnishings, art, and porcelain—in the United States. A sixteen-member gardens and grounds subcommittee focused on the landscape. It was chaired by Anne Lane, the wife of Mills B. Lane Jr. First Lady Betty Sanders served on the committee, along with Laura Maddox Smith, daughter of the original owners of Woodhaven. The landscape architects Hubert B. Owens and William C. Pauley served as advisers.

Daugherty was invited to serve on the committee, which addressed smaller details pertaining to the newly designed gardens as well as the historic landscape. When Robert Maddox sold Woodhaven, he had hoped that the elaborate gardens his wife had designed and managed for decades would be preserved. Photographs from 1967 showed the historic terraced bowl garden intact but in need of restoration. Discussions regarding the primary function and the restoration of the historic garden are evident in the gardens and grounds committee minutes throughout 1967 and 1968.[23] The committee determined that the primary purpose of the historic terraced bowl garden was to provide a beautiful view from the west side of the executive mansion. The committee discussed the possibility of the space also being used as a garden theater for informal performances, as it had been during the Woodhaven days. Efforts were made to remove invasive plants from the terrace beds and to maintain the existing boxwood. The historic tennis court was expanded to regulation size, and the half-pergola structure was preserved. Additions to the landscape included a new greenhouse on the east side of the property near

Among these were southern and sweetbay magnolia, southern red oak, tulip poplar, red maple, white pine, eastern redbud, dogwood, fringe tree, yaupon holly, native azaleas, oakleaf hydrangeas, rhododendrons, and Carolina jessamine. Traditional southern plants included China fir, gingko, Burford holly (*Ilex cornuta* 'Burfordii'), boxwood, and forsythia.[21] Daugherty was an early proponent of using native plants. Regarding their benefits, he said, "I try to look at the natives primarily because natives always know what to do. They know how to behave. They know the soil, or they wouldn't be here."[22]

Because construction costs were higher than anticipated, the state auditor, Ernest Davis, pondered

the former Maddox-era carriage house (referred to as the barn), which was retained. The former vegetable gardens, small orchard, and hennery no longer existed when the state purchased the property. Laura Maddox's playhouse, the servants' quarters, and remnants of an old hothouse for overwintering tender plants had been removed during the construction of the executive residence.

The Georgia Governor's Mansion opened in January 1968 and since then has been home to eight first families—the Maddoxes, the Carters, the Busbees, the Harrises, the Millers, the Barneses, the Perdues, and the Deals. Many of the first families raised their children there. All have hosted public events at the mansion, and all have added their own elements to the gardens and grounds.

The mansion's first occupants, Governor Lester Maddox and First Lady Virginia Maddox (no relation to the Maddoxes who owned Woodhaven), established a fruit and vegetable garden fifty yards from the east wing. There they grew corn, okra, squash, and watermelon. Virginia Maddox frequently used the garden's bounty for family meals and small gatherings.[24] Governor Maddox requested a number of additions to the property: a substantial entrance gate, a tall brick-and-wrought-iron fence along West Paces Ferry Road, and a guardhouse.[25] Although grateful for the work of the Fine Arts Committee, Maddox disbanded it in June 1968, stating that the committee's duties had been fulfilled; he also expressed the first family's need for privacy.[26] The gardens and grounds committee was terminated as well, which put a stop to the efforts to restore the historic terrace bowl garden.

In 1969, a substantial addition was made to the ravine area on the northwest section of the grounds. The Georgia Botanical Society, in concert with Edward Daugherty and the Atlanta landscape architect and nurseryman Norman C. Butts, created a one-acre native garden with rustic pathways and steps. Together they designed, gathered, and planted an impressive collection of trees, shrubs, and other plants native to Georgia and the southeastern United States. The garden was intended to provide an avenue for visitors to learn about Georgia's rich horticulture and enjoy the beauty of the state's flora. The native selections included dogwood, redbud, fringe tree (*Chionanthus virginicus*), Allegheny serviceberry,

common witch hazel, inkberry, American holly, yaupon holly, mountain laurel, oakleaf hydrangeas, rosebay rhododendron (*Rhododendron maximum*), mapleleaf and Blackhawk viburnums, southern wax myrtle, devil's walking stick (*Aralia spinosa*), sassafras, sourwood, and Blue Ridge blueberry (*Vaccinium pallidum*).[27] Between 1969 and 1975, the native plant collections were expanded extensively and maintained by members of the Georgia Botanical Society.[28]

When Governor Jimmy Carter, who would later serve as the thirty-ninth president of the United States, and First Lady Rosalyn Carter came to the executive residence in 1971, they embraced the extensive grounds. Rosalyn Carter, wishing to have fresh flowers daily, cultivated flowering plants in the greenhouse and on the grounds. A rose grower who had met the first lady during a private tour sent her 120 rosebushes, which became the basis for a rose garden located behind the mansion. A former peanut farmer from Plains, Georgia, Governor Carter added a border of peanuts around the rose garden so visitors could see how peanuts were grown.[29] The first lady started an effort to restore the historic terrace bowl garden. In 1974 she had a full-color booklet about the governor's mansion created, with the proceeds going toward the garden restoration. Laura Maddox Smith and her brother, Baxter Maddox, also lent old photographs of the garden to assist in the restoration efforts.[30] The expense, however, prevented a complete restoration, although the fountain, statues, and some of the boxwoods were preserved.

During Governor George Busbee and First Lady Mary Beth Busbee's residence in 1975, a tornado tore through Buckhead. It uprooted over fifty trees and caused extensive damage to the executive residence, requiring significant repairs to be made to the mansion and much work to clean up the grounds. During their tenure, the long-planned swimming pool was constructed north of the West Garden, bringing much enjoyment for their children and grandchildren as well as to future first families.[31]

During Governor Joe Frank Harris's administration, beginning in 1983, the mansion's gardens gained an enthusiastic and sympathetic patron. First Lady Elizabeth Harris was known for her love of gardens and believed that "the grounds of the Governor's Mansion should display something for natives to be proud of and give visiting dignitaries an impression of Georgia horticulture and plants."[32] Many people and organizations supported her efforts. On the east side of the property, she expanded the vegetable garden, added an herb garden, and established a fruit orchard with apple, cherry, peach, pear, and plum trees. She also added more native Georgia plants to the woodland areas as well as over four hundred rosebushes and a perennial garden. Each year she gave her husband a tree, expanding the site's tree canopy. In 1985, with the support of the first lady, Laura Maddox Smith donated a small memorial garden that she dedicated to her parents, Lollie and Robert Maddox.[33] It contained a paved circle with a long bench, a millstone with a dedication plaque, and two containers with evergreen shrubs. Staff members created a new rose garden in Elizabeth Harris's honor near the area behind the mansion where Rosalyn Carter's rose garden still thrived. In 1989, Elizabeth Harris received a Certificate of Merit from the Garden Club of Georgia for her outstanding horticultural work on the mansion grounds.[34]

During the tenures of Zell Miller and Roy Barnes, the governor's mansion continued to serve as a private residence and a public facility, hosting staff meetings, tours, special events, and many distinguished guests, including President Bill Clinton, during Miller's administration. Before and during the Olympic Games, held in Atlanta in 1996, the mansion was a hive of activity, welcoming many international visitors.[35] In 2000, the gardens were featured in the Garden Club of Georgia's annual pilgrimage, just as they had been in the first pilgrimage, in 1937.

When George "Sonny" Perdue, the state's first Republican governor since 1868, moved into the mansion at the opening of 2003, the building was in urgent need of repair after having served seven first families for thirty-five years.[36] Many of the original furnishings selected by the Fine Arts Committee had become worn and needed attention. In 2005, Mary Perdue created the Friends of the Mansion, Inc., a nonprofit organization dedicated to preserving and restoring the mansion's remarkable collection of antiques. Her work was focused on restoring furnishings on the first floor.[37] When several severe thunderstorms toppled numerous trees on the site in 2008, the Perdues chose to highlight the significance of

conserving natural resources in the state by planting a wide range of drought-tolerant and disease-resistant trees on the grounds.[38] Other changes included the addition of a playground and a rope swing behind the mansion for the Perdues' grandchildren and other visiting children to enjoy.[39]

Georgia's eighty-second governor, Nathan Deal, and his wife, Sandra, like their predecessors, have maintained a vegetable garden and an orchard on the mansion grounds and have used the garden's abundance for family meals and for small gatherings. Improvements include the construction of a building on the northeast side of the property to house a few state troopers, who previously resided in the old barn, and the addition of a concrete heliport located southeast of the Fountain of Progress. The old barn now houses administrative offices. The adjacent greenhouse, filled with myriad plants, is used by the staff and the first lady.[40] The Deals had a permanent tent installed over the West Garden after a guest passed out from the heat. First Lady Sandra Deal continued the work Mary Perdue had begun by forming a ten-member Executive Fine Arts Committee to guide the restoration and preservation of the mansion's antiques, with a focus on the second floor.[41] When the Robert L. Staton Rose Garden at the Fernbank Museum of Natural History closed in 2012, its remarkable collection of two hundred floribunda and hybrid tea roses was relocated to a large sunny area near the west gate.[42]

Today, the grandness of the governor's mansion, the exquisite collection of antiques, and the gardens and grounds still impress visitors. Much of the design work done by Edward Daugherty in the 1960s remains, including the East, West, and Spring Flower Gardens. Visitors to the West Garden continue to be delighted by its breathtaking view of the historic terraced bowl garden. The west side of the West Garden now contains an oval bed with two crape myrtles surrounded by benches and pots with small shrubs and flowers. Plantings in the adjacent Spring Flower Garden have been simplified to a central lawn of zoysia grass edged with boxwoods and a small palette of perennials. The East Garden continues to be used as a private space for the first family and small gatherings. The rolling hill in front of the mansion is maintained as a shaded lawn filled with an array of trees. Annuals adorn the entrance and exit drives onto West Paces Ferry Road. The landscape is cared for by Kirk Talgo, the grounds manager, and an eight-person staff consisting of state prison trustees.

The garden features remaining from the Robert Maddox days include the roadway system, which Daugherty widened and paved in the 1960s; the tennis court, surrounded by stucco-covered marble columns; and the terraced bowl garden. Although the structure of the terraces remains, the five terraces once lined with boxwood and filled with roses and other flora are now planted with grass. The staircases and concrete planters dotting the terraces still exist, as does the pergola on the north side of the terraced bowl garden. The circular pool with a fountain in the sunken bowl garden remains, as do the four Italian marble statues.[43]

Most of the rare collection of Georgia's native plants installed by Daugherty and the Georgia Botanical Garden no longer exists. Concerns about the safety and protection of the first family led the State of Georgia in 1975 to place further restrictions on public access to the grounds.[44] The Georgia Botanical Society, with some assistance from the state, transplanted the majority of the native collection to other locations, including the Mary Howard Gilbert Memorial Quarry Garden at the Atlanta History Center, located nearby on West Paces Ferry Road.

The site currently faces a major challenge: the continuing loss of one-hundred-year-old oak, hickory, and pine trees from the Robert Maddox era. These mature trees, many coming to the end of their life cycles, frequently suffer from structural damage or fungal diseases. The grounds manager started an initiative in recent years to replant the grounds with native oaks to address this inevitable loss.[45] These efforts at the governor's mansion are part of a broader, citywide movement to sustain Atlanta's urban forest.

Urban forests are critical to the health of Atlanta and its citizens. According to Trees Atlanta, a nonprofit that protects and expands the city's tree

Foliage along the native woodland garden walk

canopy: "Current estimates indicate that 80% of the U.S. population lives in urban areas. As more rural land becomes urbanized, the role of urban forests and urban tree canopy becomes increasingly important."[46] Urban trees not only beautify a city but are also key to its environmental health by lowering the air temperature, reducing the amount of heat absorbed by paved surfaces and structures, reducing energy consumption, decreasing air and water pollution, helping stormwater management, and providing habitats for native pollinators, birds, and other wildlife.[47] Although Atlanta has the densest urban tree canopy in the nation,[48] its tree cover is being threatened by the city's rapid development and the age of its forest. Many of the city's trees were planted in the early twentieth century and are coming to the end of their life expectancy. Because large shade trees take decades to mature, every effort to plant trees, whether at the Governor's Mansion, on other public land, or private property, is critical to Atlanta's future and its sustainability in the twenty-first century and beyond.

Sculpted boxwood plantings with a central urn and a nearby fountain at the Hills and Dales Estate

Hills and Dales Estate

CONSIDERED THE "apotheosis of all Georgia box gardens," the Hills and Dales Estate is home to the historic Ferrell Gardens, one of the best preserved nineteenth-century designed landscapes in the southeastern United States.[1] It is also one of the most significant historic sites in LaGrange, which lies seventy miles southwest of Atlanta near the Chattahoochee River border. Beginning in the 1840s, Sarah Coleman Ferrell created a series of intricate terraced parterre gardens, filling them with Christian symbolism and incorporating an interesting and diverse selection of plants; her work forms the foundation of today's Hills and Dales Estate. The women who came after her, Ida Cason Callaway and Alice Hand Callaway, carefully built on Ferrell's vision. For over 170 years, these three generations of southern women tended this iconic antebellum landscape, each leaving an indelible mark.

Sarah Coleman Ferrell first came to the frontier town of LaGrange in 1832 when she was fifteen. The year before, her father, Mickleberry Ferrell, had purchased 405 acres a mile from the center of town and established a cotton plantation.[2] Sarah attended the new Troup County Academy, where she met her double first cousin, Blount Ferrell, who taught at the school. They married in 1835 and moved to the territory of Florida to reside with Blount's parents. When Sarah and Blount permanently returned to LaGrange in 1841, Sarah's father gave the young couple eighty acres from the lands he had purchased a decade earlier.[3] It was there that Sarah Ferrell began fashioning her garden. Her background and role in society had a strong influence on the richness and complexity of the gardens she spent decades creating. This included her witnessing the disappearance of the Georgia frontier, her sophisticated education, her place in antebellum society as a plantation mistress, and her deep Christian faith.

You know how I have ever loved beautiful plants and flowers. I do not say they were a part of my life; they were life itself. My idolatry has gone so far as to feel that Heaven must be the home of flowers, and without them would be incomplete. Wicked, was it not?
—Sarah Coleman Ferrell, 1901

East façade of the Neel Reid–designed mansion

Sarah had been born in 1817 in Jones County, Georgia, northeast of Macon in what was then the rugged frontier. During her school years, she watched firsthand the wilderness being tamed into towns surrounded by cotton plantations.[4] By the time she arrived in LaGrange, a similar transformation was taking place there. Located on the lower Piedmont plateau on the Alabama border, Troup County was one of five counties created in 1826 on land ceded by a small group of Creeks in 1825 in the Treaty of Indian Springs.[5] A land lottery in 1827 brought land-hungry cotton farmers, and they established many new towns, LaGrange among them. Designated the seat of Troup County in 1828, it was named after the French estate of the marquis de Lafayette, an American Revolutionary War hero who visited the area in 1825. The area's mild climate, rich soil, and abundant water supply made the county an ideal location for cotton plantations. During the antebellum era, Troup County was the fourth-wealthiest and the fifth-largest slaveholding county in Georgia. LaGrange became a sophisticated oasis for white plantation society on the edge of the frontier, serving as a center of commerce,

government, and education that boasted several schools.[6] By 1860, the prosperity of the plantation class could be seen in the more than one hundred Federal and Greek Revival–style mansions erected throughout the town.

Over the years, through purchase and inheritance, Blount Ferrell added to the original plot of land that Sarah's father had given them. By 1870, he owned a 265-acre farm for cotton cultivation and a 102-acre farm for raising milk cows and swine and growing winter wheat, corn, oats, potatoes, and cotton. He also owned a cotton plantation in Chamber County, Alabama, just to the west of Troup County.[7] By 1888, Blount had amassed nearly 800 contiguous acres to the north and northwest of the Ferrell home. In addition to managing his plantations and extensive landholdings, Blount was a lawyer and later became a judge.

Sarah's status as a member of the planter class dictated the path her life would follow. A planter's status was signified by elaborately designed gardens, a grandiose main house, expensive furnishings, and large numbers of slaves. Ferrell Gardens was no exception. Slavery in the antebellum South relieved

Extensive boxwood gardens laid out in a series of terraces along the south façade

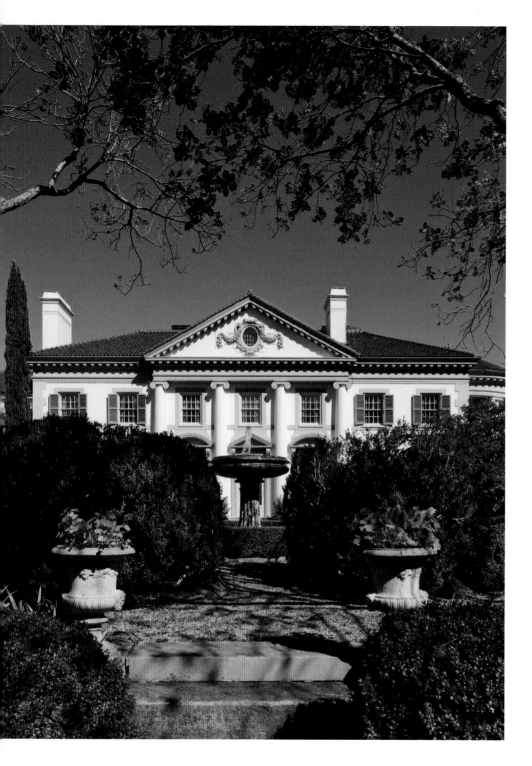

Neel Reid–designed fountain on the first terrace

Americans in Ferrell Gardens. It is likely that a few of them worked solely as gardeners and acquired skills and knowledge about gardening and plants.

Sarah's participation in gardening was not limited to supervision. A letter dated July 25, 1860, from Sarah to Blount states: "You can imagine how busily I work every evening with the watering pot. Some of the shrubbery, I fear will be lost at last."[9] A photograph from around 1870 depicts Sarah in her garden with hands that were "conspicuously sinewy and large, not delicate," according to the historian Catherine Howett.[10] Her schooling had given her a strong foundation for her later horticultural pursuits. Unlike most on the frontier, Sarah had received a comprehensive education, while in Jones County and in LaGrange, that gave her an in-depth knowledge of botany, drawing and painting, history, music, mathematics, science, and Latin and Greek.[11] As described by family and friends, gardening was her life's work, a true obsession. Sarah's own words, written to a friend in 1901, a few years before her death, offer a deeper understanding of her passion for gardening: "You know how I have ever loved beautiful plants and flowers. I do not say they were a part of my life; they were life itself."[12]

Sarah's deep Christian faith played a major role in her passion for gardening, reflecting the mid-nineteenth-century notion that the creation of a garden was an act of religious piety that would have a positive effect on the character of her family and her community. Unlike most intricately patterned gardens of this period, hers was infused with spiritual messages conveyed by iconography and plants mentioned in the Bible.[13] The creation narratives in Genesis had a paramount influence on her.[14] Those accounts are woven throughout the fabric of her design, as Buckner and Carole Melton explain in *Fuller E. Callaway: Portrait of a New South Citizen*: "The stories of how God created and brought order to the world naturally complemented Sarah's own observations during the settling of western Georgia as well as Florida. In the first chapter of Genesis, God commanded Adam and Eve to exercise dominion over the earth and to subdue it. For Sarah, this wasn't an abstraction. For her first twenty-five years and more, it was a hard fact that she daily witnessed being fulfilled. And, of course, the ultimate symbol of this domination in Genesis was a garden."[15]

wealthy plantation mistresses of daily household chores and offered them an opportunity to pursue one or several of the "genteel arts." For Sarah Coleman Ferrell, her passion in life was gardening.

Sarah Ferrell's garden was not only an indication of her family's wealth but also a testament to her vision as a gardener and to the work of the enslaved African Americans who helped her make that vision a reality. By 1850, Blount and Sarah Ferrell owned thirty-four enslaved people.[8] Unfortunately, existing records do not detail the specific involvement of African

South façade of the house with sculpted boxwood parterres

Blount and Sarah lived in a one-and-a-half-story Gothic Revival framed house sited on the high point of the landscape. It featured brick foundations, gables, bay windows, and a portico.[16] The surrounding land had already been shaped into terraces, which led the Ferrells to name their new estate "The Terraces," and set the groundwork for how Sarah would lay out her garden.[17] She implemented her intricate landscape design in stages over decades, methodically filling the six terraces of gardens with a wide array of plants.[18] Her design embraced the prevailing regional aesthetic of formalism, yet her work was also "highly personal and idiosyncratic."[19] Four common elements are integral to her design: using terracing as the primary underpinning of the design; using local quarried stone for the terraces, walls, and steps; employing dwarf English boxwood (*Buxus sempervirens* 'Suffruticosa') to create formal patterns and shapes and to edge beds and pathways; and incorporating Christian and Masonic symbolism. Each terrace had its own theme and name: the Upper Terrace, Sentinel Avenue, Bower Avenue,

Labyrinth Avenue, Magnolia Avenue, and the Valley.

On the Upper Terrace, next to the south façade of the house, were two boxwood parterres containing mottoes shaped into half circles, the pair making a full circle symbolizing Sarah and her husband's oneness. For her motto, Sarah selected "God is love." For Blount, who, besides being a lawyer and judge, was a Freemason, she chose *Fiat Justitia*, a Latin legal phrase meaning "let justice be done," paired with the Masonic symbol of a compass.[20] On the second-highest terrace, Sentinel Avenue, named for its central aisle of tall cedars, Sarah weaved messages of freemasonry and Christianity into the boxwood: the freemason's butterfly, expressing the metamorphosis of the human soul from birth to resurrection; the freemason's circle, signifying eternity; and the Christian cross. The third-highest terrace was named Bower Avenue after the bowers that Sarah placed at each end of the garden's long path. In the 1860s, a local minister who was a friend of Sarah's used Bower Avenue as a quiet retreat where he crafted his sermons.[21] Family members likewise found

Bower Avenue an ideal place for contemplation and prayer. The fourth terrace, Labyrinth Avenue, contained a maze of winding, irregular walks edged in boxwood.[22] Some speculate that Sarah included this labyrinth as homage to similar patterns found in medieval Christian churches, while others believe that it represents the Masonic view of life's anxieties. The fifth terrace, the longest of all, was dubbed Magnolia Avenue. At the east end was a garden entrance where Sarah spelled out the word *God* in gigantic letters formed of dwarf boxwood. On the opposite end, she planted a cluster of grapes formed in clipped boxwood, representing the Old Testament story in which spies sent into Canaan by Moses to survey the land returned with a bunch of grapes so massive it required two men and a pole to transport it.[23] On the west side of the garden was an area known as the Sanctuary, or Church Garden, which contained boxwood sculpted into church furnishings, including a pulpit, a life-size organ, a bishop's chair, pews, a lyre (or harp), and an offering plate (a circular bed once planted with yellow flowers symbolizing coins).[24] Sarah added a miniature cascade created with boxwood instead of water. The Valley, the sixth and lowest terrace, had an ornate square summerhouse and was enclosed by an iron fence and stone retaining walls.

In addition to boxwood, Sarah cultivated a wide variety of trees and plants, showing her passion for horticulture as well as her interest in using plants associated with the Bible. Of particular note were the cedar trees (*Juniperus virginiana*) and the shittah tree (*Acacia seyal*), which are mentioned together in Isaiah 41:19: "I will plant in the wilderness the cedar, the shittah tree, and the myrtle, and the oil tree."[25] Sarah placed cedars throughout the terraces and lined her driveways with them; she planted a shittah tree on the Upper Terrace. She included other trees from the Old Testament that had sacred uses, including bay, cypress, fir, myrtle (*Myrtle communis*), olive, palm, and pine, as well as flowers such as roses. In addition, the garden contained an array of plants common to antebellum Georgia gardens, such as dwarf boxwood, crape myrtle, Eastern red cedar, southern magnolia, tea plant, and Chinese wisteria. She searched far and wide for exotic specimens, including the Chinese fir, Chinese parasol tree, and ginkgo.

Sarah continued to garden during the tumultuous years of the Civil War. Union troops marched through LaGrange in April 1865 but did not pillage or destroy Ferrell Gardens. According to legend, a Union officer in charge of the troops spared the site because when he entered the gate he saw the word *God* in boxwood. After the war, Sarah's husband planted seven pine trees in a grove at Ferrell Gardens in memory of loved ones lost at the Battle of Seven Pines in Virginia.[26]

After three decades of continuous work, Sarah opened Ferrell Gardens to the public in the late 1860s. It became a popular spot for visitors. Newspapers and other publications often featured the site. An article in the 1872 *LaGrange Reporter* deemed the garden the "finest in 30 states."[27] An 1881 promotional publication for LaGrange said of it that "many who have traveled extensively have pronounced it unequaled by any private garden in America, and one gentleman of taste declared that while it lacked in extent it surpassed in taste the world famed gardens of Versailles."[28] Sarah shared flowers from her garden

The singular "GOD" boxwood along the east end of the garden

OPPOSITE: Religious-themed iconography, throughout the gardens, reflecting Sarah Ferrell's deeply held beliefs, as shown by her personal motto, "God is Love"

Plants Grown by Sarah Coleman Ferrell That Are Still Cultivated at the Hills and Dales Estate

American holly (*Ilex opaca*)

Banana shrub (*Michelia figo*)

Bay [laurel] (*Laurus nobilis*)

Boxwood

    Dwarf boxwood (*Buxus sempervirens* 'Suffruticosa')

    "Hedge" box (most likely *Buxus sempervirens*)

    Tree boxwood (*Buxus sempervirens* 'Arborescens')

Caladiums (*Caladium bicolor* or × *hortulanum*)

Carolina cherry laurel [wild olive] (*Prunus caroliniana*)

China fir [Chinese pine] (*Cunninghamia lanceolata*)

Chinese parasol tree [Varnish tree] (*Firmiana simplex*)

Chinese wisteria (*Wisteria sinensis*)

Crape myrtle [crepe myrtle] (*Lagerstroemia indica*)

Eastern red cedar (*Juniperus virginiana*)

English ivy (*Hedera helix*)

English laurel (*Prunus laurocerasus*)

Fig (*Ficus carica*)

Ginkgo [maidenhair tree] (*Ginkgo biloba*)

Japanese cryptomeria [Japanese cedar] (*Cryptomeria japonica*)

Lady Banks rose (*Rosa banksiae* 'Lutea')

Loquat [Japan plum] (*Eriobotrya japonica*)

Mimosa (*Albizia julibrissin*)

Oakleaf hydrangea (*Hydrangea quercifolia*)

Oregon grape holly (*Mahonia aquifolium*)

Pomegranate (*Punica granatum*)

Rhododendron [rosebay or great laurel] (*Rhododendron maximum*)

Southern magnolia (*Magnolia grandiflora*)

Tea [Asian tea plant] (*Camellia sinensis*)

Tea olive (*Osmanthus fragrans*)

Plant names in square brackets are historic common names that differ from current plant names.

The plant list was compiled from extensive sources by Jo Phillips, horticultural manager, and the horticultural staff at the Hills and Dales Estate. The list is included with the permission of the Fuller E. Callaway Foundation, Hills and Dales Estate.

with others, leading the *LaGrange Reporter* to call her a "Floral Priestess."[29]

Following the deaths of Sarah in 1903 and Blount in 1908, Ferrell Gardens sat neglected for several years until Fuller E. Callaway, a textile magnate and businessman, purchased it in 1911.[30] Callaway was a native of Troup County. As a young merchant, he had met Ida Jane Cason while she was attending the Southern Female College in LaGrange. They were devout Christians dedicated to each other and to their ambitions. They married in 1891. Their early interest in gardening was evident in the extensive plantings, seen in period photographs, surrounding their modest home on West Haralson Street in LaGrange.

By the 1910s, Fuller Callaway's involvement in the textile industry, railroads, the insurance business, and banking had made him well known throughout Georgia and the South. His success as a textile producer later brought him to the attention of national and world political leaders during World War I. In 1919, President Woodrow Wilson appointed him to the Conference on Industrial Relations.[31] As Fuller's prominence grew, the Callaways needed a home befitting their status, which for Fuller included fine gardens. The Terraces had made a lasting impression on him in his youth, when he often visited "Miss Sarah" and her gardens. After the Callaways purchased the Ferrell estate, they renamed it Hills and Dales for its sunny hills and shady dales. Two years later, in 1913, they commissioned the prominent Atlanta architectural firm of Neel Reid and Hal Hentz to replace the existing Gothic Revival house with a more opulent residence that would better complement the gardens.[32]

When the Callaways hired Hentz & Reid, it was the leading Beaux Arts architectural firm in Atlanta. Its projects included private residences, commercial buildings, and institutional buildings for wealthy and influential clients in Georgia, Florida, and other southern states. Reid, only twenty-eight at the time, already had extensive architectural experience. He had studied at Columbia University's School of Architecture and the École des Beaux-Arts in Paris, and had worked in New York. He mostly designed Colonial Revival–style houses, to which he added a variety of classical details in a single design.[33]

For the Callaway project, Reid was inspired by the work of Charles A. Platt, a leading New York architect and landscape designer during the Country Place era. Reid was particularly influenced by Platt's adaptation of Italian villas set in formal gardens.[34] The formality of Sarah's garden lent itself to the Italian Renaissance style, which emerged in Italy in the sixteenth century. In keeping with one of the core principles of Italian Renaissance garden design that was evident in Platt's work—locating the villa

A cluster of grapes in boxwood below a large gingko tree

above the garden so that each could be admired from the other—Reid placed the Callaway mansion on the site of the old Ferrell home. Completed in 1916, the Callaway mansion resembles an Italian villa, although Reid dubbed his design "Georgian Italian" to highlight the architectural styles he drew upon.[35] The house's white stucco edged with stone and its red tile roof reflect distinctly Italian elements. The two-story southern façade with seven bays crowned by a pediment supported by four Ionic pilasters harks back to the popularity of Greek Revival architecture in antebellum Georgia. The eastern portico features a two-story semicircular entrance. In its symmetry, formalism, and classicism, the Callaway home was an appropriate marker of the family's status and offered a regal welcome to Hills and Dales' many visitors.

To strengthen the relationship between the Italian architecture of the mansion and the antebellum Ferrell Gardens, Reid added such classical features as fountains, statuary, benches, and urns, which the Callaways and their visitors could admire as they strolled through the terraces and as they looked out from the villa perched atop the gently rolling hill. The repetition of these features throughout the terraces created a sense of unity within the garden. On the Upper Terrace, on the southern façade, Reid placed a large jetted Italian-inspired fountain, which he designed specifically for the Callaways. He added a circular reflecting pool in the sunken garden of the sixth terrace, providing another destination for the family and their friends to enjoy. He suggested adding traditional southern plants such as azalea, boxwood, jonquil, gardenia, southern magnolia, and

In the Church Garden, a specimen Chinese fir planted by Sarah Ferrell, surrounded by a formally planted boxwood maze

Historic well in the Church Garden

Chinese wisteria throughout all six terraces, which brought further cohesion to the design. Reid placed the twentieth-century amenities the Callaways needed—a garage, greenhouse, and a garden workroom—discreetly out of the way on the edge of the terraces. The official opening of Hills and Dales was held on June 15, 1916, in an elaborate celebration of Ida and Fuller Callaway's twenty-fifth wedding anniversary.[36]

To guide them in their future plans for the historic garden, the Callaways commissioned a management plan. The resulting "Report on the Improvement and Maintenance of the Property of Mr. Fuller E. Callaway, LaGrange, GA," created in 1916 by W. B. Marquis, a landscape architect working for the P. J. Berckmans Company, is one of the most informative surviving documents from this period.[37] It details the state of Ferrell Gardens at the time, including roadways, pathways, walls, structures, garden designs, and plant material. The report became invaluable to the Callaways and their staff as they worked to preserve the key features of Ferrell Gardens while contemplating changes that would suit the new villa and the Callaways' twentieth-century needs as well as determining how to maintain such a complex site.

During these years, Ida Callaway played a vital role in the development and care of the gardens. In the early stages, she worked directly with Neel Reid as the villa was being built and the corresponding Italian-inspired features were added to the garden. She later worked with Marquis to preserve the majority of Sarah's design and plants and to add new elements and plant selections that would be sensitive to Sarah's vision for the garden yet express her own ideas.

After a tour of Europe in 1921, Ida was inspired to enhance the Upper Terrace, adding mottoes clipped into boxwood half circles: *ora pro mi* (Latin for "pray for me") from the Callaway coat of arms and the words "St. Callaway." This boxwood parterre was placed on the other side of the large central fountain, mirroring the circular boxwood parterre containing the Ferrell's mottoes "God is love" and *Fiat Justitia*.

On the second-highest terrace, referred to as Sentinel Avenue in the Ferrell days, Ida, in concert with Reid and Marquis, added a number of elements that gave it an Italian feel: a formal boxwood hedge, classical statues, and flowering trees, the last meant to enhance the terrace's evergreen background. *House Beautiful* described the effect in 1932:[38]

> A broad, straight gravel path is bordered on the upper side by sheared specimens of *Buxus sempervirens Arborescens*, forming a loose hedge, with seats of Italian design placed in it every thirty feet. This terrace is terminated at each end by statuary. On the other side of this walk there is a lower hedge of *Buxus sempervirens*, bordered by ancient cedars overgrown with English ivy. Here also are Carolina cherry trees, interspersed with crape-myrtle, whose bark of gray with white patches, like sycamore trees, and watermelon-colored blooms, are so effective against the evergreen background. Along this walk, the illusion of Italy is complete.[39]

On the third terrace, once called Bower Avenue, wooden benches were placed at each end of the long pathway, along with pedestals holding the sculpted heads of Aratus and Sophocles.[40] Traditional southern plants and classical statuary were added to the fourth, fifth, and sixth terraces. Like Reid and Marquis, Ida Callaway was keen on using plants familiar to the South, paying tribute to the Ferrells and their southern heritage. Another passage from the 1932 *House Beautiful* article describes the lushness of the gardens:

> Large southern magnolias, willow oaks, cedars and cherry-laurel, box bushes, and various other types of broadleaved evergreens give both specimen and mass-effect. Informality prevails, and the eye is lost in the luxuriance of evergreen growth. At the east end of this terrace an old pergola supports a mass of wisteria, full of color during the blooming period, and leading to a well with stone wellhead and Italian iron tripod. A succession of flowers, starting with the early flowering old-fashioned jonquils, lend color to the shady beds. Beds too shady for flowers are carpeted with English ivy and periwinkle, and bordered with dwarf box.[41]

Ida established Florida Lane on one of the lower terraces, filling it with tender and tropical plants from Florida.[42] *Garden History of Georgia* describes this area as "the interesting Florida garden with its masses of pink and blue hydrangeas, papaya, orange and lemon trees, and blossoming oleanders."[43] On the sixth terrace, known as the Valley by the Ferrells and dubbed the Sunken Garden by the Callaways, Reid added a circular pool along with a large

ornamental curved stone bench. The view from this bench provided a clear view of the terraces to the grand house. A 1920 *Country Life* article describes this area:

> Steps lead to the sunken garden whose stone walls are covered with ivy and moss, and topped by cylinders of box. The central feature of the sunken garden is the pool, a single jewel in a setting of emerald box by day—by night, a cluster of stars. Here are more magnolias and hemlocks. A Confederate jasmine vine runs to the top of one of the magnolia trees and on

Lower terraces, featuring long walkways bordered in boxwood

Whimsical miniature bronze deer grazing on mondo grass

Magnolia-espaliered garage located northwest of the mansion

Pool house with fountain

another is the yellow jasmine vine. There are flowering pomegranates, a flowering peach, and flowering pear trees. Against the walls are fine clumps of peonies, and the pendant blooms of the drooping deutzia add much to the picture.[44]

Ida made other additions to the grounds, including a new vegetable garden northwest of the house, to provide food for the family and their many visitors, and a rose garden next to the greenhouse, for enjoyment.

Like the Ferrells before them, the Callaways invited visitors to explore and enjoy their gardens. And like Sarah before her, Ida felt she had a duty to share this gift with the community. She once expressed this sentiment by writing, "Life is short, and as we pass this way but once, why not strew our paths with rose petals, so as to leave fragrance on life's way?"[45]

In February 1928, Fuller Callaway died at Hills and Dales at the age of fifty-seven. Ida continued to care for the house and gardens, enjoying time with her children and grandchildren and visitors from near and far. She hosted a luncheon at Hills and Dales for the Garden Club of America in honor of the one-hundredth anniversary of Ferrell Gardens. She died in the spring of 1936. In the summer of that same year, Fuller E. Callaway Jr., his wife, Alice Hand Callaway, and their two children moved to Hills and Dales.

Born in LaGrange in 1907, Fuller E. Callaway Jr. spent most of his childhood at Hills and Dales. Like his father and his brother, Fuller Jr. was a successful manufacturer and businessman. In 1935, he succeeded his brother, Cason, as president of Callaway Mills, which they had established together in 1932 from the network of industries their father had started. In 1930 he married Alice Hinman Hand of Pelham, Georgia, forming a partnership with shared Christian values and a drive for philanthropic work. Alice Callaway played a key role in every aspect of her husband's life, including their support of local churches, hospitals, libraries, schools, and other resources for LaGrange and its citizens.[46]

When the younger Callaways moved to Hills and Dales in 1936, Alice embraced the gardens just as the women who came before her had done. Although only twenty-three at the time, Alice took her responsibility seriously. For over six decades, she

Plants Grown by Ida Cason Callaway That Are Still Cultivated at the Hills and Dales Estate

Azalea (*Rhododendron sp.*)
Banana (*Musa sp.*)
Bearded iris (*Iris germanica*)
Calla lily (most likely *Zantedeschia aethiopica*)
Camellia (*Camellia japonica*)
Carob tree (*Certonia siliqua*)
Carolina jessamine [yellow jasmine vine or yellow jessamine] (*Gelsemium sempervirens*)
Confederate jasmine (*Trachelospermum jasminoides*)
Flowering quince (*Chaenomeles speciosa* or × *superba*)
Gardenia [cape jasmine or cape jessamine] (*Gardenia jasminoides*)
Larkspur (*Consolida ajacis*)
Mophead hydrangea (*Hydrangea macrophylla*)
Oleander (*Nerium oleander*)
Pansy (*Viola* × *wittrockiana*)
Peony (*Paeonia lactiflora*)
Petunia (*Petunia sp.*)
Pink dogwood (*Cornus florida* f. *rubra*)
Poppy (*Papaver sp.*, likely *P. somniferum*)
Rose (*Rosa* 'Empress of China' and *Rosa* 'President Herbert Hoover')
Sweet William (*Dianthus barbatus*)
Tall phlox (*Phlox paniculata*)
Tulip (*Tulipa sp.*)
Viburnum (*Viburnum sp.*)
Zinnia (*Zinnia elegans*)

The plant list was compiled from extensive sources by Jo Phillips, horticultural manager, and the horticultural staff at the Hills and Dales Estate. The list is included with the permission of the Fuller E. Callaway Foundation, Hills and Dales Estate.

worked diligently to preserve and protect the historic garden, and also to leave her own signature on it. She was a dedicated plantswoman. Among the notable changes she made was to increase the diversity of plants. Alice worked in the garden and greenhouse every day, keeping extensive records and studying countless gardening books, amassing a lifetime of horticultural knowledge. When interviewed by the famed English garden designer and writer Rosemary Verey in 1983, Alice said that "the main joy of gardening for me, aside from growing beautiful, healthy plants, is finding rare ones and growing them successfully."[47] She, like Ida before her, had a dedicated and knowledgeable staff to help her.

Plants Grown by Alice Hand Callaway That Are Still Cultivated at the Hills and Dales Estate

American beech (*Fagus grandiflora*)

American wisteria (*Wisteria frutescens*)

Angel's trumpets [datura] (*Brugmansia suaveolens*)

Azalea (*Rhododendron alabamense*, 'Appleblossom', 'Bridesmaid', 'Coral Bells',
  'Hinodegiri', 'President Claeys' or 'President Clay', 'Pride of Mobile',
  'Salmon Beauty', 'Snow', 'Vittatum')

Chinese fringe tree (*Chionanthus retusus*)

Chinese pistache (*Pistachia chinensis*)

Columnar Japanese plum yew (*Cephalotaxus harringtonia* 'Fastigiata')

Dawn redwood (*Metasequoia glyptostroboides*)

Dove tree (*Davidia involucrata*)

False indigo (*Baptisia australis*)

Fragrant snowbell (*Styrax obassia*)

Fragrant wintersweet (*Chimonanthus praecox*)

Franklin tree (*Franklinia alatamaha*)

Golden rain tree (*Koelreuteria paniculata*)

Iris (several, including *I. cristata, florentina, siberica, tectorum*)

Italian cypress (*Cupressus sempervirens*)

Japanese evergreen oak (*Quercus myrsinifolia*)

Japanese stewartia (*Stewartia pseudocamellia*)

Magnolia (several, including *M. ashei, denudata, fraseri, kobus,
  officinalis* var. *biloba, salicifolia, stellata, tripetala, × soulangeana,*
  'Dark Shadow', 'Lennei', 'Pristine', 'Wada's Memory')

Maidenhair fern (several, including *Adiantum capillus-veneris, hispidulum,
  macrophyllum, raddianum* 'Variegated Tessellate')

May Day tree (*Prunus padus* var. *commutata*)

Orange tea olive (*Osmanthus fragrans* f. *aurantiacus*)

Saw-toothed oak (*Quercus acutissima*)

Seven-son flower (*Heptacodium miconoides*)

Weeping dogwood (*Cornus florida* 'Pendula')

White redbud (*Cercis canadensis* f. *alba*)

The plant list was compiled from extensive resources by Jo Phillips, horticultural manager, and the horticultural staff at the Hills and Dales Estate. The list is included with the permission of the Fuller E. Callaway Foundation, Hills and Dales Estate.

Alice and Fuller began to make their mark on the gardens soon after arriving at Hills and Dales. In 1937, they hired the landscape architect J. Leon Hoffman to help Alice add more variety to the flora. Other modifications occurred over time. On the second terrace, they replaced the aisle of tall cedars with azaleas on one side and a row of golden rain trees (*Koelreuteria paniculata*) on the opposite side, to shade the stone benches that had been added by Ida.[48] Alice replaced Ida's rose garden, adjacent to the greenhouse, with an herb garden; in 1983, she hired the herb specialist Rosemary Louden to redesign it. On the site that once held Ida's vegetable garden, just below the entry drive in full view of the courtyard, Alice added the visually stunning Ray Garden in 1950. The beds were arranged in a spoke design with a lacy metal gazebo in the center. At first, Alice used the site to grow roses and ornamental conifers. By the 1980s, the beds were filled with azaleas, iris, *Alyssum saxatile*, variegated liriope, and daylilies.[49] In 1984, Alice commissioned the noted blacksmith Ivan Bailey to create a unique iron bird gate, which she placed near Sarah Ferrell's *God* wrought in clipped boxwood on the fifth terrace.

Alice and Fuller added new structures to accommodate their family's needs, including a swimming pool and bathhouse in 1940–41. The bathhouse, located northwest of the house, was designed to harmonize with the architecture of the house and garage. The Reid-designed greenhouse from 1916 was remodeled in 1948; it is maintained today much as it was during Alice Callaway's time. The first section contains begonias, orchids, succulents, and other tropical plants. The center section houses Alice's collection of ferns, and the third section holds calla lilies from Ida Callaway's original tubers as well as orchids and succulents.[50]

Like Sarah Ferrell and Ida Callaway, Alice frequently opened the gardens to visitors. In 1937, the gardens hosted visitors as part of the Garden Club of Georgia's first statewide garden pilgrimage. When the pilgrimage was resurrected in 1996, Hills and Dales was a featured site. Alice welcomed residents of LaGrange, students from Georgia colleges and universities, and many others to experience the history, grandeur, and beauty of Hills and Dales.

Fuller E. Callaway Jr. died in 1992, and Alice Callaway in 1998. The property was then bequeathed

Ray Garden, added by Alice Callaway

HILLS & DALES
ESTATE
1916

HISTORIC HOME OF THE FULLER E. CALLAWAY FAMILY ❦ LaGrange, Georgia

Contemporary map of the Fuller E. Callaway Estate, Hills and Dales Estate, watercolor. Courtesy of the Fuller E. Callaway Foundation

Greenhouse

Greenhouse still in use

Window to the
greenhouse office

to the Fuller E. Callaway Foundation, with the request that it be used for the instruction and enjoyment of the public. In 2004, the Hills and Dales Estate formally opened as a house and garden museum. The thirty-five-acre site features a visitor center, where guests can explore educational displays about the rich history of the estate. Tours of the house and garden are offered. Included within the Vernon Road Historic District, which is listed in the National Register of Historic Places, Hills and Dales provides visitors a sense of history, an appreciation for preservation, and the pleasure of exploring the beauty of the house and gardens.

Hills and Dales is an inspiring example of three women's continuous care and dedication: Sarah Coleman Ferrell, whose devotion to God and passion for rare and exotic plants formed the bedrock of her nineteenth-century garden; Ida Cason Callaway, who, with her husband, Fuller E. Callaway, created the Hills and Dales estate, including an architecturally significant home designed by Hentz & Reid, and preserved and enhanced the garden in the early decades of the twentieth century; and Alice Hand Callaway, who, with the support of her husband, Fuller E. Callaway Jr., worked tirelessly for sixty-two years to preserve and protect the garden of her foremothers while adding generously to the plant diversity. Although the landscape has evolved over time, the essence of Sarah Ferrell's masterpiece remains today. The garden's history reflects the decisions of all three guardians of the site.[51] Hills and Dales serves as a reminder of the value of preserving our rich southern garden heritage for enjoyment today and years to come.

"Well," circa 2015

"Well," circa 1933, from
Garden History of Georgia

Remnants of stone pillars, in the Lullwater Conservation Garden,
at the site of Patriots' Bridge on Lullwater Creek

Lullwater Conservation Garden

ON A SUNNY AFTERNOON in June 2014, the Lullwater Garden Club hosted a celebration honoring the one-hundredth birthday of longtime member Jean Givens. The setting for this happy occasion was the Lullwater Conservation Garden, where, over the years, numerous milestones in the club's history have been recognized. Located in Atlanta's historic Druid Hills neighborhood, the Conservation Garden is a woodland area and bird sanctuary of just over six acres. What began in the early 1930s as a desire by the newly formed Lullwater Garden Club to develop a "retreat for nature lovers, a sanctuary for birds and a place in which to study Georgia's native flora and [wild] life" has grown into a long-term commitment to a landscape that offers beauty and tranquility in the midst of a major metropolitan city.[1] The Lullwater Garden Club is unusual in that it owns and maintains its own garden, which it generously shares with the public.

The Lullwater Conservation Garden is a fitting component of the Druid Hills neighborhood. Druid Hills, "one of the finest turn-of-the-century suburbs in the southeastern United States," attracted some of Atlanta's most influential and affluent citizens.[2] Listed in the National Register of Historic Places and designated a Landmark District by the Atlanta Urban Design Commission and a Historic District by DeKalb County, the neighborhood is known for the quality of its architecture and its landscape. Frederick Law Olmsted produced plans for the new suburb in 1893 for the developer Joel Hurt; after Olmsted's retirement, the plans were completed by his successor firm, Olmsted Brothers. Olmsted's original design was somewhat altered when developers, led by Asa Candler (of Coca-Cola fame), purchased the property from Hurt, but Olmsted's basic concept and vision for the area remained intact. Olmsted believed in the power of the landscape to restore the human spirit. His design

Morning in the garden! Birdsong and sweet-voiced tranquillity bid me welcome.—Inscription on the plaque at the entrance to the Lullwater Conservation Garden for Druid Hills respected the natural contours of the topography, creating a parklike setting in which the large lots were nestled. He designed a number of parks too, although the Lullwater Conservation Garden was not among them.

The vision for the Lullwater Conservation Garden was described in a 1933 issue of the *Atlanta Journal*: "At Lullwater Road and Lullwater Parkway a pylon entrance of rustic stone will be constructed later. To the front of this entrance and on either side of the walks there will be a planting of shrubbery of a formal nature, making a gradual and delightful transition from the residential atmosphere to that of the forest primeval. The keeper of this entrance will be the immortal wren, a gatekeeper's lodge being provided in each of the pylons."[3] This inviting entrance is now distinguished by a stone walkway, colorful plantings, and two large stone pillars, each rustic tower housing a built-in bird's nest. Bronze plaques identify the Lullwater Conservation Garden and Bird Sanctuary. Stone steps descend into an open

Stone pillars marking the main entrance to the garden

grassy area surrounded by trees and shrubs, including a Chinese fir, magnolias, camellias, azaleas, and dogwoods. The remains of an early rock garden are evident, and stone benches provide opportunities for relaxation. This sunlit section of the garden often serves as a pleasant gathering place.

The main pathway continues toward a forest-like setting; its entrance is also marked by two stone pillars. From there, footpaths wind through uneven terrain, passing pine trees, oaks, native rhododendrons, hosta, and numerous other types of vegetation. As the original designers envisioned, a walk through today's garden reveals numerous varieties of "native trees and shrubs, flowers and ferns."[4] Trees Atlanta has identified six species of champion trees, "the largest of each tree species inside I-285,"[5] in the conservation garden: yellowwood (*Cladrastis kentukea*), American beech (*Fagus grandifolia*), Carolina silverbell (*Halesia carolina*), mountain laurel (*Kalmia latifolia*), tulip poplar (*Liriodendron tulipifera*), and black gum (*Nyssa sylvatica*).

Chinese fir and azaleas bordering the open area in the southern end of the garden

Open area in the southern end of the garden, including stone benches, remnants of a rock garden, and flowering plants and shrubs

An early stone well and the Patriots' Bridge Memorial Garden are also part of Lullwater's woodland landscape. Paths lead to three wooden bridges that cross the ravine and culverts at Lullwater Creek. Bird feeders are hung throughout the trees. The main path eventually connects to the garden's northernmost point of access. There, stone steps lead to a boulder with a simple plaque recognizing the Conservation Garden and Bird Sanctuary. Visitors are often seen walking through these woods, enjoying a brief retreat from the pace of urban life.

The Lullwater Conservation Garden was the brainchild of the Lullwater Garden Club. In the late nineteenth century, women's clubs became popular social organizations across the United States, and they soon became identified with particular causes. Interest in gardening was gaining in popularity, and garden clubs emerged, not only as social and educational outlets, but also as a way for women to contribute to their communities. In 1891, Georgia's first garden club, the first in the country "with a constitution and bylaws," was formed in Athens.[6] The Garden Club of Georgia, a nonprofit statewide group composed today of nearly 400 garden clubs, held its organizational meeting in 1928. The Lullwater Garden Club was a charter member.[7]

The twenty-six members of the Lullwater Garden Club came together for their first meeting on June 22, 1928.[8] Projects began almost immediately. Besides sponsoring flower shows, sending bouquets to local hospitals, and assisting nearby neighbors—including the Druid Hills School and the Emory Shopping Center—with landscaping, the club began to plan a conservation garden.[9] The selected site was a somewhat oblong tract of woodland with a small creek, just below street level in the

Woodlands
and plantings
surrounding the
open area

Pathway bordered by
may apples leading into
the woodland path

members' neighborhood. In 1930, they received permission from the landowner to establish a garden on the property.[10]

Susan P. Phillips, the group's conservation chairman in the late 1930s, explained the concept for the garden complex: a "semi-formal garden" served "as a park-like entrance to the lovely conservation garden," and "the two gardens have been separated and tied together by hundreds of mountain laurel and rhododendrons, and a gateway of time-darkened stones has just been completed that leads directly into the wild garden from the semi-formal one."[11] The practical reason for this arrangement was explained: "It was thought advisable to make a park-like entrance to the strictly native garden, so that vandals, attracted to the spot, might know that this was a project sponsored by a garden club, rather than just a wooded spot from which choice specimens could be taken. And then, a restful spot by the side of a brook in a setting of grass and flowering shrubs is attractive to everyone."[12]

The Atlanta architect Eugene C. Wachendorff prepared plans and drawings for the garden.[13] Trails were laid out, and a bridge was constructed over the creek.[14] DeKalb County officials provided fieldstone for the pylons and retaining walls and assigned part-time labor from the Civil Works Administration to the project.[15] (Although most of the property is within the city limits of Atlanta, its northern edge is included within unincorporated DeKalb County.) The landscape architect William C. Pauley designed a wooden sign for the conservation garden.[16] W. B. Baker, a biology professor at nearby Emory University and a club member's husband, generously gave botanical advice and remained a lifelong friend of and adviser to the Lullwater Garden Club.[17] By 1938, "one thousand seventeen native trees, shrubs, and bulbs," as well as "thousands of wild flowers, ferns, and rhododendron," had been planted.[18] This was in addition to the eastern red cedar installed specifically for the enjoyment of wintering birds.[19] A rockery enhanced the landscape, and a rustic well was constructed.[20] Members spent long hours in the garden and raised money by sponsoring such events as a horse show and by transforming the garden into a country fair during the Atlanta Dogwood Festival.[21]

During World War II, "maintenance and beautification" of the Conservation Garden continued as one of the club's annual projects, but of necessity,

Lullwater Creek

those activities were focused merely on keeping the grounds clean and safe.[22] Members of the Lullwater Garden Club, like Americans all across the country, redirected their energies toward winning the war. The Conservation Garden itself became part of the war effort when the club donated its metal bridge to a local scrap drive.[23]

When the war ended, the country was ready for life to return to some sense of normality. The club, no exception, eagerly turned its attention to "true garden club work."[24] To redress the lack of improvements during the war years, members decided to replace "thousands of bulbs" in the Conservation Garden.[25] Other priorities included general maintenance and the construction of a new bridge over Lullwater Creek.[26] In her "President's Report of 1952–1953," Mrs. James T. King described the garden as "a source of great satisfaction."[27] She made this additional observation: "As in the past, we have planted a large part of this area in grass, but in other sections we have left in the natural so as to be a haven for birds."[28]

Woodland path winding through the forest

Lullwater Conservation Garden: serenity in the city

The club soon faced a crisis that put the future of the Lullwater Conservation Garden in jeopardy. While planning new landscape projects in 1964, members attempted to contact the Candler estate, the owner of the property, to request permission to install running water in the garden. Much to their surprise, they discovered that Emory University was the current owner, and it had proposed selling the land to the City of Atlanta for use as a park. Although that sale did not materialize, word spread that a developer was interested in the acreage. The club realized that the Conservation Garden was in danger and that immediate action was needed. Owning the land was the only way to ensure its protection. Emory was approached, and discussions proved fruitful.[29] The university agreed to sell the approximately six acres for $1,500, and a nonprofit corporation was chartered to handle legalities.[30] Funds were raised, and in October 1964, Lullwater Garden Club, Inc., took possession of the property. The deed stipulated that use was to be limited to "a Park or Beautification Area."[31] If that condition was not met, the land was to be returned to Emory.[32]

The purchase of this tract was a major achievement as well as a considerable commitment. The acquisition included additional woodlands, so decisions had to be made about the best way to approach the design and care of the larger landscape. The solution was "to keep it as much as possible a natural woodland area, to make suitable plantings," and "to lay out a nature walk from one end of the garden to the other."[33] Stone steps and benches were added, three bridges constructed, and fieldstone paths set. Over seventy-five species of native plants were introduced, many specifically selected to attract birds. Ferns were relocated and seedlings planted. Weeds and poison ivy were painstakingly attacked, and the disposal of dead trees became a necessary task.[34] The south end's formal garden was made into a more "naturalistic setting," and the entire tract was designated a bird sanctuary.[35]

Fund-raising was, and continues to be, a necessity. A special event occurred in 1968 when the club and the Druid Hills Civic Association held the first tour of Druid Hills homes and gardens. The Conservation Garden was one of five featured landscapes. Its share of proceeds, approximately $1,600, was a welcome addition to the club's bank account.[36]

Today, the club holds an annual plant sale to coincide with the spring tour of homes in Druid Hills.

The Lullwater Garden Club understands the importance of the garden to its members and to the surrounding community. A summary report of club activities in 1965 and 1966 explains: "So near to the very heart of our busy bustling City of Atlanta this garden is literally a 'green belt' that is so necessary not only for esthetics but also for our mental and physical needs in this era of brick and cement."[37] In 1976, when the country celebrated its bicentennial, the Lullwater Garden Club became a cosigner of the Fernbank-Atlanta-DeKalb Bicentennial Conservation Covenant, confirming a commitment to preserving over 450 acres of parks, private gardens, and forest, including the Conservation Garden.[38]

Among its functions, the Conservation Garden serves as a place where members can express their responses to personal, local, and national events. For instance, when Hollywood came to Druid Hills in the spring of 1989 to film *Driving Miss Daisy*, adapted from an award-winning play written by the Atlanta native Alfred Uhry, a club member's home was selected to represent the residence of the main character. The Conservation Garden became the cast and crew's "base of operations" for approximately ten weeks, as well as the site of the party celebrating the

Pathway and early stone well

end of filming.[39] When the world came to Atlanta in the summer of 1996, newly planted pansies in the Conservation Garden welcomed the Centennial Olympic Games.[40] When the nation's heart was broken on September 11, 2001, the club responded by planting eleven 'Cherokee Princess' dogwood trees in memory of the individuals lost on that tragic day.[41]

In 2006, members dedicated the Patriots' Bridge Memorial Garden as "a tribute to the men and women who sacrificed and served this great country during times of war" and in remembrance of the club's actions during World War II.[42] This garden area includes a granite bench and bronze commemorative plaque surrounded by native plants and camellias. The restful setting overlooks a stone pier in Lullwater Creek, a remnant of the metal bridge donated during World War II and a symbol of the patriotism of the women of the Lullwater Garden Club.[43]

Honoring the memory of deceased members by planting shrubs, usually camellias or azaleas, dates from the club's earliest beginnings. A Memorial Garden was established at one time on the garden's south end; however, over time the placement of shrubs has become less formal. An especially poignant remembrance was planted to honor two members who perished in the Orly plane crash of 1962, an event that dramatically affected Atlanta's cultural community.[44]

Although the Conservation Garden offers a respite from modern life, it is not unaffected by being located in a heavily populated urban environment. In the 1930s, Lullwater Creek, a tributary of Peavine Creek, was a small gentle stream that flowed through the property.[45] By the 1960s, flooding and its impact on the landscape were becoming concerns.[46] Over the next several decades, as the banks of the creek began to erode and tree roots were exposed, the number of fallen trees and damaged bridges increased. Summer droughts and bad storms contributed to the destruction, but there was a larger problem. After consulting a number of sources, the club realized that the prime culprit was a by-product of urban development. After heavy rains, runoff from impervious surfaces such as streets, driveways, and roofs found its way into the creek. This excess storm water roared through the streambed, causing serious problems. Watershed management of Peavine Creek and its tributaries needed to be addressed. The Peavine Watershed

Alliance, organized in 1997 by Patricia White, a club member, brought together organizations and local governments in an attempt to tackle what has proved to be a difficult, ongoing issue.[47] In 2012, the garden's master plan, prepared by the landscape architect Spencer Tunnell from the Atlanta firm of Tunnell and Tunnell, contained recommendations to combat erosion and stormwater damage, including the installation of granite curbing and the use of diverse plant material to promote the garden's overall health and to help stabilize the streambeds.[48] The work, which is being done in phases, will take several years. The Lullwater Garden Club received funds from the Garden Club of Georgia's Historic Landscape and Garden Grant program to support this project.

The club's initial vision of the Conservation Garden was a romantic one. As the landscape matured, members learned some practical lessons and modified their approach to the garden's development. By the mid-1930s, they realized that the "Conservation Garden soil is porous and summer drouths caused a great loss of plants and shrubs."[49] Their response: "More attention was given to the study of plants that could do with less water."[50] In the mid-1950s, the club acknowledged that many of the plantings did not fare well in the garden's soil. Also, plants requiring intensive labor and regular watering were quite impractical. A change in approach was needed: "Acceptance of 'survival of the fittest' practice along with efforts toward maintaining the natural beauty seems most prudent."[51] By the 1970s, this strategy more closely resembled a "letting it go back to nature" policy, which led to some unpleasant results related to an increase in invasive plants.[52] The current philosophy is to introduce more native plants and remove nonnative invasives.

The Lullwater Garden Club has adapted to numerous challenges. It now confronts the difficulties of managing a conservation garden in a twenty-first-century urban setting. Complex problems such as water management and the protection of native plants must be dealt with when tending an extensive woodland tract within a residential neighborhood. Today, the garden's continued healthy existence is even more important than when it was first planned. It is a significant refuge for birds, plants, wildlife, and people, and a model for those concerned with the preservation of similar environments.

OPPOSITE: Large specimen trees and a vibrant understory

Palmetto Garden, on the southwestern side of the house
at Millpond Plantation

Millpond Plantation

MILLPOND PLANTATION, a winter retreat and hunting plantation with a lavish home and elaborate ornamental gardens, was created between 1903 and 1910 by the Cleveland businessman Jeptha Homer Wade II.[1] It is an extraordinary example of a Country Place–era estate developed in the Red Hills region of Georgia by the renowned landscape architect Warren H. Manning. It is also significant for its vital role in the conservation of old-growth longleaf pine forests.

Recognized by governmental agencies and conservation groups for its ecological importance, the Red Hills are home to some of the last remaining longleaf pine forests in North America. Stretching between Thomasville, Georgia, and Tallahassee, Florida, the 300,000-acre region is abundant in biological diversity, scenic beauty, historic resources, and a variety of cultures. Its subtropical climate means hot, humid summers and mild, cool winters. The topography features rolling hills, plentiful lakes, fertile soils, valley terrain, and pine forests.

White settlers came to the region as a result of the land lottery of 1820 and seized the opportunity to work its rich soil. The wealthy slaveholding class established large slave-based cotton plantations and built grand white-columned Greek Revival–style mansions, sometimes with elaborate, symmetrical high-style gardens. After the Civil War, some planters worked their land through sharecropping or tenant farming, and others sold off acreage at extremely low prices. The 1880s brought a tourist boom to Thomasville and Thomas County as well-to-do northerners sought sanctuaries with a warm climate, rest, and outdoor pursuits, including hunting, fishing, and horseback riding.[2] Between 1880 and 1930, many of the old plantations were merged, replaced, or expanded as wealthy northerners established winter homes and quail-hunting estates. The native longleaf pine forests provided an ideal habitat for bobwhite quail.

I am quite willing to give my brief reason for building a winter home at Thomasville. In looking about the South I found Northern Georgia and Carolina a little too cold and bleak and not sufficiently green in winter to be attractive, and middle Florida too humid, and not bracing enough for vigorous outdoor exercise. Of the places between these extremes, none struck me so favorably as Thomasville.

—J. H. Wade, *Thomasville Times-Enterprise*, August 26, 1904

209

Awe-inspiring house
and gardens at Millpond
Plantation

In the winter of 1903, Wade and his wife, Ellen Garreston Wade, visited the Red Hills, which "aroused within him an ambition to walk in paths of his own making in Thomasville."[3] Wade was the grandson of Jeptha Homer Wade, a founding member of Western Union Telegraph and a philanthropist from Cleveland. Inspired by his love of nature and the climate of the region, Wade purchased the old Linton Mill place two miles south of Thomasville. The property had once been owned by Thomas Clark Wyche, who by 1860 had amassed 1,600 acres for his slave-based plantation, raising cotton, corn, and livestock and operating a gristmill.[4] Alice Wyche Linton inherited the land upon her father's death in 1870. By 1885, she and her husband, John Linton, had expanded the property to 3,000 acres; they ran the plantation under the sharecropping system.[5]

When Wade purchased the property in 1903, he turned Millpond Plantation into a winter retreat and hunting plantation. In striking contrast to the Greek Revival antebellum plantation homes in Thomas County, Wade commissioned the prominent Cleveland architectural firm of Hubbell and Benes to design a 38,000-square-foot Spanish Revival–style villa and complex of buildings, including a hunting

lodge, stables, kennels, and a water tower.[6] Wade had connections with the firm through family members, including his grandfather, who had commissioned it to design residences as well as commercial and public buildings in Cleveland.[7] Wade also hired the up-and-coming landscape designer Warren H. Manning of Boston to design the grounds of the sprawling three-thousand-acre estate.[8] The architectural historian William R. Mitchell Jr. reflects that the design of Millpond is unique in Georgia for its "modern twist to the concept of a Renaissance villa, combining Prairie School horizontality with formal landscape gardens, surrounded by a wild southern forest."[9]

Warren Manning was a prominent landscape architecture practitioner in the Country Place era. He worked for the prestigious Olmsted firm from 1888 to 1896, specializing in horticulture and planting design.[10] While at the Olmsted office, he developed the foundation of his resource-based approach to design, embracing the principle of genius loci, or "spirit of place," in which garden and landscape designs were adapted to their locations. He also, according to the landscape historian Robin Karson, "gained sophisticated design skills, primary among

Southeastern side
of the house

Live oaks along the
southeastern edge of
the lawn

Formal array of pathways lined in boxwood and laurel, radiating from the northwestern side of the main house

them an approach to laying out landscapes that integrated a response to nature with strong spatial planning."[11] Manning evaluated his design and planning projects from an environmental viewpoint, conceptualizing projects as parts of larger regional systems. This design method contrasted with that of practitioners who were stylistically oriented.[12] He garnered knowledge about cutting-edge mapping and planting techniques from Charles Eliot, a partner in the Olmsted firm. The method involved preparing maps of an area's vegetation and then overlaying them with sheets detailing topography, water features, and road layout.[13] Like Olmsted and Eliot, Manning understood the value of landscape design for both private and public benefit, executing projects that linked natural systems with progressive social goals.[14]

Manning established his own Boston-based firm in 1896, operating one of the largest landscape architecture offices in the United States in the early twentieth century. His career comprised more than 1,600 landscape design and planning projects throughout North America, ranging from small residences to grand estate gardens, college campuses, subdivisions, parks, and burgeoning industrial towns.[15] Manning was not designing other estates in Georgia at the time Wade hired him. Wade may have been introduced to Manning through Hubbell and Benes, or may have had heard about him because of his national network of prominent clients, his earlier work with the Olmsted firm, or his articles in popular magazines such as *Country Life*. Regardless, the marriage of Jeptha Homer Wade, Hubbell and Benes, and Warren Manning created a unique and vast Country Place–era estate amid the longleaf pine forests of the Red Hills.

Not long after purchasing Millpond, Wade began devising plans for his new estate. As the developer of Wade Park in Cleveland, later home to the Cleveland Museum of Art, Wade's grandfather had had a keen interest in public spaces, ornamental gardens, and the natural world. Thus, it is not surprising that Wade became involved in developing the grounds at Millpond as well as managing its longleaf pine forest. An *Atlanta Constitution* reporter wrote in 1905: "Mr. Wade himself is genuinely fond of his estate. He gets up at 6 o'clock each morning and from then until dark is on his horse, enjoying the beauties of nature that his place guarantees him. Just at this particular time, when thousands of different plants and trees are in full bloom, Mill Pond place is irresistible."[16] Wade oversaw the leveling of a hill to create a clear view of an existing pond from the main house.[17] Moreover, he envisioned a series of garden rooms around the house, filled with roses, palms, poppies, dogwoods, crabapples, lilies, shrubs, ferns, and tropicals.

Wade charged Manning with analyzing and designing the land at large. In keeping with Manning's resource-based approach, he conceptualized the project from an environmental viewpoint as part of the larger longleaf pine forest system. To that end, in the fall of 1904 he developed an extensive survey of the area's topography, vegetation, woodlands, fields, roads, streams, pond, and plantation-era cemetery.[18] He detailed areas of tall open pine woods with undergrowth; low land with magnolias and young pines, and high land with young pines, oaks, tupelos, and dogwoods; swampy and bushy forest areas with oaks, magnolias, tupelos, and inkberry bushes; and remnants of old cotton fields filled with low weeds and grasses.[19] Manning developed site and planting plans that respected the pine forests and native plant species.[20] North of the house he allocated spaces for formal garden rooms around the mansion, and he allocated space for an orchard, an integrated four-part vegetable and cut-flower garden, a water tower, stables with pasture, chicken coops, a cottage for the superintendent, and a lodge for those who came to hunt quail. He developed a road system that protected the longleaf pine woods and old roadways.[21] As a reminder of the land's function as a nineteenth-century plantation, Manning incorporated the two

Clipped boxwood and laurel contrasting with the landscape beyond

The garden, still much as it was in 1933

existing tree-lined dirt roads that meandered for almost a mile from the main road through longleaf pine forests and fields, providing an authentic arrival experience to a Red Hills plantation. He also devised a subtle entrance drive that led from the dirt plantation roads and looped in front of the mansion's main entrance.

Manning admired the longleaf pine woods and the rich native-plant palette and advised Wade that they should be protected. Longleaf pine forests and savannas were once one of the most extensive woodland ecosystems in North America, blanketing more than ninety-two million acres across the southeastern United States. In the 1770s, William Bartram, the famous eighteenth-century explorer and naturalist, traveled through the region and wrote of their majesty: "A magnificent grove of stately Pines, succeeding to the expansive wild plains we had a long time traversed, had a pleasant effect, rousing the faculties of the mind, awakening the imagination by its sublimity, and arresting every active, inquisitive idea, by the variety of the scenery, and the solemn symphony of the steady Western breezes playing incessantly, rising and falling through the thick and wavy foliage."[22] Today, less than 5 percent of this habitat remains, and even that continues to be threatened by outdated forest conservation practices, habitat fragmentation, timber harvesting, invasive exotic species, and encroachment from development.[23]

Research over many decades has revealed the inner workings of this unusual ecosystem. Longleaf pine forests are among the most biologically diverse natural communities in North America.[24] Although there are valley areas where longleaf pines (*Pinus palustris*) live amid oaks, magnolias, hickories, and beech, and other places where they mingle with fellow pines such as loblolly, slash, and shortleaf, a longleaf pine forest contains almost no other kind of tree. Such a dynamic ecosystem, according to the authors of *Longleaf, Far as the Eye Can See*, is exceptional: "Longleaf has turned the concept of a forest upside down, subverting all our preconceptions about what a forest should look like and be. A longleaf forest is richest precisely where typical forests are most impoverished. . . . Stranger still, longleaf doesn't discourage competition from other plants in the way oaks and hickories do. Longleaf thrives by

encouraging other plants to grow in its thin shade."[25] Its diverse understory is home to rare plants and animals not found anywhere else. It "contains from 150 to 300 species of groundcover plants per acre, more breeding birds than any other southeastern forest type, about 60 percent of the amphibian and reptile species found in the Southeast—many of which are endemic to the longleaf forest—and at least 122 endangered or threatened plant species."[26]

Like most at that time, Manning and Wade were unaware of the importance of fire to the health and survival of the longleaf pine ecosystem and the native flora and fauna within it, including the disappearing bobwhite quail population. Dubbed a fire-climax community by ecologists, longleaf pine forests depend on fire.[27] It is the instrument responsible for the forest's diversity. Fire encourages seed germination of the trees and the renewal of the abundant plant life on the forest floor while decreasing competition from less fireproof trees.[28] Wade employed the practice of burning the longleaf pine forests infrequently, but over time was unsatisfied with the results, noting that the site was "brush choked" and had a "marked falling off in their quail supply."[29]

Northwest garden, from *Garden History of Georgia*

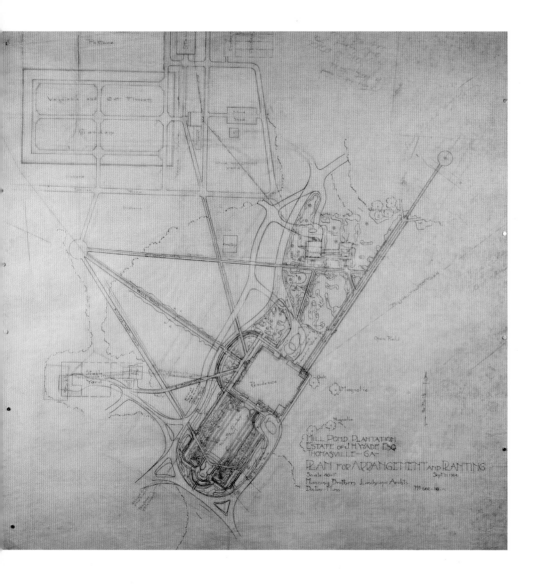

Plan for Arrangement and Planting, Mill Pond Plantation, Estate of J. H. Wade, Esq., Thomasville, Ga., September 21, 1904, no. 602–10, Warren H. Manning Papers, MS 218. Courtesy of the Special Collections Department, Iowa State University Library

In the 1920s, Wade received crucial advice from Herbert L. Stoddard, one of the most important southern conservationists of the twentieth century. In 1924, Stoddard was hired by the U.S. Bureau of Biological Survey to study the habitat and history of quail in the Red Hills region and to help implement land management measures that would safeguard the quail's stability in the area.[30] He later published *The Bobwhite Quail: Its Habits, Preservation, and Increase* (1931), a seminal work in the field of wildlife management and the first comprehensive study of the quail. After comparing, over several years, plantations in the Red Hills that burned their entire forests every two years versus those, including Millpond Plantation, that burned infrequently, Stoddard realized something counterintuitive: "The parklike woodland landscape he first encountered in the Red Hills—that aesthetic so attractive to quail hunters— was actually the result of frequent fire. This likely came as no great surprise to locals in the region."[31]

Because of the destructive logging practices of the late nineteenth and early twentieth centuries, many foresters believed that fire would make the reforestation of pine unfeasible, and they launched educational campaigns to curb the practice. Stoddard and a few others opposed this viewpoint, espousing that the use of fire was vital to maintain the longleaf pine forests.[32] Wade followed Stoddard's advice and found that burning his longleaf pine forests more frequently increased their health and vitality. The forestry management practices that Stoddard developed are still in wide use.

Against the naturalism of Millpond's larger landscape, in and around the house Manning created a lush, intimate environment where the Wade family and guests could enjoy a variety of formal gardens and pathways rich with plants that complemented the Spanish Revival–style mansion and enticed the senses. Influenced by old Spanish houses, Hubbell and Benes incorporated into the mansion a ten-thousand-square-foot central courtyard, onto which all the first floor rooms opened. A steel-and-glass pyramidal roof capped the courtyard, which Manning divided into four quadrants with a brick herringbone-patterned floor and a pool and fountain at the center beneath a large pergola covered in bougainvillea.[33] According to *Garden History of Georgia*, Manning's choice of plant material created a "tropical atmosphere."[34] Manning covered the Spanish arches around the periphery of the courtyard in creeping fig and filled the space with sago palms, banana shrubs, tea olives, cast iron plants, varieties of *Camellia japonica*, English ivy, liriope, and other tropical flora.

Extending the formality of the house, Manning flanked three sides of the mansion with elaborate gardens and walks and left the fourth side open, with a smooth lawn dotted with live oaks and magnolias. The entire complex of gardens, surrounded by a splendid forest of live oak, magnolia, pine, dogwood, and redbud, featured three garden rooms: the Palmetto Garden to the south, the Court (or Camellia) Garden to the west, and the Rose Walk and Garden to the north. Manning defined most of the garden pathways with boxwood or laurel. Gardens were filled with a variety of palms, fragrant shrubs, *Camellia japonica*, laurel, holly, wisteria, and a plethora of climbing and shrub roses. Although

Palmetto Garden, terminating in a reflecting pool shaded by palm trees

Walks, filled with boxwood, laurels, and camellias, along either side of the Palmetto Garden

Vine-covered trellis
defining the pathway

Through a live oak
toward the Tea House
and the Rose Walk

these garden rooms and walks were distinctive, Manning's design masterfully connected them to one another and to the larger site. A unique element found throughout the gardens were the Spanish Revival–style arbors covered in Chinese wisteria or roses. These arbors punctuated exit and entry points to the gardens and created visual cohesion between the garden rooms and the architecture of the mansion.

In the Palmetto Garden, the most extensive of the three gardens, Manning created an intricate design feature: a complex series of linear and diagonal paths around an elongated rectilinear lawn that terminated in a large water basin surrounded by a variety of palms. *Garden History of Georgia* remarks on how the water "mirror[ed] the fronds of the palms on its clear green surface."[35] Boxwood-lined linear pathways were bisected by diagonal paths leading to outer linear pathways, where beds edged in boxwood were filled with a variety of fragrant shrubs, camellias, and palms. Manning dubbed these outer walkways "perfume walks."[36] Creating a highly unusual geometric pattern, these diagonal pathways were reminiscent of a Frank Lloyd Wright–designed stained-glass window.

Pathways also featured prominently in the Court Garden and the Rose Walk. Manning divided the semicircular Court Garden with three diagonal pathways and lined the resulting four pie-shaped sections with boxwood; the mansion's west patio offered a striking view of this fan-shaped pattern. The Rose Walk consisted of a five-hundred-foot-long pathway that Manning extended from the covered porch on the north side of the mansion through the woodlands until it terminated at an octagonal observation platform.[37] This long avenue was bordered on each side by garland posts covered with climbing roses; hundreds of shrub roses filled the areas adjacent to the posts. The design included three diagonal five-hundred-foot-long walks that connected the three garden rooms to a circular Spanish Revival–style concrete pergola designated the Tea House.[38] According to *Garden History of Georgia*, the pathways to the teahouse were "pleached alleys, each bordered with a different variety of fruit tree."[39] One can easily imagine the ladies of the Wade family and their guests taking tea under the pergola draped in Chinese wisteria.

By the time of Wade's death in 1926, he had expanded his estate to almost ten thousand acres.[40] The property has since remained in the hands of descendants. Photographs published in 1933 show the Palmetto Garden and Rose Walk thriving, and the mansion draped in creeping fig and Chinese wisteria.[41] Much of Manning's design remains today, including the inner Courtyard Garden, Palmetto Garden, and Court Garden, although some of the plant material has changed. The Chinese wisteria that adorned the mansion was removed in the 1980s because of its strain on the tile roof. The allées of fruit trees were lost to the native forest, but the pathways to the teahouse pergola remain. In the mid-1980s, the posts strewn with roses, the dominant feature of the Rose Walk, were removed; only the five-hundred-foot path to the woodlands remains.

Today, the continued devotion of Wade's descendants has ensured the health of Millpond's historic and ecological resources. In the early 1960s, Millpond Plantation was divided into three 3,300-acre tracts (Arcadia Plantation, Millpond Perry Plantation,

Through the walkways toward the house

Glass atrium roof

Planters at each corner of the atrium

Fountain in the atrium

and Millpond Sedgwick Plantation) for Wade's descendants. All three tracts, collectively referred to as Millpond Plantation, were added to the National Register of Historic Places in 1976. In 1979, a 200-acre old-growth longleaf pine forest located on Arcadia Plantation (owned by Jeptha Homer Wade III) was placed in a conservation easement, the first of its kind in Georgia. This tract, known today as the Wade Tract Preserve, is one of only a few old-growth longleaf pine forests that have been managed with fire for decades, and the only stand dedicated to research purposes. According to the Tall Timbers Research Station, the organization that conducts research on the Wade Tract Preserve and oversees its management, "The history of research conducted on the Wade Tract, coupled with the extreme rarity of this old-growth forest type, make it one of the most important ecological research sites anywhere."[42] In 1995, Helen Greene Perry, another Wade descendant, entered the entire Millpond Perry Plantation into a conservation easement with the Nature Conservancy. In 2013, under the stewardship of the Sedgwick family, direct descendants of the Wade family, this easement was transferred to the New England Forestry Foundation to allow for consolidated oversight of the care of the land at Millpond. Millpond Plantation is a historic and ecological jewel in the Red Hills region of Georgia—a lasting tribute to the vision of Jeptha Homer Wade II, a significant example of the design genius of Warren H. Manning, and a model for the conservation of longleaf pine forests.

Arcade surrounding the central atrium

Oakton's six-square garden with fruit, vegetables, and ornamental plantings

Oakton

OAKTON, the majority of whose original antebellum and Victorian structures remain, along with an 1870s-era formal six-square kitchen garden, is the oldest continuously occupied residence in Marietta. Built in 1838, Oakton has been home to five families—the Irwins, Allens, Wilders, Andersons, and Goodmans. During its more than 175-year history as a family home, Oakton has also functioned as a small farm in the 1830s; endured the pressures of war and, later, suburban development; and been sensitively adapted to support the current owners' business endeavors. Because of its longevity, Oakton provides a rare look at how the changes made by successive owners reflected the needs and circumstances of each period, and how those changes were achieved in a way that respected the site's historic integrity.

Marietta, twenty miles northwest of Atlanta, was incorporated in 1834 and named the seat of Cobb County, which was one of ten northwestern Georgia counties carved out of Cherokee lands. The Western and Atlantic Railroad selected Marietta for its hub in the 1830s, lending further prominence to the nascent community. Business thrived. During the Civil War, the Union army invaded Marietta in the summer of 1864, and in November of that year, General Kilpatrick's cavalry burned the town, a vital strike in Sherman's March to the Sea. After the war, Marietta, along with the rest of the South, began the long road to economic recovery. During World War II, Marietta was transformed from a rural county seat into a major industrial center when the Bell Aircraft Corporation opened the Bell Bomber Plant in 1942 to assemble B-29s and other fighter planes. The site later became home to Lockheed Martin, one of the world's largest defense contractors. Today, Marietta is known for the historic character and charm generated by its many commercial and residential buildings that remain from the 1840s to the 1950s.

Oakton is beautiful.
—Anne Page Wilder,
June 19, 1889

Boxwood-bordered half-moon garden in front of the 1838 home

Vitex at the top of
the winding drive

Oakton owes its birth to Judge David Irwin. Arriving in the area in the mid-1830s, Irwin, a pioneer citizen of Marietta, served as the first judge of the North Georgia region and later codified the state laws of Georgia. In 1835, he acquired twenty acres on Cassville Road (now Kennesaw Avenue) and directed the building of a Greek Revival cottage and a series of outbuildings, including slave quarters, a detached kitchen, a barn, an outhouse, and cold frames. When the property was completed, in 1838, Irwin named it Oakton.[1] Because of his work as a circuit judge, Irwin traveled extensively throughout northwestern Georgia, using Oakton as a base. Besides serving as a home for Irwin, his wife, Sarah, and their children, it contained a small-scale farm, which was maintained by nineteen enslaved African Americans.[2]

Irwin's ownership of the property was brief, as was that of its next owner, George Allen, a South Carolinian who purchased Oakton in the late 1840s. He sold it to Drucilla Wilder, through her trustee E. W. Russell, in 1852. Between 1854 and 1869, Drucilla's husband, John Randolph Wilder, purchased additional surrounding land, ultimately amassing 325 acres.[3] John Wilder was vice-consul to the Russian government in Savannah and a prosperous cotton exporter in the city. Like many wealthy families who retreated to the hills of North Georgia to escape the oppressive heat and diseases of the coastal South, the Wilders maintained their primary residence in Savannah, using Oakton as their summer home until the Civil War brought the chaos of war to Marietta.

Few documents survive from Oakton's early period, and no archeological work has yet been conducted at the site, making it difficult to ascertain exactly how Oakton functioned. Ruins of a two-story antebellum stone structure, which served as a tannery owned by Wilder and his partner, J. B. Glover, remain on the bank of Noses Creek, part of the original Oakton property. Before the Civil War, both Wilder and Glover were slave owners, and it is likely that the tannery was operated by their enslaved African Americans or others hired from local farmers.[4] During this period, Oakton may have

Oakton, near downtown
Marietta

operated like other small slaveholding households in
the region, in which a large portion of the acreage
was devoted to grain crops and livestock, both of
which were worked by a small number of field slaves.
The buildings that sat close to the owner's residence,
such as the kitchen, dairy, smokehouse, and well,
defined the work yard, a space where domestic slaves
performed many of the household tasks, such as preparing and preserving food, cooking, and washing
clothes and dishes.[5] A kitchen garden of fruits, vegetables, and herbs was likely located near the work
yard. The wealth of the owners at Oakton from the
1830s to the 1860s makes it likely that the landscape
contained a small pleasure garden with ornamental
trees and shrubs.[6]

Perched atop a hill with a full view of Kennesaw
Mountain from the west side of the main house,
Oakton occupied a strategic location in the Civil
War, attracting Major General William W. Loring,
a Confederate officer who commandeered the house
as his headquarters in the summer of 1864 during
the battles around Kennesaw Mountain.[7] The 1939

American epic movie *Gone with the Wind* was partially responsible for uncovering Oakton's role in
the Civil War when the renowned Atlanta illustrator Wilber G. Kurtz, who was hired as a historian
and technical adviser to ensure the movie's historical
accuracy, discovered evidence identifying the military occupation of many Georgia residences, including Oakton.[8]

After the Civil War, John Wilder continued to
prosper through his investments and as a board
member of the Central Rail Road and Banking Co.
of Georgia. The Wilder family began spending more
time at Oakton, undertaking a major expansion of
the house in 1879. Wilder hired a local contractor
named W. Bayliss Carnes.[9] Two wings containing
six rooms were added to the Greek Revival cottage,
and the façade was transformed into one suitable
for an elaborate, early Victorian–style residence. The
expansion added three porches with highly ornamental square columns grouped in pairs (the two side
porches were later enclosed and turned into parlors),
double front doors topped with arched moldings,

and bay windows decorated with ornamental brackets. The house still maintains this appearance. The Wilders likely also added or upgraded the smokehouse, milk house, fire tower, two wells, and other outbuildings, which are located in a tight cluster south of the main house.

During this period, the Wilders also made significant modifications to the grounds. While on a trip to Europe in 1868, the couple met a Scottish gardener named William Annandale and convinced him and his wife, Jane Clark Annandale, to move to Marietta to further develop and maintain Oakton's grounds. Shortly thereafter, the Annandales started a family, eventually raising twelve children at Acorn, a nearby property with a two-story farmhouse that Wilder built for them.[10] Although records do not exist, practices of the period suggest it is likely that Annandale also managed the tenant farms located on the land once worked by enslaved African Americans.

It was under Annandale's skill that Oakton's landscape changed dramatically—a landscape still evident today. During the late 1860s and early 1870s, Annandale brought much elegance to the property. The 1933 description in *Garden History of Georgia* provides insight into the variety of design elements and plants he added:

These [grounds and gardens] cover an area of some twenty-five acres on a low, ridge-like hill, approximately fifteen hundred feet in length. The face of this hill is divided into three sections; in the center a five acre lawn is shaded by splendid oaks, Norway spruce and cedars, and was originally hedged on three sides by euonymus. A double driveway meets in front of the house, which crowns the hill. To the left there was formerly a well stocked deer park, now a pasture; to the right an orchard. Immediately in front of the house is a lovely little half moon rose and lily garden of simple design, its beds outlined in

Large fountain in the six-square rear garden

Potting shed

very dwarf box. Giant yews, clipped and bound to a formal slenderness, flank the walk from the garden to the flower encircled house. An avenue of lilac and crape myrtle leads to the former deer park, and a path bordered by bulbs and Louis Phillippe roses to the orchard.[11]

Two tulip poplars (extant) flanked the ends of the half-moon retaining wall enclosing the rose and lily garden, creating an overlook above the front lawn as it slopes toward the road a hundred yards away. Two paths, one made of river sand and edged with brick, intersected at the center of the half-moon. A dry stone wall separated this garden from the front drive, reinforcing the passage of one space to another. Massive ornamental urns adorned each end of this upper space, providing dramatic focal points for guests approaching by carriage.

Around 1870, Annandale also created a one-and-half-acre kitchen garden outlined in boxwood (*Buxus sempervirens* 'Suffruticosa') west of the main house. Like most formal landscape designs of the time, as well as those of the earlier antebellum period, Annandale's plan was inspired by the

European tradition of using straight lines, right angles, and axes of symmetry. For the kitchen garden, Annandale created six squares, each measuring approximately sixty by sixty feet and enclosed by a picket fence. Three of the squares sit on the same terrace, and the remaining three are located on the terrace below. The original entrance to the garden was on the pathway closest to the rear of the main house. A grape arbor once ran the length of the garden, shading a path that led to an extensive fruit orchard. Since this was a functioning vegetable and fruit garden, Annandale made the paths wide enough to allow for a cart carrying manure and tools. A detailed description of this kitchen garden appeared sixty years later in *Garden History of Georgia*: "Beyond kitchen, well, smoke house and dairy is an acre and a half of garden enclosed by a picket fence; here we find apple, fig, pear, quince and cherry trees.... The box bordered beds contain small fruits and berries, musk cluster and Malmaison roses, peonies, iris, narcissus, jonquils and snowdrops, a mint bed, long borders of sweet lavender and knotted rows of herbs and seasonings. The seven

Cutting garden outside
the back door

Outbuildings alongside
the cutting garden

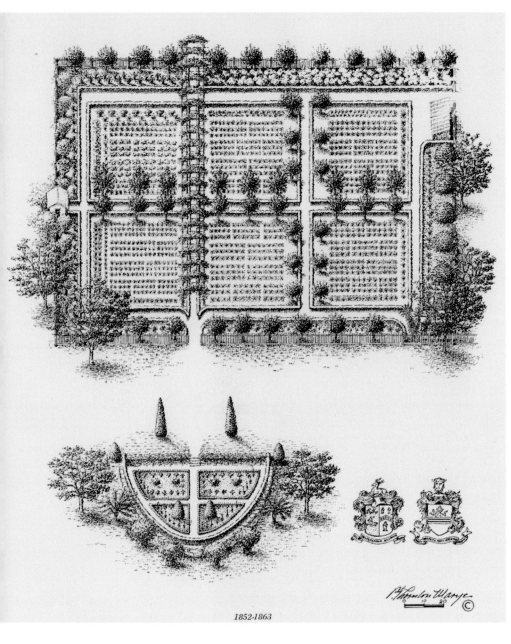

1852–1863

Oakton site plan, P. Thorton Marye, *Garden History of Georgia*

varieties of vegetables formerly thought necessary to any dinner can still be gathered here."[12] The illustration of the six-square kitchen garden that appears in *Garden History of Georgia* was drawn by the Atlanta architect P. Thornton Marye. He had been a guest of the Wilder family at Oakton decades earlier, in 1902, according to an *Atlanta Constitution* social column.[13]

Wilder did not live to enjoy the beauty of his expanded house and grounds, dying in his sleep at Oakton in 1879, shortly after arriving from Savannah to oversee the improvements at the property.[14] Oakton passed to his son Joseph John "J. J." Wilder and his wife, Georgia Page King Wilder, who continued the tradition of using the property as a summerhouse while keeping their primary residence in Savannah. They continued the relationship with

the Annandale family, too. An 1885 legal agreement between J. J. Wilder and William Annandale lends further insight into the arrangement as well as the grounds at Oakton: "The said Wm. Annandale on his part agrees to take the same care of the premises including the family dwelling house, outbuildings, yards & garden as he has heretofore done, mending the fences & keeping the flower beds & hedges in good order. He also agrees to supply the family living at Oakton with vegetables & fruit produced upon the place free of charge—also all milk & butter they may need for which moderate rates shall be paid."[15]

Two 1880s-era letters written by J. J. and Georgia's only child, Anne Page Wilder, provide a glimpse into the property's activities and its gardens, with romantic descriptions of her playing outside with a child who is pretending to be a caterpillar and of delicious peaches and blackberries brought to her by Annandale.[16] This generation of Wilders made other improvements to Oakton, adding a three-story board-and-batten carriage barn in 1890 and purchasing three elaborate six-foot-tall cast-iron planters in Italy for the gardens.

Following the death of J. J. Wilder in 1900 and the tragic death of Georgia Wilder in August 1914 at a railroad crossing near Oakton, the property passed to their daughter, Anne Page Wilder Anderson, who was married to Jefferson Randolph Anderson, a prominent attorney, a state senator from Savannah, and a direct descendant of Thomas Jefferson.[17] The Wilder family's ownership of Oakton lasted nearly ninety years until 1939, when it was sold to Robert McAlpin Goodman Sr., a Marietta native and engineer and the grandson of Robert McAlpin Goodman, founder of the *Marietta Journal*.[18]

After serving in World War II, Goodman and his wife, Dorothy Stephens Goodman, made the most extensive alterations to the 325-acre estate since Annandale. They kept intact the five acres containing the historic house, outbuildings, and formal gardens; to offset taxes and the expense of maintaining the property, they developed the remaining land into a small residential subdivision with large wooded lots.[19] Goodman's design for the subdivision partially shielded the historic house and gardens from view. Goodman and his wife enhanced the landscape at Oakton by adding brick pathways and a statue of the Madonna and child on a pedestal where the two paths intersect in the historic half-moon rose and lily garden, a row of beech and cedar trees along the lower drive south of the main house, and a large Oregon grape holly off the upper drive north of the main house. They erected a small chapel in the lower level of the 1890s carriage barn.[20]

The stewardship of the Goodman family continued into the next generation. Robert McAlpin Goodman Jr. and his wife, Barbara Walker Goodman, inherited Oakton in the late 1970s after seven of their eight children were grown; their youngest son, Will, was the only one who grew up at Oakton. Like Robert's parents, he and Barbara maintained the historic structures and gardens at Oakton. They enhanced the elegance of the home's interior, remodeled the basement into a shooting range in 1978, and in 1988 added a swimming pool in one of six original squares of the 1870s-era kitchen garden.[21]

In 2002, Oakton came into the possession of Will Goodman and his wife, Michelle, becoming the home where they raised their family. Will had spent his childhood exploring the grounds, and his passion for Oakton's gardens had inspired him to become a landscape architect. Devoted to Oakton and its history, Will and Michelle Goodman have championed adaptive reuse as the avenue for Oakton to thrive in the twenty-first century.[22] Today, the following structures have been restored: the main house, smokehouse, milk house, well house, cold frames, and carriage house, which contains Will's landscape architecture office on the top floor. Although the Goodmans have not attempted to restore the landscape precisely to its Victorian-period configuration, they have maintained the historic drive, front lawn, mature trees, thin line of historic daffodils north of the main house, half-moon garden, and formal kitchen garden with its historic boxwood while adapting the site to accommodate contemporary needs. In one of the six garden squares, Will created an Italian garden using one of the historic cast-iron planters as its focal point. In the other squares, the Goodmans have experimented with pairing ornamentals with fruits, including varieties of apples, pears, figs, and blueberries, and an array of vegetables, paying homage to the garden's original purpose. Cradled by the smokehouse, milk house, and well house south of the main house, they added a kitchen and ornamental garden for daily use. They

Vegetable garden

also garden organically, using the 1870s cold frames for creating compost.

In addition to Will's landscape architecture practice, the property is home to Michelle's full-service event-planning and floral design business. Michelle uses cut flowers from the garden in her floral designs, and the family uses edibles for their meals and to sell at the local Marietta Farmer's Market. The Goodmans have used these resources to teach hands-on gardening and floral design workshops at Oakton and have generously opened their home for small events for friends and for fund-raisers to benefit Marietta's historic preservation efforts. In January 2015, the Goodmans placed Oakton for sale. As of the summer of 2017, Oakton is still for sale, and the fate of this rare gem in Marietta is unknown.

Included in the National Register of Historic Places in 1975 as part of the Northwest Marietta Historic District and in the locally designated Kennesaw Avenue Historic District, Oakton is a significant and distinctive historic site, in part for having one of the only extant 1870s formal kitchen gardens in the state. By changing and adapting over time to the preferences and needs of its owners, Oakton has become a survivor that today provides visitors a glimpse into Georgia's antebellum and Victorian landscape heritage.

"See Rock City" along a bluff atop Lookout Mountain in northwest Georgia

Rock City Gardens

THE WORDS "See Rock City" conjure images of barns along quiet old rural roads painted with the famous slogan. Many Georgians and visitors to the state recall visiting the site as children, experiencing the terrifying thrill of walking across the Swing-A-Long Bridge, watching elder relatives struggle through Fat Man's Squeeze, seeing the amazing vista of seven states from Lover's Leap, and reveling in the delightful dioramas filled with quirky gnomes and fairy-tale characters in the Fairyland Caverns and Mother Goose Village. Today, many people's gardens proudly display the iconic red birdhouses with black roofs and "See Rock City" painted in large white letters. Indeed, although most know Rock City as a world-famous tourist attraction, fewer are aware of its fascinating history and its significance as one of Georgia's rarest historic landscapes, created amid unusual, distinctive geological formations.

Rock City Gardens, located atop a broad ridge called Lookout Mountain in northwestern Georgia, offers astonishing views of Lookout Valley to the west and the Chattanooga Valley to the east. The mountain extends eighty-four miles from downtown Chattanooga, Tennessee, through Georgia into downtown Gadsden, Alabama.[1] It and Sand Mountain to the southwest form the southern edge of the Cumberland Plateau. The two-mile-wide Lookout Valley separates the two mountains. Lookout Mountain contains remarkable geological wonders along its ridge. Over millions of years, erosion and weathering have shaped the mountain's concentration of limestone, sandstone, and shale formations into peculiar forms.[2]

The mountain's broad, flat ridge has been home to many people over the ages. For thousands of years, Native Americans inhabited the vicinity; most recently, the Creeks and Cherokees resided there until the early nineteenth century. One of the missionaries who came to the mountain in 1823 to convert the Cherokees, the Reverend Daniel S. Butrick,

Commanding view to the southeast from the Overlook

Confederates back into Georgia and opened the path for Sherman's Atlanta Campaign and march to Savannah in 1864. Today, Lookout Mountain is home to the Chickamauga-Chattanooga National Military Park, the first and largest national military park, authorized by Congress in 1890. Like Rock City Gardens, it is one of the top twenty-five tourist destinations in Georgia.

After the Civil War, Chattanooga became a major industrial hub of the New South.[5] By the 1880s, the city was home to foundries, railroads, mills, and other businesses. As pollution and noise increased in the closing decades of the nineteenth century, the wealthy turned to the ridges and mountains surrounding the city, including Lookout Mountain, for places where they could build idyllic homes. In the last three decades of the nineteenth century, tourism inched its way up Lookout Mountain. Publications in the 1870s wrote of its strange rock formations, citing many of them as wondrous sites to behold.[6] In the 1880s, railroads, roadways, and an incline railway were built to make access to the pinnacle of the mountain easier. Entrepreneurs constructed fancy hotels to accommodate visitors. Early tourist sites included Natural Bridge Park, with its interesting rock formations, and the parks commemorating the Civil War battles.[7]

Tim Hollis, a historian of popular culture and a Rock City expert, said about the promise of this area: "Clearly, Rock City was sitting there as it had for several million years, waiting for some individual with the uncommon foresight to develop it to its full potential."[8] Two locals did just that: Garnet Carter and his wife, Frieda, both East Tennesseans by birth. In 1905, Garnet Carter, a salesman, married Frieda Utermoehlen, a gifted artist and musician. Following a stint in Cincinnati, where Carter worked for his father, the couple arrived in Chattanooga in 1910. After trying his hand at several business ventures over the next decade, Carter saw the opportunity to develop both a sought-after residential suburb on Lookout Mountain and an engaging tourist attraction.

In 1924, Garnet Carter and his partner, Oliver Andrews, purchased hundreds of acres on the mountain for a residential subdivision. Because Frieda was passionate about European folklore, Carter dubbed the new neighborhood Fairyland. He gave the streets names such as Cinderella and Peter Pan

described the terrain in his diary as "a citadel of rocks," a place with gigantic boulders laid out in a way that would allow for streets and paths.[3] After the Cherokees were forcibly removed following the Indian Removal Act of 1830, white settlers, mostly farmers from Virginia and the Carolinas, moved to the area for its plentiful agricultural land.[4]

During the Civil War, the area was the site of two significant battles. The Battle of Chickamauga, the largest Confederate victory in the western theater and the second costliest battle of the Civil War, with 16,170 Union and 18,454 Confederate casualties, occurred in September 1863. The Battle of Lookout Mountain and the Battle of Missionary Ridge, known collectively as the battles for Chattanooga, occurred in November 1863. The Union victories pushed the

Falls cascading from the bluff at Lover's Leap

Enchanted Trail winding through rock formations

Roads, Red Riding Hood and Wood Nymph Trails, and adorned the neighborhood with imported German statues of elves, gnomes, and folktale characters. The first lots were listed for sale at the close of 1924.[9] The following year, Carter built a luxury hotel, the Fairyland Inn, and his brother constructed an even larger one a few miles away.[10] In 1926, Oliver Andrews sold his interest in the venture to Carter. Garnet Carter invented miniature golf and built the first course adjacent to his hotel. He patented the game and franchised it throughout the country as Tom Thumb Golf.[11] After the stock market crash in October 1929, the number of upscale tourists coming to the area dwindled, and Carter looked to the general tourist public to keep his businesses going. In 1930, a spelunker named Leo Lambert turned Ruby Falls, a 145-foot waterfall located more than one thousand feet beneath the mountain's surface, into a tourist attraction, and the stage was set. Rock City Gardens was soon born.

Rock City Gardens, located on the eastern ridge of Lookout Mountain close to the north summit, became a forty-two-acre tourist destination surrounded by single-family residences to the north, south, and west. The heart of the site was a fourteen-acre rock garden that featured the 4,100-foot-long Enchanted Trail and its surrounding natural and man-made rock formations and gullies, fairy-tale statuary, and a wide array of flora. Its informal design and curvilinear circulation patterns were the result of the site's mountainous topography and natural rock shapes, the garden's vernacular style, and the site's slow and methodical growth over eight decades.[12]

Rock City began as the Carter's private garden. Within the seven-hundred-acre Fairyland neighborhood, the Carters had set aside land where they could fashion an estate for themselves. Covered with huge rock formations and dotted with narrow tunnels and winding paths, their property on Lookout Mountain had been known locally as "rock city" since the early 1800s. Here in 1928, Frieda Carter set forth her vision, designing one of the most spectacular and unusual rock gardens in the United States. She used string to lay out the Enchanted Trail, a four-foot-wide dirt trail that became the backbone of the garden, and incorporated the site's large rock formations and other natural features into her

Rock formations along the Enchanted Trail

Photo from *Garden History of Georgia*

Bridge, and Gnomes Overpass—to span chasms on the property.[13] He crafted two reinforced-concrete-and-stone bridges, Stone Bridge and Stone Arch Bridge. At the entrance to the Enchanted Trail, the Chattanooga architectural firm of Crutchfield and Law, in partnership with Frieda, designed a small hexagonal stone gatehouse with a conical roof, like a gnome's hat.[14] Other significant features along the trail included the Grand Corridor, the Needle's Eye, Pulpit Rock, Shelter Rock, Fat Man's Squeeze, and Tortoise Shell Rock.[15] Frieda's beloved statues of gnomes and fairytale characters were embedded throughout the site to add whimsy. *Garden History of Georgia* describes these curious displays:

> Many little figures add to the charm, the mystery and the interest of the place. On a wide platform under an overhanging rock an orchestra of gnomes stands ready to play fairy music. Others serve as guides, standing at points of interest along the Trail to show the different locations. On a shadowy slope within the cavern sits Rip Van Winkle, awakened from his nap of twenty years, watching, in dazed fashion, the gnomes as they roll their ten pins down the hill. In a barberry thicket Red Riding Hood and the Wolf delight the children who visit the garden.[16]

To make the trail easier to navigate, stone stairways were built, and a weathered rustic rock wall that complemented the natural geological treasures enclosed the entire site.

Rock City Gardens abutted the mountainside's dense forest, which was filled with ash, birch, dogwood, elderberry, hemlock, hickory, holly, maple, oak, pine, sweetgum, wild crabapple, serviceberry, and a plethora of other flora.[17] The garden itself burst with native flora—azaleas, mountain laurel, rhododendron, partridgeberry, trailing arbutus, galax, spiderwort, and rare coral moss covering the rocks. The treescape was rich, shaped by the rock formations and openings in the land. As *Garden History of Georgia* described it: "Late trees, like the white oak and ash abound. Twisted, stunted, windblown pines, hemlocks and dogwood add a picturesque note, while in more sheltered places the trees are symmetrical and luxuriant."[18]

Rock City Gardens opened on May 21, 1932, with an admission fee of fifty cents. The following year, Frieda Carter received the Garden Club of America's horticultural bronze medal of distinction for her

design. The trail snaked its way through the large rock crevices and caverns, terminating at a gigantic rock outcropping known as Lover's Leap. A knowledgeable amateur gardener, she planted native trees, shrubs, and flowers.

The Carters both realized the appeal her creative work would have for tourists. In 1930, they began making improvements to the garden to accommodate the public, adding many new features and wonders. Frieda assembled a team to help implement her ideas, including her friend Annie Pendley; Orville York, an employee; Don Gault, the Fairyland superintendent; and a cadre of locals. Gault designed three suspension bridges—Swing-A-Long Bridge, Sky

Arched stone bridge crossing the trail

Stone bridge crossing
a ravine

a row of gas pumps as well as a restaurant, gift shop, restrooms, and offices. Designed by Crutchfield and Law, the Colonial Revival–style building was made with random-course rubble exteriors using local stone, creating a perfect complement to the natural rock found throughout the site. Modifications were made to the garden, too. To provide direct access to the attractions, the garden's main trailhead was moved to the rear of the Trail Entrance Building.[20] A new cliffside path was set out along the mountain bluffs overlooking the Chattanooga Valley, and safety improvements were made along the entire trail. The Carters continued to enhance the landscape with more plants and more ceramic characters. A deer park was added along the trail in 1940.

The Carters' private residence, named "Carter Cliffs," was constructed in 1936, south of the gardens. Designed by Halbert Grant Law, with contributions by Frieda Carter, the Colonial Revival–style residence featured a rubble exterior of local stone, a cross-gabled slate roof, and a west-facing main façade containing a broad porch with Doric columns and a bell-shaped roof. The east façade contained a front-gable two-story porch with a balustrade and a massive Palladian window, giving a broad view of the Chattanooga Valley for the family to enjoy.[21]

The decades following World War II brought changes to Rock City Gardens. Two parking lots enclosed by stone walls were built on the west side of Patten Road in 1946 to accommodate the growing number of automobile tourists. A building called the Tag House was erected near the parking area so that employees could affix large "See Rock City" bumper stickers on cars.[22] The old parking lot in front of the Trail Entrance Building was transformed into a plaza with a new souvenir shop and a coffee shop. Later, in the 1950s and 1960s this area was expanded to include administrative offices, updated restrooms, and more dining options.[23] Fairyland Caverns, an enclosed crevasse featuring gnome dioramas, and High Falls, a 140-foot man-made waterfall, was added in 1947. In 1951, following a tragic fire in the nearby Fairyland subdivision, Carter had a firehouse and gas station built on Patten Road across from the gardens. The last important expansion occurred in 1964 with the opening of Mother Goose Village. Designed by the Chattanooga firm of Selmon T. Franklin Architects, this windowless gambrel-roofed

efforts in "preserving and making accessible to all this strange and impressive spectacle of nature."[19]

Rock City Gardens' popularity soared in the following years. In 1935, Garnet Carter began one of the country's most iconic advertisement campaigns. He hired a sign painter named Clark Byers to travel the nation's highways and offer to paint farmers' barns in exchange for allowing him to adorn the structures with the three simple words: See Rock City. This distinctive black-and-white message appeared far and wide, driving thousands to the gates of Rock City Gardens.

Visitors arrived at Rock City Gardens, located six miles from downtown Chattanooga, by wending their way up Highway 58 to Patten Road. To better accommodate the throng of tourists, especially those arriving by car, amenities were added in 1937, including the Trail Entrance Building and Main Gift Shop. This combined building had a parking lot and

Flowering plants and stone structures along the path

Along the trail

Rock City Gardens Historic Plant List

TREES

American holly (*Ilex opaca*)
Black gum (*Nyssa sylvatica*)
Chestnut oak (*Quercus prinus*)
Flowering white dogwood (*Cornus florida*)
Fringe tree (*Chionanthus virginicus*)
Hemlock (*Tsuga canadensis*)
Redbud (*Cercis canadensis*)
Sourwood (*Oxydendrum arboretum*)

SHRUBS

Flame azalea (*Rhododendron calendulaceum*)
Mountain laurel (*Kalmia latifolia*)
Rhododendron (*Rhododendron* sp.)

PERENNIALS

Columbine (*Aquilegia canadensis*)
Cross vine (*Bignonia capreolata*)
Dwarf crested iris (*Iris cristata*)
Fame flower (*Phemeranthus teretifolius* or *Talinum calycinum*)
Trillium (*Trillium catesbaei, erectum, cuneatum, grandiflorum*)
Violet (*Viola sororia*)
Wild geranium (*Geranium maculatum*)

National Register of Historic Places, "Rock City Gardens," item 7, page 9. This list is based on the research of George Schimpf, retired director of horticulture for Rock City Gardens (1987–2017). These plants were mentioned in historical newspaper clippings and are still growing in Rock City Gardens.

building constructed of concrete and stone rubble walls contained dioramas of fairy tales.[24] From the late 1940s through 1965, other support buildings, including concessions, a greenhouse, and maintenance buildings, were added; all adhered to the overall naturalistic design of Rock City Gardens.

Few changes occurred at Rock City Gardens thereafter until the 1990s. In 1991, the Cliff Terrace Restaurant and Gift Shop were built adjacent to the overlook area. Other additions included new restrooms and concessions. The firehouse and gas station across Patten Road was renovated and reopened in 1999 as the Cornerstone Station, which housed a coffee shop and a gift shop. Located adjacent to Rock City Gardens is Grandview, the former home of Garnet Carter's uncle, built in 1930. It was purchased

and converted into a special-event facility in 2005. The same year, a new ticket building was added to the main entrance plaza. In 2007, as part of the seventy-fifth anniversary of Rock City Gardens, the former Carter Cliffs driveway was turned into Legacy Lane, an accessible trail leading to a section of the gardens that guests with limited mobility could enjoy. Carter Cliffs remains a private residence.

Today, Rock City Gardens remains much as it was in the 1930s, despite alterations made over time, with a unified design aesthetic and harmony between the natural and the man-made.[25] Natural stone has been used in buildings, terraces, pathways, and raised planter beds throughout the landscape. Two-foot-high rock walls line the paths through the interior of the garden, and taller rock walls capped with stone crenellations and iron railings define the exterior boundaries. The pathways that Frieda Carter designed have been minimally altered; the changes made were done for the safety of visitors. Many of the historic garden gnomes remain on the property. Historic and modern seating and tables were built with stone, rustic wood, and wrought iron. Original wrought-iron signs atop poles guide visitors along the trail, and a few of the features are marked with neon signs in 1940s-era script. The flora of Rock City Gardens have been enhanced over the decades, and it is now home to over four hundred species of blooming plants, shrubs, and trees.

Follow the Enchanted Trail to get a peek into the marvelous world of Rock City Gardens. Visitors enter the Enchanted Trail through the Trail Entrance Building on the southwest corner of the property. After descending a flight of paved steps, the path passes through the bottom of the Grand Corridor, a thirty-foot-long smooth limestone cavern lined with planting beds filled with American holly, red maple, sweet gum, rhododendrons, and ferns.[26] The trail abruptly turns to the south toward the Needle's Eye, a tight crevice between twenty-foot-tall rock formations. As the path curves, it passes through several giant rock outcroppings before arriving at an overlook into Gnome Valley, a huge enclosure that contains gnome statues engaged in various pursuits. Also included is a gnome-like house, an arched structure with tiny doors and windows and a windmill, once part of a deer shelter. Nearby is the sizable Mushroom Rock, a natural mushroom-shaped rock formation.

The trail continues through a wooded area containing numerous native trees and shrubs before moving toward the raised Gnomes Overpass, a series of man-made concrete-and-stone arched footbridges spanning the Grand Corridor. The overpass ends at the Goblins Underpass, a man-made concrete-and-sandstone arched passage that runs beneath Legacy Lane, which features interpretive signs and artifacts about the history of Rock City Gardens. Visitors surface from the Goblins Underpass onto the elevated, walled portion of the Enchanted Trail, which twists through a number of large rock formations. The trail continues past the recently added Wild Bird Observation Deck to Shelter Rock, a natural hollow in a rock formation decorated with musical gnome statuary. Just past Shelter Rock, the trail splits. To the north it continues to the intimidating Swing-A-Long Bridge, a 180-foot long cable suspension bridge; to the south, it leads to the Great Stone Bridge, a large man-made double-arched stone-and-concrete bridge. The two paths unite again at the main overlook area on the east side of Rock City Gardens.[27]

To arrive at the overlook, visitors cross over High Falls, the 140-foot waterfall that emerges from within the mountainside, via the ten-foot-long man-made arching concrete-and-stone Sky Bridge. They then encounter Lover's Leap, a natural cliff located 1,700 feet above sea level that offers a stunning panoramic vista of the Chattanooga Valley to the east and the bluffs of Lookout Mountain farther to the north. From the overlook, visitors can see seven states (Tennessee, Kentucky, Virginia, North Carolina, South Carolina, Georgia, and Alabama) by using a semicircular sandstone sign that points to their locations along the horizon. A three-foot-tall concrete-and-stone rubble wall encloses the entire section. On the opposite side of the overlook, guests pass the historic stone gazebo. Adjacent to the overlook across a large stone terrace are modern amenities, including the Seven States Flag Court, the Cliff Terrace Restaurant, Prospector's Point, and the Rock City Pavilion.

The journey along the Enchanted Trail resumes just north of the overlook area. Visitors see a rock formation called Tortoise Shell Rock before descending a long flight of sandstone steps into Fat Man's Squeeze, a sheer limestone chasm that measures only twelve inches wide in some places.

The trail then plummets almost twenty feet into an underground cavern, passing under both the Great Stone Bridge and the Swing-A-Long Bridge. The path crosses over the Stone Arch Bridge, a forty-foot-long man-made concrete-and-stone bridge supported by three Gothic-style arches. Up a stone step and through a small tunnel, the path opens to the cliffside route, which runs along a blasted-out shelf and overhang that snakes along the lower wall of the bluff overlooking the Chattanooga Valley.[28] Visitors then walk through Rainbow Hall, a covered passageway with red, yellow, green, and blue stained-glass windows set into the stone wall.

The Enchanted Trail continues to loop around and arrives at Observation Point, a man-made cantilevered platform with iron railings. It offers views of the valley to the east and of High Falls and Lover's Leap to the south. Visitors next arrive at the 1000-Ton Balanced Rock, a massive boulder balanced on a pair of upended stones, before arriving at the Cave of the Winds and the Hall of the Mountain King, both

"1000-Ton Balanced Rock" along the Enchanted Trail

Entrance to Fairyland Caverns

Gnomes and
constructed rock formations
in Fairyland Caverns

defined by enormous smooth rock formations that create a tunnel passageway below overhangs. Within this space are a fountain, benches, and a diorama showing gnome statues operating a moonshine still. The trail exits the Hall of the Mountain King through a Gothic archway into a small courtyard. Visitors continue up a series of low stairs through Magic Valley, a wooded corridor encased by limestone walls. The path passes Galoochee, the Stone Witch, a natural rock formation that resembles a big-nosed witch in profile. The Enchanted Trail then arrives at the entrance to Fairyland Caverns. Recessed into the

rock face just a few feet before the Fairyland Caverns entrance is a two-story Bavarian-style painted board-and-batten structure dating to 1946.

The entrance to Fairyland Caverns (from 1947) is distinct, featuring a wrought-iron sign adorned with Little Red Riding Hood and the Wolf set atop the cutout lettering "Fairyland." Embedded in the rock wall beneath the lettering is a sign that reads "Caverns." Entering the caverns, the trail passes through a wrought-iron gated arch to the Diamond Corridor, a ten-foot-wide passage-way covered with rocks accentuated with quartz

Mother Goose Village

Fairy-tale vignettes in the cavern

Stone gatehouse, circa 1930s

Birthplace of Tom Thumb Golf

crystals, pyrite, and painted coral on the walls and ceiling.[29] Gnome statues hanging from walls and suspended from the ceiling welcome visitors. The caverns are filled with scenes populated with gnomes and illuminated by ultraviolet lights, which make the painted ceramic figures glow. The trail leads deeper into the caverns, twisting and turning through a series of lighted dioramas of fairy tales recessed into the rock walls. Early diorama artists include the Atlantans Charles and Jessie Sanders, and, later, Kenny Saylor.[30]

The path through Fairyland Caverns snakes toward Mother Goose Village. From a large central platform there, visitors can view intricately designed scenes depicting Mother Goose nursery rhymes, Grimm Brothers folktales, and European fairy stories sculpted by Jessie Sanders. The scenes—such as the Cow That Jumped over the Moon; Mary, Mary, Quite Contrary; Humpty Dumpty; Little Miss Muffet; and Puss n' Boots—are enhanced by ultraviolet light. As visitors depart Mother Goose Village, they are beckoned by the final diorama—Rub-A-Dub-Dub,

Light show in
Rainbow Hall

Three Men in a Tub—with figures moving back and forth across the water. Once outside, the trail passes a turning waterwheel within a water fountain. The Enchanted Trail ends at the east side of the Trail Entrance Building and adjacent to Main Gift Shop, where visitors can purchase souvenir postcards and booklets and the famous "See Rock City" birdhouses. Today, the Enchanted Trail, the soul of Rock City Gardens, retains 90 percent of its original configuration, including the orientation of the paths, gnomes, and other features.[31]

Thanks to the brilliance of Frieda and Garnet Carter, and the sensitive care given to the site by their descendants, more than half a million people visit Rock City Gardens annually. The world-famous tourist attraction has been featured in hundreds of publications and was named one of "America's Iconic Places" by *National Geographic*.[32] Rock City Gardens certainly fulfills its mission to "create memories worth repeating for our guests and partners," beckoning visitors to See Rock City again and again.

Historic fountain on Salubrity Hall's east patio

Salubrity Hall

SALUBRITY HALL, once the winter retreat of the wealthy northerners Olivia and John Herbert, is an exceptional example of a Country Place–era estate developed in the Summerville area of Augusta in the late 1920s. The site is also significant for its story of rebirth in the twenty-first century, thanks to the careful attention of the current owners, Karon and Don Williamson, and the landscape architect William T. Smith. The property is appropriately named Salubrity Hall both because of its historical roots as a salubrious site and because it is conducive to the well-being of its residents and all who are fortunate to experience its beauty.

Augusta, the second-oldest and currently the second-largest city in Georgia, was established on the western bank of the Savannah River in 1736. By the late 1700s, it had become a thriving manufacturing center. The city played an important role in the American Revolution and later served as the temporary capital of the new state of Georgia between 1785 and 1795.[1] Augusta was home to a large inland cotton market. Local farmers brought their cotton to the city to be shipped to the port of Savannah via boats down the Savannah River, or to Charleston, South Carolina, by rail. Augusta continued to prosper in the antebellum period because of improvements in transportation. Completed in 1845, the Augusta Canal, a source of water, power, and transportation, attracted cotton mills, ironworks, and other manufacturers along its banks, making Augusta one of the few industrial centers in the South. The year 1845 brought a railroad link between Augusta and Atlanta, connecting the city with more markets around the country. To support the war effort, the Confederate Powder Works was established. It was a critical producer of ammunition for the Confederates during the Civil War. Augusta's economy rebounded from the war with the expansion of the Augusta Canal in 1875, which brought the construction of large textile mills and

The gardens in Augusta are numerous and beautiful. Each is lovely for some special characteristic all its own. Here, truly, one sees why Augusta is known as the "Garden City of the South."—Mary C. Alexander, *Garden Gateways*, 1940

Semicircular drive and oval-shaped boxwood-bordered lawn

ironworks; the city's population grew as farmers and their families moved to Augusta to work in the mills.

In the early twentieth century, Augusta was named the "Garden City of the South" because of its plethora of private gardens. *Garden History of Georgia* highlighted some of these high-style landscapes, such as Green Court, Highgate, Le Manoir Fleuri, Morningside, and Sandy Acres.[2] Many of the estates with elaborate gardens were found in Summerville, located on the sand hills west of Augusta. Among these was Salubrity Hall, the private estate of the tobacco heiress Olivia Antoinette ("Etta") Helme Herbert and her husband, the attorney and businessman John Warne Herbert Jr. of New Jersey.

Summerville, commonly called "The Hill" or the "Sand Hills," was founded in the late eighteenth century as a small village. Augusta's proximity to the river and surrounding marshland made the town uncomfortable during the hot summer months.

Prosperous Augustans came to The Hill to construct summer homes where they could take advantage of Summerville's clean, healthy air and escape the oppressive heat and malaria found in the city below. Belief in the area's healthy environment is seen in surviving place names such as Monte Sano (Spanish for "Mount Health") and Mount Salubrity.[3] By the 1850s, it had become a year-round community, and more permanent buildings were constructed. With the construction of several large hotels in the 1890s, including the Partridge Inn and the Bon Air Hotel, Summerville was transformed into a fashionable winter resort and golf capital.

By this time, electrified streetcars provided easy access between Augusta and its suburbs and nearby villages. Summerville and other surrounding communities primarily served wealthy northerners, some of whom built luxurious residences where they could escape the harsh northern winters and enjoy golf year-round. The City of Augusta annexed Summerville in 1912, and when much of Augusta's downtown business district and residential neighborhoods were devastated by fire in 1916, Summerville underwent a building boom. Many fine homes in the most popular styles of the time were built there.[4] In 1931, Summerville became the site of the Augusta National Golf Club, developed by Bobby Jones, the famous golfer, and the entrepreneur Clifford Jones. Home to the world-famous Masters Golf Tournament, the club was built on the former grounds of Fruitland Nurseries, one of the first commercial nurseries in the South, which had been founded by the Berckmans family during the antebellum period.

The Herberts, who owned homes in Helmetta, New Jersey, and New York City, came to Summerville in 1926. They purchased a large tract of land on which to build a winter retreat. They named their estate Salubrity Hall, after the Ladies Academy at Mount Salubrity, a girls' school that had stood on the site since the 1790s. The school had been built by Thomas Sandwich and founded by Sandwich's wife, who taught the girls reading, writing, arithmetic, and needlework; they publicized the institution as Mount Health.[5] Located near the Augusta Country Club, the tract was ideal for the Herberts; an avid golfer, he was one of the founding members of the nearby Augusta National Golf Club, and she was an artist who wanted to express her love of design and horticulture. The Herberts hired the notable Augusta architectural firm of Scroggs and Ewing to design an 11,000-square-foot English Tudor country house. Portions of the late eighteenth-century structure that housed the academy, particularly the old timbers, were incorporated into the new mansion, which was completed in 1928.[6] To give it an appearance of age, the mansion featured sixteenth-century stained glass, a grand Celtic fireplace imported from Europe, and a brick, stucco, and decorative half-timbered exterior with casement windows, a slate roof, and elaborate chimneys. The estate included a large carriage house, a modest caretaker's cottage, and extensive gardens designed by Olivia Herbert.

Olivia created five gardens at Salubrity Hall: a formal garden, a sunken garden, a rose garden, an arabesque garden, and a wild garden. The four formal garden rooms surrounded the mansion, and the

naturalistic wild garden sat at the edge of the property, producing an ideal balance within the landscape. The scheme paid homage to the European grand gardens that Olivia had visited during tours abroad. Her devotion to plants led Olivia to cultivate many traditional southern plants, including azaleas, boxwood, and camellias; native plants; and an extensive array of perennials, roses, and bulbs. She imbued her landscape with elaborate structures, including two pergolas and a teahouse, as well as fountains,

Curbside plantings of the estate

brickwork, stonework, urns, and statuary that lent an air of age.

Olivia placed the formal, rectangular garden on the west side of the mansion. Its main feature was a large quatrefoil-shaped pool and fountain that sat at the center of an open grass lawn; the pool's edges were punctuated by four urns. One side of the garden held a "weeping willow drooping over a semi-circular marble seat,"[7] and another contained a brick patio with an impressive rose-covered pergola made of antique columns and flanked by old iron grillwork. The back of the pergola was composed of "weather-beaten brick, with a niche for a leaden figure of a boy holding a tray of flowers."[8] The north side of the garden contained a decorative balustrade overlooking a bronze dragonfly fountain, which was

"cleverly screened on two sides by a graduated planting of junipers and yews."[9] The formal garden was filled with a large collection of irises.

Brick steps from the formal garden descended to a boxwood-bordered walk that led to the sunken garden. The sunken garden featured a small pool bordered by irregular rocks surrounded by large old English boxwood. The two additional formal gardens were located behind the mansion. A rose-draped pergola led to the rose garden, which contained, at its center, a Swedish porcelain fountain surrounded by plantings of low-growing junipers and blue hyacinths.[10] Adjacent to it was the rectangular arabesque garden, framed by two rows of flowering crab trees. It had a central lawn flanked on each side by planting beds laid out in arabesque patterns of scrolling

Quatrefoil fountain in the west garden

Formally planted herb garden in a corner of the west garden

Rose-covered pergola in the west garden

and interlacing ornamental designs. These beds ran north to south and were filled with perennials and bulbs, including narcissi, tulips, and irises.[11]

Olivia placed the wild garden on the far northeast corner of the estate, beneath a wooded area of the property filled with native pines and oaks. A winding dirt path through the garden led to a sizable one-room Tudor Revival–style structure that served as a teahouse where the Herberts could serve light refreshments to guests. The path was bordered by native shrubs, including yaupon (*Ilex vomitoria*), Carolina cherry laurel (*Prunus caroliniana*), mountain laurel (*Kalmia latifolia*), and flame azaleas (*Rhododendron calendulaceum*). Closer to the teahouse were masses of Indian and Kurume azaleas.[12] Many types of bulbs were naturalized throughout the woods, and Carolina jessamine and woodbine climbed many of the trees.

During her nearly two decades of wintering at Salubrity Hall, Olivia Herbert generously opened her gardens to the public to benefit local charities. For an event for the Woman's Auxiliary of St. Paul's Church in March 1935, the *Augusta Chronicle* announced to its readers: "Flower lovers in Augusta will welcome the opportunity tomorrow to enjoy the beautiful informal and formal gardens of Mrs. John W. Herbert at Salubrity Hall. Mrs. Herbert is being most gracious in giving Augustans and visitors a chance to enjoy the lovely flowers which are now in full bloom in her garden."[13] The property was included on many garden tours throughout the 1930s and 1940s, including the Garden Club of Georgia's pilgrimages between 1937 and 1941.[14]

Salubrity Hall went up for sale in April 1946. Olivia Herbert had died the previous August at the age of eighty-two, eleven years after the death of her husband. The listing in the *Augusta Chronicle* advertised it as "the famous winter home and garden of the late Mrs. Olivia A. Herbert in Augusta, Georgia, and one of the most outstanding in the entire Southland."[15] Between 1947 and 2002, the estate changed hands nine times, and as the decades rolled by, most of Olivia Herbert's formal and informal gardens were lost. In the late 1940s or early 1950s, the wild garden and the wooded areas were subdivided into smaller lots, including the northeastern corner containing the teahouse. During that period, the building was enlarged into a single-family home

White blooming annuals and perennials in the west garden

Below the west garden railing, a sunken garden containing a pool

that maintained the Tudor Revival style of the original structure. Elizabeth Robinson Anderson and her husband currently live in the former teahouse; she grew up there, and in 2007 she inherited it from her parents, Clara and Frank Robinson Jr., who had purchased it in 1959.[16]

In 2003, Karon and Don Williamson, the current owners of Salubrity Hall, purchased the remaining portion of the property containing the mansion, roughly three acres. By that point, time had taken its toll on both the house and the gardens. Their first priority was to restore the once-elegant English Tudor country home to its 1920s grandeur, which was a significant undertaking because of the complexity of the

architecture. The Williamsons restored the large carriage house and stabilized the caretaker's cottage. They turned their attention to the gardens in the summer of 2006, hiring Bill Smith, an Atlanta landscape architect and owner of William T. Smith and Associates, which specializes in residential garden design. Over the past twelve years, Smith and the Williamsons have collaborated on reviving what remained of the original gardens and designing a series of new garden rooms that echo elements of the past while meeting twenty-first-century needs. Smith used a blend of historic plants with newer cultivars.

When the Williamsons purchased the property, the large oval lawn in the center of the broad

East garden, from *Garden History of Georgia*

semicircular drive was filled with a group of trees that obscured the house. Smith suggested they be removed so that the impressive front façade would be visible, as it was during Olivia Herbert's day. He called it "the best five-minute advice he has ever given."[17] The oval lawn is now surrounded by a low-clipped boxwood hedge. The brick gutter and curb running along the front drive were also restored.

The most intact historic garden remaining on the property was the formal garden on the west side of the mansion. Smith restored the surviving historic features, including the quatrefoil-shaped pool with fountain and surrounding lawn, the brick patio with its brick wall and iron grillwork, and the balustrade. The Williamsons outfitted the patio with a wrought-iron table and chairs for outdoor entertaining. Smith designed a number of new elements inspired by the original garden features. In place of the original four urns that stood at the edges of the pool, Smith added four large round planters filled with Boston ferns. No photo documentation exists showing the design of the original rose-covered pergola. Nonetheless, Smith climbed up the brick wall to determine the original anchor points and created an elaborate pergola in scale with the mansion.[18] The

now-lost dragonfly bronze statue has been replaced by one featuring two angels.

Smith added a stunning semicircular white garden on the far western edge of the formal garden with an array of shrubs such as slender deutzia (*Deutzia gracilis* 'Nikko'), gardenias (*Gardenia jasminoides* 'Frost Proof' and 'Grif's Select'), hydrangeas (*Hydrangea paniculata* 'Lime Light', 'Quick Fire', and 'Tardiva'), tea olives (*Osmanthus fragrans*), spireas (*Spiraea prunifolia* 'Plena' and *Spiraea × vanhouttei*), hammocksweet azaleas (*Rhododendron serrulatum*), roses (*Rosa* 'Iceberg'), and a variety of viburnums. The white garden, located on the west side of the formal garden, is also home to numerous white-flowering perennials, including asters, clematis, daisies, daylilies, dianthus, garden phlox, and verbena. Seasonal color comes from *Cleome spinosa* 'Helen Campbell', Queen Anne's lace (*Daucus carota*), delphinium (*Delphinium* 'Galahad'), foxgloves (*Digitalis* 'Emerson' and *D. purpurea* 'Camelot White'), salvia (*Salvia coccinea* 'Snow Nymph'), and *Zinnia angustifolia* 'Crystal White'.[19]

Smith added a parterre herb garden inside the formal garden adjacent to the house; Karon Williamson enjoys cooking with fresh herbs. In keeping with the original brickwork found on the property, Smith

OPPOSITE: Large perennial garden to the east

Series of distinct garden rooms behind the main house

added a brick pathway to connect this small garden to a doorway on the west side of the house, giving ready access to the family. The square garden is surrounded by low-clipped boxwood. The garden is divided into four boxwood-lined sections with a diamond-shaped center.[20] The central diamond is home to an antique urn, and each section holds a large planter containing gardenia topiary filled with herbs (sage, thyme, rosemary, and others). The pathways through the herb garden are bordered by brick and filled with smooth gravel. A small new circular

brick patio with convex brick steps leads off the west side of the house to provide a small space for the family to eat outdoors.

The only surviving historic element in the sunken garden is the grotto-like niche surrounded by a small pool composed of irregular stone. Smith and the Williamsons decided to pay homage to the original garden by transforming it into a grotto garden. The garden is reached by descending two historic sets of brick steps laid in a chevron pattern. The pool is surrounded by bluestone and brick set in a diamond

East perennial garden in bloom

Magnolia-lined alleé along the western edge of the property

pattern and flanked by two cast-iron benches. Boxwood and a variety of ferns and wildflowers are planted throughout.

Nothing remained of the historic rose and arabesque gardens. In their place, Smith added three new gardens—a vegetable and fruit garden, a motor court with an open lawn, and a perennial garden—along the back of the mansion, in keeping with the Country Place–era scale of the original gardens. Karon Williamson's ties to rural Georgia (she was raised on her family's farm in Baxley) and her love of cooking prompted her desire for a vegetable garden. The rondel-shaped vegetable garden, which Smith placed directly across from the grotto garden, is defined by a circular lawn accented in the middle by a two-level circular platform made of stone. At its center is a large decorative planter filled with a giant Boston fern. A bed filled with annuals and edged with brick surrounds the platform. The corners of the lawn are divided into four sections, each marked by a wooden bench overlooking the platform. Each section contains eight triangular trellises, used for vegetables, and is filled with fruits, herbs, and vegetables: tomatoes, okra, melons, beans, figs, and more. The outer edges of the four sections contain beds of woody shrubs, including camellia, clethera, gardenia, hydrangea, oleander, spirea, and viburnum.[21]

The Williamsons wanted a place where their children could play outdoor games and a functional area for hosting parties for family and friends as well as events for charitable benefits. To accommodate those wishes, Smith added a large motor court, connected to the existing driveway, directly behind the house; an open lawn lies beyond. He paved the motor court with terra-cotta-colored stone inset with a double row of bricks that form a cross and intersect at a historic millstone.[22] A brick border encloses the entire court. Smith selected the brick and stone to complement the property's historic brick and stonework. A set of convex brick steps descends from the motor court onto the open grass lawn, which is surrounded by ten live oak trees. A bed of *Azalea indica* 'Mrs. G. G. Gerbing' lines the wooden fence at the back of the estate.

The large perennial garden occupies much of the eastern portion of the property. This rectangular space is enclosed by hedges of clipped boxwood punctuated by an opening on each side marked by tall conical evergreens. The perennial garden can be reached by descending a brick staircase that connects

Walled path leading
to the west garden

to the brick patio on the east side of the house, which features a restored wall fountain. Smith continued the use of brickwork in the perennial garden: a brick-lined pathway frames the garden's outer perimeter and bisects the garden from the east and west entrances. The center of the perennial garden consists of a lawn sculpted into three overlapping circles, the largest at the center. Deep perennial borders, much like those of the famed early twentieth-century English garden designer and horticulturist Gertrude Jekyll, flank the lawn; they are planted with perennials in complementary cool colors of blues, purples, pinks, and whites. Several varieties of foxgloves emerge strikingly in early summer.

As it has been since its earliest days, Salubrity Hall continues to be admired for its noteworthy architecture and gardens. In 2008, the Williamsons received a preservation award from Historic Augusta for their restoration of the mansion. Because of its architecture and importance in the history of Augusta, Salubrity Hall is a contributing site to the Summerville Historic District. Listed in the National Register of Historic Places, the district claims one of the most extensive collections of historic residences and gardens in the state of Georgia, displaying myriad architectural and landscape styles and periods. The Williamsons have upheld Olivia Herbert's tradition of opening the gardens to the public for the benefit of local groups. In 2014, they hosted Historic Augusta's famous Cotton Ball, which supports the organization's mission "to preserve historically or architecturally significant sites in Augusta and Richmond County, Georgia."[23] With the restoration of the mansion and the revival of its gardens, Salubrity Hall once again emanates elegant charm.

OPPOSITE:
Front edge of
the property

Chippewa Square, with a monument to General James Oglethorpe, the founding father of Georgia

Savannah Squares

THE MENTION OF Savannah conjures up images of charming cobblestone streets filled with evocative historic architecture and its famous squares, teeming with moss-draped live oaks, blooming azaleas, tranquil fountains, and statues commemorating historical figures and events. Internationally recognized for its rich history, cuisine, and hospitality, Savannah is also a landmark in the history of urban planning in North America. Based on Oglethorpe's eighteenth-century plan, the city's squares are a key component of the uniqueness and allure of the city. In the second half of the twentieth century, the squares played a vital role in the preservation and revitalization of Savannah's downtown. Today, locals, along with millions of tourists, enjoy the history and beauty of Savannah and its extraordinary squares.

Led by James Edward Oglethorpe, colonists founded Savannah in 1733 after George II signed a charter that established Georgia as the thirteenth colony and created a governing board of Trustees.[1] Savannah, the oldest city in Georgia, was sited eighteen miles from the Atlantic Ocean on a steep bluff above the mouth of the Savannah River. Oglethorpe managed the economic and political development of the new colony.[2] He and the founders sought colonists with the skills to make the new colony a success and create a commercial outpost for the neighboring colony of South Carolina.[3] Possessing one of the largest seaports on the East Coast, Savannah quickly became a thriving commercial center, exporting cotton, rice, and other agricultural goods. It was also Georgia's largest city from its inception until the 1860s.

Following the American Revolution, Savannah served as Georgia's first capital until 1786. Its role as an international shipping center, which continued during the antebellum period, was anchored around the slave economy and the agricultural production of cotton and rice.[4] Although the city fell to Union troops at the close of

Savannah is one of the most striking cities in the Union, regularly built on a high sandy bluff, with a very regular ground-plan, and numerous picturesque houses standing at intervals with rich gardens between them. Its whole plan and arrangement fit it for the climate. The broad rectangular streets are lined with luxuriant Melia and Locust-trees, and there are frequent open squares with grass-plats.
—Charles Joseph Latrobe, *The Rambler in North America*

1864, General William Sherman decided not to destroy it, despite an earlier pledge to do so. By the early 1870s, Savannah had rebounded from the war by continuing to export cotton grown in inland Georgia.[5] From the 1880s until the 1920s, Savannah was the world's top producer of naval stores—shipbuilding materials garnered from southern pine forests, such as timber, rosin, and turpentine.[6] After the cotton industry was decimated by boll weevils in the 1920s, the city transformed itself into a national leader in both the paper-pulp and food-processing industries.[7] Savannah played a key role during World War II as one of the country's most active shipyards for the building of ship transports.[8] After the Georgia Ports Authority acquired waterfront acreage in Savannah, port operations expanded in the late 1940s and into the second half of the twentieth century.[9] The economy was also bolstered by the development of Hunter Army Airfield and nearby Fort Stewart in the early 1940s. From the mid-twentieth century to the present, Savannah's economy has been driven by its port, manufacturing, and the military. Tourism, although modest for much of its history, has been a vital part of Savannah's economy since the 1990s.

The history and beauty of Savannah's historic district, as well as myriad cultural amenities, have made Savannah one of the top tourist destinations in the United States for decades. In the 1950s, major historic preservation efforts began to protect its wealth of historic buildings, landscapes, and Old World charm; this drive was spearheaded by the Historic Savannah Foundation, established in 1955. Since no local zoning laws were in place to safeguard historic buildings, the foundation created a broad strategy to foster preservation through private-sector involvement. Its efforts resulted in hundreds of the city's oldest structures being saved during the second half of the twentieth century.[10] The Historic Savannah Foundation, one of the most respected local historic preservation organizations in the country, has served as a model for like-minded groups. In 1966, the Savannah Historic District was designated a National Historic Landmark. At the heart of the district and its thriving tourism industry are the Savannah squares.

The plan Oglethorpe developed for Savannah, according to the historian Beth Reiter, is one of the most studied in the history of American city planning.[11] Some scholars view it as a descendant of seventeenth-century Northern Ireland settlements created by the British, while others support the claim that inspiration for the plan came from Oglethorpe's friend and architect Robert Castell, who was a proponent of Roman urban-planning principles.[12] Others argue that Savannah's plan was heavily influenced by the plan for London conceived after the Great Fire of 1666.[13] In 2012, the scholar and urban planner Thomas D. Wilson claimed that Oglethorpe's plan, besides being a dynamic force in urban planning, was an Enlightenment-era demonstration in which Oglethorpe set forth his utopian ideas of agrarian equality.[14] As Wilson explains, "The legacy of the original physical design—once intended to support a complex, humanistic plan—can readily be seen today in the form of a blended environment that accommodates nature and formal structures equally well. It is a city interpreted from its civic squares, city parks, promenades, tree-canopied streets, and a dense urban forest, elements that contribute to a rare urban aesthetic evolving from the exceptional composition originally conceived by Oglethorpe."[15] Regardless of its origins and true intent, the city that Oglethorpe created out of the wilderness was groundbreaking.

Oglethorpe laid out Savannah from north to south, leading away from the river. The plan consists of a grid of identical divisions called wards. Each ward featured wide streets, smaller lanes dividing rows of building lots, and a central green space, now referred to as a square. The east and west sides of the squares contained large trust lots for public buildings such as churches, government buildings, markets, and stores.[16] The north and south sides contained forty smaller "tithing" lots for private residences.[17] The planners hoped that each square would serve as the heart of the commercial, religious, and social activities in the ward. Oglethorpe's original six squares and surrounding wards were duplicated over the next 150 years until there were twenty-four squares and associated wards.[18] This revolutionary plan has stood the test of time, helping the city to flourish, as the authors of *Savannah Square by Square* explain: "Over the decades, as Savannah endured fires, economic crashes, wars, and even devastating outbreaks of mosquito-borne tropical fevers, the

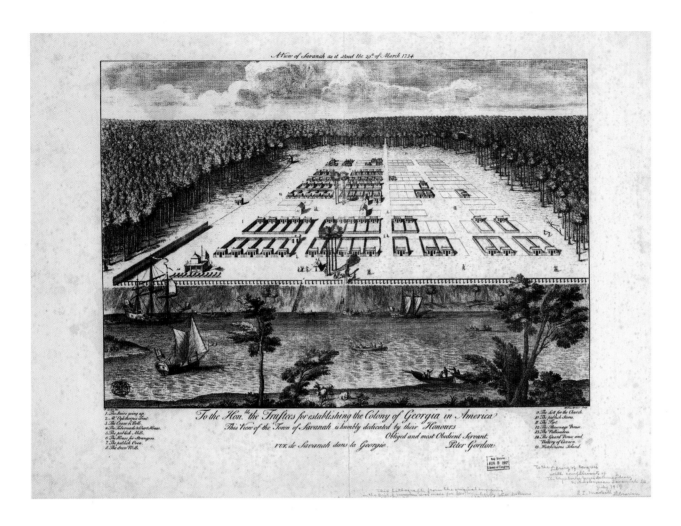

system of squares and lots held firm, providing a template for the architectural, economic, and spiritual life of the city."[19] Remarkably, the squares "allow for more open space in Savannah than in any city layout in history."[20]

In the eighteenth century, the Savannah squares were not the lush green spaces they are today. Rather, they were utilitarian, composed of sandy soil and containing little ornamental vegetation. Public wells made the squares muddy, and they were frequently used for dumping refuse.[21] In the nineteenth century, the city began to make improvements, installing iron fencing, statues, monuments, fountains, and plantings of ornamental trees and shrubs. In the early twentieth century, the addition of oak trees, wide brick walkways, and more statues, monuments, and fountains turned the squares into the parklike spaces we know today. As time passed, the squares became home to masses of azaleas, camellias, and other ornamentals. Misguided city planners threatened the squares in the twentieth century, wanting to cut roads through them.[22] By the mid-1950s,

preservation activists had turned the tide, demonstrating to the government and the community the value of the squares to Savannah's historic fabric. Today, twenty-two of the original twenty-four squares remain.

Although each square is distinctive, certain consistent features bind them all visually. They are encompassed by beautiful historic houses and structures showcasing numerous architectural styles from the eighteenth century to the mid-twentieth century.[23] Many of the homes feature elaborate gardens and ornamental iron fences and gates. The squares are enveloped by broad streets, many of which are made of historic tabby, cobblestone, or brick. Within each square are wide brick pathways and comfortable iron and wooden benches. The squares contain large Southern live oaks (*Quercus virginiana*), their twisted branches filled with resurrection fern and Spanish moss.[24] Beneath the oaks are a symphony of azaleas (*Azalea indica*), colored striking pink and red, subtle salmon, and white.[25] Many contain ground covers or lawn spaces, too. Some quintessential

Johnson Square, with its fifty-foot obelisk honoring
the Revolutionary War hero Nathanael Greene

examples of the Savannah squares indicate their
overall character and ambiance.

Of the six squares developed by Oglethorpe
between 1733 and 1746, Johnson Square was the first,
named for Robert Johnson, who served as the royal
governor of South Carolina from 1730 to 1735. The
square's central feature is a fifty-foot-tall obelisk
honoring the Revolutionary War hero Nathanael
Greene.[26] It is the oldest monument in Savannah,
dating to 1830. Around the monument are two contemporary, unadorned, circular concrete fountains.
Anchoring Derby Ward, Johnson Square was created as the heart of the city. In the colonial period,
the area and its surrounding trust lots were home
to the Trustees' store, the public oven and mill, a
house for visitors, and a church, where the stately
nineteenth-century Christ Church, Georgia's first
Christian congregation, now stands.[27] The square
was the city's public meeting place, hosting many
political and civic events, including famous orations
by James Monroe in 1819, the marquis de Lafayette
in 1825, and Daniel Webster in 1845. From the early
twentieth century to the present, Johnson Square
has served as the city's financial center, home to
numerous banks located within some of the city's
tallest buildings.

Located along Bull Street south of Johnson
Square, Wright Square, the centerpiece of Percival
Ward, was the second square that Oglethorpe laid
out. Originally named Percival Square, in 1763 it was
renamed for James Wright, the royal governor. The
focus of Wright Square is an opulent monument with
four polished red granite columns and carvings signifying agriculture, art, commerce, and manufacturing.[28] The monument was erected in 1883 in honor of
William Washington Gordon, the city's mayor from
1834 to 1836, the founder of the Central of Georgia
Railroad, and the grandfather of Juliette Gordon
Low, who founded the Girl Scouts of America.[29] A
large rough-cut granite boulder in a corner of the
square serves as a memorial to Tomochichi, chief
of the Yamacraw.[30] Tomochichi helped Oglethorpe
in the establishment of the city by serving as the
key mediator between Native Americans and the
English settlers during the 1730s.[31] The National
Society of the Colonial Dames of America in the
State of Georgia dedicated the monument in 1889.
Tomochichi's remains are believed to be buried

somewhere within Wright Square. Today, two court-houses border the square, one from the 1890s in the Renaissance Revival style, and the other an 1889 Romanesque Revival–style building. Wright Square is home to the Lutheran Church of the Ascension, completed in the late 1870s, with an incredible 225-foot steeple.[32]

One of Savannah's most-photographed squares, Chippewa Square was named for the Battle of Chippewa, an American victory in the War of 1812. Laid out in 1815, the square is the hub of Brown Ward. Many significant historic buildings surround the square, including one of the city's best-known landmarks, Independent Presbyterian Church. First constructed in 1819 and rebuilt after a fire in 1889, it is considered the mother church of Georgia Presbyterians. Other nearby notable buildings include the antebellum Philbrick-Eastman House, a Greek Revival mansion with cast-iron fencing; the Foley House, dating to 1896; the Six Pence Pub; and the Savannah Theatre, the nation's oldest continuously operating theater, identified by its large illuminated "Savannah" sign.[33] The showpiece of Chippewa Square is a statue depicting Georgia's founder, General James Oglethorpe, with his sword drawn; it is guarded at the base by four lions, each holding an inscribed shield—one with the Oglethorpe family crest, one with the seal of the colony, one with the seal of the state, and one with the seal of the city.[34] The 1910 bronze statue was created by the sculptor Daniel Chester French and the architect Henry Bacon, who collaborated on the design of the Lincoln Memorial in Washington, D.C.[35] Visitors frequently flock to Chippewa Square to see the place where the movie character Forrest Gump sat on a bench and declared to his neighbor, "Mama always said life was like a box of chocolates . . . You never know what you're gonna get."

Madison Square, located in Jasper Ward, was named for the fourth president of the United States, James Madison. Set out in 1837, the square features a striking bronze statue atop a marble base; dedicated in 1888, the work depicts Sergeant William Jasper attempting to save his unit's colors during the 1779 Battle of Savannah during the Revolutionary War.[36] A large marker on the northwest section of the square signifies the southern edge of British defenses during the battle.[37] The square also commemorates,

with two cannons on its south edge, the first two highways built in Georgia, the Ogeechee Road, between Savannah and Darien, and the Augusta Road, between Savannah and Augusta. The most beloved aspect of Madison Square is the daily echo of the chimes of St. John's Church, built in the 1850s.[38] Its neighboring parish house, the former Green-Meldrim House, is one of the finest examples of Gothic Revival architecture in the South. Dating to 1853 and designed by the architect John Norris, the house boasts a restored parterre garden. Other historic buildings around the square include the Masonic Temple, with its symbolic architectural

Wright Square, with its large monument to William Washington Gordon, a Georgia entrepreneur and the grandfather of Juliette Gordon Low

Isaiah Davenport
House, near Columbia
Square

details, and the Greek Revival–style Sorrel-Weed House, dating to 1841.[39] Another nearby historic building is the 1892 Savannah Volunteer Guards Armory, which was restored by the Savannah College of Art and Design in the late 1970s.[40] The college—SCAD, as it is popularly known—trains students in preservation design as a part of its curriculum and has been instrumental in the preservation of a number of Savannah's historic buildings.

Named for the female personification of the United States, Columbia Square and its ward were set out in 1799. The square boasts many historically significant houses, most notably the Davenport House, a two-story brick Federal-style mansion dating to around 1820. Savannah's twentieth-century preservation movement jelled here in 1955 when seven local women organized to save the house from demolition.[41] The Historic Savannah Foundation emerged out of this effort, and today the organization's offices are located in the nearby Abraham

Sheftall House, dating to 1818.[42] The renaissance of Columbia Square began in the 1970s when descendants of Noble Jones, one of Savannah's early settlers, moved a fountain from Wormsloe Plantation to the square. Jones had been instrumental in the establishment of the colony as well as in constructing Wormsloe (discussed elsewhere in this book), a portion of which today is a state historic site.

Laid out in 1799, Greene Square and its ward were named in honor of the Revolutionary War hero Nathanael Greene. In the nineteenth century, the square became a center for Savannah's African American community.[43] In 1802, the Second African Baptist Church was formed, and the congregation built a wood-and-stone church on one of the square's trust lots. Eight years later a house was built for the pastor of the church, Henry Cunningham. On January 12, 1865, the church was the location of a meeting between Union general William T. Sherman, U.S. secretary of war Edwin Stanton, and twenty local

Telfair Museum, near
Telfair Square

African American leaders to discuss the treatment of freed slaves by Sherman's troops.[44] Four days after the meeting, Sherman issued Special Field Order Number 15, which had been approved by President Lincoln. This order appropriated as Union property land ranging from Charleston, South Carolina, to the St. Johns River in Florida, redistributing almost 400,000 acres in forty-acre segments to newly freed African Americans. The order was later revoked by President Andrew Johnson.[45] Since 1925, the Second African Baptist Church has been housed on the original site in an elegant brick building with elaborate stained-glass windows. In the second half of the twentieth century, the church's congregation played a seminal role in the civil rights movement in Savannah, its members actively participating in the nonviolent protests calling for the integration of the city. The square itself, like seven other squares, is a true neighborhood square; it is a simple, contemplative space devoid of grand monuments and massive fountains.

Lafayette Square and Ward were named for the marquis de Lafayette, a key aide to George Washington during the American Revolution. He visited Savannah in 1825. Laid out in 1837, the square features an ornamental fountain installed by the National Society of the Colonial Dames of America in the State of Georgia in 1983 to commemorate the 250th anniversary of the founding of Georgia as a colony. Considered one of Savannah's most beautiful squares, it is surrounded on every side by historic landmarks. Lafayette Square is dominated by the Cathedral of St. John the Baptist, a monumental 1876 French Gothic structure with twin spires that can be seen from many spots around the city.[46] Other historic buildings include the antebellum Andrew Low House and its remarkable parterre garden, the Second Empire–style Hamilton-Turner House, the Italianate Putzel House (erected in 1888), and nearby the Battersby-Hartridge House, which is home to one of Savannah's last remaining antebellum town

Cathedral of
St. John the
Baptist towering
above the fountain
at Lafayette
Square

gardens.[47] The Andrew Low House and garden and the Battersby-Hartridge Garden are discussed elsewhere in this book.

The story of Savannah's squares is one of loss and redemption. In the 1930s, two squares—Elbert Square and Liberty Square—were destroyed to clear the way for U.S. Highway 17. Elbert Square, established in 1801, was named for Samuel Elbert, a Revolutionary War hero and Georgia governor. Today, the Savannah Civic Center blankets the square's original location.[48] Liberty Square, dedicated in 1799 to the Sons of Liberty, an organization of Savannah patriots during the American Revolution, is today the site of the 1970s-era Chatham County Courthouse.[49] Ellis Square too was destroyed, but received a second life. Established in 1733, it was one of the four original squares laid out by Oglethorpe. Named for Henry Ellis, the second royal governor of Georgia, the square served as a public market place from the mid-eighteenth century until 1954, when it was demolished to make way for a parking garage. In 2006, the city tore down the garage and resurrected Ellis Square, creating a new public space with lighted, dancing fountains, a public event area, and a visitor center.[50] Over the last century, many other Savannah squares have undergone improvements, including the renovation of Greene, Madison,

Historic First African Baptist Church near Franklin Square

Live oaks, Warren Square

Troup, Warren, and Washington Squares by the renowned Savannah landscape architect Clermont Lee, whose work was funded by the Mills B. Lane Foundation.[51]

Two of Savannah's green spaces, Colonial Park Cemetery and Forsyth Park, complete the montage that makes the Savannah squares such a significant part of this historic city. Established in 1750, the six-acre Colonial Park Cemetery served as Savannah's principal burial ground for more than a hundred years.[52] Among its unique features are the fifty above-ground brick vaults. When it became a city park in 1896, curvilinear paths, benches, and ornamental plantings were added.[53] A beautification project

in 1897 led to the removal of dozens of headstones to make space for public walkways. The gravestones were fastened to a brick wall on the east side of the cemetery and remain there today.[54] Colonial Park Cemetery is filled with ornamental trees such as crape myrtles and dogwoods.

Often called Savannah's last square, Forsyth Park is a thirty-acre park that many consider one of the most outstanding public spaces in the United States.[55] It got its start in 1841 when the Savannahian William B. Hodgson set aside ten acres of what was then a pine forest for Hodgson Park. It was renamed Forsyth Park in 1851 to honor John Forsyth, a Georgia governor, U.S. senator, and secretary of state. Forsyth

Entwined live oak limbs,
Pulaski Square

Colonial Park
Cemetery, the final
resting place of many
notable Georgians

Southern end of Bull Street, terminating at Forsyth Park,
with its monumental 1858 cast-iron fountain

donated an additional twenty acres for the park.[56] Over time, the park was enclosed with an iron fence, and the pine trees were replaced by broad walkways and ornamental plantings.[57] The masterpiece of the park is a large ornamental cast-iron fountain, erected in 1858, that has made Forsyth Park one of the most iconic places in the city. A woman sits at the apex of the two-tier fountain, and beneath her jets spray water into the lower pool, which is filled with statues of swans and tritons. During Savannah's Saint Patrick's Day celebration, the water is dyed green during a ceremony that launches the parade.[58] The Fragrant Garden is also located in Forsyth Park. Established in 1963 by local garden clubs, the walled garden captures the aroma of a wide variety of trees, shrubs, and flowers; it was designed to be enjoyed by the visually impaired, too, with plaques written in braille.[59] After decades of neglect, the Fragrant Garden was restored and reopened in the early 2000s by a community initiative led by the Trustees' Garden Club of Savannah.[60]

Lording over the park is the Confederate Monument, the tallest monument in Savannah. It is joined by a number of other monuments. The park is overlooked by noteworthy historic buildings such as Hodgson Hall, home of the Georgia Historical Society since 1876. Directly across Drayton Street from Forsyth Park is the acclaimed Candler Oak, a live oak that is one of the oldest trees in the city, thought to be about three hundred years old. In 2001, the Candler Oak was designated a Georgia Landmark and Historic Tree by the Georgia Urban Forest Council and was added to the Champion Trees National Register in 2004. The tree is protected by a conservation easement held by the Savannah Tree Foundation.[61]

Today, Savannah's twenty-two squares, all descendants of Oglethorpe's plan, are jewels in the crown of a vibrant city with a rich and complex history. The Savannah squares embody the ethos of the city, a place that values its history, beauty, and the millions of tourists who visit each year. Savannah's unique plan influenced the design of other Georgia cities, particularly Brunswick's six squares, laid

out in 1771, and served as the underpinning for the eighteenth-century towns of Hardwick and Wrightsborough. Some scholars and urban planners believe that many of the principles embodied in Oglethorpe's plan may be applicable to contemporary city planning. Thomas Wilson argues this position: "The Savannah ward plan, and its underlying planning paradigm, warrant further investigation by city planners and urban designers. Just as New Urbanism is a reinvention of traditional town planning, the broader practice of city and regional planning can begin reinventing itself by examining an inspired historic and humanistic plan."[62] Nearly three hundred years later, it is remarkable that Oglethorpe's vision still holds valuable lessons.

Troup Square, slightly off the beaten path, featuring flowering cherry trees and a centrally placed armillary sphere

Diana, Goddess of the Hunt, at the head of the pool
in the Stephenson-Adams-Land Garden

Stephenson–Adams–Land Garden

THE ATLANTA LANDSCAPE ARCHITECT William C. Pauley described gardening as "a fine art, just the same as sculpture, painting, music and architecture are fine arts," and defined a landscape architect as "an artist that studies Nature and supplements her beauties."[1] Pauley's artistry can be seen in the garden he designed for the residence of businessman H. Warren Stephenson and his wife, Helen, known today as the Stephenson-Adams-Land House in Atlanta's historic Druid Hills neighborhood.[2] Associated with Frederick Law Olmsted, Druid Hills boasts grand eclectic and revival-style houses set amid a parklike setting. In the development's formative years during the early twentieth century, many of its houses had professionally designed gardens like that of the Stephenson house on Ponce de Leon Avenue, the area's main thoroughfare. For over eighty-five years, this backyard oasis has been a place of beauty and reflection. To date, only minimal changes have been made, a testament to the strength of Pauley's design and to the level of enjoyment it has given the three families who have been its stewards.

Listed in the National Register of Historic Places and designated a local preservation district by both the Atlanta Urban Design Commission and DeKalb County, Druid Hills has been described as "one of the finest turn-of-the-century suburbs in the southeastern United States."[3] Recognized both for its outstanding architecture and for its "exceptionally high quality" landscape, Druid Hills was originally designed by Frederick Law Olmsted with later involvement by the Olmsted Brothers firm and others.[4] The suburb developed in different stages; the first, beginning around 1908, was at its southern edge along the Ponce de Leon corridor, where the Stephensons built their home in 1931.

The establishment of Druid Hills coincided with a period when a renewed interest in America's early history was expressed through architecture. Public and private buildings were constructed in the popular Colonial Revival style, with gardens that likewise reflected

Nobody will love it as much as I do.—Mary Young Land, October 26, 2015 this influence. These formal gardens called to mind pre-Revolutionary landscapes with their geometric patterns, axis walkways bordered on either side by flower beds, and, often, a distinctive focal point.[5] Twentieth-century enhancements included sunken gardens, sculpture or statuary, grass panels, and perennial borders.[6] The early twentieth century was also a time of intense interest in gardening in the South, and women's clubs and garden clubs gained in popularity.

Working in conjunction with William Pauley was the architect James T. Mitchell, whom the Stephensons hired to design their house.[7] The two men were not strangers, having been paired on other projects in Atlanta and Columbus, designing houses and landscapes for prominent businessmen and their families. They were familiar with Druid Hills and comfortable in dealing with clients to create high-quality residences similar to those found throughout the neighborhood. Residents likely knew of Mitchell's and Pauley's work. In 1926, B. Earle Yancey hired the two to design his house and garden on Ponce de Leon.[8] Pauley was involved with other projects in the popular suburb. The gardens he designed on Ponce de Leon alone included the residences of Thomas A. Martin and Henry Heinz. For Martin, Pauley created "plans for the grounds and garage, a pool, flower garden, and a profile for the drive and a planting plan for the grounds" in 1928.[9] This work was typical of what he produced for a number of his clients. In 1929 and 1930, he prepared preliminary and detailed landscape plans for the Heinz property; however, the impact of the Depression prevented the project's completion.[10]

When Stephenson hired Pauley, the young landscape architect's practice was thriving. Following his 1916 graduation from Purdue University, where he studied horticulture, Pauley entered what is now the University of Massachusetts Amherst, completing graduate work in landscape architecture. An Indiana native, Pauley settled in Atlanta after serving in World War I and quickly found employment, gaining practical knowledge by working with several landscape firms and nurseries. With both education and experience, by 1923 he was ready to establish his own business. In *Pioneers of American Landscape Design* (2000), the landscape architect and historian Spencer Tunnell observed that "although architecture as a profession was well established in Atlanta, no professionally trained landscape architect had set up a practice there before Pauley."[11] In later years, Pauley earned the distinction of being named the first registered landscape architect in Georgia.[12]

Pauley's practice benefited from the growth and prosperity that Atlanta experienced in the 1920s. He received many commissions to design the gardens and grounds of private homes and estates. Toward the end of his career, when Pauley prepared a list of his projects, he gave special mention to Bankshaven, a private residence in Newnan. He wrote that it was "the last job, I know of, in Georgia, and probably in the Southeast, which covered so much ground, at a time when people were cutting down on acreage."[13] William Banks Sr. hired Pauley in 1928, and

Stone path leading
to the front door

Stephenson-Adams-Land House and garden in parklike Druid Hills

Curvilinear drive extending from the front to the back of the property

they worked together over many years to create an elaborate landscape. In William Mitchell's *Gardens of Georgia* (1989), he identifies Bankshaven as "one of the major gardens in Georgia and the nation," describing it as a "landscaped park" with "300 acres, five major gardens, and a broad lawn leading to a ten-acre lake."[14] In later years, when writing of his work on the estate, Pauley modestly said that "the Garden developed, and turned out to be very satisfactory."[15]

After the financial devastation of the Depression, jobs of this nature became rare, but Pauley was open to other opportunities. His practice grew more diverse and over time included not only residences but also churches, colleges, garden club shows and projects, parks, cemeteries, public housing, hospitals, and children's homes. Pauley designed projects throughout Georgia as well as Tennessee, Alabama, South Carolina, and Florida. His long and rewarding career lasted until his retirement in 1968 and included being named a Fellow of the American

Society of Landscape Architects (FASLA) in 1965.[16]

The Stephenson property covers a little over an acre. Located on the eastern edge of Druid Hills at the corner of Ponce de Leon and Ridgecrest Road, it sits directly across from Deepdene Park, one of the six planned parks in Olmsted's initial design for the suburb. In notes about the project, Pauley mentions that James Mitchell "did a very good job with the house."[17] Set back from the roadway, the elegant two-story brick Colonial Revival residence features a symmetrical façade with horizontal stone belt coursing, double-hung six-over-six windows, and dormers. A curved flagstone path leads to the striking front entrance, with its pilasters and broken pediment. Throughout Druid Hills, the setting was (and remains) fairly consistent, suggesting "informal 'English' landscaping with an emphasis on broad, undulating lawns and casually disposed trees, shrubbery, flower gardens, and walks."[18] The Stephenson property maintained this pattern. Although a few trees and shrubs dotted the front

yard, with foundation plantings of English box-wood, the overall appearance of Pauley's design is that of a wide, open lawn that rises slightly from the street level to the house.

It was behind the house, however, that the major feature of the Stephenson landscape was found: the formal terraced garden designed by Pauley. As the patterned brick drive traversed the front lawn along the west side and under the porte cochere, it curved at the back of the property to meet Ridgecrest Road, creating an uninterrupted space where Pauley placed the garden. A brick patio or terrace immediately off the rear porch provided a view into the garden, which Pauley divided into two additional levels. Steps led from the patio up to the middle terrace, which had a rectangular lily pool at its center, bordered by grass. Brick walks on either side of the grass were shielded by "thickly planted peren-nial borders."[19] Pauley used low American boxwood hedges to delineate the northern and southern edges of this level. The brick walkways continued up

steps into the "upper garden of perennials," where, on either side, were "two semi-circular rose gardens, themselves enclosing grass panels, and screened by twin hedges of Rugosa roses."[20]

In "The Art of Gardening," a presentation Pauley gave to the Garden Club of Columbus in 1931, he theorized that "a garden should have some dominant feature or some climax," which could be a "central planting" or "an unusual setting for a fountain, gar-den seat, etc."[21] He chose as a dominant feature for the Stephenson garden the summerhouse, or gazebo, "of ornamental iron work," which he placed at the apex of the upper terrace; it looked down through the garden back toward the house.[22] Sheltering two wrought-iron benches and a small table, this struc-ture contained a "stone slab in the floor," which dis-played "the points of the compass and inform[ed] the visitor that the exact elevation on which he stands is 1007.4 feet above sea level."[23]

Spencer Tunnell has observed that in Pauley's work there was "a balance between the formal

Terrace garden in the backyard

aspects of landscape architecture and its interdependence with architecture and the naturalistic aspects of the site."[24] Pauley believed that a landscape architect "studies the setting and the house proper and ties them together making a perfect ensemble."[25] At the Stephenson property, he took into account the lot size and topography as well as the spatial needs of a rear yard that had to accommodate not only the garden but also a garage and a drive. Most especially, he devised a formal landscape appropriate to the formality of the Colonial Revival house. The result of his careful attention was a garden that appeared to extend from the residence, an intimate landscape anchored by a geometric layout and a calming lily pool that culminated in an eye-catching architectural feature.

When describing some of Pauley's Atlanta-area projects, Tunnell notes that his selection of plants "reflects the broad range of plant material that thrives in Atlanta's interzonal location."[26] Pauley's horticultural expertise enabled him to provide his clients with recommendations that ensured beauty, variety, and hardiness. For the "thickly planted perennial borders" in the Stephenson garden, he chose, among others, "azalea—Indica alba, Hemerocallis gold dust, columbine, Maid Marian phlox, bronze snapdragons, and stokesia"; his plans for the perennials on the upper terrace showcased "phlox-Von Lassburg, Iris-Lord of June, heuchera, and hardy candytuft."[27] A little over twenty years after Pauley designed the Stephenson garden, he returned to prepare a plant survey and revised planting plan for the couple in December 1953.[28] He made only minor recommendations to add texture and color to the landscape.

Within five years of Pauley's additional work, the Stephensons had sold the property to Dr. Oscar S. Adams. In the twenty-seven years he and his wife, Frances J. Adams, lived in the house, they appear to have made few alterations to either the residence or the grounds, aside from perhaps minor changes to plant material.[29] When the current owners, Dr. William C. "Bill" Land Jr. and his wife, Mary Young Land, first considered purchasing the property, in 1985, they were drawn to the stately architecture, with its curving entry staircase, as well as to the garden.[30] They were unaware of the Pauley connection, but as the Lands learned more about the house and its landscape, they realized they had a responsibility

Rear garden, from *Garden History of Georgia*

to take care of this special place. Together they made a conscious decision to protect the historic integrity of the garden and to maintain the intent of its original design as closely as possible. Any changes made were not taken lightly.[31]

To give themselves time to study the garden, the Lands refrained from making any alterations. Eventually, Mary Land decided that it needed to be refreshed and replanted. She hired the Atlanta landscape architecture firm of Spencer and Spencer and Associates to devise a new planting plan that would blend Pauley's plant recommendations with new selections.[32] Regarding the layout of the garden, however, the Lands made only minimal changes to Pauley's design. On the east side of the house, a path originally led from the front lawn into the formal garden, but as traffic continued to increase

OPPOSITE:
Rectangular lily pool

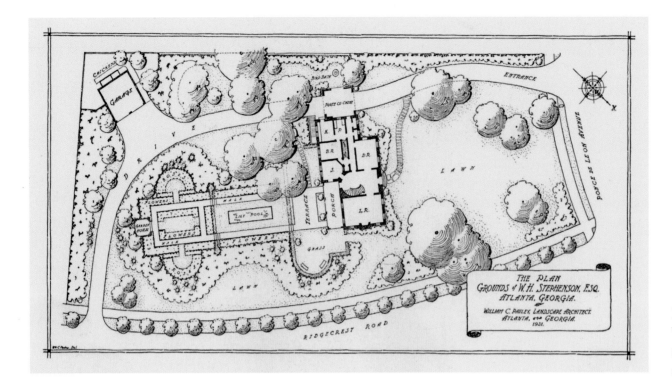

Landscape plan by William C. Pauley, from *Garden History of Georgia*

H. W. Stephenson Residence, Partial Planting List, 1931

White Indian azalea (*Azalea indica* 'Alba')

Boxwood (*Buxus sempervirens*)

Japanese flowering quince (*Cydonia japonica*)

Golden bell (*Forsythia × intermedia*)

Rose of Sharon (*Hibiscus syriacus* 'Totus Albus')

Cassina berry (*Ilex cassine*)

Holly (*Ilex opaca*)

Carolina cherry laurel (*Prunus caroliniana*)

English laurel (*Prunus Laurocerasus*)

Glossy privet (*Ligustrum lucidum*)

Yates apple (*Malus* 'Yates')

Nandina (*Nandina domestica*)

Pecan (*Carya illinoinensis* 'Stuart')

Flowering almond (*Prunus glandulosa*)

Osmanthus (*Osmanthus fortunei*)

Anthony Waterer spirea (*Spiraea × bumalda* 'Anthony Waterer')

Japanese snowball (*Viburnum plicatum* f. *tomentosum*)

Wisteria (*Wisteria sinensis*)

Planting Plan, Mr. H. W. Stephenson's Residence, Atlanta, Ga., 1931, William C. Pauley Architectural Drawings Collection, 0082M, Georgia Archives. In some instances, the botanical names originally included in Pauley's planting list have been updated with the current botanical name.

on Ponce de Leon, the Lands enclosed that space with a cherry laurel hedge to provide additional privacy. This secluded circular spot became their white garden, where white flowers, mostly annuals, bloom in the spring.[33] They removed the central section of the American boxwood hedge between the garden's lower and middle terraces to enhance the sightline between the porch and the gazebo.[34]

The ephemeral nature of landscapes means that some change is inevitable. A number of years ago, the Lands hired the Atlanta landscape firm Pope-Ozlo and Associates to address matters in the front yard. Lightning strikes had resulted in damaged trees that, once removed, opened up the lawn.[35] To soften the area around the front of the house, mondo grass was installed and oak trees were planted, although the original flagstone path and foundation plantings of English boxwood remained. As years passed, mature trees and shrubs died throughout the grounds. These included a cedar, dogwoods, and tea olive; some have been replaced. Oaks, tulip poplars, and dogwood still remain from the original design.

Working with this landscape for over thirty years has given Mary Land much pleasure. While respecting the garden's original design, she has introduced her own style. With a single glimpse of the statue *Diana, Goddess of the Hunt*, she envisioned it standing amid the boxwood hedge overlooking the lily

pool, where it resides today. She has added tulips, daffodils, elaeagnus, laurels, and pansies as well as 'Queen Elizabeth' and 'Lincoln' roses to the garden. [36] She has simplified it, too. She no longer uses perennial beds and now employs a yard service to manage maintenance and planting.

A former president of the Lullwater Garden Club, Mary Land and her husband, Bill, are pleased to share the garden with others. It has been used for entertaining, and guests have enjoyed wandering throughout its terraces. The property was included as part of a local tour of houses and gardens. The space, however, has been mostly one of personal satisfaction for the Lands. Seeking a quiet and peaceful setting, Mary Land has fond memories of climbing onto the porch roof to write and look out over her garden. [37]

A visitor to the 1930s garden would find the 2016 landscape reassuringly similar to the original in many ways. The garden's terraces framed by flowers and boxwood, its central lily pool, brick walks, and gazebo all remain intact. Yet it gracefully reflects the attention and tastes of its most recent owners. The garden of the Stephenson-Adams-Land House serves as a legacy of William C. Pauley, one of Georgia's most distinguished landscape architects. Unfortunately, many of his designs have disappeared or have been unrecognizably altered. It is fortunate that the original owners of this residence were interested in developing such a garden, and that subsequent owners have maintained it and have understood and appreciated their roles as its guardians.

Gazebo with original garden furniture

Upper terrace fountain cascading between twin staircases at the Swan House

Swan House

TUCKED AWAY from the posh and busy streets of Buckhead is an oasis evocative of an earlier time—Swan House, an iconic house and gardens that have graced Atlanta since 1928. Considered a masterpiece of the famed Atlanta architect Philip Trammell Shutze, the house and gardens provide a glimpse into the lifestyle of the Inman family during the 1920s and 1930s. With many rooms resplendent with exquisite furnishings, an elegant exterior, and luxuriant gardens, Swan House is one of Atlanta's most recognized landmarks.

By the third decade of the twentieth century, Atlanta had become the business and financial heart of the Southeast. The chamber of commerce's "Forward Atlanta" campaign, established in 1925 to promote the city and its advantages, generated 20,000 jobs, launched almost 800 new businesses, and expanded the economy by $34 million.[1] Between 1900 and 1940, the population tripled, and downtown swelled with buildings and people. During the 1910s and 1920s, the availability of trolley lines and automobiles, coupled with a housing shortage, sent many middle- and upper-class Atlantans in search of suburban neighborhoods north and east of the city.

By the 1920s, the northern suburb of Buckhead had become a fashionable residential enclave. As a result of suburban migration, the area grew from a population of 2,600 in 1920 to over 10,000 in 1930.[2] Some prominent families purchased large tracts of land in the area and commissioned leading architects, landscape architects, and interior designers to build and decorate their estates. Among these were Edward Hamilton Inman and his wife, Emily MacDougald Inman.

Heir to a fortune amassed by his grandfather and father through the cotton industry, railroads, banking, real estate, manufacturing, and other ventures, Edward H. Inman remained involved in these family business interests. As a leading figure in the business and political worlds of Atlanta, he served as president of Kimball House Company,

As to the landscaping, whatever has been done was with the Italian garden in England in mind.
—Philip Trammell Shutze, regarding Swan House

vice president of Atlanta Woolen Mills, and director of several banks. He was also a member of the Atlanta City Council and the Fulton County Board of Commissioners. Inman was a key figure on the national stage, serving in the administration of President Woodrow Wilson during World War I and as a presidential adviser on the international cotton trade following the war.[3]

Edward and Emily married on June 19, 1901, and had two sons, Hugh Theodore in 1902 and Edward Jr. in 1912.[4] In 1909, they commissioned a Tudor-style house on 15th Street in Ansley Park. After several fires at their home, the family moved to the Biltmore Hotel in 1921. Shortly thereafter, the Inmans hired the firm of Hentz, Reid, & Adler to design an estate for the twenty acres they acquired in 1924–25 in the Peachtree Heights Park neighborhood (now called Peachtree Heights West).[5] The Inmans were among the wealthiest and most fashionable of Atlanta's citizens. They wanted their new home to be a place where they could entertain and enjoy family and friends among large, lavish rooms and elaborate gardens. After two years of planning, construction

of the house and gardens began in early 1926 and was completed two years later.

Philip Trammell Shutze, a lead associate in the firm of Hentz, Reid, & Adler (later Hentz, Adler, & Shutze), was the architect chosen by the Inmans. Shutze, a graduate with honors from the Georgia Institute of Technology in 1912 and from Columbia University's School of Architecture in 1913, won the Prix de Rome in 1915, the most prestigious architectural award of the time. The prize afforded Shutze three years of study in Italy. For forty years, he designed many of Atlanta's most refined homes and buildings, including Tryggversson for Andrew Calhoun, Knollwood for W. F. Kiser, the Floyd McRae House, the Patterson-Carr House, Citizens and Southern National Bank, Spring Hill Mortuary, the Temple, and the Academy of Medicine. Of the influences on Shutze and his significance in American architecture, the architectural historian Robert M. Craig wrote: "The Beaux-Arts traditions that informed his education and career molded an academic architect of the first order, known during his career as America's greatest living classical architect. The Columbus native was a designer of skill, with a masterly sense of proportion and scale, and a talent seldom rivaled by his contemporaries."[6]

For the Inmans, Shutze created a masterpiece of classicism, adapting English and Italian classical architectural styles. His design work drew on his formal education; his own photographs, notes, and sketches from his study abroad in Italy; and his extensive personal library and collections. These varied influences are evident in Swan House, which Craig named "Shutze's ultimate eclectic design."[7] Sources for Shutze's design for the house and gardens included the Palazzo Corsini in Rome for the cascade fountain, Duncombe Park in Yorkshire for the massive Doric portico on the east facade, Marble Hill House in Richmond (England) for the wall ornament around the grand staircase, Mereworth Castle in Kent for the pedimented

View from the upper terrace on the west side of the house, with the grounds falling away toward the Andrews Road gates

Elaborately designed fountain

doors in the stair hall, Branham Hall in Yorkshire for the horseshoe staircase descending from the west façade, and Badmitten House in Gloucestershire for the brackets and pediment on the west façade.[8] As he did throughout his career, Shutze unified the house and its interiors with the surrounding landscape. For garden design, Shutze was influenced by the gardens he studied in Italy, as the architectural historian Elizabeth Dowling explains: "Whenever the opportunity presented itself, Shutze designed a landscape similar in many ways to those he had seen in Italy. In the hilly terrain of Atlanta, he typically placed buildings in elevated positions that visually dominated their sites, and he then surrounded the buildings with natural box or clipped box parterres to integrate the man-made geometry of the house with the wild nature of the untouched landscape. He often used a pink or yellow stucco building as an accent in the green landscape."[9]

Shutze sited the Inman residence on an elevated position within the hilly and wooded landscape by using a reverse design plan. The house faces Andrews Drive, set back quite a distance from the street. The main entrance, however, is at the back of the house. The landscape architect Spencer Tunnell explains the placement: "This mysterious arrangement allows the street façade and foreground to be treated as a completely ornamental set piece. The house is treated in a manner similar to a casino in an Italian villa."[10] Although Shutze placed the driveway on axis with the façade, it soon disappears into the woodlands along the side of the house. This allows the dramatic composition of the house, terraces, and cascading fountain to be unfettered by automobiles.

Shutze's use of English and Italian architectural styles is seen most readily in the two façades he created for Swan House. The symmetrical west façade overlooking Andrews Drive is Italian Baroque in derivation. The three-bay stucco façade features a large horseshoe staircase leading to a heavily framed central doorway, topped with a segmental pediment with a large sculptural decoration at its apex. A large circular window called an oeil-de-boeuf ("ox eye") crowns the west façade; two stone figures on the roofline represent Summer and Autumn.[11] The main entrance on the east façade is Anglo-Palladian in style. Its most striking feature is the large pedimented portico with four Roman columns

Tufa-encrusted urns punctuating the walls throughout the garden

supporting a heavy entablature and cornice. The portico serves as a porte cochere. Centered beneath the portico, the rusticated entry door is capped with a fanlight containing a swan motif. The Inman residence became known as Swan House after the swan motifs found throughout the house. The entrance is flanked by pedimented niches housing massive decorative urns.

To create elegant interiors, Shutze worked in tandem with the prominent Georgia-born New York decorator Ruby Ross Wood and Emily Inman. All three were influenced by Elsie de Wolfe, recognized as the most important force in American interiors between the two world wars. Like the house and gardens, the interior of Swan House contained a balance of eclectic styles. The furnishings were a blend of fine antiques from different periods and styles, quality reproductions, and contemporary pieces. During the construction of the house and gardens, Emily traveled extensively in America and Europe to collect an impressive array of antiques for the residence.[12]

Shutze's devotion to classicism could be seen in the design of the circular entrance hall, which serves as a prelude to the stair hall, the grandest space in the house. The entrance hall features a paired series of Ionic columns and a concentric

Swan House garden façade elevation, watercolor on paper, Philip T. Shutze, ca. 1928. Courtesy of the Kenan Research Center at the Atlanta History Center

checkerboard-pattern floor with an encircled star at its center, all made from black and white marble. The checkerboard marble floor continues into the stair hall, where the centerpiece is the curved floating staircase.[13] Shutze placed the three main rooms off the stair hall. He fashioned the library around an ornate seventeenth-century lime wood overmantel carving the Inmans acquired from an English manor house. Edward used the library as a home office, and Emily later hosted friends for tea, bridge, and conversation there. The morning room, the female center of the house, served as a living room and housed Emily's collections of porcelain, silver, glass, and fans. This striking green room features a Siena marble fireplace with a Chinese pediment above, all enclosed by fluted Corinthian columns. With its exquisite antiques and bold chintz-covered sofa, the morning room was used to entertain guests after supper and for relaxing privately. The largest room in the house was the opulent formal dining room, which featured English wallpaper hand-painted in a chinoiserie style, a French Aubusson rug, and Portuguese rainbow plaid taffeta draperies. The first floor contained the family's private breakfast room, a spacious and modern butler's pantry, and a kitchen that could accommodate cooking for family meals and large dinners.

The family and guest bedrooms were on the second floor. The third floor held servants' rooms, storage spaces, and two attic spaces. The butler's

pantry, kitchen, and third-floor rooms were used by the domestic servants. The Inman family required a sizable staff to maintain the extensive property and serve the needs of the family and its guests. At times, the staff included housemaids, a nursemaid or nanny, a chauffeur, a professional caterer, and a gardener. As was typical in the Jim Crow South, the majority of the staff was African American; however, from 1927 until the late 1940s, the main gardener for the family was a white man named James Marion Self, who lived nearby on Pharr Road. Self maintained the lawn and gardens, tended the cows and barn nearby on the property, and did odd jobs.[14] Quarters for the male staff members were located above the garage, which was also designed by Shutze. Located east of the house, the six-car garage housed Edward's collection of automobiles. He was one of the first automobile owners in the city and one of the first Atlantans to be issued a driver's license. Edward and his chauffeur, Grant Carter, were a successful racing team. Some of their trophies were displayed in the library.

For the landscape around Swan House, Shutze, as he did with the house and its interiors, combined several styles. As Dowling explains: "To reflect the dual stylistic nature of the house, Shutze composed a landscape conceived from Italian themes and filtered through the English experience."[15] He created a sense of history and instant age with stone walls with niches, fountains, large urns and pots, obelisks, statuary, and mature natural and clipped boxwoods. He used the surrounding forest to give the house a green backdrop and sense of place in the natural terrain of the southern Piedmont.

For the entrance court on the east façade, Shutze created a serene landscape that balanced the imposing portico and provided a sense of enclosure. Opposite the portico, he designed a high stone wall broken by three arched niches and "two circular stairways ascending to a terrace above,"[16] where there was an expansive view of the house and surrounding woods. The three inner niches were filled with ivy. In between the house and the high wall he placed a grass court encircled by an elliptical drive. For the façade facing Andrews Drive, Shutze emulated classic Italian garden design, seen in his use of terraced lawns, retaining walls with recessed arches, massive stairs, and a cascading fountain containing five basins. Just below the house, he positioned the cascading fountain as the focal point of the terraced lawn, which was bookended

between two flights of broad steps. This elaborate feature, which *Garden History of Georgia* describes as "a series of cascades like great lotus leaves which descend along the stairways bearing water plants on their mirror surfaces,"[17] was inspired by Shutze's visit to the Palazzo Corsini in Rome with his classmate Edward Lawson. The cascade and its enclosing walls taper inward toward the house. Shutze's use of this forced-perspective device amplified the apparent length of the stairs and cascade, magnifying their presence at the base of the house.[18] At the bottom of the fountain, the manicured lawn of grass ramps leads down to a concave stone retaining wall and the lower terrace, which was adjacent to the entry drive. The wall was inset with seven semicircular niches filled with clipped ivy and draped in masses of a pink semi-double hybrid musk rose. *Rosa* 'Paul's Scarlet Climber' twines up large stone obelisks placed at both ends of the stone wall that encloses the sides of the lawn.[19] Shutze added two quatrefoil fountains to the grass-covered terrace. The quatrefoils hold

Motor court entrance on the east side of the house

Imposing columned entrance portico

OPPOSITE: High stone wall flanked by circular stairs opposite the motor court entrance

it, Shutze placed twin pairs of Ionic columns supporting broken pediments that frame a statue of an eagle, two large urns, and a stone bench beneath. This component was inspired by Shutze's studies at the Villa La Pietra in Florence, Italy.[20] In between, Shutze divided the garden into four symmetrical quadrants with a fountain in the center, bordered by two perennial beds along outside walls adorned with tufa-encrusted urns.[21] *Garden History of Georgia* describes the layout: "This garden is rectangular in shape and features box and gardenias. The central fountain basin has a petal-shaped outline that is repeated in the generous boxwood plantings of the formal beds. Against the walls are straight line beds for perennials and annuals and tall crepe myrtle trees on the inside and Magnolia grandiflora on the outside soften the lines of the walls."[22] Shutze's simple planting scheme produced primarily a green garden containing an evergreen palette of English box (*Buxus sempervirens* 'Suffruticosa'), English ivy (*Hedera helix*), and lilyturf (*Liriope muscari*) within the parterres, punctuated with standards of white wisteria (*Wisteria floribunda* 'Alba'). Pathways were made of crushed limestone, and the beds were edged with simple terra-cotta tiles. The bordering perennial beds running perpendicular to the house helped draw the eye to the terminus of the garden at the Ionic columns and also provided a space for color that Emily desired in her garden. An avenue of redbud trees, "shading wide bands of blue scillas" (*Hyacinthoides hispanica* syn. *Scilla hispanica*), led from this walled garden to the surrounding forest, which was filled with native trees and shrubs.

In April 1931, only three years after they moved into the house, Edward Inman died of a heart attack at age forty-nine. Following her husband's death, Emily invited her eldest son, Hugh T. Inman II, and his family to move into Swan House. Hugh, his wife, Mildred, and their two young children, Samuel and Mildred (who were known as Sam and Mimi) lived in the house until the late 1940s.[23] With her husband's passing and the uncertainty brought about by the Great Depression, Emily educated herself about business and finance. The daughter of a women's suffrage leader, Emily believed that women should be capable of handling their own business matters. She invested wisely in the stock market and took an active role in business.

religious symbolism, representing the Gospel writers Matthew, Mark, Luke, and John.

To provide a transition between the contrasting architectural styles of the two façades, Shutze placed a rectangular walled boxwood garden on the south side of the house. He designed the space, with Emily Inman's advice, in keeping with the Italian-inspired formal gardens seen in England in the late 1800s. Attached to the house on one end of the garden is a large vaulted screened porch that offered a shaded retreat during hot summer months and gave the family another space to entertain. Opposite

Formal boxwood garden on the south side of the house

Boxwood garden from the porch, from *Garden History of Georgia*

Emily Inman lived at Swan House until her death in 1965. For over three decades, she hosted luncheons, mint julep parties, and elegant dinners at her exquisite home for her family, friends, and guests. During the Garden Club of America's annual meeting in Atlanta in April 1932, she welcomed members to her estate.[24] She was a member of Peachtree Garden Club, established in 1923 as Atlanta's first garden club. The gardens were featured on numerous Garden Club of Georgia pilgrimages in the 1930s. The gardens declined in the last years of her life.

Before her death, she entered into negotiations with the Atlanta Historical Society for the sale of the house and grounds. In 1966, a bequest from Walter McElreath, one of the Atlanta Historical Society's founding members, enabled the organization to acquire the Inman estate. The property included Swan House and most of its furnishings, the formal landscape, and the estate's 26.3 acres. In the summer of 1967, the Atlanta Historical Society, which was founded in 1926, moved from 1753 Peachtree Road to Swan House, and the house was opened to the public as a house museum. The same year, the society hired James C. Wise to convert the Inman garage and servants' quarters into a tearoom and gift shop

known as the Swan Coach House Restaurant, which has been leased by the Forward Arts Foundation since that time. An art gallery was added to the restaurant in 1984 to further serve the foundation's mission to enrich the Greater Atlanta community by promoting and supporting the visual arts. The barn was razed in 1968.

Two society trustees, Louise Richardson Allen and Anne Coppedge Carr, chaired the newly formed landscape advisory committee to direct work on the grounds. They initially enlisted the help of fifteen local garden clubs. The Atlanta Historical Society's resources were challenged by the purchase of the Inman estate, the alterations to the garage, and the addition of driveways and parking areas for the staff and visitors. Little was left to pay for the care of the landscape. The committee coordinated the garden clubs, which ultimately numbered thirty-five, each taking responsibility for a specific area. A volunteer committee of three Atlanta landscape architects, Edward L. Daugherty, Edith Henderson, and Dan Franklin, reviewed the maintenance and improvement plans and met regularly with the landscape advisory committee. Franklin turned the service area on the north façade into a kitchen garden (named the Old Lamp Post Garden) in 1968.

Ornamental
fountain in the formal
boxwood garden

Until the early 1980s, the garden clubs volunteered both labor and financial resources to maintain and improve the grounds. Many of these garden clubs are still actively involved with not only the Swan House gardens but also many other gardens throughout the property, which is now a history museum owned by the Atlanta Historical Society and operated as the Atlanta History Center. A professional garden staff has overseen the grounds since 1980.

Other changes came to the Swan House gardens between the late 1960s and the 1980s. Some of the more prominent additions included two statues in the boxwood garden, *A Hunter Standing with His Dog* and *A Maiden Standing with a Young Man on One Knee*, donated by Ann Grant in the late 1960s. The statues, which stand at either end of a long stone bench, are still located near the east entrance to the garden. The bench was purchased by the Pine Tree Garden Club. In 1971, a white marble elephant named Ambrose was acquired by the Atlanta Historical Society and placed in the stone circle down the pathway from the west entrance of the boxwood garden. Mrs. William D. Ellis donated a Victorian playhouse (circa 1890) to the society in 1980. Originally constructed in downtown Atlanta on Peachtree Street, the tiny cottage moved progressively north as its young occupants outgrew it. Its fifth address is Swan House, where in 1981 it was nestled into the woodlands just east of the boxwood garden. Elaborate wrought-iron gates were added to the Andrews Drive entrance in 1982. Designed by W. Caldwell Smith, the gates were funded by the Forward Arts Foundation.

Attention was brought to the walled boxwood garden in 1995 when the Atlanta landscape architect Spencer Tunnell began a faithful restoration, which was completed the following year. He approached the effort in "three parts: an examination of the original documents and photographs from 1933–1975, an extensive investigation to determine what had actually been built and planted, and a determination of change during the last 68 years."[25] When the Atlanta Historical Society acquired the property, the field of landscape preservation was hardly known and rarely practiced. Unfortunately during that time, most of the original plant material except for the boxwood and English ivy were removed.[26] Crusher run, a mixture of granite sand and small gravel, was spread over the original crushed limestone pathways in order to better accommodate visitors. Over many years, the crusher run covered the terra-cotta tiles that had originally lined the beds, resulting in extensive drainage problems. The restoration included removing azaleas and other plants added by garden clubs in the late 1960s and 1970s, hauling out decades of crusher run and returning crushed limestone to the pathways, reestablishing the terra-cotta edging, removing volunteer trees that crowded the garden and obscured Shutze's design, installing new drains and repairing existing ones, and installing large English boxwood in original locations.[27] The restoration, dedicated to the longtime Atlanta History Center supporter Caroline Sauls Shaw, was granted an Atlanta Urban Design Commission Award of Excellence in 1999.

In the entry court, the terrace above the high wall with the ivy niches, the highest elevation on the property, was not cultivated during the Inmans' time at Swan House. Although Shutze had designed a circular domed temple and an approach flanked by recumbent sphinxes for this location, neither was realized. In 1998, a plan to embellish the area was enacted. Peyton and English Robinson donated funds to establish a garden to memorialize their parents, H. English and Ermine Robinson. Spencer Tunnell researched and designed the garden to ensure a style consistent with the rest of the Inman estate. The garden includes a demilune gravel terrace with a planting bed in a wide arc behind it. It is punctuated by a large old white oak and enclosed by *Eleagnus frutescens* 'Fruitlandii'. The bed is planted with rhododendron, hosta, wild ginger, and toad lily. The Robinson family gathered to dedicate the garden on May 18, 2001.

The garden staff has continued to be watchful of the historical accuracy of the Swan House gardens. In 1996, workers removed the English ivy that had run uncontrolled over walls, obscuring original stonework and suffocating native trees and plants in the adjacent forest; they left only the original ivy plantings in the boxwood garden and the ivy niches. The staff removed all the thorny elaeagnus (*Elaeagnus pungens*) from the landscape in 2000, which, like the ivy, was growing unchecked. In the fall of 2002, the staff planted Fruitland silverthorn (*Elaeagnus pungens* 'Fruitlandii') in two areas where it had been planted during the Inman era: along the walls bordering the terraced lawn on the Andrews Drive façade, and on either side of the entrance to the motor court. These elaeagnus plantings are maintained regularly to keep them in bounds. Other plants appropriate to the 1930s period were added during this time, including yellow Lady Banks roses (*Rosa banksiae* 'Lutea') on either side of the horseshoe staircase, and both the double yellow and the double white Lady Banks roses (*Rosa banksiae* 'Alba Plena') draping over the edge of the retaining walls nearest the west façade. Tunnell was hired again in 2004 to oversee the removal of the 1960s-era kitchen garden and to return the space to its 1930s appearance. In 2005, diseased American boxwood along the west façade of Swan House were replaced with healthy ones, and the later addition of a gravel walk in front of the house was removed and planted with grass, as it had been during the Inman era. In 2009, the English boxwood (*Buxus sempervirens* 'Suffruticosa') in the boxwood garden, which was not well suited to this site, was replaced with *Buxus sinica* var. *insularis* 'Justin Brouwers', a cultivar of Korean boxwood.

Since 2014, major funding from the Goizueta Foundation and the generosity of other supporters has allowed additional improvements to be made to the Swan House gardens. Drains have been fixed, paths leveled, and over ten thousand pounds of limestone gravel spread in the boxwood garden; major repairs have been made to all the fountains; the lawn has been restored; once-buried curbstones

Formal boxwood garden with axial paths providing access from the sides

along the original driveway have been raised and reset; and a new gravel path has been added along the house's west façade to resolve the ongoing problem of grass suffering under heavy foot traffic.[28] In 2014, the historic gardens of the Atlanta History Center were named the Goizueta Gardens, honoring the Atlanta philanthropist Olga C. de Goizueta.[29] In November 2015, the Garden Conservancy funded a grant for the removal of five mature self-sown southern magnolias (*Magnolia grandiflora*) just outside the wall of the boxwood garden. They were crowding the crape myrtles, preventing their full growth and reducing their flowering, as well as that of the wisteria standards and peonies located within the garden. The grant funded the replacement of Shutze's redbud allée, most of which had reached the end of their typically short life spans, along the stone ramble leading from the boxwood garden to the woodlands beyond. The rediscovery of redbud stumps around the stone circle at the end of this path allowed for a more accurate representation of the original intent of Shutze's design. The woodlands surrounding Swan House were adopted by the Peachtree Garden Club in 1967 and today contain an extensive trail surrounded by trees, shrubs, ferns, and wildflowers native to the Georgia Piedmont.

With its exquisite, classically styled architecture and accompanying landscape, Swan House is one of the most notable and photographed landmarks in Atlanta. It was listed in the National Register of Historic Places and, in 1989, was named a protected Landmark Building by the Atlanta Urban Design Commission. The house, including the interiors and furnishings, underwent a four-year $5.4 million restoration, completed in 2014 and led by the Atlanta architectural firm of Lord Aeck Sargent. The house has been the site of the Swan House Ball, the Atlanta History Center's annual fund-raising gala, since 1985. It is frequently the backdrop for print and media advertising and was the setting for scenes in the 2013 film *The Hunger Games: Catching Fire* and the 2015 film *The Hunger Games: Mockingjay, Part 2*.

Today, the Inman estate makes up the bulk of the Atlanta History Center's grounds, which were expanded in the mid-1990s with the acquisition of adjacent properties. In addition to the Swan House

gardens, the Atlanta History Center interprets five others: the state's most comprehensive native plant garden, ten acres of Swan Woods as a protected Piedmont forest, an Asian plant garden, a modern garden featuring rhododendrons and azaleas, and the Smith Family Farm, showcasing the landscapes and vernacular gardens that rural Georgians sustained for pleasure and utility in the 1860s. In these six gardens, visitors can experience "a walk through time that highlights important changes in Atlanta's landscape, from the period preceding European settlement to the present day."[30]

Boxwood garden from a path, from *Garden History of Georgia*

Iconic arch, installed circa 1857, leading into the Academic Walk on the University of Georgia's North Campus

University of Georgia

North Campus, the President's House and Garden, and the Founders Memorial Garden

---

THE UNIVERSITY OF GEORGIA is the oldest and largest educational institution in the state. Among its many heritage sites are three significant historic landscapes: North Campus, the President's House and Garden, and the Founders Memorial Garden. Spanning almost 150 years, these landscapes represent a range of design styles in Georgia, from early nineteenth-century campus design and formal antebellum residential gardens to twentieth-century Colonial Revival gardens.

In 1785, the Georgia General Assembly passed a charter to incorporate the University of Georgia, the first college in the United States to be established by a state government, which helped set the framework for the American system of public higher education.[1] Because of other priorities, it was not until sixteen years later, in 1801, that a committee finally selected the site for the new college. The university's trustees chose 633 acres along the west banks of the North Oconee River among the gently rolling hills of northeastern Georgia, setting aside thirty-six and a half acres for the campus proper. An 1801 article in the *Augusta Chronicle* provides a detailed account of the land that was chosen:

> The site of the University is on the south side, and a half a mile from the river. On one side the land is cleared; the other is wood-land. On the cleared side are two ample orchards of apple and peach trees; forming artificial copses, between the site and the river, preferable to the common under growth of nature.
>
> What little vapour rises at any time from the river is always attracted by the opposite hills, towards the rising sun.
>
> About two hundred yards from the site, and at least three hundred feet above the level of the river, in the midst of an extensive bed of rock, issues a copious spring of excellent water; and, in its meanderings to the river, several others are discovered.[2]

The trustees named the place Athens, after the epicenter of classical culture in Greece.[3] Like many early American colleges and universities, the University of Georgia was intended to, among other goals, tame the wilderness into a pastoral landscape and transform it into a civic setting by erecting structures in architectural styles inspired by ancient Greece and Rome.[4] In Athens, these ideals had to work in concert with the existing lay of the land—the hills, valleys, and springs, along with the North Oconee River of the Georgia Piedmont.

By September 1801, the first university classes were being taught in a log structure. Five years later, the city of Athens was incorporated on land adjacent to the college, and by the 1820s, the town had grown into a thriving hub for textile manufacturing, commerce, and trade. By the early 1830s, it even had a popular tourist attraction, the university's lush four-acre botanical garden, once located on the campus's northwest edge. By midcentury, Athens was well known for its many stately homes and beautiful gardens. The town had become a cultural center in Georgia, attracting distinguished scholars and prominent persons.

NORTH CAMPUS

Et docere et rerum exquirere causas
(To teach and to inquire into the nature of things.)
—The University of Georgia's original motto, 1785

Of the over six hundred acres purchased on behalf of the university in 1801, almost all the land except for the thirty-six and a half acres allotted for the campus was sold or rented to provide income for the nascent college. Those thirty-six and a half acres comprised the majority of what is now known as North Campus, originally bounded by Broad Street (originally Front Street) on the north, Jackson Street on the east, Baldwin Street on the south, and Lumpkin Street on the west. It served as the university's campus for the next 100 years. The design for the campus had a kinship to that of Yale University in New Haven, Connecticut, which produced the University of Georgia's first two presidents.[5] The University of Georgia adopted the quadrangle plan, which was popular at the time for U.S. college campuses; it was characterized by a large rectangular lawn-filled courtyard strewn with pathways and trees and surrounded by buildings. Until the twentieth century, the university's quad contained only nine buildings.[6] Opened in 1806, Old College, originally called Franklin College, after Benjamin Franklin, was the first permanent building erected on campus; today it is the oldest building in Athens.[7] Located at the far edge of the quad, a good distance from Broad Street, it is a large three-story brick building based on Connecticut Hall at Yale University. Since the designers were unsure in which direction the campus would grow, they designed identical front and back facades. For the next fifteen years, Old College

housed the classrooms, dining hall, and dormitory for the entire study body.[8] Over succeeding decades, the landscape of North Campus was strongly defined by the construction of new buildings as the needs of the college expanded, as well as by the straight and diagonal pathways laid between the structures.[9]

The eight additional buildings erected during the 1800s flanked the sides of the quad—five on the west and three on the east—fronting the two main pathways that terminated at Old College. They displayed common architectural styles of the era.[10] On the west side was the Federal-style Demosthenian Hall, constructed in 1824, and the Greek Revival–style Chapel, completed in 1832. The Chapel quickly became a landmark on the campus and for the surrounding community. The west side was also home to New College, designed in the Federal style in 1832. Last were the Ivy Building, dating to 1832, a portion of which held the first permanent library, and the university's second library, dating to 1859. In 1903, these two structures were joined to create the Holmes-Hunter Academic Building, a Beaux Arts–style structure. On the east side of the quadrangle was Phi Kappa Hall, a Greek Revival–style structure with a temple-front façade. Completed in 1836, it was intentionally sited across the quadrangle from the home of the school's rival literary society, Demosthenian Hall. The east side was home to another Greek Revival–style building, the Lustrat House, a faculty house completed in 1847, as well as Waddell Hall, built in 1820 in the Federal style.

From 1801 until the early 1880s, the campus landscape was primarily utilitarian, made up of dirt paths

interspersed with existing native trees—hickories, oaks, and pines—which were retained for beauty and shade, as well as a few ornamental plantings. In 1830, ornamental trees were planted on the quadrangle, including tree of heaven (*Ailanthus altissima*), black locust, and chinaberry tree (*Melia azedarach*).[11] A wooden fence was constructed around a portion of the campus in 1833 to keep out livestock, which often roamed freely throughout the adjacent town.[12] The University of Georgia's most revered icon and traditional entrance, the Arch, was installed around 1857, and the adjoining ornamental fence, running along Broad Street, was added to the landscape around the same time.[13] Located on Broad Street at the terminus of College Avenue, Athens's main thoroughfare, both were made of cast iron at the local

foundry. Patterned after the Great Seal of Georgia, the famed Arch comprises three fluted columns, representing the state motto of "Wisdom, Justice, and Moderation," with a crosspiece and half-circle at the top. The Arch, which originally stood at sidewalk level, featured iron gates.[14]

An 1850-era lithograph depicts an idealized view of the campus from Broad Street, with formal pathways bisecting a manicured lawn and groupings of trees, all of which are set among grand buildings.[15] An 1875 photograph of the campus from Broad Street shows several impressive buildings, less formalized paths, denser tree cover, and much less polished grounds.[16] Regardless of the level of refinement, the campus remained in keeping with the quadrangle plan.

Northern end of the quadrangle, with Old College

Historic lithograph of the quadrangle, from *Garden History of Georgia*

OPPOSITE: Quadrangle, with a large lawn filled with trees and pathways and surrounded by buildings

Significant improvements came to the campus landscape around 1880 when Young Harris, a trustee of the university, took up the cause. In the summer of 1879, Harris engaged John Meeker, a wealthy local farmer, to address the "unsightly grounds" in front of Moore College, located on the western edge of the campus. Completed in 1876, Moore College housed the College of Agriculture and Mechanic Arts. For the new Second Empire–style building, according to a Chancellor's Report of 1881, Meeker designed "graceful terraces that admirably harmonize with, and set off with greater impressiveness, the architectural building that crowns their summit."[17] Meeker donated his time and talents, and Harris funded the plan. The series of terraces were constructed from Moore College diagonally to the intersection of Broad and Lumpkin Streets. Around the same time, Harris brought P. J. Berckmans, of Fruitland Nurseries in Augusta, to the college. Berckmans donated his services to draft and execute a plan to improve the grounds, and donated more than two hundred ornamental trees as well.[18] Additional trees were paid for or furnished by locals during this period.[19]

More alterations occurred behind Moore College as a result of the university's athletic programs.[20] The rough, weedy area behind the building served as a parade ground until the 1880s when it became a field for the university's first baseball and football teams. In 1892, it was the site of the first intercollegiate

football game in Georgia, in which the University of Georgia trounced Mercer University, 50–0.[21] In 1896, the area was named Herty Field for Charles H. Herty, a chemistry professor and the coach of the university's first football team.

Throughout the last two decades of the nineteenth century, the trustees continued to address problems on the campus. In 1882, they noted the dire need for a drainage system, as well as functional walkways to connect Moore College with the other buildings on the campus, since "students in winter have to bog their way between one Lecture room and another."[22] They noted that a small portion of the grounds still needed to be graded and sodded. These improvements were made in the 1880s. A groundskeeper position was established in 1892. Around that same year, three arc lamps were installed on the campus, and four tennis courts were put in near Broad Street.[23] A photograph from 1900 provides a look at the central quadrangle of North Campus, showing an impressive academic village with a formal quad containing wide vistas of lawn, diagonal and straight walkways, and groupings of trees and ornamental shrubs, all bordered by stately buildings.[24]

The first half of the twentieth century further defined the North Campus as expansion beyond the original borders became imperative to the institution's growth. With the assistance of alumni, the college repurchased most of the land it had sold in the early 1800s, along with additional property, ultimately amassing more than a thousand acres by 1930. Between 1900 and 1949, over a dozen buildings were erected on the North Campus. As a consequence, additional quads, or open spaces, were developed. Named for Allen D. Candler, Georgia's governor from 1898 to 1902, Candler Hall was constructed in the Exotic style in 1901. The same year, North Campus became home to Denmark Hall, which served as the campus dining hall. The first LeConte Hall was built in 1905. It was renamed Meigs Hall in 1937 in honor of the university's second president, Joseph Meigs. In 1904, Terrell Hall was constructed in the Beaux Arts style on the basement remnants of Science Hall, a Richardsonian Romanesque building that was destroyed by fire in 1903. The Science Hall cornerstone was recycled as the cornerstone for Terrell Hall. The first fireproof building came to the campus in 1904 with the university's third library,

Holmes-Hunter
Academic building

which became home to the Georgia Museum of Art after World War II and now serves as the Administration Building.

Other additions to the landscape included a sundial donated by the Class of 1908 to mark the location of Toombs' Oak, a majestic oak that once stood in front of the Chapel. When the tree fell in 1908, the sundial was placed there to serve as a symbol of one of the university's most endearing legends, the story of Robert Toombs. As a young and boisterous student, Toombs was dismissed from the college, only to return decades later to give a great oration under

the oak tree, drawing students and faculty from far and wide. The legend says that the oak was struck by lightning on the day of Toombs's death. Students still share the story of Robert Toombs today. In 1914, twelve cast-iron lampposts with electric lights, called the "White Way," were installed along the sidewalk in front of the Academic Building, Demosthenian Hall, and the Chapel.[25]

In 1913, Peabody Hall was erected for the School of Education. Designed by the notable Georgia architect Neel Reid, a large Neoclassical building called the Commercial-Journalism Building (now called Brooks Hall) was completed in 1928, housing the School of Commerce and the Henry Grady School of Journalism for many years.[26] Joe Brown Hall, a Georgian-style building, was constructed in 1932 and named for Joseph E. Brown, Georgia's governor from 1857 to 1861. The same year saw the completion of Hirsh Hall for the School of Law, a Georgian-style building topped with a cupola containing the scales of justice. In 1938, Baldwin and Park Halls were erected, as was the second LeConte Hall, named for the notable nineteenth-century scientists John and Joseph LeConte, both graduates of the university. Gilbert Hall, which served as the campus infirmary from 1945 until 1997, was built in 1942, and the current façade was added in 1975.

Between 1950 and 2000, only five major buildings were added to North Campus, including the Greek Revival–style Ilah Dunlap Little Memorial Library (commonly referred to as the Main Library) in 1952.[27] In 1957, Morris Hall was built as a student residential hall. Named for the former University of Georgia president Harmon W. Caldwell, the seven-story Caldwell Hall was built in 1981. It held both general classrooms and the College of Environment and Design until 2012, when the College relocated to the renovated Visual Arts Building, completed in 1960 and located on Jackson Street. Dean Rusk Hall, named for the U.S. secretary of state in the Kennedy and Johnson administrations, was erected in 1996. The following year saw the birth of Sanford Hall, the 38,000-square-foot home of the business college. The North Campus acquired a 1,200-space parking garage in 1999 called the North Campus Parking Deck, located between Jackson and Thomas Streets on axis with the east side of Old College.

Other key facets of the North Campus landscape today include three distinct gardens—Founders Memorial Garden, the Presidents Club Garden, and the Latin American Ethnobotanical Garden—as well as the Hubert B. Owens Fountain and the resurrected Herty Field. Located behind Old College on the north end of the quad near the Main Library, the Presidents Club Garden was created in 1973 to honor high-level donors to the university. Funded by the Athens businessman Elmer Schacht, the garden has a brick plaza surrounded by ornamental shrubs and seasonal flowers; a brick wall features plaques that commemorate the donors.[28]

In 1989, an octagonal flower bed was removed and an octagonal fountain was installed on an open brick plaza on the east side of Old College in honor of Hubert Bond Owens. The Hubert B. Owens Fountain memorializes the man who pioneered landscape architecture in Georgia and served on the University of Georgia's faculty for forty-five years. During his tenure, he founded the Landscape Architecture Department, was the first dean of the School of Environmental Design, and was the primary landscape designer for the North Campus. Owens also designed the Founders Memorial Garden, which honors the twelve women who in 1891 established the Ladies' Garden Club of Athens.[29]

The Latin American Ethnobotanical Garden opened in 1998, adjacent to Baldwin Hall. Managed

Holmes-Hunter building and the Academic Walk, from *Garden History of Georgia*

Herty Field with
cascading fountain

Expanded campus to
the south

OPPOSITE: Fountain memorializing the landscape architect
and faculty member Hubert Bond Owens

by the Latin American and Caribbean Studies Institute, it focuses on the field of ethnobotany, the study of the relationship between people and plants. Constructed of recycled materials, this multilevel garden includes over 150 culturally significant plants from Latin America and the Caribbean and serves as a place for research, teaching, and community outreach.[30] In 1999, Herty Field, which was once used as a football field and parade ground, was converted from a parking lot to an open lawn space and enhanced with a grand fountain.[31]

The original design and stately old buildings of the North Campus, along with its landscape of plentiful trees and ornamentals scenic vistas, has produced one of the most beautiful campuses in the United States. Because of its significance, the North Campus was listed in the National Register of Historic Places in 1972. Although some changes have occurred to the landscape over time, the quadrangle plan dating to the university's inception has remained largely intact. The iconic Arch still welcomes students, and many trees grace the North Campus, such as black walnut, elm, gingko, green ash, pecan, red maple, southern magnolia, tulip poplar, and an array of oaks—black, chestnut,

laurel, pin, scarlet, northern red, Oglethorpe, southern red, water, and willow.[32] A self-guided walking tour of the trees was developed in the 1990s as part of the Campus Arboretum initiative. Landscape preservation efforts are ongoing, including the preservation of the old lampposts in 2014, work on the Arch in 2015, and a turf restoration project on two sections of lawn on the original quad in 2016.

The University of Georgia is a comprehensive land- and sea-grant institution with an enrollment of over 36,000 undergraduate and graduate students and a workforce of over 10,000. In 2016, it was ranked twenty-first among public universities in the *U.S. News & World Report*'s "Best Colleges" edition.[33] Of its seventeen schools and colleges, four pertain to the study of the land: the College of Agriculture and Environmental Sciences, the Daniel B. Warnell School of Forestry and Natural Resources, the College of Environment and Design, and the Eugene P. Odum School of Ecology.[34] Although the main campus now contains 463 buildings on 762 acres, along with many greenspaces, the landscape of the North Campus remains the historic heart of the University of Georgia.

PRESIDENT'S HOUSE AND GARDEN

The large box garden has a particularly dignified design carrying heavy plantings of magnolia, cedar of Lebanon, cherry laurel and tree box.—*Garden History of Georgia*

Although established as a college town, Athens can trace its growth and prosperity to its role in the cotton trade.[35] This fall-line community was located in proximity to numerous cotton plantations. Enterprising businessmen built mills in Athens, and the coming of the railroad brought wider trade opportunities. In the years before the Civil War, Athens attracted a fairly affluent population, and many residents built houses that reflected their positions. The railroad contractor John Thomas Grant was one of them. In the late 1850s, he built an impressive Greek Revival–style residence on Prince Avenue, one of the town's most attractive residential areas, and it later became home to the presidents of the University of Georgia. Its landscape is distinctive: an antebellum parterre

town garden, one of the few remaining in the state, and a rear yard designed by Hubert Bond Owens, who was eventually honored with the title of dean emeritus by the university he served so long and well.

Around 1855, Grant, who owned a plantation southwest of Athens in Walton County, purchased lots on Prince Avenue to build a town house for his wife, Martha Cobb Jackson, and himself. A small Greek Revival cottage on the property was moved, and in its place, Grant built what has been described as "possibly the most elegant Greek Revival house left in Georgia."[36] Completed in 1858, this grand two-story frame building with raised basement is distinguished by a two-story colonnade. Fourteen fluted Corinthian columns resting on brick pillars spaced along the wide porch surround the front and sides of the building and support the roofline's classical entablature. On the first level, the five-bay façade has a central entrance with transoms and sidelights; directly overhead and complementing this entry is a doorway with transoms and sidelights opening onto a balcony. The roof, like those of many Piedmont houses of its date and style, has no pediment.

When building such an impressive residence in this period, it was a common practice to plant an elaborate ornamental garden. The relationship between the house and garden usually resulted in a formal appearance that emphasized structure, organization, and control.[37] In *The Early Architecture of Georgia*, Frederick Nichols describes the Piedmont's Greek Revival landscape: "The site of the big houses of up-country Georgia was of paramount importance. In general, formal gardens were laid out on the southern front since the houses usually were oriented in that direction. Box hedges often defined the flower beds, and in the 1840's and 1850's they assumed the free-form shapes that characterized Victorian gardens. . . . The rear, or north side, was given over to kitchens, offices, service buildings, and slave quarters."[38]

Nichols's overview aptly describes Grant's property. The formal front garden, south of the house, was divided by a central walkway that led from the property's entrance to the house's front steps. The walk was flanked by symmetrical cutwork parterres. Both parterres featured a central circle surrounded by beds of varying geometric patterns. The box-bordered beds, according to James Cothran's *Gardens and Historic Plants of the Antebellum South*, contained, among other plants, "bulbs, peonies, iris, daylilies,

Antebellum Grant-Hill-White-Bradshaw House, with monumental gingko tree

Greek Revival–style house
and formal landscape

violets."[39] Pathways filled with sand were found throughout the yard.[40] Cothran mentions a fence on the garden's southern edge and a hedge enclosure on the east and west sides.[41] This garden was designed to be seen by anyone looking down from the house or strolling through the grounds. Although the garden's designer is unknown, oral tradition credits "an itinerant Irish gardener."[42]

The grounds behind the house were arranged in keeping with the rural character of the area, where large houses on large lots were the norm, and the structures and agricultural features needed to sustain them were part of the landscape.[43] The rear yard included not only the cottage that had been moved but also a "barn, carriage house and stable buildings" in addition to "orchards, vegetable garden and pasturage."[44]

Only a few short years after the house was built, the nation went to war. After completing his service in the Confederacy, Grant moved to Atlanta and sold the Athens property to Benjamin H. Hill. A well-known state politician, Hill was married

to Caroline Holt. Their son, Charles, eventually bought the Prince Street residence and owned it until the mid-1880s. Soon after, James White, a prominent Athens banker and businessman, and his wife, Julia Ashton White, moved into the house. The property remained in the hands of the White family until 1949.

The Whites' daughter, Rosena, who married William F. Bradshaw, was active in the Garden Club of Georgia, and the Prince Street property reflected her interests. She carefully tended to the formal parterre garden. Its boxwood beds and the plants in them, according to *Garden History of Georgia*'s description in 1933, would have been a magnificent sight: "Filling the beds are cape jasmine, evergreen bush (euonymus), Mahonia aquifolia, winter jasmine, yucca, cassinas, pittosporum, tea and tea olive, flowering quince, Persian and European lilac, forsythia, althea, weigela, sweet syringa, sweet shrub, snow ball, bridal wreath spirea, ribbon grass, roses and bulbs."[45] When leaving the front garden, guests walked under "arched openings through cedar hedges" that led to

Large boxwood parterre with central walk

Rear courtyard garden

Panoramic view of the large rear lawn

OPPOSITE: Colonial Revival–style rose garden designed by Hubert Bond Owens

"tree planted lawns" on the east and west sides of the house.[46] *Garden History of Georgia* states that many of the plants in the front and side yards were "original" or "careful replacements."[47]

Rosena Bradshaw focused her attention on the area behind the house as well. There in the old service yard stood the early Greek Revival cottage, along with a kitchen building and a well.[48] In 1927, Bradshaw began converting the rear acreage's rural landscape into "a beautiful stretch of lawn and garden."[49] What had once been a farm-like setting eventually contained "a rose walk, arbors, shady bowers, and terraced flower beds."[50] To achieve this, she used the services of Craig Orr, a well-known garden designer in Athens.[51] A picket fence surrounded much of the property.[52]

As an acknowledgment of the achievements in her own gardens and in her club work, Rosena Bradshaw was named, in the late 1930s, cochair of the Garden Club of Georgia's committee in charge of the proposed development of Founders Memorial Garden at the university. Before her death in 1941, she was able to ensure that the project was underway.[53] During World War II, Julia B. Rahr, the daughter of William and Rosena Bradshaw, lived in the house while her husband served in the military. The Bradshaw family's stewardship of the property ended in 1949 when the University of Georgia Foundation, in cooperation with the Bradley Foundation of Columbus, Georgia, acquired the Prince Street house and its grounds. The university planned to adapt the residence to its new use as the

Pierced brick wall and entrance gate separating the rose garden from the surrounding lawn

home of the school's president and to its role as a highly visible symbol of the university. A committee of ten was formed to plan the improvements to the house as well as to select the furnishings; another committee, consisting only of Hubert Owens, was appointed to prepare the grounds.[54]

When work finally began on the property, the front garden was in need of attention. Its basic design, however, remained intact. The garden's appearance, along with that of the house, was important for supporting the site's new purpose and the increased number of visitors it would receive. Owens's work in the front garden respected the site's historic integrity. He removed and replaced dead plant material

and installed gravel walks between the beds and in the central walkway.[55]

Owens redesigned the landscape behind the house "to function as a garden for the president of a growing university."[56] This space was to be used for entertaining large groups of faculty, students, parents, and other visitors. About his work, Owens said, "So I had the gardens in the central area at the rear of the residence transferred to the east and west sides [of the back yard]. The rear gardens were replaced with an expansive lawn, extending from the rear portico steps to the north boundary."[57] Behind the house on the lot's east boundary, he installed a new Colonial Revival rose garden with a sundial at

Sundial and axial paths in the rose garden

Formal walkway leading to the rear of the property

Gazebo at the rear of the garden

Over the years the landscape has continued to be adapted to contemporary needs while still reflecting its history. American boxwood has replaced English box in the front garden. A brick walk with brick edging now leads from the picket fence at the entrance of the garden to the main house. Two large magnolias thrive in the parterres. Outside the fence directly in front of the property stands a large gingko tree, a local landmark known for its brilliant fall color. The lawn on the west side of the house is now a parking area, landscaped with Encore azaleas and a cherry tree. On the house's east side is a grass lawn with trees. The Greek Revival–style cottage and another historic outbuilding face each other on the east and west sides of the rear courtyard. Between them is a grass panel surrounded by a brick walk with raised brick planters, two of which contain large crape myrtles. From there the yard opens onto the large manicured lawn. On the east side of the property near the historic cottage is the former rose garden, its beds now filled largely with herbaceous perennials. *Camellia sasanqua* and *Camellia japonica* still provide autumn and winter color along the brick walk leading to the stone terrace and an early twentieth-century gazebo.[62] The rear yard and west walk contain red oaks, native azaleas, dogwoods, maple, anise, cedar of Lebanon, willow oak, spirea, and yaupon holly, among other shrubs and trees. The property is well maintained by the university's Facilities Management Division.

The first university president to live in the house was J. C. Rogers.[63] Since then, all the school's presidents have stayed there for at least part of their tenure. The President's House, listed in the National Register of Historic Places in 1972, represents the University of Georgia. The house and its five acres are the setting for numerous special events. Luncheons, dinners, and receptions are held here, many celebrating student achievements, recognizing faculty and staff, and hosting university-associated groups and individuals. Over time, and as an understanding of the grounds has evolved, the property's significance has increased, serving "as an important example of the union of architecture and landscape architecture within the context of the Greek Revival period in Georgia's piedmont."[64]

its center and surrounding geometric beds.[58] From there, a camellia walk with plants designed to bloom during football season led to a stone-terraced area, probably from the Bradshaw years, where "annuals, perennials, and bulbs" were planted.[59] On the west side of the rear lawn, Owens designed a walk of azaleas with evergreens and flowering shrubs as background. At the property's northernmost boundary, space was set aside for a vegetable and fruit garden.[60] Owens incorporated a rear courtyard behind the main house, installed brick walks throughout the grounds, and paved the drive leading to the residence.[61]

FOUNDERS MEMORIAL GARDEN

It is felt that the most appropriate memorial would be a living garden, a place of beauty and inspiration which would reflect the vitality and growth of the garden club movement. If this garden could also serve an educational need it would fulfill the highest possible ideal and would become a moving force for the future as well as a satisfying tribute to the past.
—Hubert Bond Owens, *Garden Gateways*, 1939

Located on the University of Georgia's North Campus, Founders Memorial Garden was constructed between 1939 and 1950 to commemorate the twelve women who in 1891 established the Ladies' Garden Club of Athens, America's first organized garden club, and fallen soldiers from World War II.[65] Built around an antebellum house, the two-and-a-half-acre Colonial Revival–style garden contains formal rooms and informal naturalistic landscapes.[66]

It was designed by Hubert Bond Owens, Professors Brooks Wigginton and Frederick W. G. Peck, and their students in partnership with the Garden Club of Georgia. In 1972, the garden and the house were listed together in the National Register of Historic Places.[67] Managed by the College of Environment and Design, today the garden serves as a living laboratory for students, a social gathering place for those in the community, and a destination for visitors to Athens.

The Colonial Revival garden, one of the most popular styles of the twentieth century, is a distinctively American creation. Rooted in the success of the 1876 Centennial International Exhibition in Philadelphia, the Colonial Revival movement was driven by Americans' widespread interest in their

Sunken perennial garden and its manicured lawn

Founders Memorial Garden, featuring formal garden rooms and a naturalistic landscape

colonial-era history, coupled with nostalgia for simpler times and a desire to escape industrialization.[68] Popular in the late nineteenth and early twentieth centuries, the style reflects a patriotic mindfulness and appreciation. Influenced by early efforts to restore colonial gardens like those at Colonial Williamsburg, Colonial Revival gardens were a departure from the outlandish bedding-out schemes in Victorian-era gardens and from the large estate gardens of the Country Place era. Most prevalent in the eastern United States, the style featured small well-ordered symmetrical gardens containing boxwood and old-fashioned perennials and roses.[69] Colonial Revival gardens encompassed both formal and informal landscapes. Formal rooms, such as a walled-parterre garden, a sunken garden, or terrace garden, were placed close to the house and linked by a strong axial plan. Informal landscapes, located

farther from the house, were naturalistic: groupings of canopy trees and flowering shrubs with ground covers and bulbs beneath them. Other common elements found in Colonial Revival gardens included arbors, clipped boxwood hedges, fountains, pergolas, stone walls, sundials, and brick walkways.[70] Antiques and aged materials were often used to add a sense of days past.[71] The Colonial Revival style was made popular in America by landscape architects such as Charles Gillette, Alden Hopkins, Ellen Biddle Shipman, and Arthur Shurcliff, as well as Hubert Bond Owens in Georgia.

Founders Memorial Garden got its start in 1936 when delegates to the Garden Club of Georgia convention voted to establish a fund for a memorial to honor the founding of the Ladies' Garden Club of Athens, whose fiftieth anniversary was approaching. In January 1939, Hubert Owens, who had worked with the Garden Club of Georgia since 1928, proposed that the memorial be in the form of a garden shared between the University of Georgia and the Garden Club of Georgia. Owens, along with the faculty and students in the Landscape Architecture department, would provide the plans and supervise the building; the Garden Club of Georgia would finance the effort; and the university would provide

funds for ongoing maintenance. Mattie Hatcher Flournoy, president of the Garden Club of Georgia, appointed Rosena Bradshaw as chair of the Founders Memorial Garden Committee, with Nina Scudder as cochair; both were members of the Ladies' Garden Club of Athens.[72] The timing was ideal for both parties because in a few months the antebellum house, also located on the site selected for the garden, was

Clipped boxwood parterre enclosed by a white picket fence behind the antebellum Lumpkin House

to become the permanent home of the university's Department of Landscape Architecture. With this initiative, the Garden Club of Georgia became the first of the National Council of State Garden Clubs to undertake a garden development project.[73]

Founders Memorial Garden was created around an antebellum house, today known as the Lumpkin House, and its adjacent buildings on an irregularly shaped sloping parcel. Constructed around 1860, the Greek Revival–style two-story house, as well as a smokehouse and kitchen building—all close to one another and all made of red brick—were located on the most heavily wooded portion of the North Campus, near the corner of Lumpkin and Bocock Streets.[74] An 1894 campus map shows asymmetrical formal gardens in front of the house.[75] The house served as a residence for professors and their families for many decades; in 1898, it became a student dining hall.[76] In the 1910s, it housed student-athletes, because of its proximity to Herty Field, and in 1920 it became the home of Mary Lyndon, the university's first dean of women. Following her death, it served as the headquarters for Phi Mu, the university's first sorority, until 1928.[77] It was a women's dormitory until the mid-1930s, when it was used for classes by the Biology and Sociology Departments.[78] The university's Landscape Architecture Department moved into the antebellum house in 1939.

A preliminary plan for Founders Memorial Garden published in *Garden Gateways* in March 1939 showed Owens's Colonial Revival design.[79] He envisioned a series of formal areas—a courtyard garden, a boxwood garden, a terrace garden, a perennial garden, and a pedestrian forecourt—that he synthesized by using strong axial connections.[80] The formal gardens were harmonized by informal areas to the north and south. Owens designed the informal spaces to combine the existing mature hardwoods with extensive underplantings of smaller ornamental trees, woody ornamental shrubs, ground covers, bulbs, and herbaceous plantings.[81]

The first areas to be installed were the boxwood and courtyard gardens. An article in the May 1940 issue of *Garden Gateways* describes the progress: "So far, a courtyard garden of cut stone and brick together with a Garden Club of Georgia museum and trophy room, remodeled from an antebellum smokehouse,

Lush plantings in the perennial borders of the sunken garden

have been finished and to the latter a bay window has been added which overlooks the newly constructed boxwood garden at the rear."[82] The courtyard garden, which was shaded by a large oak, contained white azaleas at the corners and a ground cover of mondo grass. Carolina jessamine and clematis vines were "trained over the old pierced brick courtyard walls."[83] Gates, nestled between gardenias, led from the courtyard to the boxwood garden, a circular parterre with a sundial at its center. A white picket fence enclosed the garden, and brick walkways delineated the space. The patterns featured in the boxwood parterre were "a conventionalized Cherokee Rose, a watermelon, a peach, and a cotton boll."[84] The four outer flower beds contained old-fashioned plants such as asters, bleeding hearts, chrysanthemums, jonquils, lilies, phlox, and pinks.[85]

The terrace and perennial gardens, located just south of the boxwood garden, had been largely completed by 1941. The terrace garden, which held a large shade tree, was separated from the boxwood garden by a brick retaining wall and a white picket fence. A low brick wall with limestone coping enclosed the garden, whose floor was composed of river gravel. Brick-edged free-form beds along the sides contained two crape myrtles, two boxwoods, and a dogwood with a ground cover of periwinkle and "1,000 Emperor and Empress narcissus bulbs."[86] The terrace garden provided a dramatic view of the

OPPOSITE: Circular parterre featuring cutwork of a peach, a watermelon, a cotton boll, and a Cherokee rose

Oval pool at the southern end of the perennial garden

perennial garden, which was five feet below. The perennial garden was reached by twin flights of brick and stone steps. An ornamental iron railing formed one end of the garden, and the opposite end held a large oval pool with limestone coping placed on axis with two ornamental iron gates.[87] The 125-foot-long garden was surrounded by a serpentine wall made of old brick; a large manicured lawn at its center had a flower bed on either side.[88] Owens called for the use of "new varieties of irises, peonies, and other spring flowering perennials, chrysanthemums and asters in the six-foot borders in this garden."[89] He also outlined the use of "specimen boxwoods, crape myrtles, tea olive, fig and ivy vines and water lilies" in the planning scheme.[90] To complete the enclosure,

he specified that nine large southern magnolias be planted around its perimeters.[91]

Because of a shortage of labor and materials during World War II, progress in Founders Memorial Garden slowed; however, maintenance and some additional planting in the existing boxwood, courtyard, terrace, and perennial gardens continued.[92] In February 1942, the Georgia State Nurseryman's Association and Landscape Contractors voted to donate plants for the project.[93] In 1943, a twin flight of brick steps with wrought-iron railings replaced neglected wooden steps at the entrance to the Lumpkin House.[94] In April 1945, Brooks Wigginton, a new instructor in the landscape architecture program, drafted a plan to extend a historic iron fence and retaining walls along the property's west boundary, which was completed later that year.[95]

Also in 1945, Louise Neely, president of the Garden Club of Georgia, proposed a living memorial garden in the form of an arboretum dedicated to the fallen soldiers in World War II.[96] Owens and the University of Georgia approved the suggestion. Under Owens's supervision, Wigginton and a new generation of postwar students created the plans to turn one-and-a-half acres on the north and south sides of the Lumpkin House into an arboretum.[97] The arboretum was designed to serve as a place not only of beauty but also of instruction for future landscape architects and horticulturists.[98]

The south part of the arboretum featured a group of forty-one *Camellia japonica* and three *Camellia sasanqua*, donated by Jeff Smith, a university alumnus, and his wife in 1949. The camellias, which lent a gradation of color, were thoughtfully placed beneath twenty mature oak trees.[99] The area contained a central lawn with masses of Kurume azaleas, bulbs, ground covers, stewartias, and gordonias, an appropriate accompaniment to the camellia collection.[100] The northern section of the arboretum was described in an October 1945 issue of *Garden Gateways*: "Most of the undeveloped area is wooded and the largest portion of it lies on a hillside where there are four existing terraces with large oak trees and a few dogwoods. Plans call for this Living Memorial to be developed into a small arboretum where 300 different species of plants will be grouped together and arranged so as to create quiet walks and pleasant vistas. Steps will connect the terraces at various points and the trees and shrubs will be labeled with both botanical and common names."[101] The northern arboretum contained a small commemorative fountain with a small tablet inscribed with the following: "In Memory of Those Who Gave Much and Those Who Gave All. 1941–1945." All the work was completed by the early 1950s. In 1954, the Garden Club of Georgia, on the occasion of its twenty-fifth anniversary, was awarded the National Council of State Garden Clubs' Silver Seal Award in recognition of the Founders Memorial Garden.[102]

The 1960s and 1970s brought new challenges to the Founders Memorial Garden. Conditions around the garden changed significantly as a result of increased

enrollment at the university.[103] New facilities were erected to the east, and large parking lots were added across Lumpkin Street. A large pedestrian corridor across Lumpkin Street from the parking lots led to a major increase in foot traffic through the garden. The turf grass around the perennial garden pool was lost because of compaction; it was replaced with cutstone paving. Additionally, drainage was a problem, and the large magnolia canopy had begun to shade out many of the border plantings in the perennial garden.

In 1988, the Founders Memorial Garden Advisory Committee—a consortium of University of Georgia alumni, faculty members, and staff and a representative from the Garden Club of Georgia—was

Statue and twin flights of steps leading to the terrace garden

Arbor with Lady Banks roses above the entrance to the courtyard

established to assist with design, management, and financial matters related to the garden.[104] The committee contacted Dan Franklin, a landscape architect and alumnus, who designed, pro bono, an improvement plan to revitalize the border plantings in the perennial garden. Work was completed later that year.[105] Problems with the plantings were further addressed in 1990 when the university heavily pruned the magnolias, eventually replacing them with a slow-growing variety. That same year, a deteriorated slate walk in the south arboretum was replaced with granite cobblestones. Following the death of Hubert Bond Owens in 1989, an arbor was built in his memory at the western end of the perennial garden, funded by the Garden Club of Georgia and completed in 1991.[106]

Other initiatives have been undertaken to guide the garden into the future. In March 2009, a formal mission statement for the Founders Memorial Garden cited a twofold purpose: "1) to commemorate the first U. S. Garden Club, its members, and those notable individuals who created and/or continue to preserve the property's buildings and gardens; and 2) to provide a resource for the study and teaching of plant material, garden design and management, historic buildings and landscapes."[107] In 2014, the Jaeger Company created a management plan to guide ongoing maintenance.[108] Two permanent staff positions were created to oversee the garden: a director, currently David B. Nichols, and a curator, currently Maureen O'Brien, both of whom also teach at the College of Environment and Design. In addition to support from the university's Grounds Department, landscape architecture students help care for the garden, working under the supervision of the garden's director and curator.

The Lumpkin House remained home to the Department of Landscape Architecture until 1956, when it relocated to the renovated Denmark Hall. From 1963 to 1998, the house served as state headquarters for the Garden Club of Georgia. Today, the Lumpkin House's first floor functions as a classroom and conference space, and the second floor houses emeritus faculty offices and the Environmental Ethics Certificate program. The former kitchen outbuilding contains the office of the garden's curator,

Part of the memorial arboretum garden north of the Lumpkin House

Peaceful solitude of the arboretum in the center of the university

and the smokehouse is still a memorial to the twelve women who established the Ladies' Garden Club of Athens.

Today, Founders Memorial Garden's formal and informal landscapes remain much as they were when they were created between 1939 and the 1950s. In 1999, the garden was named one of the top 100 landscapes of significance in the United States by the American Society of Landscape Architects, and it received the honorable Blue Star Memorial designation by the Garden Club of Georgia in 2015. Just as it was conceived of over seventy-five years ago by Hubert Bond Owens and the Garden Club of Georgia, the Founders Memorial Garden is a vital teaching resource for the University of Georgia. Its over three hundred varieties of historic trees, shrubs, and perennials serve as a laboratory for studying landscape design and horticulture. The site also serves as a public garden for the enjoyment of faculty, students, and visitors.

These three historic places are physical reminders of the rich history of the city of Athens and the University of Georgia. The North Campus reflects the intentions of the university's founders and those who spearheaded its subsequent growth. The President's House and Garden stand as a testament to early business leaders who helped Athens prosper and to those who have served as presidents of the university over the last six decades. And the Founders Memorial Garden celebrates the legacy of the women in the state who have long advocated for the value of gardens as places of beauty, learning, tranquility, and necessity.

OPPOSITE: Along the stone walkway in the arboretum garden is a fountain and plaque dedicated to fallen soldiers.

Herringbone brick walk bordered by a triple hedge of boxwood and cherry laurel at Valley View

Valley View

LOCATED IN scenic rolling hills in the vicinity of Cartersville in northwestern Georgia, Valley View is home to a vernacular Greek Revival–style historic house with original interiors and furnishings, historic outbuildings, a working farm with fertile lands, and one of the finest intact antebellum landscapes in the Southeast.[1] Overlooking the Etowah River Valley, the property exhibits a rare level of historical integrity; minimal changes have occurred since the antebellum period. The stewardship of five generations of the same family has made Valley View an exceptional beacon of history amid an area in Bartow County undergoing increased growth and development pressure in the twenty-first century.

Native Americans lived in the rich plains of the Etowah River Valley for thousands of years before white settlement came to the area.[2] In the first half of the nineteenth century, enticed by plentiful natural resources and fertile land made available in the land lottery of 1832, settlers formed several small towns and communities along the Etowah River. In 1832, Cass County was established, and Cassville was designated its seat the following year. In the late 1830s, Cass County's population rapidly expanded as Georgia reaffirmed the Treaty of New Echota, in which the Cherokees ceded all of their lands to the United States, and a statewide economic boom attracted farmers and planters from other states, particularly South Carolina. Beginning in the late 1830s through the 1850s, a series of plantations and farms were developed along the lower Etowah River in the fertile river valley. Completion of the Western and Atlantic Railroad by 1850 provided local farmers and planters with greater access to state and regional markets and helped them maintain and expand their landholdings. With the increase in cotton prices in the 1850s, farmers and planters devoted less acreage to corn and livestock and more to cash crops such as cotton and wheat. In 1861, the county was renamed Bartow County in honor of Colonel Francis S. Bartow, the

A large brick house was built and a dignified formal garden laid out. . . . Passing the entrance gates one drives through a quarter of a mile of lovely woods before reaching the house, which overlooks a wide valley. The garden's most distinguished feature is triple hedges bordering the central walk, formed of Carolina cherries and box.

—*Garden History of Georgia*

Antebellum Greek Revival–style house and the boxwood parterre gardens

first Georgia officer to fall on the field at Manassas, Virginia.[3] Union troops destroyed Cassville in 1864, and Cartersville became the county seat in 1867.

Those who prospered in the years before the war built sophisticated houses and formal gardens. The masterpiece among these fine plantations was Valley View. In the early 1840s, James Caldwell Sproull, a successful planter from the Abbeville district of South Carolina, established a large cotton plantation on approximately two thousand acres along the Etowah River.[4] James and his wife, Eliza Marshall Sproull, likely named their plantation Valley View for the phenomenal vista it offered of the rolling terrain of the Etowah River Valley below and the low-peaked mountains in the distance. The grounds encompassing the plantation contained large pastures, groves of native trees, and cultivated fields of

cotton and wheat.[5] The Sproulls also bred horses, sheep, and cattle.[6]

The exterior and interior of the Sproulls' commanding vernacular house indicate the influence of antebellum plantation homes of the Carolinas and Virginia. The exterior was designed in the Greek Revival style, popular at the time in the South, where it was well suited to the desire of the wealthy class to build fine houses that reflected its status. According to family records, the house, which was placed on a bluff above the river overlooking the broad valley below, was erected over a seven-year period, completed around 1848.[7] The house is composed of a two-story brick I-house with two one-story brick wings extending perpendicularly toward the rear. Ionic columns create a majestic portico, underneath which is a wide porch that wraps around the sides and a second-floor gallery. The structure has few common walls, and there is no access between the front portion of the house and the two wings. A two-story brick wall extends from the sides of the I-house onto the portico, creating a brick façade to hide the adjoining one-story wings.[8] At the rear, the wings form a U-shaped courtyard. Wrapping around this courtyard is a square-columned gallery onto which the rooms at the back of the house open. In addition to the Ionic columns, architectural details including the heavy entablatures with framing pilasters around the first-floor doors and windows and the second-floor door onto the gallery, suggest the Sproulls' stature.[9] It is likely that the master builders of Valley View were Glazner and Clayton, who constructed the nearby Stilesboro Academy in 1859 and other buildings in the area.[10]

Like other planters, the Sproulls paid great attention to the interior and the furnishings, displaying the family's prominence. James brought a German cabinetmaker named Vitenger, known as "Mr. Witey," to Valley View from South Carolina. Vitenger, who lived with the family, created the staircase, wood-grained paneling, and door trim for the handsome central hallway, as well as woodwork throughout the house. Vitenger made much of the furniture, including bedsteads, cabinets, tables, a washstand, and a crib.[11] Rebecca Sproull Fouché, the daughter of James and Eliza Sproull, explains in her memoirs the family's relationship with Vitenger: "He had a bedroom, a workshop, a place to keep and dry his lumber, and always a seat at our table."[12] Lumber from walnut trees on the property was used for some of the interior woodwork and furniture.

Portions of interior walls in the house were adorned with milk-based decorative painting, including painted wainscot paneling; *faux bois*, or wood graining, on the trim, doors, and plaster wainscots; and *faux marbre*, or marbling, on a fireplace mantel. This trompe l'oeil, or "deceive the eye," decorative painting, was popular in the antebellum period as part of the Federal and Greek Revival styles, as a way to make lesser woods like pine resemble more expensive types like maple, mahogany, and oak. At Valley View, the pine doors are grained in a maple-combed pattern, with the trim elaborately painted to look like oak graining on the casing. Two backbands

painted to look like an opaque cherry on the inner band and walnut on the outer band create a pleasing tricolor pattern. This pattern was used on the wainscots, baseboards, and staircase trim and on the panels of the staircase landing.[13]

As was typical of antebellum plantations, the outbuildings erected closest to the main house defined the work yard.[14] At Valley View, two brick outbuildings, a smokehouse and a two-room detached kitchen and weaving room, both dating to the late 1840s, were located behind the main house.[15] Farther to the west were slave quarters.[16] By 1860, according to the Cass County census, the Sproulls owned thirty-seven enslaved African Americans.[17] These structures were likely occupied by domestic slaves who labored in the nearby work yard, outbuildings, and main house, preparing and preserving food, cooking, washing clothing, sewing, weaving, and performing other household duties.[18] The location of the slave quarters for those who worked in the fields is unknown.

Landscape plan of Valley View by P. Thornton Marye, from *Garden History of Georgia*

Gated walkway leading to the front entry, dividing the parterres

Family oral history indicates that enslaved laborers were the ones primarily responsible for constructing the buildings at Valley View and for transforming the land into a cotton plantation. Little information remains, however, about the enslaved people who lived and worked at Valley View. No journals or other documents have survived to explain the specific involvement of African Americans in the construction of the house and outbuildings or their role in the formal gardens, work yard, and agricultural land. Because of the intricacy of the formal gardens, it is likely that a few enslaved individuals worked primarily as gardeners.

The Sproull family's sophistication was reflected in the grand house with its detailed interior and fine furnishings, and also in the site's formal boxwood gardens, which are as old as the house itself. Eliza laid out the formal gardens, which were surrounded by a decorative picket fence.[19] The central herringbone-patterned brick walk stretched from the entrance gate to the front steps of the house.

The walk was flanked by two parterre gardens, one in the pattern of the sun and one of the moon.[20] Like most parterre gardens in the antebellum South, the formal boxwood gardens were designed to be viewed from the second floor of the house. Triple hedges of clipped boxwood and cherry laurel bordered the walkway.[21] According to Rebecca Sproull Fouché's memoirs, the boxwood "was brought from the old Marshall home in Abbeville District, South Carolina, in a bag strapped on to Mother's trunk behind the carriage."[22] Her memoirs also shed light on the ornamentals grown in the formal garden: "Mother loved evergreens, roses, violets, cape jasmines, tulips, mignonette, hyacinths, etc., and there was room for all her favorites because the hedge was always kept one yard square and the boxwood one foot. I have never seen such lovely straw-colored double hollyhocks elsewhere, and violets seemed indigenous to the soil. It seems to me that they were always in bloom."[23] She further describes a special green rose grown by

Triple hedges and parterres flanking the walkway

her mother, vegetable gardens, and "a magnificent peach and apple orchard."[24]

In 1864, upon hearing the news that Union forces were in route to the valley on their way to Atlanta, the Sproull family took refuge in Alabama, leaving Valley View in the care of the cabinetmaker, Vitenger.[25] Union general John Schofield and his troops occupied the site for a few days; officers used the second floor of the house for living quarters. Horses were kept in the parlor to protect them from Confederate snipers, and the piano was used as a horse trough.[26] When the Sproulls returned to the area at the end of the war, they discovered that Valley View and its garden had survived.

James died at his beloved Valley View in 1866. After his death, his son Charles, known as Charlie, continued the farming operations on the property with sharecroppers. Valley View struggled financially during the Reconstruction period, but had become prosperous by the later part of the nineteenth century.[27] Charlie died of consumption in March 1883 at the age of thirty-three.[28] Eliza, his mother and James' widow, continued to reside at the property until her death in 1906.

The second generation of descendants at Valley View was Rebecca Caldwell Sproull, the daughter and eldest child of James and Eliza Sproull. Rebecca married Major Robert Turnbull Fouché at Valley View in 1868.[29] The couple had two children, James Sproull and Kitty Florence. The family lived in nearby Rome, Georgia, where Robert practiced law, and managed Valley View as a farm from 1883 to 1899.[30] In later years, the Fouchés enjoyed Valley View as a summer retreat.[31] Rebecca's memoirs provide detailed descriptions about her mother's garden before the Civil War but few details after the war and through the closing years of the nineteenth century.

Between 1899 and 1962, the third generation of descendants, James Sproull Fouché and Edith Carver, who married in 1909, owned Valley View. James, known as "Sproull," served as the commercial attaché to the American legation in Romania from 1918 to 1933.[32] While he and Edith were abroad, cousins of the Sproulls, the Auchmuty family, lived at Valley View.[33] Sproull and Edith returned to Valley View a few times while on leave. Following Sproull's retirement from the diplomatic corps, they

House and gardens atop a rise on the edge of a broad meadow

made Valley View their permanent home.[34] Sproull and Edith adorned Valley View with many antiques, paintings, and decorative items that they had collected during their travels through Europe and Asia, contributing another layer of interest and history to the main house. In the 1940s, they installed electricity in the historic house. Sproull purchased numerous tracts of land that previously had been inherited by other family members, reuniting some of Valley View's original acreage. Photos in the family archives show the main house and garden in the late 1800s and early 1900s looking much as they were described in the antebellum period.[35]

In the 1930s, the Fouchés added a brick water tower near the south side of the antebellum smokehouse. By 1933, many antebellum-era plantings were still growing at Valley View, according to *Garden History of Georgia*: "The garden bounded on one side by Carolina cherry and by bush wistaria on the other, shows original plantings of well trimmed dwarf box borders, tree box, Carolina cherry, English laurel, euonymus, Norway spruce and fir, Persian lilacs, crape myrtle, mock orange, flowering holly, cape jasmine, Pyrus japonica and forsythia."[36] Several varieties of old roses flourished in the gardens too, including "Maman Cochets, Malmaisons, dailies, both red and pink, moss roses, and a highly valued green rose."[37] The site was home to cedar, locust, and oak trees as well as lilies, narcissus, and violets.[38] Other significant landscape features documented in the 1930s include vegetable gardens and orchards.[39]

Parterre viewed from the balcony

One parterre in the pattern
of the sun

One parterre in the pattern
of the moon

The fourth generation to care for Valley View was Dr. Robert Fouché Norton Sr. and his wife, Helen Goodwin. Robert and Helen married in 1940; the couple had four children. In 1962, Robert inherited the property from his aunt, Edith Fouché, who had had no children. By this point, the property had shrunk to 540 acres.[40] The Nortons resided in Rome, Georgia, enjoying Valley View as a second home for three decades. Like the generations before them, their devotion to Valley View was strong, and they worked arduously to preserve the house and its furnishings, outbuildings, and formal boxwood garden. Family photographs from the 1960s and 1970s show the house and formal boxwood garden preserved much as they were in the mid-nineteenth century.[41] They established a nursery for boxwoods so that the formal boxwood garden could be maintained in the original patterns using clippings of the original boxwood. For safety, they installed a railing on the second-floor gallery of the main house, one that was in keeping with the character of the structure, and they added a well in the work yard. To help maintain and preserve Valley View, the fourth generation sold portions of the land, reducing the acreage to 275.[42] To help sustain the site, the Nortons leased a one-hundred-acre field for row crop farming, a practice that continues today. They retrofitted the historic house with modern plumbing and converted two rooms to new uses. Remarkably, aside from these updates, the house has seen very little change since its construction in the late 1840s. In 1974, the Nortons nominated Valley View for listing in the National Register of Historic Places. The nomination was approved the following year.

In the late 1980s, Valley View was passed down to the Nortons' children: Jane Norton Finger, Florence Norton Reisgies, and Dr. Robert "Bob" Fouché Norton Jr., who spent many of their childhood days at the site. To preserve the historic character of the house, they decided to keep the property unoccupied. One of the descendants built a modern house seventy-five yards away. Valley View continues today as a viable farming operation. In recent years, crops grown at the farm include corn, oats, soybeans, and winter wheat.

Like the generations before them, Bob and his wife, Mary, as well as Bob's sisters, Jane and Florence, are devoted to the preservation of Valley View, even

Boxwood nursery in the side yard

down to the detail of preserving, in two iron pots near the smokehouse, the historic green rose (*Rosa chinensis* 'Viridiflora') grown by Eliza Sproull in the antebellum period. They have conducted thorough historical research, amassing extensive records about the property from the 1840s to the present. They organize family workdays and keep detailed records of the rehabilitation work conducted on the home, outbuildings, furnishings, and garden. In the 1990s, the family expanded the boxwood nursery and created a boxwood preservation program. Chris Hastings, an Atlanta-based ornamental horticulturist, master arborist, and boxwood expert who has served as an adviser to the Nortons, describes their efforts: "The Norton family has implemented a sustained conservation effort to preserve the boxwood gardens at Valley View Farm. This program includes restorative pruning, insect/disease control, soil

Rear courtyard,
flanked by the wings
of the main house

nutrient management, and plant propagation. Their work is lauded as a paradigm for historic boxwood care. In addition, the information they have gathered and documented has become a valuable resource for boxwood caregivers throughout the state and the Southeast."[43] In 2007, the executive director of the Georgia Trust for Historic Preservation praised Valley View for its outstanding significance "as a high-style, brick, Greek Revival rural historic house that retains an extraordinary degree of its original integrity, as a documented historic landscape of great significance immediately surrounding the house, and for the rich farmland of the property."[44]

As part of their ongoing efforts to ensure that Valley View is preserved well into the future, the fifth generation of descendants has put in place a number of measures. In 1999, the family set up the Valley View Fund to support the preservation efforts of the home, garden, and farm operations.[45] They also, in 2009, placed seventy-five acres surrounding the antebellum home, outbuildings, and formal garden in a conservation easement held by the Mountain Conservation Trust of Georgia, permanently protecting the historic landscape and the viewshed.[46] For their outstanding commitment to Valley View, in 2015 the Norton Family was presented the Georgia Trust's Excellence in Stewardship award.[47] Valley View is also important as one of the only properties in northern Georgia owned by the same family—the descendants of James and Eliza Sproull—since the late 1840s. Love and devotion for Valley View have been instilled in the sixth generation of descendants, ensuring that it will endure into the twenty-first century and, it is hoped, beyond.

Massive 1913 arched gate marking the entrance to Wormsloe

Wormsloe and Wormsloe State Historic Site

WHEN NOBLE JONES landed at Yamacraw Bluff in 1733 as a member of James Oglethorpe's party of English settlers, he was determined to take advantage of the opportunities available in the new colony of Georgia. He planned to stay only a short while, but soon found himself building a productive and profitable life in the fledgling settlement of Savannah for himself, his wife, Sarah Hack Jones, and their three children: Mary, Noble Wimberly, and Inigo.[1] In addition to owning a residence in town, in 1736 he was granted five hundred acres on the Isle of Hope peninsula, which he named Wormsloe.[2] There on a bank of land overlooking the Jones Narrows waterway near the Skidaway River, a site deemed critical to the defense of Savannah, Jones constructed a house made of tabby and wood. He surrounded the house with eight-foot-high fortified tabby walls, which provided a base of operations for a small garrison of marines who guarded Savannah against attack from the Spanish and their Indian allies. It is interesting to speculate whether Jones would be surprised that over 280 years later, his descendants still live on the land, and that thousands of tourists annually visit the remains of his fort and enjoy the site's beauty and history.

Less than ten miles from downtown Savannah, Wormsloe is part of Georgia's Lowcountry, which is marked by forests and salt marshes. Wormsloe is historically, culturally, and environmentally significant. Its striking landscape has been, and continues to be, a major factor in its appeal and importance. Both its natural and man-made features enhance the beauty of this serene and special place.

Today, the estate is both privately and publicly owned. The State of Georgia acquired the majority of Wormsloe's acreage in 1973 for the benefit of its citizens, and opened the Wormsloe State Historic Site in 1979. A small portion of the land containing Wormsloe, the traditional family seat, is still home to Jones's descendants.

Wormsloe was now more than two hundred years old, the last survivor of the handiwork and dreams of the early Georgians, those who came with Oglethorpe and soon thereafter. Noble Jones's neighbors and acquaintances on the Isle of Hope and in the surrounding regions had built their estates and given them proud names, but time had gnawed them all away. . . .
But Wormsloe continued.—E. Merton Coulter, *Wormsloe: Two Centuries of a Georgia Family*

For most of its existence, Wormsloe was considered a country estate, its owners having other property and residences. Although fields were cleared and crops were planted, Wormsloe's agricultural production was never the primary source of income for Noble Jones and his descendants.[3] They nonetheless experimented with ways to improve Wormsloe to make the land productive and attractive.

When Noble Jones arrived in the New World, he brought his skills as a surveyor, carpenter, and man of medicine. He was a loyal subject of King George II, holding numerous public offices in the new colony. His interest in botany led him to pursue the production of crops compatible with the Lowcountry's climate. With varying degrees of success, Jones grew grapes, figs, pomegranates, plums, and oranges.[4] He planted white mulberry trees on Wormsloe as part of the colony's experiment with silk production, as did his daughter Mary, who inherited the estate after her father's death.[5] With Mary's passing, Wormsloe, according to her father's wishes, was deeded to her brother, Noble Wimberly. Unlike his father, Noble Wimberly Jones was an ardent patriot. He held political office and actively supported the fight for American independence. A physician, he served as the first president of the Georgia Medical Society, which he and his son George helped establish.[6] Noble Wimberly probably used Wormsloe as a hunting retreat.[7]

George Jones carried on the family tradition of holding public office and practicing medicine. Also a good businessman, he bought property and increased the family fortune. After his plantation burned, he moved to Wormsloe, which he had inherited from his father. In 1828, George Jones abandoned the original fortified tabby house and built a new frame residence about a mile northeast, along the river. Over the years, that building experienced numerous major

changes but today still serves as the family home. With Jones's death in 1838 and that of his wife, Eliza Smith Jones, in 1857, Wormsloe passed to their son, George Frederick Tilghman Jones.

This new generation brought much change. The spelling of the estate became "Wormsloe" rather than "Wormslow," and the spelling of some of the family names changed. "Wimberly" became "Wymberley," and, more radically, "Jones" became "De Renne." George Frederick Tilghman Jones, after several transformations, became known as "George Wymberley Jones De Renne." Those closest to him called him "Wymberley."[8] He earned a medical degree and was a successful investor but was more inclined toward the world of books.[9] Wymberley, who had a strong attachment to Wormsloe, funded improvements to the estate and increased its acreage. He established an oak avenue leading from the north side of the house to the public road and planted "cedars of Lebanon, deodars, Irish yew," along with camellias, Carolina jessamine, and aloes on the grounds.[10] Wormsloe's fields reflected Wymberley's experiments with improving and modernizing agricultural production, and two rows of cabins for the enslaved people who lived and worked on the land were built near the riverbank south of the main residence.[11]

The exact number of enslaved African Americans who lived on Wormsloe over the years is not known; however, their population was probably greatest in the nineteenth century.[12] Labor-intensive sea island cotton was grown as a commercial crop, so additional workers would have been needed.[13]

The De Renne family was able to hold onto the estate during and after the Civil War. Upon his death in 1880, Wymberley provided generously for his wife, Mary Wallace Nuttall De Renne, and their family, but he designated the Pennsylvania Company for Insurance on Lives and Granting Annuities as executor of his estate to ensure that his grandchildren, not his four children, would eventually inherit his holdings.[14]

Wymberley and Mary's son, Wymberley Jones De Renne, had been sent to Europe as a boy to escape the turbulence of the Civil War. There he received most of his formal education, but returned

Historic allée of about four hundred live oak trees lining the entry drive

Wormsloe's main house, surrounded by naturalistic and formal gardens

to New York to obtain a law degree. Seeking his fortune, he moved to Texas and married Laura Camblos Norris of Philadelphia. An estrangement from his family resulted, but Wymberley Jones De Renne returned to Wormsloe in 1891 and rented the estate from the Pennsylvania Company for nearly twenty-five years.[15] Under Wymberley J.'s direction, Wormsloe became a working farm, with dairy cattle and truck gardens, but it was also known for its beautiful grounds.[16] Wymberley J. employed a full-time gardener and had a greenhouse installed.[17] To enhance the approach to the residence, he planted shrubs and ornamentals.[18] On the north and south

sides of the house, he added circular pools with fountains showcasing "graceful bronze waterbirds."[19] The southern grounds included reflecting pools, small wooden bridges, and a gazebo.[20] To amuse his three children, "statuettes of elves and gnomes" were placed throughout this landscape, and a playhouse was built for their enjoyment.[21] In honor of his son, Wymberley Wormsloe De Renne, he created a new oak avenue of four hundred live oak trees on what had been a path that led from the tabby ruins of the fortified house to today's Skidaway Road.[22] Later he added a stone arch to mark this entrance to Wormsloe. An active member of the Georgia

Historical Society, Wymberley J. was interested in books and genealogical research. To house his collection, he built a massive Greek Revival library southeast of the house and facing the river. This repository of priceless volumes, completed in 1908, used concrete construction, marble steps, and a tile floor in order to be fireproof.

With the death in 1916 of Wymberley Jones De Renne, the last surviving child of Wymberley and Mary, the estate passed to their grandchildren, in keeping with Wymberley's will. Wymberley Wormsloe De Renne, Elfrida De Renne Barrow, and Audrey De Renne Coerr Howland, all children of Wymberley Jones and Laura De Renne, were the beneficiaries. The siblings decided that Wymberley W. would take over Wormsloe, and the sisters assigned their shares of the property to him in 1917.[23]

Wymberley Wormsloe De Renne's life underwent several major changes quickly: in 1916, he graduated from Columbia University, saw the death of his father, and acquired Wormsloe. In 1918 he married Augusta Gallie Floyd of Savannah and began his service in France during World War I. Upon his return to Georgia, he, like many of his forebears, invested in real estate, but the results were disastrous and set the stage for financial difficulties that would eventually result in his losing Wormsloe.

Rectangular formal garden with axial walkways and a central pool

Cherokee roses climbing a wrought-iron fence at the east end of the formal garden

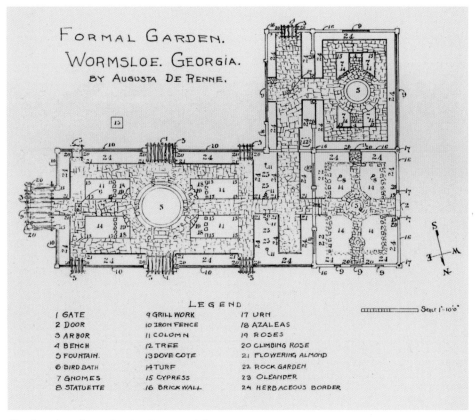

Garden plan, from *Garden History of Georgia*

Wymberley W.'s wife, Augusta, was an avid gardener. Active in both the Garden Club of Georgia and the Garden Club of America, she was known for her expertise in historic plant material and garden design.[24] Soon after her marriage, she planted flowers around the library, beginning what was to become an elaborate expansion of Wormsloe's ornamental landscape. By 1925 she had begun the design for a formal Colonial Revival garden, adjacent to the south façade of the main house, for which she would receive much acclaim.[25]

Emerging in the late nineteenth and early twentieth centuries, the popular Colonial Revival style represented a growing interest in America's past, especially in its colonial heritage. Although based on historical precedent, the resulting designed landscapes were often romantic interpretations of this early period. Colonial Revival gardens were known for their symmetry, geometrically patterned beds, and axial walkways. Usually located near the main residence and often enclosed, the gardens were filled with texture and color from perennial plants, shrubs, and trees.[26] Throughout the landscape, elements such as sundials and fountains, as well as historic remnants, provided visual interest.[27] Augusta De Renne incorporated all these features into her design.

Wormsloe's Colonial Revival garden was composed of three interconnected garden rooms arranged in an L-shaped form. The first, a rectangular garden, was enclosed by low brick walls topped by brick columns and decorative ironwork. Freestanding marble columns said to be from the old Spalding mansion on Sapelo Island were prominent features, as was an arbor-covered southern gate with a dovecote standing just outside it.[28] The other two garden rooms were added in 1928: the gnome and the sunken (or west) gardens, both partially enclosed by six-foot-high walls made of brick taken from the chimneys of former slave cabins.[29] All three rooms were connected by walkways made of flagstone that had once been used as ship ballast, and all featured a central focal point.[30] The rectangular garden had at its center a circular pool and fountain containing Wymberley Jones De Renne's bronze waterbird. The west garden displayed a "well-head supported by a circular base of square cobbles from the streets of old Savannah," and the gnome garden featured a cast-iron fountain in a circular pool.[31] Throughout

Central fountain with axial paths leading to
interconnected walled garden rooms

Brick walls and wrought
iron in the garden

the gardens, the grass surfaces were laid out in geometric shapes, and plant-filled borders lined the
walls. They also contained statuary, gnome figurines,
urns, Spanish jugs, stone benches, a sundial, and a
birdbath.[32] A partial list of plants included roses,
azaleas, violets, daisies, hyacinths, verbena, blue sage,
pansies, marigolds, nasturtiums, yellow callas, and
jonquils.[33] *Garden History of Georgia* noted that "blue
larkspur, pale pink, and valerian are used extensively
at Wormsloe, and the native yuccas and palms lend
a tropical flavor."[34]

As their financial situation grew more critical,
Wymberley W. and Augusta opened the estate to
the public for a fee. Wormsloe Gardens quickly
became a popular tourist destination, offering the
opportunity to see a picturesque formal garden; historic structures, including the ruins of the fortified
tabby house that Noble Jones had built, as well as
a former slave cabin; a landscape developed over
generations; and the Lowcountry's natural beauty.
When describing Wormsloe in 1933, *Garden History*

of Georgia stated: "It is almost impossible to separate
the old from the new, as the informality of its plan
and planting has admitted of a constant intermingling of the two. In every phase it is a record of the
development of coastal Georgia."[35] The 1927 opening
of the garden to the public coincided with the emer-
gence of the automobile as a source of increased
mobility for a growing segment of Americans,
spurring people's desire to travel. Wormsloe benefited from the nascent tourism industry. By the time
Wormsloe Gardens closed in 1938, thousands of
people had passed under its stone arch.

The success of Wormsloe Gardens was not
enough to ease the De Rennes's financial worries,
however. Wymberley W., Augusta, and their children left Wormsloe in 1938. They eventually moved
to Athens, where Wymberley W. accepted a position with the University of Georgia as curator of
the De Renne Library, consisting of his father's rare
book and manuscript collection, in addition to other
special acquisitions. Augusta continued her involvement with garden clubs and established a garden at
her new house.[36]

Determined that the estate would remain in
the family, Elfrida De Renne Barrow purchased
the property. In 1938, she and her husband, Craig
Barrow, a physician and chief surgeon for the
Central of Georgia Railroad, made Wormsloe their
home. A noted poet and founding member of the
Poetry Society of Georgia, Elfrida was interested
in the state's history and active in Savannah's early
preservation movement. In 1951 she established the
nonprofit Wormsloe Foundation, whose purpose in
part is to encourage historic research and the preservation of historic records and sites.[37] The work of the
foundation has included the publishing of a number of scholarly articles and books; as a result, there
has been a long and fruitful relationship between
the foundation and the University of Georgia Press.
Elfrida Barrow was posthumously honored in 2008
as one of Georgia's "Women of Achievement."

The Barrows discontinued public tours of the
property. They made major modifications to the main
residence, which took on a Neoclassical appearance
with the addition of a six-column two-story porch
and a curving double stairway on the north façade.
While the formal garden and grounds were no longer as ornate as when Wormsloe Gardens existed,

they retained their beauty. *Georgia: A Guide to Its Towns and Countryside* (1940) provides a glimpse of the landscape: "The grounds, carpeted with large-leaf Algerian ivy, are shaded by lofty oaks that form a dark setting for the azalea and camellia bushes, many of which grow as tall as young trees."[38] Over the years, Elfrida generously allowed Wormsloe to be used as a site for charity tours, educational visits, and special events.

Elfrida Barrow took a naturalistic approach to Wormsloe's landscape and believed that nature should determine the appearance of the grounds. She filled in the circular pool on the north side of the house.[39] She hired two caretakers to maintain the property and keep the paths cleared. The Algerian ivy, a delicacy for the deer, soon disappeared.[40] When Craig, her husband, died in 1945, Elfrida had a small family cemetery, surrounded by walls of brick from the old rice mill's chimney, constructed on land south of the house. Upon her death in 1970, she was buried there next to her husband.

When Craig Barrow Jr., a financial adviser, and his wife, Laura "Dolly" Bell Barrow, took over Wormsloe, they continued many activities begun by Elfrida. Craig Jr. shared his mother's interest in historical research and strongly supported this aspect of the foundation's work. He and his son especially encouraged the publication of William M. Kelso's classic *Captain Jones's Wormslow* (1979), which reported on the findings of archaeological excavations of the tabby ruins conducted in 1968 and 1969. Craig Jr. also preferred to have the main residence shielded by vegetation from the entry road and waterway. Dolly served as president of the Trustee's Garden Club, a member club of the Garden Club of America, and was a recipient of its Medal of Merit award. She devoted her energies to numerous civic organizations, to historic preservation in Savannah, and to the Wormsloe Foundation. Most importantly, Craig Jr. and Dolly shared Elfrida's love of Wormsloe and concern about its future.

In 1961, Elfrida Barrow had donated 750 acres of the estate to the Wormsloe Foundation, keeping the remaining acreage for the family's use. By the time Craig Jr. took over, he had to take decisive action in order to protect the entire site. Mounting development pressures and changing tax laws meant that solutions were needed if Wormsloe was to remain intact. In 1972, the Wormsloe Foundation,

Path leading into Craig's Garden

the Nature Conservancy, and the State of Georgia worked together to ensure Wormsloe's future and to protect its historic, cultural, and environmental integrity. Through their efforts and the support of the General Assembly, Wormsloe became one of the first properties acquired by the state in 1973 as part of Governor Jimmy Carter's new Heritage Trust program. In that same year, Wormsloe was listed in the National Register of Historic Places. In 1978, the Barrows granted a façade and conservation easement to the State of Georgia for the nearly fifty acres of property that remained in family hands, including the main house, helping ensure its long-term preservation.[41] The family donated acreage around the one remaining former slave cabin to the Wormsloe

Foundation.[42] Today, the family estate includes the main residence, originally built by George Jones; the formal garden, first planned by Augusta De Renne; Wymberley J.'s library, with its tall palms leading from the front steps to the water; Elfrida Barrow's family cemetery, where Craig III's parents and grandparents are buried; G. W. J. "Wymberley" De Renne's original oak drive; and numerous outbuildings associated with the site's history.

The current owners, Craig Barrow III and his wife, Diana Deas Barrow, and their two young children, Thornton and Kathryn, moved to the estate in 1986. Craig III, a financial adviser, has continued his family's interest in history and scholarship through active involvement in the Georgia Historical Society and

Craig's Garden

Walled garden, circa 1933, from *Garden History of Georgia*

West walled garden, circa 2015

as founding chairman of the advisory boards of the University of Georgia's Libraries and the University of Georgia Press. Like her mother-in-law, Diana is a long-standing member of the Trustees' Garden Club, and was awarded its Medal of Merit. Recipient of the Creative Leadership Award, Diana has held numerous offices on the national level of the Garden Club of America.

The Barrows' early years at Wormsloe were centered on raising a family, so it was not until the late 1990s, with a few exceptions, that they began to focus their attention on improving the landscape around the house and library.[43] When they moved to Wormsloe, the circular area in front of the house (the north side) contained mostly trees; in 1990, the Barrows added beds. What was once a small kitchen garden between the house and garage was enclosed with brick and enhanced with beds and a cherry tree.[44] Bronze sculptures placed around the grounds feature coastal wildlife: a heron by Geoffrey Smith,

an owl by Roger Martin, and a red-tailed hawk by Paul Rymer.[45] A sentimental favorite near the formal garden is of the Barrows' two small children feeding a fawn named Bambi. It was cast by the Dallas sculptor Barvo Walker in honor of the Barrows' twenty-fifth wedding anniversary.[46] To maintain the grounds, the Barrows use a tree service to ensure the health of the old oaks and a landscaping service to take care of edging, maintenance, and seasonal planting. Craig III prefers a landscape in which overgrown vegetation is cut back, and views of the grounds and marsh from the house are kept open.[47]

Diana recalls a specific moment when the couple reassessed their approach both to the formal garden and to the grounds. Advice they received from a close friend and several landscape architects as they prepared to host approximately six hundred people attending the Garden Club of America's 2012 annual meeting helped them determine what direction to follow: "What they all led us to realize

Wormsloe library overlooking the Skidaway River

OPPOSITE: View along the Skidaway River

was that having large gardens of planted flowers was superfluous to the magnificent vistas we had surrounding us with the water, the trees, and the scrubs—that was what we should focus on."[48] This decision resulted in a new boxwood hedge around the library, the removal of shrubs blocking the view of the river from the east side of the house, the subsequent planting of a yew hedge, and replacement of "worn out" azaleas with dogwood on the eastern grounds near the water. An unexpected discovery came when Craig III cleared out "a very long sunken garden of Formosa azaleas" and uncovered an acorn-shaped fountain that probably dates from the 1890s.[49]

On the grounds east of the house are rows of camellias that brighten the winter months. Camellias were first planted in mass on the north and east

sides of the house in 1961 when Elfrida Barrow, who enjoyed these colorful shrubs, was given a number of them. Craig Jr. and Dolly later had camellias planted between the house and boat dock on the river. When Craig III and Diana came to Wormsloe, they moved the camellias found throughout the grounds and used them to enhance the walk on the east side of the house.[50]

The L-shaped form of the enclosed formal garden remains basically as it did when planned in the 1920s, although it is no longer filled with flowers. The garden is primarily green, largely in response to the feeding habits of the property's deer population. The rectangular garden room nearest the house is no longer enclosed on three sides by brick walls. Low brick walls with coping frame the south side; on the east is a low brick wall topped with decorative iron

Panorama of Jones Narrows near the Skidaway River

work; and on the north no wall exists, only simple brick edging. The garden room's focal point is a low circular pool edged in brick and surrounded by a small grass border. Brick walkways and grass surfaces complete the space. On the west, near the two walled garden rooms, are two oblong beds installed by Dolly Barrow; these beds were subsequently framed with dwarf boxwood and planted with crape myrtles by Craig III and Diana.[51] They moved standard boxwood from other parts of the grounds to create a hedge along the wall of the west garden.[52] That room has at its center a circular bed that contains a large fern and is edged with bricks. Grass covers the garden floor. Its southern wall contains decorative grillwork that allows a glimpse into the adjoining room, now known as "Craig's Garden." Once the gnome garden, this enclosed, southernmost space is named for Wormsloe's owner, who enjoys working in this quiet and peaceful setting. In half shade, this gated landscape is enclosed by brick walls lined with creeping fig vine; the west wall is topped with decorative ironwork. Protected from the deer, the beds lining the garden walls have featured *Fatsia japonica*, geraniums, hostas, pittosporum, agapanthus, greenfly orchid (*Epidendrum magnoliae*), cast-iron plant (*Aspidistra elatior*), and ligularia. Ferns line the brick walk, and a resurrection fern perches on a branch of a moss-covered live oak. The garden's center contains a circular bed for annual planting. For visual interest, small statues are scattered throughout this garden room.

When talking about Wormsloe, Craig III exclaims: "Look to the future."[53] He understands that its long-term security cannot be taken for granted. The property must adapt to twenty-first-century needs and interests. One way to achieve this is by exploring Wormsloe's immense potential for scholarship.

In 2007, the Wormsloe Institute for Environmental History was formed to study the site's historical and physical development through an interdisciplinary approach. Six years later, the Wormsloe Foundation donated approximately fifteen acres, which includes the site of the former slave cabins, to the University of Georgia's new Center for Research and Education at Wormsloe. Visiting faculty members and students use the remaining historic cabin, which has undergone major renovations over the years, as well as two additional buildings constructed in 2016, for housing and research. The foundation, the Institute for Environmental History, and the Center for Research and Education encourage scholarship relevant not only to Wormsloe but also to Georgia's coastal resources. Projects are diverse. They include a report of Wormsloe's cultural landscape, a study of invasive parasites in coastal waterways, an analysis of the impact of constructed wetlands, and research on butterfly habitats. Bringing together scholars in fields such as history, landscape architecture, geography, ecology, and engineering provides opportunities for collaboration and new discoveries.

The Barrows take seriously the responsibility of caring for and ensuring the future of Wormsloe. They maintain the long-standing tradition of sharing the estate's beauty with visitors and special groups. As a result, they have been honored and recognized for their stewardship. In 2014, Craig III was named a Preservation Hero by the Library of American Landscape History. Reflecting on their work, Diana Barrow said, "What we are really proud of are our efforts to preserve and enhance our beautiful surroundings and to do justice to this wonderful gift with which we have been blessed."[54]

WORMSLOE STATE HISTORIC SITE

It would be a catastrophe to lose Wormsloe.... This is a tract granted to Noble Jones by King George II, rich in history and beauty.—Governor Jimmy Carter, budget message, January 11, 1973

When Governor Jimmy Carter presented his budget proposal to the Georgia Legislature in the winter of 1973, he described the new Heritage Trust program, in which significant natural and historic sites would be identified and recommended for possible acquisition by the state. One of these special places was Wormsloe, historically significant, especially as part of the state's early colonial history, and environmentally important as a relatively undeveloped coastal area. When requesting funding, Governor Carter spoke with urgency: "The clock of commercial development is ticking away our chances, and the bulldozer of misguided progress is awaiting the signal to destroy your heritage and mine."[55]

The opportunity to acquire Wormsloe came at a time when concern for the environment and historic preservation had captured the public's attention. In 1966, Congress passed the National Historic Preservation Act, setting the stage for a federal and state partnership to promote the identification and protection of historic places. The first Earth Day occurred in April 1970, and in December of 1970, the U.S. Environmental Protection Agency was formed. That same year, the Georgia Legislature passed the landmark Coastal Marshlands Protection Act. In addition, the nation was anticipating its upcoming bicentennial celebration.

Governor Carter's budget request passed, allowing the state to acquire 750 acres from the Nature Conservancy in 1973. Today's site contains approximately 1,200 acres and includes both Long and Pigeon Islands, tracts also associated with Wormsloe's history. The Department of Natural Resources is the state agency in charge of the historic site's management. Before Wormsloe opened to the public in 1979, the agency carried out environmental, site, and interpretative planning. A visitor center and museum were constructed, along with the site superintendent's residence, a maintenance facility, and a parking area. Walking trails were laid out. The site's interpretation would focus on its colonial history and the importance of the tabby ruins and their association with early English settler Noble Jones. William Kelso's report on his archaeological excavations of the ruins in the late 1960s proved an invaluable resource.

It was during the early planning stages that the Department of Natural Resources faced a serious challenge. Shortly after taking over the property, the agency became aware of the southern pine beetle's presence in Wormsloe's forest. Knowing the potential for this pest to damage the loblolly pines, the department reluctantly decided that cutting down both diseased and healthy trees was necessary in order to keep the infestation from spreading within the site as well as to neighboring properties. This action affected a larger land area than originally anticipated.[56] As a result, most of the pine trees in today's forest are less than forty years old.[57]

Entering the historic site from Skidaway Road, visitors first pass under Wymberley Jones De Renne's stone arch, inscribed "1733 Wormsloe 1913." Greeting them is the image most often associated with the property and most often photographed: a stately

Tabby ruins at the Wormsloe State Historic Site

Tabby ruins at the
Wormsloe State
Historic Site

Tabby ruins, from *Garden
History of Georgia*

avenue of approximately four hundred live oaks, also planted by De Renne. On the immediate right is the gatehouse, which Wymberley Wormsloe De Renne built in 1917 as the superintendent's cottage, where visitors now purchase their passes; the building was rehabilitated in 1997. Driving under the moss-covered oak canopy along the mile-and-a-half-long roadway, visitors can briefly glimpse the privately owned residential complex that belongs to Noble Jones's descendants. At the end of the avenue, guests are directed to the parking area, which is surrounded by trees. The 1970s-era visitor center and museum, featuring a brief film, exhibits, and bookshop, provide background information before the short walk through the woods to the tabby ruins. A short distance from the old fort is the former burial place of Noble Jones, his wife, Sarah, and their son Inigo. Although the graves have been removed, Georgia Wymberley Jones De Renne erected a stone monument in 1875 to mark their original resting place. The historic site provides an observation deck for an unobstructed view of the marsh and Jones Narrows.

In 1998, Governor Zell Miller issued an executive order dedicating the Wormsloe State Historic Site as a Heritage Preserve. He expressed his desire that Wormsloe be protected for future generations so that it could be used "for scientific, historical, educational, and aesthetic purposes" and that it "be kept essentially in its present state."[58] The Wormsloe State Historic Site contains an increasingly rare yet significant cultural component of the architectural heritage of the coast: tabby construction. Tabby, a mixture of lime, shell, sand, and water, forms an extremely hard surface, making it a useful building material that historically was found along the coastal areas of Georgia, South Carolina, and Florida. The tabby ruins no longer overlook an active waterway, as the site did when Noble Jones first constructed the fortified house across from Jones Narrows. The dredging of the Atlantic Intracoastal Waterway and construction of the Diamond Causeway in the 1960s changed the tidal flows and salt marsh around Wormsloe, creating a dense marsh that prevents ships and large boats from sailing through it.[59] The ruins, however, can still provide insight into colonial defenses, building construction, and the way in which the early settlers might have lived. As part of the site's interpretation and emphasis on living history, a colonial-life area has been established. A small hut and several primitive shelters have been constructed to illustrate how soldiers and, possibly, indentured servants and the enslaved were housed in the eighteenth century.[60]

Changes appear to be underway at the site. Plans are under consideration for the construction of a new visitor center, and parking may be moved closer to the front gate and farther from the tabby ruins. With tourist numbers close to seventy thousand annually, the dedicated site staff works daily to maintain the crucial balance between a positive visitor experience and the protection of the site's fragile natural and historic resources.

Dating from the founding of the English colony, Wormsloe is one of Georgia's earliest and most significant historic sites. Besides illustrating the achievements and interests of many generations of an American family, it reflects the state's history as seen through the family's experiences. From the early colony, the formation of the young nation, the antebellum life of the affluent and the enslaved, the Civil War and its aftermath, the state's recovery and growth, the twentieth century and its many cultural, political, and technological changes—Wormsloe was part of it all. Unlike many historic places, this property and its landscape, both natural and man-made, have been protected through the determination and concerted efforts of its owners. May historian E. Merton Coulter's 1955 observation, "But Wormsloe continued," remain true for generations to come.

Flagstone steps leading from the naturalistic hillside garden to a spring garden with a rock-work pool in the Zahner-Slick Garden

Zahner–Slick Garden

THE ZAHNER-SLICK house and garden are located in the northwest Atlanta neighborhood of Peachtree Heights Park, one of the most significant early twentieth-century landscaped suburbs in the city. Developed by Loyer and Kenyon Zahner beginning in 1926, the garden is a valuable example of a sophisticated landscape designed by a homeowner without professional assistance—one that has survived into the twenty-first century. The design combines elements of both formality and naturalism. Today, the current owners, Barbara and Charles Slick, not only have been stewards of this historic garden but also have helped it flourish.

In cities across the United States, suburbs first emerged on a large scale in the late nineteenth and early twentieth centuries because of increased industrialization, a growing middle class, and improved transportation, which allowed people to commute longer distances. As cities became increasingly crowded, noisy, and polluted, those with means sought places to create fashionable houses. In Atlanta, Peachtree Heights Park was one of the first such large-scale residential neighborhoods to be built north of the city. In the early twentieth century, major changes were occurring along the Peachtree Road corridor north of Peachtree Creek in the Buckhead area. For much of the previous century, the area had largely consisted of farms and hardwood forests. During the 1910s and 1920s, the expanding streetcar lines and the growing popularity of automobiles further contributed to the growth and development of Peachtree Road. Real estate developers seized the opportunity to turn these picturesque lands into moneymaking ventures. In 1910, Walter P. Andrews and Eretus Rivers, developers of the Peachtree Heights Park Company, acquired from the estate of the pioneer Atlantan Wesley Gray Collier land located off Peachtree Road a few miles north of downtown Atlanta, which they turned into a huge landscaped residential park named Peachtree Heights Park.

Does everyone know the garden in the half evening light, when all sharp outline is blended into one luxuriant composition of flower forms, paths, and fountain, held in a mass of green that is unlike that of day? And do we all know it by moonlight, when all green is gone and distant corners are lost in darkness, while perhaps a white evening-primrose opens its bloom to the summer night and stands pale and cool with the moon's rays upon it, and its long shadow cast across the pathway? It is at these moments that our gardens are of unspeakable worth to us and we begrudge no care that has gone to their making.
—Loyer Lawton Zahner, ca. 1930

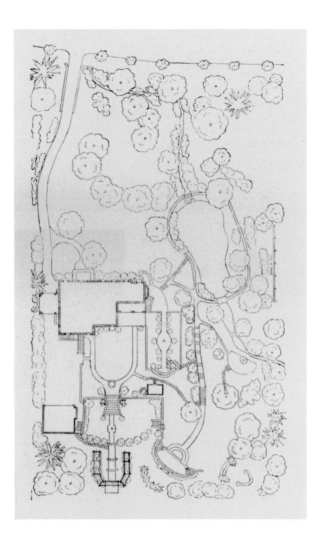

Garden plan, from *Garden History of Georgia*

Besides being an early example of a suburban neighborhood, Peachtree Heights Park is notable for being the only known suburb designed by Carrère and Hastings, one of the outstanding Beaux Arts architecture firms in the United States. The firm's large body of work encompassed buildings, interiors, and gardens and grounds. Among its prestigious public commissions were the New York Public Library, the House and Senate Office Buildings in Washington, D.C., and the Memorial Amphitheatre at Arlington National Cemetery. The firm was also notable for designing extravagant country estates for American elites.[1]

In collaboration with the civil engineer Frank Stone Tainter of E. A. Stevens & Co., Carrère and Hastings designed a plan for Peachtree Heights Park that capitalized on the natural terrain, with a curvilinear street pattern arranged in harmony with the rolling hills. Woodward Way and Habersham Road coiled up gentle hills toward the north, and Nacoochee and Rivers Roads stayed mostly in the bottomlands near streams. Carrère and Hastings

preserved a number of the natural streambeds as parks and divided the land into generously sized lots. Peachtree Battle Avenue, the main thoroughfare, was bisected by a vast landscaped park in its median.[2]

The planned suburb was publicized by the developers as "the best of city and suburban life," and lots went on sale in May 1911. Over the next three decades, influential, wealthy Atlantans moved to Peachtree Heights Park. By the early 1930s, more than three-quarters of the lots had been built; the area was largely completed by 1940.[3] The neighborhood contained some of the finest early twentieth-century residential architecture in Atlanta designed by leading local firms, including Hentz, Reid & Adler (later Hentz, Adler & Shutze), Tucker and Howell, Pringle and Smith, and Cooper and Cooper. Styles included Georgian, Italian, Regency, and English Tudor. Notable local landscape architects including William C. Pauley and William L. Monroe Sr., along with nationally recognized landscape architects such as Robert Cridland and Ellen Biddle Shipman, designed elaborate gardens for some of the houses. In general, a naturalistic design approach was followed: stately homes were set a good distance from the road amid wide, sweeping front lawns with informal groupings of native shrubs and large stands of trees, producing a visual consistency throughout the neighborhood.[4] Listed in the National Register of Historic Places in 1980, the Peachtree Heights Park Historic District is known today as Peachtree Heights West.

Kenyon Benedict Zahner and his wife, Harriet Loyer Lawton Zahner, came to Peachtree Heights West in 1926. Not long after their marriage in 1921, the Zahners had begun searching for a lot north of Atlanta that was near a streetcar line and a school and was ample enough to accommodate their garden plans. After a two-year search, they found a site in Peachtree Heights West on the north side of Peachtree Battle Avenue near the intersection of Woodward Way. They approached the developer Eretus Rivers in March 1924 and negotiated the expansion of the lot lines to include a small stream and ten extra feet of woodlands. Kenyon Zahner described the property at the time of purchase: "There are oaks, beech, hickory, gum, pine, poplar, maple, 23 dogwoods, and other trees. The lot

Zahner-Slick Garden, with many original design elements

Walled formal garden on the side of the house

is covered with wild azalea, all shapes and colors. Other wildflowers and ferns are there. It is ¼ mile from [the street] car line and from the best school in Fulton County."[5]

Born in 1892, Kenyon B. Zahner was a native Atlantan, a lawyer, and an executive, like his father, of the Union Central Life Insurance Company for Georgia and Alabama.[6] Both his parents were distinguished citizens, and he grew up among the social elite in the city. In June 1921, Zahner married Harriet Loyer Lawton in her hometown of Summerville, South Carolina.[7] Loyer hailed from a notable South Carolina family.[8] Her mother and father's three-acre garden in Summerville contained a large vegetable garden on one side of the property, and on the other side was an ornamental garden sanctuary that they named "Paradise." Loyer was strongly influenced by her family's passion for gardening as well as by the gardens of Lowcountry South Carolina.[9] Loyer, who had a deep passion for garden design and horticulture, was a founding member of the Primrose Garden Club, established in Atlanta in 1928, serving as its president in 1932 and 1933.[10] The mission of the club was "the study and culture of flowers, landscapes, gardening, protection of Nature, trees, plants, and birds, and the encouragement of civic planting."[11] An avid gardener, she wholeheartedly embraced the club's ethos in the planning, creation, and care of her garden on Peachtree Battle Avenue. In the early 1930s, Loyer presented a paper called "Design in the Garden" to local garden clubs. It highlights her deep knowledge of the history of garden design in Europe and America: "By studying European examples we can improve the design of our home surroundings, but when we attempt to copy any particular example in its entirety it is usually cumbersome and out of place. It is not art to copy an Italian, French or English garden, but from all of them we can obtain suggestions and adapt them to our needs."[12] Her presentation demonstrated her understanding of the principles of laying out a garden, too, which is evident in the well-designed, balanced scheme she created for her own garden.[13]

After purchasing the lot in Peachtree Heights West, the Zahners hired the Atlanta architectural firm of Burge and Stevens to design a two-story clapboard house to sit at the crest of a gently rolling hill.[14] It was one of the firm's earliest residential

Walled garden, from *Garden History of Georgia*

commissions. Over time, the Zahners transformed their property into a showplace. They later rehired Burge and Stevens to expand the house into a grand two-story brick Georgian Revival house. Loyer, with the help of her husband, designed a series of formal garden rooms and informal landscaped spaces that gradually filled their one and a third acres. The home's front façade featured a pediment with an oculus that provides a visual anchor. There were pediment-topped dormers on either side, quoins embracing the corners and central section, and an elaborate front entry supported by two columns crowned by a fan-shaped entablature. Foundation plantings of large boxwood added near the front façade reinforced the character of the Georgian Revival architecture. The house, the gently undulating drive, and a small motor court capped by a garage at the rear were sited on the eastern portion of the property, leaving generous uninterrupted space for a broad front lawn and for the Zahners to realize their garden plans.

Unlike many of their neighbors in Peachtree Heights West, the Zahners did not hire a professional landscape architect or designer to create their garden world. They both loved the outdoors and did extensive work in their garden. Loyer designed, planted, and tended the beds, and Kenyon laid out the brick and

stone pathways. The stone retaining walls throughout the property were made of local granite. The Zahners also hired African American workers to move boulders, plant trees, and perform other tasks to help their landscape vision come to life.

An artist with the land as her canvas, Loyer created a balanced composition, fashioning formal garden rooms and terraces closer to the house and developing naturalistic design elements on the far west side of the lot, which was heavily wooded and included a natural stream and a man-made pond and waterfall. Great thought was given to the pathways through the garden rooms; the goal was to provide a seamless way for family and guests to enjoy their wonders. Weathered rock, historic brick, mature boxwood, and antique wrought-iron gates added an air of age throughout.[15] Loyer's keen interest in horticulture manifested itself in the wide array of ornamental trees, shrubs, perennials, roses, and bulbs she chose.

Among the formal components Loyer designed were a horseshoe-shaped garden, a number of terraces, a rose arbor, a spring garden with a rock-work pool, and a walled garden. In her garden talk, Loyer emphasized the importance of the axis in garden design, calling it "the backbone of any planting plan which relates a garden to the house or to any other parts of the formal outdoor planting."[16] In her garden, she created a strong axis line that led from the back of the house through the horseshoe-shaped garden up a broad flight of granite steps to a series of terraces that terminated on axis at the middle of a curved cedar arbor embraced by climbing roses. The horseshoe-shaped garden had a central lawn and two perennial borders with brick pathways that mimicked the horseshoe curve, against a backdrop of formal clipped boxwood hedges. The arbor served as an outdoor sitting room and featured garden furniture and old ornamental oil jars used as planters.[17] Set against the background of a long privet hedge with a row of eleven pink *Camellia japonica* in front, the rustic arbor was draped with grapevines, jasmine, and a plethora of climbing roses. An early-1930s drawing by Loyer of the rose arbor shows her avid interest in climbing roses. She planted a variety on the arbor, including American Pillar, Dr. Van Fleet, Gold of Ophir, Maman Cochet, Mary Wallace, Paul's Scarlet, Pink Cherokee, Ophelia, and Silver Moon.[18] Planting

Rock-work pool

beds on this terrace also burst with iris, lilies, peonies, and violets.

Near the west side of the house, Loyer designed a formal sunken walled garden, harking back to old European gardens. The rectangular garden was enclosed by rough granite walls with stone buttresses along one side. A decorative iron gate flanked by two urns and a millstone embedded in the ground at the garden's entrance welcomed visitors. A flagstone path lined with small English boxwood bisected the space, widening into an oval in the center of the garden, which featured a bird fountain. The far end held a long rock seat built into a curved rock wall, with urns of ivy embracing each side. Loyer's beloved roses filled the planting beds.[19] On the path above the elegant walled garden was a refined wooden playhouse with a small pediment above its doorway that nodded to the Georgian Revival architecture of the house.

Near the rear west corner of the property, Loyer created a spring garden with an exquisite half-moon rock-work pool. The garden was bordered by cedar, juniper, spring flowering shrubs, and more of her beloved roses trained on chains looped from weathered posts. A broad flagstone terrace led to two flights of curving rock steps that descended to a rock-work pool with an arched grotto. Chinese

OPPOSITE: Colors at dusk, appearing as an iridescent apparition

Stone steps leading to the rear terrace

wisteria that Loyer had brought from her childhood home in South Carolina draped over the rock wall along the back of the pool. She planted a pink Japanese weeping cherry near the pool so that its "beauty might be doubled by reflection."[20] To the edges of the pool, Loyer added a bog garden filled with white Siberian iris, yellow lemon lilies, and blue Japanese iris.

To balance these formal garden spaces, Loyer imbued the woodland garden on the west side of the property with naturalistic components that reflected patterns found in nature. Pathways meandered through the area, including a long flight of granite steps that connected the spring garden to the woodland garden. A central feature was the man-made pond with a waterfall fed by the natural spring. Under the umbrella of native hardwood trees, Loyer added native azalea and rhododendron, redbud, fringe tree, dogwood, and other woodland plants. Large boulders and rocks were skillfully placed on one of the banks of the pond to create pockets for planting an array of specimens, including ferns, astilbe, daphne, dog-tooth violet, trillium, wild geranium, and water-loving plants such as waterlilies, cattails, and swamp iris.[21]

Loyer's splendid landscape of formal garden rooms and large woodland garden was well known in the 1930s. The writer of a 1930 *Atlanta Journal* article was impressed by the Zahners' efforts: "A quiet, peaceful afternoon spent with Mrs. Kenyon Zahner in the gardens of her own creation is indeed a joy and a revelation when one understands that it has all been accomplished by Mr. and Mrs. Zahner's own observance and efforts."[22] Loyer frequently hosted her fellow Primrose Garden Club members in her garden, and in April 1932 she welcomed members of the Garden Club of America for a luncheon to enjoy the masterpiece she had created.[23]

The Zahners sold their house in 1939, and since then the property has had a number of owners. Over time, some garden features were lost, including the curved cedar arbor, the weathered poles with chains for climbing roses, and plant material that succumbed to disease and age. Little is known about the changes to the garden during the ownerships of Pamela and Harold T. Patterson (1939–44) and Harriet and Clifford C. Early (1944–68), aside from

Statue gracing the garden

the Earlys adding a sizable wooden chicken coop north of the garage.

When Bill and Virginia Epstein acquired the property in 1968, the basic structure of Loyer's design was still intact, and the Epsteins began an effort to conservatively renew the gardens and make changes to suit the family's needs and horticultural preferences. In the horseshoe-shaped garden in 1974, they built a swimming pool surrounded by flagstone, yet preserved the historic stone walls and staircase along with the old boxwoods. Working in collaboration with the renowned Atlanta garden designer Ryan Gainey, the Epsteins extensively enriched the plant palette throughout the property with an emphasis on adding white and fragrant varieties adjacent to the rock-work pool. In 1985, they added five sculptures by the American artist Wheeler Williams in prominent locations around the gardens. Virginia Epstein further expanded the flora in the late 1980s by adding

Pathway along the lower edge of the property, leading to the pond

Masses of azaleas defining the
border of the front lawn and
separating it from the naturalistic
hillside garden below

Oakleaf hydrangea providing shade for the
koi and a resting place for a dragonfly

plants with golden foliage, including yellowwood (*Cladrastis kentukea*), yellow twig dogwood (*Cornus sericea* 'Flaviramea'), golden leaf spirea, yellow berried nandina, and variegated yucca.[24] The property was next owned by Jerald Portman (1994–97).

As owners of the property since 1998, Barbara and Charles Slick have enjoyed, enhanced, and lovingly cared for the gardens and grounds. They hired the Atlanta architect Ward Seymour to renovate the house to address modern needs, but kept the façade and the footprint intact. They also worked with the Atlanta landscape designer Esther Stokes and the landscape architect Edward L. Daugherty, a nephew of the Zahners, to address changing needs and to add an incredible flora medley throughout the property. One of the challenges Daugherty solved was to design a small flagstone parking area off the main driveway in front of the house. Barbara Slick,

an avid gardener, knowledgeable plantswoman, and Peachtree Garden Club member, works in the garden daily, assisted by a gardener. She meticulously maintains the landscape and has enhanced the garden by adding new plant material, pathways, areas for entertaining, and decorative features.

In the horseshoe-shaped garden, Barbara added Japanese maples and ferns around the original stones leading from the pool added by the Epsteins, to balance the space against the large clipped boxwood hedges. The east side of the pool contains low clipped Korean boxwood–bordered beds with large groupings of cast iron plants and a hedge of large American boxwood as a backdrop. Other plantings around the pool include Otto Luyken English laurel (*Prunus laurocerasus* 'Otto Luyken'), fatsia, cryptomeria, smoke tree, and a yellowwood. The north axis of the two historic terraces above the pool now

Path circumnavigating the pond

Dogwood in bloom, contrasting with the stone dam

terminates at a classical female statue added by the Epsteins. Off the northernmost terrace, which once held the rustic cedar arbor, Barbara added a gravel path that connects to the historic dry-laid flagstone terrace. She placed an iron gazebo and garden furniture nearby for outdoor entertaining.

The walled garden still remains west of the house, and Loyer's core design is intact. Modifications made over time include the removal of the original entry gate and adjacent urns. Large stone finials now adorn the entrance, and variegated ivy covers the stone walls. The central flagstone pathway inside has been replaced by a boxwood-bordered bed of similar shape, filled with perennials, with a large black urn at the center surrounded by gravel pathways. The Slicks added an overlook with a stone staircase to the west side of the house so that they could enjoy the view of the walled garden from above. The playhouse remains behind the walled garden; its entrance is covered in Confederate jasmine. The spring garden includes an open lawn surrounded by an array of plants, including English and Korean boxwood, hemlock, hydrangea, loropetalum, pittosporum, viburnum, tea olive, hosta, and holly fern. In the center of the rock-work pool, Barbara added a fountain designed by the Georgia artist and blacksmith Ivan Bailey. A pathway that leads from the pool area past the garden shed to the spring garden is lined with yews on the left and *Camellia japonica* 'Pink Perfection' on the right.

In the woodland garden, the large pond is thriving with water lilies, swamp iris, fish, turtles, and toads. Barbara added stone paths on the northwest side of the pond, and gravel paths on the east side. She lined them with myriad plants, including varieties of *Camellia japonica*, *Azalea indica* 'Mrs. G. G. Gerbing', *Hydrangea macrophylla* 'Nikko Blue', oakleaf hydrangea, bay magnolias, forsythia, winterberry, aucuba, redbud, bald cypress, rhododendron, and many varieties of ferns. The gravel paths wind around to the front of the property, terminating at the lower area of the driveway. There are also two wooden bridges around the pond, one added by the Epsteins and the other by the Slicks. Barbara has enhanced the plantings around the historic rock staircase that descends into the woodland garden with double oakleaf hydrangea, Kousa dogwood,

Seating area for contemplation

cast iron plant, hosta, hellebore, strawberry begonia, Christmas fern, and much more. The Slicks use the Earlys' chicken coop behind the garage, and Barbara has nestled herbs and vegetables in garden beds nearby.

Ninety years after its inception, the Zahner-Slick garden remains a strong, balanced composition. Loyer Zahner's thoughtful combination of formal and informal elements has stood the test of time. The plants, paths, stonework, and metalwork meant more to Loyer than their mere beauty and utility. She believed, as she told her fellow gardeners in the talk she gave to garden clubs around Atlanta, that gardens are essential to everyone's health and happiness: "From the earliest times there were gardens and the world is the better off today for the touch of gentleness and calm they have given to all who knew them. Let us all have gardens, for we shall be but following the footsteps of those of past ages, and but expressing the love of the garden that has been in our hearts for generations. Above all, let us have a sense of seclusion in our flowered space, that the calm and peace shall in no way be broken."[25] Thanks to the Epsteins and Slicks, the Zahner-Slick garden still evokes gentleness and calm to all those who walk down its paths.

APPENDIX

List and Status of Gardens Documented through the Georgia Historic Landscape Initiative from *Garden History of Georgia, 1733–1933*

Each entry in the Appendix contains the following: The garden name as originally listed in *Garden History of Georgia*; the garden's period of construction, significance, and development; the garden's current status; and a quotation from *Garden History of Georgia* regarding the garden. The appendix is arranged by county and then by city.

The authors did not correct the spelling of botanical names or common plant names quoted within *Garden History of Georgia*. Any instances of misspelled words were likewise left uncorrected. In a few cases, the authors have inserted a word or an individual's name for clarification.

꙳ Indicates a site that is open to the public

Baldwin County

MILLEDGEVILLE

Mr. and Mrs. Miller S. Bell Garden

Early twentieth century

The historic garden and house no longer remain.

"The sunken garden on the property of Mr. and Mrs. Miller S. Bell was planned with great care under the direct supervision of its owners. The garden is at its best in springtime when iris and tulips and many dainty rock plants in the crannies of the walls are all in bloom. A generous planting of shrubs of varied heights and shapes encloses the entire property and gives it a delightful seclusion from the world outside." (345)

Greenacre, or the Judge and Mrs. E. R. Hines Garden

Early twentieth century

The historic garden and house no longer remain.

"The rock garden at Greenacre, viewed of a morning in early spring, is a picture to be remembered. Strolling leisurely down the 'Old Road' there comes a sense of nature's perfection in the hush of the new day. On either side are great masses of blossoms— low ones—spilling over the rocks—English daisies, dwarf tulips, wild iris, and pansy faces, still wet with dew. From the 'Old Road' there branches off a woodland pathway leading on to a flagstone terrace, and, from the old mill-stone embedded there, a lovely view opens on the various rock gardens and terraces that merge and blend into a colorful whole." (339)

Westover Plantation

Antebellum

Portions of the historic garden remain. The original outbuildings remain. The original house burned in 1954, and another one was built on the original house's foundations. The privately owned site is listed in the National Register of Historic Places.

"A double circular drive shaded by an avenue of elms, magnolias and cedars leads from the gate to the base of the formal garden in front of the house. It consists of two rectangular and two circular beds edged with dwarf box, as is this whole central division, which contains a formal planting of cedars, crape myrtle, pomegranate, tea olive and Cape jasmine." (82)

Williams-Ferguson Garden

Antebellum

Portions of the historic garden remain. The original house remains. The site is privately owned.

"The box garden lies on either side of the front walk and consists of circles enclosed in rectangles. There are formal box tree plantings, and groups of Pyrus japonica, pomegranates, crepe myrtle, sweet syringa, German myrtle and vitex, both blue and pink, the latter a rare specimen. On each side of the house, leading from the garden toward the rear, is a wide box bordered walk forty feet long. Handsome red cedars encompass the garden, those on the west carrying a glorious mantle of wistaria, the growth of one hundred and twenty years." (81)

Bartow County

ADAIRSVILLE

ɞ Barnsley Gardens

Antebellum

Portions of the historic garden remain, and some facets of it have been restored. Ruins of the original house remain and have been stabilized. The original kitchen wing of the house was turned into a museum. The privately owned site is now part of the Barnsley Resort, which is open to the public. The site is included in the National Register of Historic Places as part of the Etowah Valley Historic District. www.barnsleyresort.com

"The entrance driveway flanked by rose and shrub plantings, divides to sweep around either side of an exquisite oval box garden, the design of which seems to have been taken from a motif in a Marseilles quilt. In its center is an antique Italian fountain of white marble. Statuary brought from Italy for its adornment was shipped North in '64. Triangular rock gardens fill the spaces between it and the drive across the terrace on which the three dwellings stand. A small box garden lies in front of the left wing; a croquet ground in front of the wing to the right." (108)

CARTERSVILLE

Valley View

Antebellum

The historic garden, the original house (with original interiors and furnishings), the original outbuildings, and a portion of the original agricultural land remain intact. The privately owned site is listed in the National Register of Historic Places individually and as part of the Etowah Valley Historic District.

"The garden's most distinguished feature is triple hedges bordering the central walk, formed of Carolina cherries and box. The garden bounded on one side by Carolina cherry and by bush wistaria on the other, shows original plantings of well trimmed dwarf box borders, tree box, Carolina cherry, English laurel, euonymus, Norway spruce and fir, Persian lilacs, crape myrtle, mock orange, flowering holly, cape jasmine, Pyrus japonica and forsythia. The roses are Maman Cochets, Malmaisons, dailies, both red and pink, moss roses, and a highly valued green rose." (110)

Bibb County

MACON

Cowles-Bond-Coleman-Cabaniss-O'Neal Place Garden

Antebellum

Few remnants of the historic garden remain. The original gazebo, carriage house, and house remain. Mercer University owns the site, which is today referred to as the Woodruff House. The site is listed in the National Register of Historic Places.

"The original four acres in which it [the house] stood were planted by Mrs. Jerry Cowles in mimosa, cherry laurel, magnolias, cedars and camellias. The principal box garden was in recent years dug up to make a tennis court. In front of the right wing is a small box maze. Part of the grounds including the peach orchard became a public park in 1879, when the handsome iron entrance gates were removed." (88)

Porterfield, or the
Mr. and Mrs. James Porter Garden

Circa 1928

The historic garden no longer remains. The original house remains and is owned by the Porterfield Baptist Church. The original barn has been converted to a private residence.

"Ornamental tree roses primly mark the path leading to the white-latticed rose pavilion in the heart of the formally planted section. This pavilion, which houses perhaps two hundred bushes, was constructed to establish the exact number of sunshine hours necessary for the best possible rose development in this section." (333)

Camden County

WOODBINE

Twin Plantations, Bellevue and Fairfield

Bellevue Plantation, 1800
Fairfield Plantation, 1798

The only remaining feature at Bellevue Plantation is the tabby ruins of the house, which was designed in the shape of an anchor. The Floyd family cemetery remains near the site of the former Fairfield Plantation. The properties are now owned by Dow Chemical.

"Two handsome homes were erected. Bellevue for the Colonel [Charles Floyd], and a mile away, Fairfield, for his son, John. An avenue of live oaks and cedars bordered the connecting road. Under its shade was a hedge-like planting of myrtle imported from Germany, edged with thousands of bulbs. Both houses had formally laid out gardens set in lawns graced by shrubs and flowering trees." (52)

Carroll County

CARROLLTON

Oak Lawn

Circa early 1800s

The historic garden no longer remains, although the original house does. The privately owned site is operated as a special-event facility.

"The house at Oak Lawn had the two-storied portico supported by twin columns and the delicately balustraded balcony seen in north Georgia houses, an initial type of the Greek Revival architecture then sweeping the State. Here the Kingsberys, both New Englanders and doubtless homesick for familiar things, did not plant the usual formal garden of the district. On either side of the box bordered, stone flagged walk leading from an arched picket gateway to the doorstep were square lawns bounded by flower-filled borders, rose beds and bands of bulbs. Two rock mounds planted in blue and white periwinkle belonged to the late fifties, giving a solemn Victorian note." (92)

Charlton and Ware Counties, parts of Brantley and Clinch Counties

Okefenokee Swamp

Home to Native American communities dating to 2500 BCE; Okefenokee National Wildlife Refuge, established in 1937 by the U.S. government

The Okefenokee Swamp is approximately 438,000 acres of peat-filled wetland. The majority of the swamp is intact and is protected by the Okefenokee National Wildlife Refuge and the Okefenokee Wilderness. It is considered one of the Seven Natural Wonders of Georgia and is the largest blackwater swamp in North America. The site was designated a National Natural Landmark in 1974.

"The swamp is approximately sixty miles long by eighteen to thirty miles wide. . . . Surrounding the inundated portion of the swamp are forests of long leaf pine (Pinus palustris) and slash pine (Pinus caribaea), with an undergrowth of saw palmetto (Serenoa serrulata), gall berries (Ilex glabra), myrtles and huckleberries. Scattered among these are found various herbaceous plants such as Eriocaulon (Pipewort), Polygala (Milkwort), and partridge peas. Upon entering the swamp from the eastern side at Folkston, one is struck by the abundance of vegetation characteristic of marsh-swamp habitat. . . . Along the banks of the canal are bay trees, Cyrilla racemiflora, Ilex Cassine and I. vomitoria, with an occasional black gum and an abundance of Leucothoe racemosa drooping over the water." (409–10)

OSSABAW ISLAND

✄ Dr. and Mrs. H. N. Torrey Garden

Gardens, circa 1920s; house, circa 1926

Portions of the historic garden remain. The original house remains. The original patio garden, enclosed on three sides by the pink stucco walls of the house and flanked by twin gardens terminating into twin tile fountains, is still intact. The garden was designed by the American landscape architect Ellen Biddle Shipman. The main house was designed by the architects Henrick Wallin and Arthur F. Comer. Buildings from the antebellum period, the late nineteenth century, and the 1920s remain on the island. The site is owned by the State of Georgia, except for the main house and the twenty-six acres surrounding it, which are owned under a life estate by Eleanor Torrey West. The state has a use agreement with the Ossabaw Island Foundation for the portion of the island that does not include the Torrey West estate. The island, which is a Georgia Heritage Preserve and is listed in the National Register of Historic Places, may be visited by the public. Ossabaw Island may be visited by the public for natural, scientific, or cultural education, research, or study. The Torrey West Estate and Garden is not open to the public. http://ossabawisland.org

"It is a long rambling plaster house of Spanish ranch-house type, an architecture appropriate not only to the native growth of palmettos and yuccas but to the historical associations here of sixteenth century Spanish occupation. The first garden made was a patio garden, developed by Ellen Shipman. The later gardens have been planned by Mrs. Torrey. Bermuda pink walls surround three sides of the patio which is the important feature of the garden side of the house. The pavement is of dark terra cotta tiles and at the centre, supported on two hexagonal stone steps is an aquarium, fifteen feet in circumference, where gold and silver fish gleam among the water plants. . . . The east wall, with its arched entrance to the forecourt, is covered with ivy and cat's claw-vine (Bignonia unguis cati) which escapes from the wall to the house, and mingles its large, golden-yellow trumpets with the lavender ones of the Bignonia Speciosa that completely covers the patio side of the house. Flanking these walls, a set of twin gardens, with an old brick walk between, terminate in twin tile fountains of a lovely blue and green color, the water spouting from the mouth of green lion heads." (349, 351)

SAVANNAH AND VICINITY

✄ Andrew Low House and Garden

Antebellum

Portions of the historic garden remain. The original house and carriage house remain. The site, owned and operated by the National Society of the Colonial Dames of America in the State of Georgia, is listed as part of both the Savannah and the Juliette Gordon Low National Historic Landmark Districts. The site is open for tours. www.andrewlowhouse.com

"The Low House is a typical Trust Lot development. The front garden retains its form and a portion of the original planting. The garden lying between residence and carriage house has been somewhat altered." (27)

Avon Hall

Antebellum

Only a few historic camellias remain. A fire destroyed the antebellum house in 1970. One slave cabin remains. The site is privately owned.

"The first garden was filled with roses and flowering shrubs; of orange trees there was an abundance. In 1865 the property was bought by William Neyle Habersham for a country home. He at once began the planting of cassena hedges, also of camellias imported from France. Of these, twenty-one varieties still bloom from November to April, many having reached the unusual height of twenty feet." (33)

Battersby-Hartridge Garden, or the Battersby-Hartridge-Wilder-Anderson Home and Garden*

Antebellum

Portions of the historic garden remain. The original house remains. The privately owned site is listed as part of the Savannah Historic District, a National Landmark District.

"A walled garden lies to the east. It has the distinction of being the oldest surviving Savannah garden retaining its original plan and planting. The oddly shaped beds outlined by double scalloped tiles were edged by violets and snowdrops, now replaced by ivy. The pride of this garden still is the original plantings of camellias of the following varieties: Don Kaleare, Camellia reticulata, Lady Hume's blush, the Ella Drayton, Legeman, Abby Wilder, alba plena, and a large, bold red and white variegated, catalogued as 'unnamed.'" (24)

* "Battersby" was misspelled in the original *Garden History of Georgia* book as "Batersby."

Bonaventure Cemetery

Antebellum

The historic cemetery is still intact, including the historic trees and plant material, the mausoleums, and the elaborate grave markers and monuments. The site is listed in the National Register of Historic Places. A world-famous tourist destination, the cemetery is open to the public, and the Bonaventure Cemetery Historical Society provides free tours to the public. www.bonaventurehistorical.org

"Imagine the effect now—these century-old trees, their arms interlacing and draped with Spanish moss, leading one in and out among monuments of brick and stone with here and there a vista through which one catches a glimpse of the sea. All along the way azaleas and camellias are planted, and in the early spring, wistaria vines festoon themselves into garlands overhead. There are many fine old cypress trees, while, in private sections, individuals have planted extensively Cape jasmines, tea olives, azaleas and camellias—now enormous in size." (427)

Chatham County Public Schools' Gardens

Circa late 1910s–1920s

The historic gardens no longer remain.

"School gardens in this county have varied horticultural histories. County schools often are close to long stretches of marshes. The fact that most of the city schools face on parks or squares, or are adjacent to them, causes one to think that the founders when selecting the site were not unmindful of the teachings of the great educator, Hermes, who maintained that 'a garden should be connected with every school so that children can, at times, gaze leisurely on trees, flowers and herbs and be taught to enjoy them.'. . . The first record of garden work by

pupils [at the Chatham Academy] dates from 1919, when this Academy became a Junior High School. Miss Ruby Rahn, science teacher, sponsored the first Junior Garden Club Garden and it has functioned through each semester." (442)

The Hermitage

Antebellum

The historic garden and house no longer remain.

"Between the mansion and the river was a sunken garden, a type rarely seen in old Georgia. The retaining walls are of brick and the flight of steps leading down to it of white marble. Square beds were separated by irrigation ditches, spanned by rustic bridges, their flooding controlled by the rise and fall of the river tide. In this garden tropical and semi-tropical plants were featured. The roses, many imported from Europe, were planted in rice field mud and reached a high state of perfection." (30)

Mrs. Thomas Hilton Garden

Circa 1925

Portions of the historic garden remain. The original house remains. The site is privately owned.

"Mrs. Hilton's garden has been placed in a sheltered spot to the southeast of the L-shaped house. A rose arbor on one side and a ligustrum and bamboo hedge on the other, complete the enclosure which gives it a delightful seclusion. On the arbor grow a succession of roses, the bloom starting in February with the Pink Cherokee, then followed by Yellow Banksia, White Cherokee, Silver Moon, and American Pillar." (374)

Lebanon Plantation

Circa 1804

Portions of the historic garden remain. The original house and outbuildings remain. The site is privately owned.

"The land approach was by a long avenue of live oaks and cedars, sections of which remain. A grove of fine old trees made a setting for the house, in front of which was a rose garden with narcissus bordered beds. Of the roses, only a Madame Lambard still wreaths the veranda to a height of fifteen feet, but thousands of old bulbs bloom each spring and two giant dark red crape myrtles have guarded the steps for more than a century. Of the fringe of flowering trees and shrubs that encircled the house and garden, there survive a banana shrub, Chinese magnolias, and a few camellias such as aeta plena, Lady Hume's Blush and Kurmii." (29)

≫ Richardson-Maxwell-Owens-Thomas House and Garden, or the Owens-Thomas House and Garden

Circa 1819

Portions of the historic garden remain. The original house and outbuildings remain. A period-appropriate garden, designed by the Savannah landscape architect Clermont Lee, was laid out in 1954. The property, owned and operated by the Telfair Museum of Art, is listed as a National Historic Landmark as one of the nation's finest examples of English Regency architecture. The site is open for tours. www.telfair.org/visit/owens-thomas

"It was enclosed on all four sides by a high brick wall topped by broken glass bottles to discourage marauders. There was a grilled iron gate on the State Street side and a solid wooden wagon gate at rear on the lane. It presented a pattern of oval and odd shaped beds edged in very dwarf box, and contained Don Kaleare, Ocse Luca, Mutabelis and other varieties of japonicas, banana shrub, sweet oleo, purple and white wistaria, rhynchospermum, English jasmine, ivy, syringa, Guernsey lilies, blue bells, white and blue flags, Roman hyacinths, narcissus, snow drops, Dutch hyacinths, ixias, anemones, asters, pansies, violets, larkspur, and many roses among which were Malmaison, Paul Neyron, cloth of gold, Marie Van Houtte, Maman Cochet and Devoniensis." (23)

Rural Felicity, or the Mr. and Mrs. Malcolm MacLean Garden

Circa 1927

A few remnants of the historic garden remain. The original house remains and has been renovated. The property is privately owned.

"A background being established [for the garden], the space was divided into three gardens, separated by high trellises, the center garden to be enclosed in shrubs, the other two to be planted in relation to the spreading fig trees. The planting was done

in such a way as to keep open a view of the marsh, so gold in winter, so green in summer. The center garden is entered from the left side by a path leading between a bed of Anthony Waterer spirea, edged with euonymous, and one of figs, which in winter shows a trunk as gray as the Spanish moss waving pennant-like from the great live oak towering above it." (375, 377)

Savannah Female Orphans Home Garden, or the Junior League Garden

House, circa 1800s; garden, circa early nineteenth century and later re-created by the Junior League of Savannah, circa 1930s

The historic garden and orphans home no longer remain. The site was sold in the late 1940s, and a car dealership was built on the site.

"At the rear of the house the garden has been made in an area enclosed in a high brick and tabby wall. While clearing this yard the workers discovered the original pattern of an old flower bed and this inspired further exploration until a complete plan was disclosed: the plan showing a formal design, a quaint heart shaped bed at the center, and paths of old brick laid in herring bone pattern. All the planting has been worked out to conform with that of old fashioned gardens in this locality, and the flowers and shrubs were selected accordingly." (424)

≫ Savannah Squares

Eighteenth and nineteenth centuries

Twenty-two of the original twenty-four squares remain. The squares are owned by the City of Savannah and are listed as part of the Savannah Historic District, a National Landmark District. The squares are open to the public.

"Savannah as laid out by Oglethorpe had building lots sixty by ninety feet, and her garden development had to conform to their narrow limits. The earliest map of the city shows the wooden palisades which enclosed them. First food stuffs and shortly afterwards flowers were planted. Turned fences were the next step, but from a very early date these flower gardens were walled and of formal pattern. Semitropical plantings mingled with roses and flowers reminiscent of the English homes of the colonists." (21)

Miss Lucy B. Trosdal Garden

Circa 1930

Portions of the historic garden remain. The original house remains. The site is privately owned.

"There are two gardens, both walled. One is a small patio garden 30 × 40 feet, opening from the dining room on the north side of the house. To the west side lies the larger garden, 90 × 120 feet. The plans are simple and in keeping with the architecture of the house. Walled gardens for privacy distinguish Savannah and add much to its old world atmosphere. A lavish use of the evergreen, camellias, azaleas, and other plant material of this section,—the design tied in with the house by means of the characteristic walls achieves for Miss Trosdal's gardens a distinct charm." (378)

Trustees' Garden

1733

The historic garden no longer remains.

"The Trustees' Garden in Savannah was Georgia's first formally laid out garden and her first experiment station. Charles C. Jones, Jr., in his History of Georgia, tells us that by order of James Oglethorpe in the spring of 1733: 'A public garden was laid out and a servant detailed, at the charge of the trust, to cultivate it. This was to serve as a nursery whence might be procured fruit trees, vines, plants, and vegetables for the private orchards and gardens of the inhabitants. It was also largely devoted to the propagation of the white mulberry, from the general cultivation of which, as food for the silkworm, great benefit was anticipated.'" (15)

Whitehall Plantation

Early 1800s

The only features that remain are an allée of live oaks and a cemetery. Most of the property was paved for container storage for the Georgia Ports Authority.

"No records survive describing the house built by Joseph Gibbons which was destroyed during the occupation of Savannah by General Sherman and replaced after the Civil War by a frame dwelling still the home of his descendants. It stands above the river in a twenty-five acre primeval grove of giant live oaks under the shade of which bloom camellias and azaleas." (28)

⚘ Wormsloe, or the Mr. and Mrs. W. W. De Renne Garden; Wormsloe State Historic Site*

Eighteenth–twentieth centuries; formal garden, circa 1920s

The eighteenth-century tabby ruins of Noble Jones's fortified residence, the Jones family burial ground, the live oak drive (circa 1890s), the original house (circa 1830, with later additions), the original 1908 library, and portions of the historic garden still remain. Noble Jones established Wormsloe in 1736, and subsequent generations have made modifications to the site, most notably Augusta Floyd De Renne, who designed a Colonial Revival garden in the 1920s. The site is listed in the National Register of Historic Place. The majority of the property is now Wormsloe State Historic Site and is open to the public; other portions, including the main house and former 1920s garden, are privately owned by original descendants and not open to the public. www. gastateparks.org/Wormsloe

"In describing this plantation it is almost impossible to separate the old from the new, as the informality of its plan and planting has admitted of a constant intermingling of the two. In every phase it is a record of the development of coastal Georgia." (20)

"The first section of the formal gardens is a walled rectangle, with a recess to the east and a flagged walk on the west side. In the recess a grille panel is used in the center of which is a medallion of Storey, the southern writer. Over the recess is a cedar arbor planted to roses, scuppernong vines, and Clematis paniculata. Four old Italian marbles from Spalding House on Sapelo Island have been used in this garden after the Pompeian manner." (370)

* Wormsloe was included in *Garden History of Georgia* twice: in part 1, "Georgia's Early Gardens," as Wormsloe, and in part 2, "Modern Gardens," as Wormsloe, or the Mr. and Mrs. W. W. De Renne Garden.

ATHENS

Beech Haven, or the
Mr. and Mrs. C. A. Rowland Garden

Early twentieth century

Portions of the historic garden remain. The original house, bridges, and stonework remain. The majority of the property is owned by Athens–Clarke County and is protected as part of the Athens–Clarke County greenway network. The site has been nominated to the National Register of Historic Places.

"Many years ago Mr. and Mrs. C. A. Rowland, of Athens, purchased a tract of over two hundred acres of wooded land on the banks of the winding Oconee, and in developing it have been careful not to destroy a single feature of the wild grandeur of rock, woodland pool, and tangled solitude." (155)

Bishop Cottage, or the Bishop Cottage Garden

Antebellum

Few remnants of the historic garden remain. The original house remains. The site, owned by the University of Georgia, is listed in the National Register of Historic Places.

"To the left of the house three terraces are planted in fruit trees, shrubs and flowers. One for many years had in its center an elm, a scion from the tree in Cambridge under which Washington stood when he took command of the Continental Army; another has a curved boundary line of box. To the immediate right of the house is a terraced bulb garden, defined by box and shaded by large flowering shrubs and a very lovely weeping box, trimmed to resemble a fringed parasol. Across a walk running along it from the street to the rear of the house, these terraces, now quite shallow, are set out in fruit trees. The fourth and final terrace is entirely given over to utilitarian planting." (74)

Box Garden, or the SAE Chapter House, or the Ross Crane Garden

Antebellum

Few remnants of the historic garden remain. The original house remains. The site is owned by the Georgia Beta Chapter House Corporation, Sigma Alpha Epsilon fraternity, and is listed in the National Register of Historic Places.

"The long walk was bordered on both sides with box from the house to the street. Outside the box borders ran paths of white sand, which were in turn edged with cypress trees and rose bushes. In time the house was sold by its builder and later owners destroyed most of the old time garden. The old magnolias on the lawn, survivors of the original garden, today are magnificent specimens." (151)

Camak Place Garden, or Camak House Garden

Antebellum

Few remnants of the historic garden remain. The original house and outbuildings remain. The privately owned site is listed in the National Register of Historic Places.

"Today finds the Camak Place, on Meigs Street, built in 1830 and occupied by five generations of that family, still standing in its original four acres of park-like planting." (73)

Grant-Hill-White-Bradshaw Place, or the University of Georgia President's House and Garden

Antebellum

Portions of the historic garden remain. The original house remains. The site, owned by the University of Georgia, serves at the President's House. The site is listed in the National Register of Historic Places.

"The large box garden has a particularly dignified design carrying heavy plantings of magnolia, cedar of Lebanon, cherry laurel and tree box. Filling the beds are cape jasmine, evergreen bush (euonymus), Mahonia aquifolia, winter jasmine, yucca, cassinas, pittosporum, tea and tea olive, flowering quince, Persian and European lilac, forsythia, althea, weigela, sweet syringa, sweet shrub, snow ball, bridal wreath spirea, ribbon grass, roses and bulbs. A screen of cherry laurel and crape myrtle secures privacy from the passer-by." (78)

Mr. and Mrs. E. R. Hodgson Jr. Garden, or the Dr. James S. Hamilton Garden

House, antebellum; garden, early twentieth century

The historic garden no longer remains. The original house remains. The site is privately owned by the Alpha Delta Pi sorority and is listed in the National Register of Historic Places.

"The garden is large, several acres in extent. It drops away from the house in three grassy terraces with steps set into the turf, but so wide are the terraces that the total effect is that of a sweeping level, the last terrace barely visible through the trees. . . . To the west of the house lies a small formal flower garden with brick paths and low box hedges. It is a spring and fall garden, in spring abloom with daffodils, narcissi, tulips, and delphinium, and in fall with asters and chrysanthemums." (148)

Mrs. E. K. Lumpkin Garden

Antebellum

The historic garden no longer remains. The original house remains. The site is home to the Young Harris United Methodist Church and is owned by the United Methodist Conference of North Georgia. The site is listed in the National Register of Historic Places.

"Two views are given of the home of Mrs. E. K. Lumpkin, in Athens, one of the front of the house, which was built in the fifties by a son of Richard D. B. Taylor, a prominent citizen, the other of Mrs. Lumpkin's parlor, where the meeting was held in January, 1891, which resulted in the formation of the Ladies' Garden Club, and the election of the first set of officers of that body. The Ladies' Garden Club has continued in existence ever since, although the name has been changed to the Garden Club of Athens. On the authority of P. J. Berckmans of Augusta, who was at the zenith of his career as a horticulturist at the time of its organization, this was the first club of its kind to be formed in America, with a president and other officers working on a parliamentary basis." (149)

Dr. and Mrs. R. E. Park Garden

Circa 1930

Few remnants of the historic garden remain. The original house remains. The privately owned site is included in the National Register of Historic Places as part of the Dearing Street Historic District.

"Hidden away behind the residence of Dr. and Mrs. R. E. Park on quaint old Dearing Street is a garden which is typical of the modern small garden. Two sections have been completed; one semi-formal, the other naturalistic. In the semi-formal garden a path encircles three sides of a space of turf in the center, which is shaded by mimosa and pecan trees. Beyond the path the borders, laid out in serpentine curves, are planted in peonies, geum, Madonna lilies, and flowering crapapple. At one side is a bird bath surrounded by iris and lilacs, and opposite is a trellis supporting a fine Lady Banksia rose which is flanked by lilacs which are in lavender bloom at the same time the rose is a mass of yellow." (153)

Dr. and Mrs. Henry Reid Garden

Circa 1930

The historic garden no longer remains. The original house remains but has been substantially modified. The site, owned by Howard Properties, is leased to a private company.

"A flat-rimmed pool, fringed in ivy, is set back in a recess of the bank and is overshadowed by tall English laurel and nandina, while around it maiden hair fern, Japanese iris and other flowers that thrive in moist soil abound. Beyond the pool the rock garden extends the length of the formally planned portion of the main garden which is divided into two sections connected by a rose hung pergola and flag stone paths under trellises of roses. In the scheme of the two gardens two features add balance to the design. At one end of the enclosure an ornamental gazing globe stands in a curve of shrubbery behind which tall poplar trees are grouped. Opposite this at the far end of the formal planting lies a curved pool holding a fountain figure and flanked by two graceful urns." (154)

Mr. and Mrs. Lamar C. Rucker Garden

Circa 1920s

Few remnants of the historic garden remain. The original house remains. The site is privately owned. The current owner has created a contemporary garden on the property, which was started in 1994. The site is included in the National Register of Historic Places as part of the Dearing Street Historic District.

"Several trees in the garden surrounding the Rucker home have survived the ravages of the War Between the States and the mutations of the lean years that followed. Flourishing in the finished beauty of the restored area are a stately gingko tree whose leaf, shaped like the maidenhair fern, turns to gold in the winds of autumn; a Kentucky coffee tree; a swamp cypress; a rare buckeye and three varieties of magnolia. In recent years a small formal garden has been added and on the east side of the house, an uncovered brick terrace bordered with boxwood has been laid." (157–58)

Mr. and Mrs. Bolling Hall Sasnett Garden

Circa 1930s

The historic garden no longer remains. The original house remains. The property is owned by the Theta Chi fraternity.

"The house was Southern Colonial, the entrance striking the keynote of the whole—spaciousness, leisurely living, a sense of ampleness and freedom—so the garden was made a place of leisurely enjoyment, a retreat from the noise and hurry of the outside world. A definite color scheme of pastel tints: cream, pink, blue and yellow, was worked out in the acid soil of shady spots, with brighter tones in the open sunlight. The relation of each mass of color to the whole scheme has been well considered in the placing of plants and the design of the garden is worked out by a fine choice of flowers. The formal planting about the house achieves its color scheme with pink azaleas, blue Phlox divaricata, daphne, and yellow pansies. Spanish and Dutch iris in the open sunlight make gay mantles of color, mixed with fleecy white gypsophila, fragrant lemon lilies and pink pentstemon. Great splashes of vivid pigments were added with German iris." (159)

Stevens Thomas Place

Antebellum

The historic garden no longer remains. The original house was moved in the early twentieth century.

"John Bishop, an English landscape gardener in charge of the University's Botanical Garden, was entrusted with the laying out of the grounds. This was done with intelligence and good taste. Oaks shaded a lawn that framed a box garden resembling two oriental rugs in a palm and crescent design, accented by Magnolia grandiflora, Japanese magnolias and cape jasmine. Between it and the front fence were rose trellises and flowering shrubs." (76)

ꝏ University of Georgia Campuses

North Campus, early nineteenth century

Founders Memorial Garden, circa 1939–50

Portions of the historic campus landscape remain. It and the historic Founders Memorial Garden, which lies within the original campus boundaries, are owned by the University of Georgia, and both are listed in the National Register of Historic Places. The campus and garden are open to the public. www.ced.uga.edu/about/facilities/founders-memorial

"In spite of its haphazard growth, this campus is well worth visiting. It is filled with traditions and mellowed with age. Its academic walk is flanked on one side by the classic columns of Greece and on the other by magnificent trees whose shadows lay a mosaic across the path that has been trod by Georgia's great since the days the Colony became a state." (455)

Misses Upson Garden

House, antebellum; gardens, early twentieth century

Few remnants of the historic garden remain. The original house remains. The property is now owned by a bank.

"To the east a formal garden, one of the most elaborate in this part of Georgia, is made on three levels. The upper level is a terrace lying along the wall of the old house and reached by low steps from the end of the high pillared porch. From the north side of the terrace, steps go down to a green garden on the second level, which is oval in shape, of smooth green turf, and planted in Italian cypress, ligustrum, junipers, and Lombardy poplars. Leading through this garden from the terrace above to the flower garden below, is a twelve-foot allee of arbor vitae." (161)

Cobb County

MARIETTA

Ivy Grove, or the Mr. and Mrs. Morgan McNeel Sr. Garden

House, antebellum; gardens, antebellum and circa 1920s–1930s

Few remnants of the historic garden remain. The original house remains and is currently being restored by the owners. The privately owned site is listed in the National Register of Historic Places as part of the Church Street–Cherokee Street Historic District, and is locally designated under a district of the same name.

"The house, surrounded by sloping green lawns, stands on a pleasant elevation in a grove of old oaks. Directly back of the house is a sizeable kitchen garden, to the west lie the flower gardens, the pecan groves and the playgrounds. The formal gardens are laid out on two levels. An arch of roses is over the entrance to the upper garden which is bound on one side by the ivy-covered brick wall and on the other by low-clipped hedges. Here are carefully planned borders, arranged for a succession of bloom. Jonquils and tulips of early spring give way to iris, fox glove, larkspur, poppies and phlox, then later perennials and annuals furnish color till frost. The garden on the lower level has a white marble pool holding goldfish and vari-colored water lilies. To the right and left of the pool are box-bordered rose beds." (337)

Oakton

House, antebellum; gardens, circa late 1860s–1870s

Portions of the historic garden remain. The original house and outbuildings remain. The privately owned site is listed on the National Register of Historic Places.

"Beyond kitchen, well, smoke house and dairy is an acre and a half of garden enclosed by a picket fence; here we find apple, fig, pear, quince and cherry trees. A grape arbor shades the path leading to an orchard at the rear. The box bordered beds contain small fruits and berries, musk cluster and Malmaison roses, peonies, iris, narcissus, jonquils and snowdrops, a mint bed, long borders of sweet lavender and knotted rows of herbs and seasonings." (116)

Coweta County

NEWNAN

Dunaway Gardens, or the Blue Bonnet Lodge, or the Mr. and Mrs. Wayne P. Sewell Garden

Circa late 1920s–1930s

Portions of the historic garden remain, and many facets of it have been restored. The privately owned site is operated by the Dunaway Gardens Foundation and is listed in the National Register of Historic Places. The site is open to the public for tours. www.dunawaygardens. com

"The sunken garden has been made against a background of rugged beauty, where a cascade dances over mossy boulders. The stream winds its way through the garden and forms three lily pools farther on. There are seven such springs on the property; and centering the sunken garden is an old-fashioned 'wishing well.'" (347)

Rosemary

Antebellum

The historic garden no longer remains. The original house has been moved.

"Berckmans, the distinguished Belgian landscape gardener, seems to have been in a playful mood when designing the garden at Rosemary. Dominated by two gigantic, sentinel-like magnolias, one of which is almost smothered in wistaria, its petal shaped beds are outlined by carefully clipped box. There are plantings of clipped tree box and many flowering shrubs." (106)

ATLANTA

Boxwood, or the Mr. and Mrs. Charles Veazey Rainwater Garden

Early twentieth century

Portions of the historic garden remain. The original house and the outbuildings remain. The privately owned site is included in the National Register of Historic Places as part of the Druid Hills Historic District. The site is also included in the Druid Hills Landmark District, a local landmark district designated by the Atlanta Urban Design Commission.

"Adjoining the house to the rear is a rectangular walled green garden used as an outdoor living-room and dining-room. Across the narrow ivy-bordered pool in the lawn is a garden figure set in a niche of the wall and shadowed by two tall cedars. Mahonia, abelia, osmanthus and English laurel afford varying foliage contrasts to the heavy clumps of English box against the side walls and the corner trees of Buxus arborescens." (251)

ᔌ Callanwolde,* or the Mr. and Mrs. Howard Candler Garden

Circa 1920s

Portions of the historic garden remain, and some facets of it have been restored. The original house and the outbuildings remain. The site is owned by DeKalb County. The county has had a long-standing partnership with the DeKalb County Federation of Garden Clubs and the Redbud District of the Garden Club of Georgia. Since 2011, volunteers with the DeKalb Extension Master Gardener program, with funding from Callanwolde and the DeKalb County Federation of Garden Clubs, have been responsible for the formal garden on the property. The Callanwolde Foundation operates the Callanwolde Fine Arts Center on the property. The site is listed in the National Register of Historic Places. This site is also included in the Druid Hills Local Historic District, designated by DeKalb County. The site is open for tours. http://callanwolde.org /tours

"Across the driveway from the house is a formal garden of perennials, the beds designed about a sun dial. A pergola hung in grape vines is at the far end and beyond this is the sunken 'rose bowl.' Hybrid teas of many colors are in the curved beds while climbing roses cover the sloping banks." (188)

* "Callanwolde" was misspelled in the original *Garden History of Georgia* book as "Callenwolde."

ᔌ Cator Woolford Gardens, or the Mr. and Mrs. Cator Woolford Garden, or Jacqueland

Gardens, circa 1920s; house, circa 1926

Portions of the historic garden remain, and some facets of it have been restored. The original house has been renovated. Original outbuildings remain and have been restored or renovated. The gardens were designed by the Philadelphia landscape architect Robert B. Cridland, and the house was designed by the Louisiana-born architect Owen James Southwell in 1926. The site is owned by the Frazer Center and is included in the National Register of Historic Places as part of the Druid Hills Historic District. The site is also included in local landmark districts designated by both the Atlanta Urban Design Commission and DeKalb County. The site is open to the public for special events. www.frazercenter. org/inclusive-community/gardens

"On a beautifully timbered hill which rises from a woodland area traversed by bold streams, the house was built to command views of the surrounding terrain. The varied character of the topography gave opportunity for gardens of different types: first and foremost the wild plantings which border the twisting bridle paths along streams and dogwood-shadowed slopes; then in open view from the portico of the house on the hill, the sunken formal gardens, one built around the clubhouse, the other laid beyond a rose hung tennis court." (275)

Mr. and Mrs. R. L. Cooney Garden, or Coon Hollow

House, 1913; garden, circa 1920s–1930s

Few remnants of the historic garden remain. The original house remains. The site, owned by the Fernbank Museum and not open to the public, is included in the National Register of Historic Places as part of the Druid Hills Historic District. The site is also included in local landmark districts designated by both the Atlanta Urban Design Commission and DeKalb County.

"From the terrace, a walk leads to a rock stairway between two hills planted with rhododendrons, kalmias and azaleas (calendulaceae) above a variety of ground covers including pachysandra, shortia, creeping ranunculus, vinca, bloodroot and Iris cristata. The hill to the right is terraced and is the nearest approach to formality. Eight levels are box enclosed, and climbing Killarney roses and large gardenias are featured in the center level." (191)

Mr. and Mrs. Thomas C. Erwin Garden

Circa 1920s–1930s

Some remnants of the historic garden remain. The original house remains. The privately owned site is included in the National Register of Historic Places as part of the Druid Hills Historic District. The site is also included in local landmark districts designated by both the Atlanta Urban Design Commission and DeKalb County.

"From the terrace steps, an expanse of lawn spreads out to a group of venerable oaks under whose leafy boughs rhododendron, ferns and laurel are serenely content. Opening from this shady spot a flight of stone steps leads down into a formal garden. A wide flagstone panel divides this area, and on either side lie box-bordered rose beds. Great tubs of oleanders and dwarf lemon trees are used with fine effect. At the far end of the garden is a semi-circular lily pool, spreading out against a luxuriant planting of shrubbery, with groups of Iris pseudacorus introduced at intervals." (197)

❧ Fernbank Forest, or the Mr. Z. D. Harrison Property

Late 1800s

The historic landscape, one of the largest old-growth urban forests in the United States, is intact. The original house no longer remains. The original barn remains. The site, known as Fernbank Forest, is owned by the Fernbank Museum and is listed in the National Register of Historic Places as part of the Druid Hills Historic District. The site is also included in local landmark districts designated by both the Atlanta Urban Design Commission and DeKalb County. The site is open to the public for self-guided tours. www.fernbankmuseum.org/explore/permanent-features/fernbank-forest

"In the forest the trees grow so dense and tall that walking amid their green silences one gets a sense of

being miles from civilization, when, in fact, Atlanta is at its edge, and Five Points, the very heart of the city, is only fifteen minutes away by automobile." (217)

Mr. and Mrs. Arthur I. Harris Garden

House, circa 1908; gardens, circa 1920s

The historic garden no longer remains. It was designed by the Philadelphia landscape architect Robert Cridland. The original house remains and has been converted for the Paideia School's administrative offices. The site is owned by the Paideia School, which serves preschool through the twelfth grade. The site is included in the National Register of Historic Places as part of the Druid Hills Historic District. The site is also included in the Druid Hills Landmark District, a local landmark district designated by the Atlanta Urban Design Commission.

"The formal garden lying to the rear of the house is connected with it by brick-paved walkways. Dim and cool in the shadow of old trees, this is a sheltered spot filled with bloom throughout the year—from the first splash of early crocus to the purple and gold of fall asters and chrysanthemums. Centering a grass panel is a sixteenth century Venetian well-head of weathered marble, pinkish in tone, and flanking the well are quaint old metal sprinkler pots brought from Dijon." (213)

Llwyn, or the Mr. and Mrs. G. W. Rowbotham Garden

Circa late 1920s–1930s

Few remnants of the historic garden remain. The original house remains. The garden was designed by the Atlanta landscape architect William L. Monroe Sr., who owned Monroe's Landscape and Nursery Company. The privately owned site is included in the National Register of Historic Places as part of the Brookhaven Historic District.

"The fact that the garden is on rising terraces makes it possible to enjoy some part of it from every window in the house, and the open door of the sunroom frames a section of the rock garden. Here is convincing proof of the fallacy of the belief that it is impossible to have a satisfactory garden beneath our Georgia pines. The carpet of grass and creeping plants, ferns, perennials, and broad-leaved evergreens, together present a picture of luxuriant growth seldom equalled by a garden in full sun." (261)

Lullwater Conservation Garden, or Lullwater Creek Conservation Project

Circa 1930s

The historic garden is intact. The site is a conservation garden and bird sanctuary. It is owned by the Lullwater Garden Club and is included in the National Register of Historic Places as part of the Druid Hills Historic District. The site is also included in local landmark districts designated by both the Atlanta Urban Design Commission and DeKalb County. The site is open to the public.

"Along Lullwater Creek in Druid Hills lies a beautiful stretch of natural woodland, irregular oblong in shape, between Lullwater Road and Lullwater Parkway. Growing here in splendid profusion are specimens of nearly all of Georgia's native trees: pine, beech, maple, sycamore, hickory, ash, elm, willow, wild cherry, poplar, and oak." (421)

Municipal Rose Garden

Circa 1929

The historic garden no longer remains. The original garden was designed by the Atlanta landscape architect William C. Pauley for the Druid Hills Garden Club. The garden was renovated by the Atlanta landscape architect Edith Harrison Henderson in the 1970s. The remnants of the garden were removed in the 1990s and 2000s as part of the restoration of Oak Grove, one of the segments of the Olmsted Linear Park.

"Shortly after its organization five years ago the Druid Hills Garden Club had the inspiration that led to the making of their Municipal Rose Garden. Today hundreds of Atlantans as well as visitors from other sections, pause on their way out Ponce de Leon Avenue to study the colorful rose display. Here a thousand roses blossom against a background of crabapple and dogwood trees, and blend their sweetness with the exotic perfume of the Cape jasmines planted near by." (417)

Mr. and Mrs. J. T. Selman Garden

Circa 1920s

The historic garden no longer remains. The original house, designed by the Atlanta architect Leila Ross Wilburn, remains. The garden was designed by the Atlanta landscape architect William L. Monroe Sr., who owned Monroe's Landscape and Nursery Company.

"Mrs. Selman's secluded small garden which opens from the rear terrace of the house is planned and carried out on simple lines and with a selection of sturdy ornamental plants to furnish a succession of color around the central lawn. From two big pines on the upper level where groups of moss-covered boulders are planted in many varieties of low creeping flowers, a path of weather-beaten flagstones leads across the grass towards a small rock-bound pool holding a fountain figure. The pool, in full sunshine, displays a wealth of water lilies and along its rim grow clumps of Japanese iris. Mimosa trees are in the background and beyond the pool a white-columned pergola living-room supports vines of wistaria, roses, Heavenly Blue morning glories and moon flowers—a combination to give succeeding bloom for all the outdoor months." (265)

Stephenson-Adams-Land Garden, or Mr. and Mrs. W. H. Stephenson Garden

Circa 1930s

The historic garden and house remain. The garden was designed by the Atlanta landscape architect William C. Pauley. The privately owned site is included in the National Register of Historic Places as part of the Druid Hills Historic District. The site is also included in local landmark districts designated by both the Atlanta Urban Design Commission and DeKalb County.

"From the driveway, a wide flag-stone walk gives on to the box-bordered brick terrace across the back of the house, and from here may be had the first full view of the formal gardens graduating upward from the lowest level. Two flights of steps ascend to a brick wall bordering a wide panel of grass, which is centered by a reflecting pool. A box hedge, trimmed low, finishes off this panel at either end, and beyond the walkways, to right and left, are thickly planted perennial borders. A massed effect in each corner is of azalea—Indica alba, Hemerocallis gold dust, columbine, Maid Marian phlox, bronze snapdragons, and stokesia." (266)

Woodland, or the Mrs. Arthur Tufts Garden

House, 1917; garden, circa 1920s

The historic garden no longer remains. The original house remains and has been renovated multiple times. The site is owned by Emory University.

"The garden is everywhere,—but what might be called the garden proper rambles in an informal manner in the sunshine near the tennis court, play grounds and kitchen garden, and uses the orchard, which is grassed, as a background. A yellow and blue garden is reached by way of a scuppernong arbor and a grass path bordered by forget-me-nots, ranunculus and valley lilies. Another garden is in pastel shades and still another in red and white. The main garden is a perpetual garden but is loveliest when the fifteen year old wall of roses: Silver Moon, Dr. Van Fleet, Caroline Testout, Christine Wright and Climbing Killarney, blend with hundreds of iris, painted daises and Madonna Lilies." (274)

DECATUR

Lazyknoll, or the Mr. and Mrs. William Nichols Garden

House, circa 1917–18; garden, circa 1920s

The historic garden no longer remains. The original house remains. The garden was designed by the Atlanta landscape architect William L. Monroe Sr., who owned Monroe's Landscape and Nursery Company. The site is privately owned.

"A typical example of a small southern blossom garden is that of Mrs. William M. Nichols at Lazyknoll—where no one has time to be lazy! The white frame house stands on the apex of a knoll overlooking a rolling lawn and the shrub-enclosed flower garden. Hidden by a screen of conifers, this garden adds to its other charms that of surprise for the approaching visitor. A rock and fern garden with flagstone court and path lies next [to] the house under a canopy formed by an apple tree and a narrow rose arbor. Separated from the formal garden by a low rose-twined fence and an ornamental white gate, the court still commands a full view of the garden's luxuriant color." (329)

Tucked-In, or the Mr. and Mrs. Bruce Hall Garden

Circa 1925–1930s

The historic garden no longer remains. The original house remains. The privately owned site is listed as part of the Clairemont Avenue Historic District, a locally designated historic district in the City of Decatur.

"The more formal garden, which is about fifty by fifty feet, is enclosed by a white picket fence, and a rustic arbor is at the far end. Climbing roses—Gardenia and Silver-moon—and Clematis paniculata grow on the fence and embower the arbor. In the garden, now eight years old, are many well considered color compositions. Pleasant combinations in the flower beds are sulphur-colored marigolds with Salvia farinacea, white nicotiana, so fragrant at dusk, snapdragons, blue lace flower and the airy graceful little annual phlox. The borders are filled with perennials of fine quality and substance; colors, soft-toned and deep, are mingled in harmony." (326)

STONE MOUNTAIN

◦ Stone Mountain, or Stone Mountain Park

Formed 300 to 350 million years ago; first tourist attraction, 1838; purchased by the State of Georgia, 1958

The site is owned by the State of Georgia and managed by the Stone Mountain Memorial Association, a Georgia state authority. The Herschend Family Entertainment Corporation has a long-term contract to operate park attractions. The site is open to the public. www. stonemountainpark.com

"In North Georgia there occur many unique areas of botanical interest to the student of Nature. One of the most interesting, in many respects, is the Stone Mountain granite region located in DeKalb County, 16 miles east of Atlanta. Here is found a mass of exposed granite rock rising 686 feet above the surrounding lowland plane, 1686 feet above sea level. It measures seven miles in circumference at the base and includes about 563 acres of exposed surface." (408)

Dougherty County

ALBANY

Miss Jane Davant Garden

Early twentieth century

The historic garden no longer remains.

"Behind the house the garden starts in twisting borders of annuals and perennials edged with the soft colored local limestone which is also used for stepping stones and for the wall which is one boundary of the garden. Vine-covered fences, a tangle of yellow jessamine, honeysuckle and roses, complete the enclosure of the charmingly informal garden plot. At the farther end is an irregular pool set in narrow rock plantings, and in the pool are lilies, poppies, hyacinths and many underwater plants, all lorded over by the stately lotus whose spicy pink blooms and huge leaf pads show in high relief against the encircling pines." (140)

Iris Court, or the Miss Cena J. Whitehead Garden

House and first garden, antebellum; second garden, 1921

The historic garden no longer remains. The 1854 house was relocated to Moultrie, Georgia, in 1965. The original house is privately owned.

"Among the specimen trees of the old garden now adding glamor to the new, are tall cedars—red, Lebanon and incense,—wild olives, hollies, magnolias, pecans and palm trees. The dogwoods have spread wide and into the fig trees a man may climb. There are thickets of the older spireas, big oleanders and pomegranates, and the air is musky when the pittosporum, gardenias and tea olive bloom. With these last three evergreen shrubs in a southern garden there is scarcely a month without some rich fragrance. The new garden, which suggested the name, Iris Court, is connected with the house by iris paths, and in the formally laid beds are many lilies, iris, phlox, and other perennials to insure a succession of bloom from early spring till late fall." (143)

Mr. and Mrs. Joseph A. Myer Garden, or the Samuel Farkas House and Garden

House, circa 1887; garden, early twentieth century

Little of the historic garden remains. The original house remains. The privately owned site is listed in the National Register of Historic Places.

"Past the lawns and iris borders which surround the house on the street side, Mrs. Myer has made her flower garden on two ascending levels by terracing the slope immediately to the rear of the house. Rock steps, flanked by two fine Italian cypresses, lead up through the center of the banks to the two garden

levels—the first one planted informally with many kinds of perennials and annuals, the upper one cut through by a flagstone walk ending at a stone bench with a pleasant outlook over the colorful ranks of bloom. The background of the rose garden, on the higher terrace, is a long rustic trellis and against the shrubbery outlines are plantings of brilliant amaryllis." (141)

Elbert County / Wilkes County

ELBERTON

Rose Hill Plantation

House, 1787, with an expansion, circa 1810; garden, circa 1810s

The only remnants of the historic garden are allées of red cedars and crape myrtles. The house no longer remains. A contemporary house now occupies the site. The site is privately owned.

"With the exception of one splendid red oak, within the house grounds of old Rose Hill, the trees were exclusively elms and cedars. A picket fence divided the gardens from the elm shaded road, and these were screened from it by a twelve-foot cedar hedge. A wide walk leading from the gate to the porch was bordered by alternate plantings of crape myrtle trees and plinth-like forms of euonymus. Similar euonymus plantings outlined a simple interpretation of English parterres. These lay between the cedar hedge and the box garden which had circular and squared beds of Dutch simplicity." (64)

Floyd County

MOUNT BERRY

Berry College, or the Martha Berry Schools

Buildings and gardens, early twentieth-century to circa 1942

Much of the historic campus landscape and numerous historic buildings remain intact. Of special note, the Ford Complex, consisting of Collegiate Gothic–style structures designed by the Boston architectural firm of Coolidge and Carlson, was named for its benefactors,

Henry and Clara Ford. *The Philadelphia landscape architect Robert B. Cridland designed much of the Berry campus landscape. Berry College is listed in the National Register of Historic Places under the Berry Schools' listing. www.berry.edu*

"A Garden for a lovely home; a campus that is a garden for America's largest school estate; and a garden to God, where stately branches of lofty poplars are lifted against the rugged rocks and tower of the Lavender Range; these are the three gardens created in Georgia for her schools by Martha Berry, founder and director of the Berry Schools for boys and girls of the eleven southern states who were low in cash but high in character qualities." (447)

House o' Dreams

House, circa 1922; garden, 1920s–1930s

The historic garden is primarily intact. The original garden was designed by the Philadelphia landscape architect Robert B. Cridland. The original house and water (or fire) tower remain. The site is owned by Berry College and is listed in the National Register of Historic Places as part of the Berry Schools' listing. There is limited public access through scheduled tours of the historic campus.

"The terrace of the house is a partly closed-in bit of the surrounding garden, for house and garden live closely together in their seclusion on the mountain top. The various garden levels are held by thick rock walls, and flagstone paths connect the lawn (where a blue peacock spreads his brilliant fan) with the garden and the lily pool. A wistaria-covered arbor offers shade from the bright sun and a frame for the panoramic view. Fragrant boxwood, lilacs and snowballs grow along the walls. A lower terrace is given over to peach trees, strawberries and raspberries. Hollyhocks, delphinium, dahlias, and chrysanthemums, and the other flowers which flourish in the borders, seem stronger, sweeter and intensified in color in this garden against the sky." (452)

⁓ Oak Hill

House, 1880s and 1920s; garden, 1920s–circa 1933

The historic garden is primarily intact and portions have been restored. The early twentieth-century garden was designed by the Philadelphia landscape architect Robert B. Cridland. The original house remains. The site

is owned by Berry College and is listed in the National Register of Historic Places as part of the Berry Schools' listing. Oak Hill and the adjacent Martha Berry Museum serve as a historic house and history museum and are open to the public for tours. www.berry.edu /oakhill

"Walks radiating from the house go southward into the formal box garden, the rose garden, and the walled garden. Northward, a golden rose-arched pathway leads to a summer house two hundred yards away, at the edge of the bluffs overlooking the Oostanaula river valley. Directly in front of the house is a wide terrace and the great oak grove from which Oakhill derives its name. Behind the house is the brick paved piazza that merges into the terraced garden, by means of a broad, ivy-clad step leading onto the grass. A wall of old English box surrounds this terrace, where the white peacocks love to strut— beautiful silhouettes against the evergreens." (448)

ROME

Rome High School Shakespearian Garden

Circa 1932

The historic garden no longer remains.

"Following the custom of several years the senior class at Rome High School in 1932 left a gift to the school. Always the seniors' gifts are to be kept and cherished by the lower classes, but this gift is to be kept and cherished with an even more precious care, for it consists of the start of a Shakespearian Garden, the first of its kind in the State. . . . The garden is laid out on the lower terrace of the school grounds and patterned after the Italian garden plans of the prevailing fashion in England in Shakespeare's day. Here are planted most of the ninety-nine flowers, herbs and shrubs mentioned in the plays, that will thrive in this climate. There are romantic nooks made by the high cut rock steps and vine hung corners. A tiny fish pond set in uneven stones holds pale water lilies and gold fish (named after characters in the plays!). A bath for the birds centers its garden and bird houses are set back in a near-by wistaria vine." (446–47)

Seven Oaks, or the Mr. and Mrs. Thomas Berry Garden

Early twentieth century

The historic garden and original house no longer remain. The site was replaced by a shopping center in 1992.

"Against the northwest side of the house is a tiny cloister garden enclosed in an ivy-hung rock wall. The intricately patterned beds are bordered with dwarf boxwood and the dominant color note in the planting is blue, but over the walls Van Fleet roses bloom in a shower of pale pink, and regale lilies are massed in the four wall corners. From the little garden a flagstone path goes out to a wide lawn and a tree-shaded swimming pool. Down a few steps from this level the path continues to the rose garden which is bounded by a high privet hedge. The inner hedges are of boxwood and the beds are laid out in formal design. The center beds hold white, yellow and pale pink roses, the next circle pink Radiance, while the outer beds are full of Purple Prince petunias through which rise standard red roses." (358)

Shorter College Court Garden

Circa 1910s–1920s

Few remnants of the historic garden remain. The site is owned by Shorter College.

"The Court is a formal garden and of a dignity not to be ruffled by the chatter of the girls as they laugh along its brick-lined walks for, though it is walled in on three sides by the ivy-covered red brick buildings, it looks out upon the northern hills and valleys in solemn contemplation. Tall sugar-berry trees, to right and to left, afford the robins and the blue birds high perches on which to sing to southern skies; and on the laurels of hunter's green cardinals hint that summer soon shall come. Below in the center walk is a white marble sundial that not only shows the time of day, but also directs attention to that part of the garden which is most beautiful—the heart or center—the lily pool. The pool is bounded by a ring of spirea which touches the gravel walk and four stately cedar trees look into the crystal water where gold fish play among the white and yellow lilies and their green lily pads." (446)

ATLANTA

Atlanta Public Schools' Gardens

Circa 1920s–1930s

The historic vegetable and flower gardens at dozens of schools no longer remain. Some of the original school buildings remain.

"The school gardens are laboratories. Here the children experiment, test soils, learn the needs of different plants, how to improve drainage, etc.—all with the basic idea of having each child carry back to his own home the desire to build a garden, plus the requisite information and experience." (433–34)

Bellvoir, or the Mr. and Mrs. J. Bulow Campbell Garden

Circa 1920s

The historic garden and house no longer remain.

"A little paved terrace at the back of the house is the first vantage point from which stretch out many alluring prospects. In the immediate foreground are old millstones paving the way to a shallow brick stairway where each step is banked in ivy, trained to keep the treads free but to cover each rise with living green. The steps lead to a lawn circled with boxwood and centered by a pool filled with the translucent pink and white of waterlilies. Beyond the pool is a green corridor, the walls of privet and ivy hedges broken by vine-wreathed arches, and stretching in long perspective between the formal gardens on either side." (184)

Boxwood House, or the Mr. and Mrs. James S. Floyd Garden

House, circa 1914; gardens, circa 1910s–1920s

The historic garden and house no longer remain. The house and remnants of the original garden were demolished in 2015.

"The gardens were planned as a continuation of the house, with each of the three main doors opening into a pleasant outdoor room. As the name denotes, boxwoods are the leading features, along with old lead brought from England and millstones laid in walks. The east entrance faces a pool built of white quartz rocks, in the center of which is a bronze figure of a kneeling boy holding a fish. Tall cedars banked with azaleas frame the picture." (202)

Boxwood House, or the Dr. and Mrs. Floyd W. McRae Garden

Circa late 1920s

Facets of the historic garden have been restored. The original house remains. The garden and house were designed by the Atlanta architect Philip Trammell Shutze.

"The garden is so keenly in keeping with the atmosphere of the house that it seems an integral part of it. A low rock wall in the background is balanced on the opposite side by the loggia, while the stone terrace of the house is continued into the garden walk. Of particular interest here, as well as on the front and side wings, is the use of vines and climbing roses. Gnarled old grape vines can be seen against the house, with Lady Ashton roses on the balustrade. Wistaria and Euonymus radicans are used effectively on the loggia wing. On the left of the picture, opposite the broad steps, an old English stone and lead fountain, dated 1769, is set into a nook which is almost hidden by crabapples and lilacs and filled with shade-loving flowers." (250)

Broadlands, or the Mr. and Mrs. Hugh Richardson Garden, or the Richardson-Allen House and Garden

Circa 1920s

The historic garden is intact. The original house remains. The site is privately owned.

"The house with its Georgian porch fronts toward the distant valley in which flows Nancy's Creek, and toward the pine-covered hills beyond; and also immediately upon a series of grass-covered, box-enclosed terraces, each of which is a decorative unit within itself. The upper terrace is flush with the Georgian porch where flower boxes add color both to the porch and to the terrace. The lowest terrace forms a sunken garden against the strong retaining wall of the highest. A quilt of small-leaf ivy covering this wall is surpassed in beauty only by the magnificent wall of boxwoods that forms the outer edge of the terrace." (258)

Dolly Blalock Black Memorial Garden at the Henrietta Egleston Hospital for Children

Circa 1928

The historic garden no longer remains. The garden was designed by the Atlanta landscape architect Norman C. Butts for the Cherokee Garden Club. This project—the club's earliest civic endeavor—was named in memory of Dolly Blalock Black, a charter member of the club.

"The garden itself is formal in design and informal in planting. The gravel terrace at the entrance, sheltered by the hedge and balanced at either end by mimosa trees, is broad enough to accommodate chairs and tables. From this level, rock steps lead directly on to the broad grass panel, circular at the far end to provide interesting detail to the design and an appropriate setting for a charming rock pool. From the low stone retaining wall of the terrace, the grass panel is bordered with narrow flower beds, broken at intervals by short paths which connect with one encircling path. Beyond this, wide borders of perennials and shrubbery give background and depth to the garden. At the far end, beyond the pool, and on a direct line with it, a low marble bench commands a view down the garden to the hospital." (415)

Mr. and Mrs. Frank Fleming / Miss Hightower Garden, or the Little Hillside Garden

Circa 1920s

The historic garden and house no longer remain. The site was redeveloped in the mid-1980s.

"The Little Hillside Garden, which specializes in native azaleas and naturalized narcissi, begins with a flagstone terrace filled with white azaleas and gardenias. The next level, reached by circular stone steps entwined with ivy, has an arch of dogwood trees at the base of the steps. From the terrace the natural slope extends west to the rear of the property and is reached by a winding path of stepping stones, bordered with wild violets of several varieties, trillium, snowdrops, and hepaticas, with narcissus grouped between. On each side of the path is a profusion of native azaleas, tall, medium and low, in shades of pale pink, apricot, orange, red, flame and rose pink, each color blending in the harmony that only nature can achieve." (200)

May Patterson Goodrum Garden, or the Mrs. James J. Goodrum House and Garden, or the Peacock House

Circa 1932

The historic garden is currently being restored by Tunnell & Tunnell, Landscape Architecture for the Watson-Brown Foundation. The historic house has been restored by the Watson-Brown Foundation. The historic house and garden were designed by the Atlanta architect Philip Trammell Shutze. The site is owned by the Watson-Brown Foundation and is listed in the National Register of Historic Places.

"Mrs. Goodrum's garden lies within the confines of a serpentine wall whose bricks, lightly washed in yellow, afford a background for beds of tulips, columbine, and Canterbury bells. Down the center of this enclosed garden stretches a miniature bowling green, hedged in with sturdy clumps of true boxwood planted to follow the winding outline of the wall. The bowling green forms the axis, with the face of the garden house at one end and at the other a latticed gazebo of McIntyre design, its graceful dome crowned with a little gilt eagle. In summer the lattice is embowered in the purple stars of Clematis jackmanii, while to right and left are giant gardenia bushes, and across the green, magnolia trees espaliered against the garden house wall, mingle their fragrance with a myriad other scents. Further along are cherry trees pinned fan-like to the yellow-washed bricks, their crimson fruit and glossy leaves thrown into high relief." (209)

Governor's Mansion, or Woodhaven, or the Mr. and Mrs. Robert F. Maddox Garden

Circa 1908–1910s

Portions of the historic garden are intact. The original house, designed by the Atlanta architect Walter T. Downing, no longer remains. The garden was designed by Mrs. Robert F. Maddox (Lollie Baxter Maddox). In the mid-1960s, the site was acquired by the State of Georgia. The Atlanta architect A. Thomas Bradbury was hired to design the new Governor's Mansion, which was completed at the close of 1967. The Atlanta landscape architect Edward L. Daugherty was hired to create a landscape that would not only serve the executive family but also the public for tours and special events. Daugherty preserved the historic terraced bowl garden.

The site is owned by the State of Georgia and still serves as the Georgia Governor's Mansion. The site is included in the National Register of Historic Places as part of the Historic Resources of West Paces Ferry Road (West Paces Ferry Road Multiple Resource Area).

"Woodhaven, the estate of Mr. and Mrs. Robert Foster Maddox, with its seventy-five acres of lawns, gardens and woodlands, has been planned entirely by the owners and in barely twenty years has acquired the mellowed air of a much older place. Originally the property consisted of a stretch of uneven but well-timbered woods ending in a deep ravine where corn and cotton straggled up the banks. In the ravine is now Mrs. Maddox's terraced sunken garden which was the first formal garden of any pretensions in Atlanta." (240)

Mrs. William P. Hill Garden, or the Old Hallman Home

Circa 1890s

The historic garden and house no longer remain. The site was demolished in 1962 for the construction of corporate offices.

"The garden, which adjoins the house on one side and on the other three sides is shut in by tall shrubs, has a very simple plan. Flagstone paths are laid between wide herbaceous borders which extend the length of both sides of an oblong stretch of lawn. Clipped biotas accent the two openings onto the lawn. At the far end are old iron benches 'for the cool of the evening' and at the other end are the steps to the veranda of the house where the outlook on the garden is framed in tangles of wistaria hanging from an old cherry tree. The wide borders are so generously planted that the procession of flowers never halts. Starting with the earliest daffodils, spring brings all the rainbow of the irises, with bright tinted tulips set in contrasting bands of blue phlox, pink thrift and spice pinks; then groupings of peonies and bleeding heart combine with early shasta daisies. June finds tall spires of hollyhocks near the sweet-scented masses of white, pink, and mauve phlox, which give way in turn to many kinds of chrysanthemums and asters for fall." (223)

Ihagee, or the
Judge and Mrs. Price Gilbert Garden

Circa 1930s

Portions of the historic garden remain. The original house remains. The privately owned site is included in the Tuxedo Park Historic District, a local landmark district designated by the Atlanta Urban Design Commission.

"The garden has three terraces one hundred twenty by twenty feet. The walls supporting the terraces as well as the steps and walkways are of weathered stone, some covered with ivy, others with climbing roses. All the paths are bordered with dwarf box and neat rows of old-fashioned white and blue hyacinths and many varieties of narcissi follow the lines of the boxwood, while beyond are wide bands of iris in some fifty varieties. These beds are permanent and practically uniform, but the space inside varies on each terrace. Perhaps there are more lilies than any other flower, for beginning with valley lilies there is some variety in bloom until late autumn." (207)

The Iris Garden

Circa 1929–1930s

The historic garden is intact. The garden was designed by the Atlanta landscape architect William C. Pauley for the Iris Garden Club. The site, part of Winn Park, is owned by the City of Atlanta and is maintained by the Iris Garden Club. The site is open to the public.

"Located in a small triangular park bounded by Peachtree Circle, Lafayette Drive and Westminster Drive in Ansley Park, is The Iris Garden, an eminently successful conservation project of the Iris Garden Club. . . . Now, by standing at the upper end of the garden, one may see at the head of the ravine a delightful little waterfall which comes dancing down over moss covered boulders to fall into a small pool. On each side of the waterfall and pool are wide plantings of iris of every color, ranging from the rarest pink to the most delicate blues which in turn shade through deep blues to royal purples; here too are all the yellows, from the pale canary hues to the oriental golds." (419)

Mrs. Richard W. Johnston Garden,
or the Johnston-Gilbert Garden

Circa 1928

This historic garden is primarily intact. The original house, which remains, was designed by the Atlanta architect P. Thornton Marye. The majority of the garden was designed by the Philadelphia landscape architect Robert B. Cridland in 1928. The upper garden was designed by W. C. Hunter in 1930. The site is privately owned.

"The first terrace is a formal green garden which adjoins the house. It is surrounded with hedges of dwarf box, occasional tree box, and other evergreens, and in the center is a small round pool bordered with ivy. From here the garden ascends through three levels to a semi-circle of grass enclosed by a tall planting of tree box, juniper, mimosa and dogwood, where an old Italian figure of Diana stands against the dark evergreens. All three terraces are bordered with wide beds of tulips and other spring bulbs combined with bleeding-heart and flowering almond; then lilies, phlox, platycodon, asters and helenium. One terrace specializes in Siberian iris in variety. There are outlines of dwarf box and liriope, and each terrace with its accents of specimen box has for a background the grass slope up to the next shrubbery." (232)

Knollwood, or the
Mr. and Mrs. William H. Kiser Garden

Garden, circa 1918; house, circa 1929

Little of the historic garden remains. The garden was designed by the Atlanta landscape architect Norman C. Butts. The historic house, designed by the Atlanta architect Philip Trammell Shutze, remains. The privately owned site is included in the Tuxedo Park Historic District, a local landmark district designated by the Atlanta Urban Design Commission.

"In ideal arrangement for this climate the series of wide terraces are made on ground sloping to the north. A long panel of grass runs down the center of the garden, divided by the central walk and cut across by lateral walks on each level. In each of the resulting squares of green is an old boxwood while bordering the middle walk is a line of clipped junipers-Ashfordii, their gray green contrasting with the tall hedges of privet which bound the two sides of the garden and, on the lowest level, form a high clipped wind-break behind the tea-house." (235)

Lane's End, or the Mr. and Mrs. Cam D. Dorsey Garden

House and garden, circa mid-1920s

Portions of the historic garden remain. The original house was destroyed by fire in 2014, and the owners rebuilt it following the original design. The garden was designed by the Atlanta landscape architect William C. Pauley, and the house was designed by Neel Reid of the Atlanta architectural firm Hentz, Reid, & Adler. The site is privately owned.

"There are two formal gardens at Lane's End, one on the house level, and also an informal rose garden. The lower formal garden, reached by steps from the side of the front terrace, is a square garden of straight line beds planted in annuals and wide bands of iris, the whole enclosed by abelia and spirea. The upper garden is rectangular, hedged in by broad-leaf evergreens, and its parterres outlined with wavy lines of dwarf box are planted informally. On the right of the house and somewhat back are a series of terraces, the dividing banks covered with pink Phlox subulata, and on the terraces roses of many varieties are grown." (196)

Mayfair, or the Mr. and Mrs. Henry Morrell Atkinson Garden / Mr. and Mrs. Jackson P. Dick Garden

Garden, circa late 1920s; house, 1929

The historic garden is primarily intact. The original house remains. The garden was designed by the American landscape architect Ellen Biddle Shipman, with later planting by the Atlanta landscape designer Constance Knowles Draper. The house was designed by the Atlanta architectural firm of Cooper and Cooper. The site is privately owned.

"The problem of a home for two families has been successfully solved in the plan of this double house and the balanced scheme is completed in the two 'Siamese' gardens with their twin old lead wall founts and almost identical planting. . . . At either side of the steps leading down into the two gardens are matched pieces of dwarf box and their duplicates flank the lead founts facing them across the central panels of turf. Box-edged flower beds are separated from the wide borders by narrow grass paths. The pattern is simple and symmetrical enough to be charming even when there is no bloom. There are

two big rounded specimens of holly-leafed tea olive (Osmanthus fortunei) for evergreen emphasis and lower clumps of tea plant (Thea bohea). Cotoneaster horizontalis is trained on the low outer walls while against the house are clipped pyracanthas. For spring, tulips, Spanish iris, and anemones are planted among the permanent old-fashioned perennials and are followed by a succession of lilies, the bulbous kinds combined with hemerocallis and funkias, to bloom till the ginger lilies of late fall add their perfume to the fainter fragrance of the tiny bloom of osmanthus." (169)

Mr. and Mrs. Edgar P. McBurney Garden

Circa early 1900s

The historic house and garden no longer remain. The McBurneys designed the garden. The site was demolished in 1966 and replaced by the Atlanta Arts Memorial Center.

"In the formal garden nearest the house the central flower beds are edged with dwarf box, a member of the garden family for nearly a century. Around this hale and hearty little old 'grandmother of the garden' are grouped her taller kindred of other varieties of box, gathered here for memories of the earlier gardens as well as for its beauty of size. . . . Leaving the formal garden a path wanders along borders of evergreens and azaleas to the pool and Tempio d'amore. The classic white architectural features in a setting of green lawns and trees are picturesque by day, but particularly so by night when the fountain sprays are illuminated by an ingenious under-water lighting device which gives rainbow tints to the high jets of water. . . . Beyond the Tempio d'amore and completely hidden from it by thickly planted evergreens is an informal Dutch garden. Emerging from the shade of a gnarled old wistaria which curtains the evergreen entrance comes the surprise of this gay little garden, the youngest of the series. Here grass paths meander between closely set irregular beds of flowers and there are two shaded platforms with garden furniture and pleasant vistas—one looking across the arabesque of flower beds and ornamental bird baths, the other facing the sunset" (244, 247)

New Oglethorpe University Grounds, or Oglethorpe University Grounds

Circa 1915

Portions of the original grounds remain. One hundred acres of the original six hundred remain. The historic buildings throughout the campus primarily remain. The site is owned by Oglethorpe University and is open to the public.

"Six hundred acres of native woodland surrounding an eighty-two-acre lake and fronting on Peachtree Road comprise the campus of New Oglethorpe. This woodland is rich in the tree, shrub and small plant life characteristic of North Georgia, and springtime brings each year its wealth of bloom: dogwood, wild crab, redbud, azaleas, hawthorns, viburnums and millions of small flowering plants. Nature has been especially generous to the Oglethorpe woods in her gift of wild flower variety, and a careful study is sure to disclose one or two species not found in other woodlands about Atlanta." (445)

Pinebloom, or the Mr. and Mrs. Preston Arkwright Garden, or the Dr. and Mrs. Glenville Giddings Garden

Circa 1915

The historic garden no longer remains. The original house remains. A portion of the original site is owned by the Veritas Church, and another portion by the Jackson Street Baptist Church. The site is included in the National Register of Historic Places as part of the Druid Hills Historic District. The site is also included in the Druid Hills Landmark District, a local landmark district designated by the Atlanta Urban Design Commission.

"The house, of English type, its foundation planting of hedges and large specimens of old boxwood, looks out over living-room terraces of grass or flagstones, bound in, too, by hedges of box, towards the gardens which are so placed as to be a part of each day's—even each rainy day's—enjoyment. The formal garden is connected with the south terrace by wide steps of gray stone, and flagstone walkways, bordered in boxwood, outline the beds designed about a circular pool edged with the same stone. The whole pattern is enclosed by graduating lines of box hedges inside a screen of evergreens, each of the four corners heightened by tall arbor vitae and, towards the lawn, by massed plantings of nandina." (165–66)

Pine Hill, or the Mr. and Mrs. Clark Howell Garden

Circa 1910s–1930s

Some facets of the historic garden remain. The original house, built in 1908, was replaced by another house, designed by the Atlanta architect Henri Jova in 1973. The original teahouse no longer remains. A tornado decimated portions of the garden in 1974. The site is privately owned.

"The twenty-acre tract comprises two beautifully wooded hills guarding a ravine of deep wildwood where a stream widens into a series of rock-bound pools and the wealth of native growth has been wisely conserved. . . . All through the ravine and the wild garden a lavish use of native rock—for bridges, draining, copings for the drives, rough-laid walls, stepping stones and tea house—is in character with the rugged beauty of woods and streams. Covered with mosses, liverworts and selaginella carpeting the borders, the rustic stone work is harmonious and vastly becoming to the natural pictures—of masses of flame or pinxter flowered azaleas, laurel, rhododendron, leucothoe and all the smaller flowers indigenous to woods such as these." (225, 227)

Rossdhu, or the Dr. and Mrs. Phinizy Calhoun Garden

Circa mid-1910s

Little of the historic garden remains. The original house, designed by the Atlanta architect Edward E. Dougherty, remains. The gardens were designed by Mrs. Phinizy Calhoun (Marion Calhoun). The site is privately owned.

"A terrace of varicolored flagstones surrounds the house on three sides, and is so enclosed by plantings of box as to make three secluded open air sitting rooms. To the north, slightly sunken below the level of the terrace, is a rectangular green and white garden where the variety in broad-leaf evergreen shrub species that outline the grass plot make interesting study. Here are found banana shrub, aucuba, mahonia, Ilex cassine and glabra, photinia, English laurel, cherry laurel, Virginia red cedar, Illicium anisatum, Viburnum tinus, euonymous, pyracantha, and crepe myrtle. White Azalea indica is banked in front of the evergreens and the brick paths are bordered by white violas and liriope. An ivy covered sundial guarded by two old-fashioned iron dogs, forms the center piece of this garden." (181)

Southlook, or the Mr. and Mrs. H. Cobb Caldwell Garden

House, antebellum; garden, circa 1909–1930s

The historic garden and nursery no longer remain. Ashford Park Nurseries was established on the site in 1909 by H. Cobb Caldwell. The boxwood garden was designed by the Atlanta landscape architect Norman C. Butts, while he was employed by Ashford Park Nurseries, for Mrs. H. Cobb Caldwell. Mrs. H. Cobb Caldwell (Mary Ashford Caldwell) was directly involved with the planning and planting of the garden. The Peachtree Golf Club and course were constructed on the site in 1947.

"Here, past the foundation planting of old boxwood lies an informal garden, an irregularly shaped lawn bordered by shrubs, boxwood and bands of lilies and spring bulbs. At the far end and to the right is the entrance to the cutting garden enclosed by a tall privet hedge. The paths through the wide beds of perennials and roses converge on an old time wrought iron summer house which is hung in star jasmine and clematis. . . . Turning back toward the house, a long walk bordered with perennials and lilies and arched overhead by mimosa trees leads to a flagstone terrace at the east side of the house which overlooks an old fashioned boxwood garden. . . . Along with the boxwood the plants typical of old southern gardens grow—such as crepe myrtle, banana shrub, fragrant tea olive and even a camellia or two." (175)

Spring Hill, or the H. M. Patterson & Son Funeral Home Garden

Circa 1928

Portions of the historic garden remain. The original funeral home, designed by the Atlanta architect Philip Trammell Shutze, remains. The garden was started in 1928 by the Pattersons, with assistance by J. D. Shannon, a local Atlanta gardener. The privately owned site still operates as a funeral home.

"The flower borders are laid in conventional design about panels of grass intersected by gravel walks. Dwarf box has been used to outline the beds, and bleeding heart, blue phlox, iris, hardy phlox, various lilies, and standard roses are in the plantings. A field stone wall bounding this sunken area displays pocket-plantings of dianthus deltoides, creeping

sedums, and similar dwarf material. Nearest the building, the wall is topped with a clipped hedge of Spirea thunbergii, and directly across in the opposite wall is a semi-circular lily pool. . . . South of the building lie the rock gardens where flowering fruit trees are used with good effect and in the background are dogwood, azaleas and other shrubs. The overflow of a rockbound spring cascades over mossy boulders down to the drip pool below." (428)

◈ Swan House, or the Mr. and Mrs. Edward H. Inman Garden

Circa 1928

The historic garden remains intact, and portions have been restored. It is part of the thirty-three acres of Goizueta Gardens at the Atlanta History Center. The original house remains and has been restored. The coach house has been converted to a restaurant and art gallery for the Forward Arts Foundation. The garden, house, and coach house were designed by the Atlanta architect Philip Trammell Shutze. The site is owned by the Atlanta Historical Society (operating under the name Atlanta History Center). The site is listed in the National Register of Historic Places and is a protected Landmark Building by the Atlanta Urban Design Commission. The site is open to the public. www. atlantahistorycenter.com

"The first terrace, as long as the breadth of the house itself, is a boxwood court of great dignity. It resembles nothing so much as two massive circular rooms connected by a short straight hall lying between the straight line of the house and the head of the double stairway leading to the next terrace below. The outstanding feature of this development is a series of cascades like great lotus leaves which descend along the stairways bearing water plants on their mirror surfaces." (228)

The Terraces

Antebellum

The historic garden and house no longer remain. The site is now home to a contemporary building that houses the Judge Romae T. Powell Juvenile Justice Center and the Mechanicsville Branch Library.

"The home of Edward Elijah Rawson was built two years after he moved to Atlanta from Stewart County. Occupying ten acres on South Pryor Street, it was for many years the show place of the community. The spacious house stood on the crest of a wide spreading and beautiful terraced hill. That these terraces were carpeted the year round in green sod was a triumph for the Scotch gardener who laid out and cared for the grounds. An unusual collection of conifers and topiary work executed in box and euonymus, vied in interest with a well designed box garden." (118)

Mr. and Mrs. Henry B. Tompkins Garden

House, circa 1922; and garden, circa 1920s–1930s

Portions of the historic garden remain. The original house remains. The garden and house were designed by the Atlanta architect Neel Reid. The privately owned site is listed in the National Register of Historic Places.

"In the center of a tapis vert is a square pool. On each side of this are two box-bordered flower beds between which are walks of old brick, laid in sand. At the back of the garden rise two curved flights of steps leading to the garage which has a rose vine clambering over its classic portico. In the semicircle between the stone stairways is a fine old Italian statue. The garden walls are completely covered with English ivy, and the planting above the walls consists of alternating roses, Silver Moon and Doctor Van Fleet, which hang over the wall. The bloom in June is profuse and the clouds of pale pink and white are very lovely against the sombre green of the ivy. Between the roses above the wall are planted flowering shrubs; forsythia, January jasmine, spirea, syringa, crepe myrtle and gardenia bushes. Beyond is a row of mimosa trees which make a background of feathery green, and their bloom is like a rosy haze." (269)

Tryggversson,* or the Mr. and Mrs. Andrew Calhoun Garden

House and garden, circa 1923

Little of the historic garden remains. The original house remains. The garden and house were designed by the Atlanta architect Neel Reid. The privately owned site is included in the National Register of Historic Places as part of the Historic Resources of West Paces Ferry Road (West Paces Ferry Road Multiple Resource Area).

"On Pace's Ferry Road, where the boundary screen is of cedars and cherry laurel, the rust tinted entrance gates frame a dramatic view of the house and its sunken gardens set far back on a tree-shadowed hill. . . . The views from the court yard look over the orchards and the distant terraced cutting gardens towards the farm and vineyards which are partly screened by pines, mimosas and thickets of bamboo. . . . The Baroque style of the house is carried on and completed in the architecture of the formal terraced gardens on the façade facing the road. Curving double stairs, separated by a wall fountain, descend from the high walled terrace of the house to a garden of boxwood and clipped ivy parterres. In the center is a fountain pool with sponge-stone ornamentation, in the side walls are niches with the same elaboration, and there are big terra cotta jars and stone pots holding aloes and azaleas. Over the soft buff-colored walls hang sprays of jessamine and climbing roses which grow from the background of the tall tree box and clustered cedars while Paul Scarlet roses twine through the balustrades and around the two Baroque statues at each side of the wide shallow steps down to the lawn." (177, 180).

* "Tryggversson" was misspelled in the original *Garden History of Georgia* book as "Trygveson."

Villa Clare, or the Mr. and Mrs. James J. Haverty Garden

House, circa 1916; garden, circa mid-1910s–1920s

The historic garden and house no longer remain. The house was designed by the Atlanta architect Edward E. Dougherty. The site was sold to the Atlanta Junior League to house the Atlanta Speech School in 1951, and it is now home to the Shepherd Spinal Center.

"The entrance to Villa Clare is a winding driveway where stately old deodars make a background for beautiful spreading pink dogwoods. The rolling lawn is bordered with a deep planting of ivy, and near the house clumps of Clara Butt tulips and iris Queen of May, brighten the foundation planting of broad-leaf evergreens. Two crouching lions guard the entrance to the Italian house whose steps and open terrace are outlined with luxuriant panels of ivy. Curving around the left wing of the house, the driveway at the back merges into a broad flagstone path which leads down to the natural terraces of the lower gardens where the retaining walls are garlanded with Silver Moon and pink Killarney rose vines." (221)

Westview Cemetery, or West View

Circa 1884–1940s

The historic cemetery, Westview Cemetery, is still intact, including the stone gatehouse, the water tower, the receiving tomb, the curvilinear circulation pattern of the roadways, the informal groves of historic trees, the elaborate grave markers and monuments, the mausoleum, the serpentine garden, the garden of time, the boxwood garden, the pool of quiet, the crab orchard fountain, the platforms of bronze statuary in sections 36 and 37, and the memorial to the Battle of Ezra Church. Thomas W. Burford was the first documented Atlanta landscape gardener to work on the site. In the late 1920s and early 1930s, the Atlanta landscape designer Constance Knowles Draper contributed to the site. The site is owned and operated by Westview Cemetery, Inc., and open to the public. www.westviewcemetery.com

"On a tract of five hundred acres of rolling, beautifully wooded land—fought over during the Battle of Atlanta—West View Cemetery was founded about fifty years ago. There is unusual horticultural interest in the hundred acres which have since been developed, for here can be found probably the finest and most varied collection of plant material in the State. The landscaping of this park-like cemetery has been in the charge of two expert gardeners—both Englishmen—(the first one, in 1896, giving his name 'Burford' to a handsome variety of Ilex aquifolia which originated here). More recent planting has been designed by Constance Draper. When the drives and sections were originally planned the best of the forest trees were carefully left to attain their present fine dimensions. Today the avenues of water oaks, willow oaks, deodars, and magnolias planted at that time are almost as impressive as the big oaks, pines, elms, maples, gums, ashes, poplars and beeches of the native groves." (430)

Wingfield, or the Garden of Governor and Mrs. John M. Slaton

House, circa 1908; garden, circa 1910s

The historic garden and house no longer remain. The garden was designed by the Philadelphia landscape architect Robert B. Cridland. The site was demolished in the 1960s and is now home to the Slaton Manor Condominiums.

"The house is connected with the garden by a brick walk and a broad-tread horse-shoe stairway outlined in low clipped hedges. At the garden level is a curved love-seat of flat stones surrounded by a planting of junipers and vinca, and the floor of each of the two garden terraces is woven of the same mellow red brick as the walk and the stairs. Centering the upper level lies a circular fountain pool where lilies, palms and cattails grow; and in each of the four large divisions is a particularly fine specimen of English laurel against which crepe myrtle blooms. Strips of grass separate the shrubs from the flower borders of annuals and perennials which complete the planting and furnish a display of brilliant color characteristic of summer gardens in Atlanta." (262)

Zahner-Slick Garden, or the Zahner Garden, or the Mr. and Mrs. Kenyon B. Zahner Garden

Circa 1926–1930s

Portions of the historic garden remain. The original house remains. The house was one of the earliest residential commissions of the Atlanta architectural firm Burge and Stevens. Mrs. Kenyon B. Zahner (Loyer Lawton Zahner) designed the garden. The site is privately owned.

"A pleasing contrast exists between the more formally treated areas and the spring garden where sunlight and shelter promote early growth. The winding flower borders have a background of woodland trees beyond the retaining walls of field stones. The upper level, reached by curving stone steps, is planted with spring bulbs, and early roses are looped on chains against a dense growth of cedars and junipers. Wistaria climbs the tall pines behind these plantings, and masses of yellow primroses with Virginia cowslip and bleeding heart, followed later by pink heuchera, bloom beneath the flowering crabs." (278, 280)

Barrington Hall

Antebellum

Portions of the historic garden remain, and facets of it have been restored. The original house remains. The site is owned by the City of Roswell and is listed in the National Register of Historic Places. The site is open to the public for tours. www.roswellgov.com/discover-us/southern-trilogy-historic-house-museums

"On the east a little circular box maze is nested in bridal wreath spirea, crape myrtle, Spanish bayonet and tiger lilies; balancing it on the west there is an informal planting of cherry laurel, lilacs, roses and sweet lavender." (112)

Bulloch Hall

Antebellum

Remnants of the historic landscape remain. An heirloom plant demonstration garden was added to the site in the 1990s. The original house remains. The site is owned by the City of Roswell and is listed in the National Register of Historic Places. The site is open to the public for tours. www.roswellgov.com/discover-us/southern-trilogy-historic-house-museums

"Bulloch Hall, built by Major James F. Bulloch of Savannah, belongs to this period and group. It is a . . . Greek Revival structure, and has the same heart shaped approach [as Barrington Hall]. The central path was bordered by cedars, of which a few remain." (113)

Mimosa Hall, formerly Phoenix Hall, or the Reid Place*

House and original garden, antebellum; garden redesigned, 1916–26

Only a few mimosa trees remain from the antebellum garden. Portions of the historic garden, designed by Neel Reid between 1916 and 1926, remain. The original house remains. The site is included in the National Register of Historic Places as part of the Roswell Historic District. In June 2017, the Roswell City Council unanimously voted to approve a resolution authorizing the purchase of Mimosa Hall to protect the historic property.

"On the twelve acres deeded John Dunwoody is a primeval grove of white and red oaks, hickories, tulip poplars, black locusts, black gum, beeches, holly, dogwood, red bud, chinquapins and black walnuts. To these were added elms. The mimosas which gave the place its later name were brought from Darien. A row of them is planted on each side of the path leading from gate to front door. A formal planting of giant cedars flanks this walk, and mimosa, cedars and Osage oranges are used at other points. To the west of the house there survive five beds of a formal garden. They are edged with stone coping. To the east is a fall of terraces planted with deutzia, syringa, Persian lilacs, flowering quince, daily roses shading from red to pink, and several varieties of old time jonquils. These terraces are partially overgrown with honeysuckle, but in the spring the old planting courageously pushes through." (114)

"It [Mimosa Hall] was later owned by General Hansell and long afterwards acquired by the late Neel Reid, architect, who restored and improved it with the rare appreciation and feeling of a true artist. . . . The formal garden is entered by a flight of steps flanked by a sweeping curved hedge of graceful line. On the steps, potted plants are used, as one season follows another. The beds are box-bordered and the paths of swept earth so often used in old gardens lead to a flat inlaid pool in the center of which is an old water jar." (361, 363)

* Mimosa Hall was included in *Garden History of Georgia* twice: in part 1, "Georgia's Early Gardens," as Mimosa Hall, and in part 2, "Modern Gardens," as Mimosa Hall or the Mrs. John Reid Garden.

Glynn County

Elizafield Plantation on the Altamaha

Circa 1790s and antebellum

Neither the historic garden nor the original house remains. Remnants of the historic sugar mill, a tower, another outbuilding, a well, and an antebellum burial ground remain. In 1935, Cator Woolford, who owned 350 acres of the original property, gave his tract to the State of Georgia for the creation of a state park. In 1945, this tract was made available by the Georgia Legislature for the establishment of Boys Estate (1945–77), a home and school for disadvantaged boys. The site is now owned by Morningstar Treatment Services.

"A large formal garden enclosed in a picket fence lay at the end of the right hand lawn. Roses were its pride. Here were the usual tropical plants always seen in this section; also spirea, cape jasmine, white and purple flags, gladioli, fuchsias, verbenas and several kinds of lilies. The beds were outlined by narcissus, snowdrops and violets which still bloom with the coming of spring." (50)

Hopeton on the Altamaha; Altama on the Altamaha

Antebellum and early twentieth century

The antebellum historic garden and house no longer remain. Foundation ruins of the original house remain, as do ruins of the sugar mill. William Dupont bought the adjacent Hopeton and Altama properties in 1914, renaming the site Altama. Dupont built a main house based on the original plantation house and added gardens. Cator Woolford bought the plantation in 1930 and built a swimming pool and "play house." Portions of the early twentieth-century gardens and the structures remain. Alfred W. Jones of the Sea Island Company acquired the property in 1944 for use as a hunting preserve. The site remains in the private ownership of the Jones family.

"The mansion, built of tabby, was distinctly Latin in type. Standing on a bluff above the Altamaha River, it was surrounded by wide Bermuda lawns, a feature peculiar to all Couper places. The land approach was by an avenue of sixty live oaks; a canal a quarter of a mile long cut through the rice fields formed the water approach. The Couper and Hamilton families used Hopeton only as a winter residence; therefore no formal garden was laid out. There was, however, an elaborate use of flowering shrubs about the lawn and houses, brought from the gardens at Cannon's Point. . . . All around were rice fields except on one side where there was a stretch of pine barren, and a thicket of live oaks, magnolias and palmettos. A wide lawn of Bermuda grass lay in front of the house, at one side of which was a long, narrow garden of simple design enclosed by a picket fence. A fine

wistaria vine grew over the porch, which was shaded by a mispilla plum. In the garden were roses, cape jasmine, crepe myrtle, oleanders, snowdrops, narcissus and violets; orange trees grew near by." (46, 48)

ST. SIMONS ISLAND

⌘ Cannon's Point

Circa 1793

The historic garden and house no longer remain. The site was established by John Couper. Foundation ruins of the plantation house and slave quarters remain. The site remains as a horticultural experiment station—citrus trees, grapes, date palms, mulberry trees for silk production, sugar cane, and olive trees from France. The site is now part of Cannon's Point Preserve, the last intact maritime forest on St. Simons Island. The St. Simons Land Trust purchased the six hundred acres in 2012. The site is open to the public. www.sslt.org /pro_cannons_point.php

"With the increase of his family and fortune a very large three-story frame house on high tabby foundations was erected, the original cottage serving as a wing. John Lord Couper's painting of his grandfather's house is the only contemporary pictorial delineation that we have of one of these Sea Island homes and gardens. As can be seen, the planting about the house was luxuriant and informal. The children's garden was laid out in beds edged in snowdrops. John Couper's vegetable garden was as famous as it was extensive. . . . Cannon's Point deserves the title of Georgia's first private experimental station. In the nursery spoken of by Fanny Kemble many horticultural experiments were conducted, first by John Couper and later by his distinguished son, James Hamilton Couper. John Couper in 1825 imported two hundred olive trees from France, from which he obtained two to three hundred bottles of oil annually." (41)

Hamilton Plantation, or the Mr. and Mrs. Eugene Lewis Garden

House, circa 1790s; garden, circa 1920s–1930s

The historic garden and house no longer remain. Beginning in 1927, Mrs. Eugene W. Lewis (Margaret Lewis), a member of the Cassina Garden Club, built formal gardens on the property. The Arthur J. Moore Museum was built on the site in 1960. The Richard

Memorial Garden was added to the site around 2010. The site is now owned by Epworth by the Sea, a Christian conference and retreat center overlooking the Frederica River.

"From the swimming pool garden, one enters between tall arbor vitae the Green Terrace overlooking the Rose Garden. The wall and steps were built of old English brick found on the plantation and coarse heavy mortar, giving a lovely texture that the English ivy and Ficus repens are not permitted to completely hide. The semi-circular back planting of the terrace is in long sweeping curves of cedar, oleander, and arbor vitae, faced down to the velvet green turf (Bermuda for summer, Italian Rye and Red Top for winter), by creeping juniper." (380)

Retreat Plantation

Circa 1790s and early 1800s

The historic garden and house no longer remain. The house burned in the early twentieth century. The avenue of live oaks, ruins of a tabby slave cabin, a slave hospital, and a greenhouse remain. In the 1920s, Howard E. Coffin, developer of Sea Island, purchased the property and created a golf resort. The original tabby corn barn was turned into the clubhouse. Portions of the site are owned by the Sea Island Golf Club; other parts are residential and commercial areas and public parks.

"Neither her rare collection of trees nor this exotic spot, but her Rose Garden was Mrs. King's [Anna Matilda Page King] special pride. It lay to the left of the house, and measured one hundred and forty by ninety feet. It was horseshoe in shape and was surrounded by a windbreak of Osage oranges trimmed like a mammoth hedge. Within this was a planting of crape myrtle and oleanders sheltering the three latticed summer houses symmetrically placed. The formal beds were edged with snowdrops, the central bed having the form of an eight-pointed star, from which the garden took its name. William Audley Couper, her son-in-law and son of John Couper of Cannon's Point, designed and laid out this garden for Mrs. King. It contained ninety-six varieties of roses and many flowers of European type." (39)

GREENSBORO

Veazey Plantation

House, circa 1868; garden, circa late 1860s–1870s

The historic garden and house no longer remain. The original house burned in the early 1900s. Following the death of Eli A. Veazey, the extensive property was subdivided and given to family members. Around 1940, the heart of the property was sold to Carl L. Batson, who sold the land to a timber company in 1965. The land has been clear cut and planted in pines.

"Set well back within the curve of the horseshoe of orchards was the house, enclosed by two fences. The outer one of horizontal boards and large gates—a warning fence—like feudal days, saying, 'Only friends enter here.' Within this fence, on each side of the swept grounds, was a group of three very large Willow oaks, overshadowing the two carriage houses where guests left their equipages. The inner fence of white pickets enclosed the house and its formal flower garden, laid out and planted by the Veazeys in 1869. Here dwarf box edged the beds, tree box accented the corners, and hedge box, bordered the walkway to the steps and mingled with the blossoming shrubs; sweet syringa, lilac, flowering quince and almond, Christmas jasmine, snowball, Cape jasmine, and spirea—along the fences. . . . Old-fashioned perennials and annuals filled the beds, while potted plants from the 'pit' came out with warm weather to increase the flower effect." (127, 129)

GRAY

Tomotavia,* or the Mr. and Mrs. T. J. Stewart Garden

House, circa 1865; garden, circa 1920s

The historic garden and house no longer remain. The property was subdivided and is now a private gated residential community.

"There are five distinct gardens that extend somewhat in the shape of a horseshoe around the sides of the rear lawn. On the northwest side lies the formal garden, typically colonial, with the small beds bordered in boxwood. This hillside garden is cut down about six feet and the incline is made into a rock garden studded with many rock-loving plants. Stone steps descend through the middle of the rockery and in the center of the garden is an old iron fountain. English junipers make accent points and the beds are kept ever blooming, filled with a succession of flowers. At one end stands a weeping willow, and at the opposite end an arch is cut in the hedge which encloses the perennial garden. Back of this garden, completely hidden by shrubbery, is a cutting garden and nursery where most of the shrubs for the place have been propagated." (335)

* "Tomotavia" was misspelled in the original *Garden History of Georgia* as "Tomotava."

Liberty County

Old Oglethorpe University Rock Garden

College, circa 1836; garden, circa early twentieth century

The historic garden no longer remains.

"Several miles from Milledgeville at Midway, on the site of old Oglethorpe University, Dr. and Mrs. H. D. Allen have built a rock garden, a memorial to the old institution which in 1860 gave its life, in giving its student body en masse to the Confederate cause. The large rocks used in the construction of the garden and the pool had been the foundation stones of the main University building. The pool is now placed on the spot from which the cornerstone of the main building was dug after the fire which destroyed it many years ago, and the cornerstone itself has been incorporated in a marker within the confines of the garden." (444)

McIntosh County

SAPELO ISLAND

Coffin-Reynolds Mansion, or the Mr. Howard Coffin Garden

Antebellum and circa 1920s–1930s

Portions of the historic garden remain. The original house remains. R. J. Reynolds hired the Atlanta architect Philip Trammell Shutze to make updates to the main house in 1937. Some of the original outbuildings remain. The site is owned by the State of Georgia, and the University of Georgia Marine Institute is housed in the site's historic farm complex. The island's Hog Hammock community is listed in the National Register of Historic Places. Sapelo Island is a state-protected barrier island.

"In the planting of the garden everything has been subordinated to the beautiful old trees with their twisted moss-covered branches which cast an ever changing pattern of light and shade on the open lawn. Arbor vitaes are used as accents along the walks and around the pool. Azaleas and camellias are in the outer borders, while yellow jessamine, white and pink Cherokee roses and wistaria vines climb up the tree trunks and add brilliant color in the spring in contrast to the sombre gray of the moss and the olive green of the live oaks." (365)

Morgan County

MADISON

Bonar Hall

Antebellum

Portions of the historic garden remain and have been restored. Of particular note is the antebellum boxwood parterre garden. The original house and outbuildings (a two-room cabin, a slave cabin, a tenant house, a carriage house, a smokehouse, and a well) remain. The privately owned site is included in the National Register of Historic Places as part of the Madison Historic District.

"The grounds show careful planning and a classical sense of balance. The lawn was surrounded by a brick wall pierced in a diamond shaped pattern. Bisecting the lawn and encircling the house is an eighteen foot walk edged by a six foot bed of bulbs. Within its borders stands a line of granite posts supporting standards of vines, between which Madonna lilies once were planted. A summer house and an orangery of matching design flank the house. The very fine boxwood garden lies to the left, outside the brick wall. It contained rare shrubs and trees, many of which still live; beyond this was a water garden of which practically nothing remains. The family burying ground, now removed, was box bordered and approached by a long walk edged by the same shrub. The vegetable garden, orchards, slave quarters and plantation buildings as usual lay to the rear." (84)

Kolb-Pou-Newton Place, or Boxwood

Antebellum

Portions of the historic garden remain. Of particular note are the antebellum twin boxwood parterre gardens. The original house and outbuildings (a smokehouse and slave quarters) remain. The site is privately owned by the Newton family and is included in the National Register of Historic Places as part of the Madison Historic District.

"The Kolb house, a severely handsome structure, boasts a rare possession, twin box gardens. Their exquisite geometric patterns are obviously the work of some one thoroughly familiar with and practised in design. The euonymus hedge fringed with crape myrtle that framed them is gone but clipping has preserved the dwarf box borders in excellent condition. Some of the tree box and one of the giant magnolias still stand. . . . Some of the old roses and lilies grow in these gardens, as do Pyrus japonica, Japanese magnolia, cherry laurel and January jasmine." (86)

Muscogee County

COLUMBUS

Bradley Olmsted Garden, or Sunset Terrace, or the Mr. and Mrs. W. C. Bradley Garden

House, circa 1912; garden, circa 1925–28

Portions of the historic garden remain. The landscape was designed by William Bell Marquis of Olmsted Brothers, Brookline, Massachusetts. It is the only Olmsted Brothers–designed landscape included in

Garden History of Georgia. The original house was converted into a museum in the late 1950s and incorporated into a major museum expansion in the 1980s. The site is owned by the Columbus Museum and is included in the National Register of Historic Places as part of the Wynn's Hill–Overlook–Oak Circle Historic District. The garden is open to the public. www. columbusmuseum.com/bradley-olmsted-garden

"Aside from the terraced rose gardens there are three features of interest at Sunset Terrace, the Fish Pond, the Swimming Pool, and the Ravine. The fish pond gets its water supply from a spring on the hillside which, summer and winter, continuously pours forth over thirty thousand gallons a day. Between the spring and the fish pond are ten little cascades twinkling over huge water-washed boulders brought from an old dam on the Chattahoochee river and each cascade empties into a pool set about with large rocks and surrounded by woodland flowers, ferns and shrubs. The swimming pool in the glade is bordered with hundreds of flowering shrubs and Japanese iris, and shaded by pine trees." (313)

The Elms

House, circa 1832; garden, circa late 1860s

The historic garden primarily remains intact. Of particular note is the butterfly-shaped parterre garden, which was designed by the second owner, Lloyd Guyton Bowers. Mrs. Lloyd Bowers oversaw the planting of the elms around the property. The current owner restored portions of the garden in the late 1990s. The original house remains. The original well remains. The privately owned site is listed in the National Register of Historic Places.

"Yet another note is struck by the delightful butterfly design of the box garden. Its form was preserved by brick edgings, as the box borders were dug up a number of years ago. Now they have been replaced, as has been much of the shrub planting. The parterre formerly filled with roses is in grass. The giant magnolia which dominates house and garden was not a part of the original scheme. At The Elms the picket fence carried pineapple finials across its front section and enclosed the service yard and buildings." (102)

Esquiline Hill

Antebellum

The historic garden and original house no longer remain. The only original feature that remains is a family cemetery. The property was established by Major Raphael Moses in the antebellum period. The property was subdivided into neighborhoods and subdivisions.

"Berckmans of Augusta was given carte blanche. He in turn sent to England for Kidd, a noted landscape gardener, who demanded a free hand and three years in which to develop the estate. In 1860 the task was finished. An avenue of crape myrtle one and a half miles long led from the road to the house. For the formal garden a design of circles and semi-circles was employed. The large beds were hedged in cherry laurel; the small beds bordered by box. In addition there was a mystic maze. The rose garden contained almost every variety then known, bulbs and garden flowers were in profusion, and rare plants were cared for in a hothouse. Near the dwelling a circular summer house formed of cherry laurel and climbing roses still affords a charming setting for the weddings of the Major's great granddaughters." (104–5)

Green Island Ranch, or the Mr. and Mrs. R. C. Jordan Garden

Garden, circa 1906, and later addition, circa 1920s; house, circa 1920

Extensive remnants of the historic landscape remain. The formal gardens were designed by John J. Brandt, a German gardener, for the early twentieth-century owner, G. Gunby Jordan. The original house burned in 1920 and was rebuilt. The 1920s-era house was designed by R. Kennon Perry of Robert and Company of Atlanta. Additions to the landscape were designed by the New York civil and landscape engineer John B. Ryer Jr. in 1922. An extensive collection of outbuildings, including a farm complex, remains. The privately owned site is listed in the National Register of Historic Places.

"The house faces northward to the view and is surrounded by extensive well-planned gardens. The obstinate hillside has been converted into terraces for the numerous garden plots and the stiff red Georgia clay has been 'tamed' by hundreds of loads of loam and sand. The gardens, formal in design, are located on three terraces parallel with the house.

A wide sweep of lawn with the original oak trees, separates the house from the gardens and stepping stones lead from the terrace porch along an ivy-covered wall to the central walk and a small fountain. Other walks lead from this center through the three terraces to circular plots in which tall urns holding clinging vines are placed. Each of the terraces is divided by clipped privet hedges into three parts, the western and middle portions devoted to annuals, and the eastern section to roses. The lower terrace, given over to native and other kinds of shrubbery, blends naturally into the hillside." (316)

Mrs. J. W. McKinnon and Miss Alsobrook Garden

House, circa 1926; garden, circa mid to late 1920s

Few remnants of the historic garden remain. The garden was designed by Mrs. J. W. McKinnon beginning in 1926. The garden was maintained and expanded with additional plant material by Mrs. T. Earle Taylor (Angie Mae Taylor) in the 1950s and 1960s. The original house and summerhouse remain. The site is privately owned.

"To the south lies the sunny garden, its beds all bordered with blue pansies. Here are several rose-covered trellises, and in the center a sun-dial rests on an old mill stone. From this garden a tiny path leads under tall ligustrums to the rear of the house, and a secluded out-door living room. This shady garden holds a mirror lily pool set in grass among cool shadows, a quiet spot walled in by evergreen shrubbery, beneath which grow many shade-loving plants and early flowering bulbs. The pathway to the right leads on to a delightful small formal garden, with grass walks and beds aglow with color. A crystal globe centrally placed reflects the varied pictures as the seasons come and go." (318)

St. Elmo

Antebellum, with later additions in the early twentieth century

Few remnants of the historic garden remain. The original house remains. The site was the setting of Augusta Jane Evans Wilson's book St. Elmo. *The privately owned site is listed in the National Register of Historic Places.*

"In its palmy days giant tropical plants were housed in a conservatory, there was a square box garden in front of the house, and additional formal gardens with statue guarded walks lay on each side. Today gardens and statuary are gone, as is the marble basin into which flowed a spring so copious that for many years it served as the water supply of the neighboring community. A blazing hedge of Pyrus japonica, giant wistaria looped from tree to tree, and a three hundred foot scuppernong arbor leading down to an enchanting lake, speak eloquently of the past and give pleasure today." (100)

Woodcrest, or the Mr. and Mrs. J. W. Woodruff Garden

House, circa 1923; garden, circa 1920s–1930s

Portions of the historic garden remain. The original house remains. The site is privately owned by a descendant of the Woodruff family.

"The gardens at Woodcrest are reached from the terrace of the house by way of a broad paved walk which curves past a tremendous old pear tree, its branches sweeping the lawn, laden each springtime with a snowdrift of bloom. Close by the picturesque old tree of a generation ago are great camellia bushes in all their shiny beauty, their colorful blossoms waning as the pear tree reaches is flowering zenith. The limestone walk shortly loses its trim formality as it leaves the open lawn to enter the shady area of the rock garden. Here under deep hanging live oaks are plantations of many native wild flowers combined with woodland shrubs and ferns; and moss covered stones bind the pools of a tiny wandering stream where water poppies, forget-me-nots and little bog flowers thrive." (319)

Oglethorpe County

LEXINGTON

Upson-Howard Place, or the Stephen Upson House and Garden

House, circa 1812; garden, circa 1820s–1830s

Little of the historic garden remains. The stone wall remains. The original house remains. The privately owned site is included in the National Register of Historic Places as part of the Lexington Historic District.

"The whole place bears a New England stamp. The stone wall of semi-dressed blocks enclosing the entire property is unique in Georgia. The usual box garden did not occupy the space between the house and street; instead there were two panels of shrub planted lawn enclosed by euonymous hedges and divided by an elaborately designed box bordered path. The terraced kitchen garden with its grape arbor, fruit trees, rose and lily beds bordered by iris and bulbs, and vegetable beds edged with herbs and small flowers were immediately left of the house. A drive shaded by red cedars led to the house, then past kitchen and quarters and continued to the barns and stables through a fine grove of oaks." (70)

Polk County

CEDARTOWN

Camelrest, or the Mr. and Mrs. Robert Campbell Garden

House, antebellum; garden, circa 1920s through mid-1950s

Little of the historic garden remains. The garden was designed by Mrs. Robert Campbell (Carrie Hitt Campbell). The original house remains. The site is privately owned.

"Deserted for many years, this century-old place has been faithfully restored by a son of the family so that once again it reflects the quaint charm of the old South. The gardens lie to the west of the house, in close relationship with it, and look out to the distant landscape of rolling pasture lands and tall cedars massed against a turquoise sky. In the foreground are groups of fine old trees. In early springtime thousands of bulbs blossom under their leafy canopy; daffodils, scillas, snowdrops, little blue hyacinths, and camassias. The perennial gardens are slightly terraced in formal design, and are built in three sections. Besides the herbaceous borders, there are a German iris garden and a rose garden containing both new and old varieties." (311)

AUGUSTA

Carnes-Howard-Thomas-Chafee Place, or the Mr. and Mrs. Harry Chafee Garden, or the Howard-Chafee Garden*

House, late eighteenth century; garden, early twentieth century

Portions of the historic garden remain. Of particular note is the original five-part ("quincunx") parterre design. Some daffodils, roman hyacinths, scilla, and snowflakes remain, too. The garden was designed by Hannah Howard. The current owner is restoring aspects of the historic garden. The original house remains. The privately owned site is included in the National Register of Historic Places as part of the Summerville Historic District, which is also a locally designated district.

"The seventeen beds of which it [the garden] is comprised were formerly edged in spice pinks. These, worn out by blooming, have been replaced by narrow copings. The bands of old fashioned blue hyacinths which outline all the beds are those set out by Mrs. Howard, as are the butter and eggs daffodils filling some of them." (56)

"The sweet scent of its flowers enveloped me and, like a magic cloak, wafted me back to its beginning." (288)

* The Carnes-Howard-Thomas-Chafee Place, or the Mr. and Mrs. Harry Chafee Garden, was included in *Garden History of Georgia* twice: in part 1, "Georgia's Early Gardens," as the Carnes-Howard-Thomas-Chafee Place, and in part 2, "Modern Gardens," as the Mr. and Mrs. Harry Chafee Garden.

Cumming-Langdon Place

Antebellum

Little of the historic garden remains except mature trees and the lawn. The original house and outbuildings remain and have been restored by the current owners. A contemporary garden on the property was designed by the Augusta garden designer Jeff Tilden for the current owners. The privately owned site is included in the National Register of Historic Places as part of the Summerville Historic District, which is also a locally designated district.

"In 1826, following the then prevailing fashion, Thomas Cumming built a summer home on The Sand Hills. To the northwest of the large, comfortable dwelling his wife, Ann, laid out a formal garden of simple design. Rectangular in shape, surrounded by a picket fence pierced by two gates, it has a round central bed, four rectangular beds and a border bed just within the fence line. The shrubs in this last are about all that remain of the planting, though the garden form can be easily followed. Flowering trees and shrubs surround both house and garden. There is a second formal garden to the west designed for Miss Sarah Cumming by Ignaze A. Pilate, a Hungarian landscape gardener, who came to Augusta with Frederick Law Olmstead [*sic*], and was later associated with him and Calvert Vaux in laying out Central Park in New York. . . . Of this garden's intricate pattern only the central bed remains." (59)

Fruitlands, or Fruitland Nurseries; later, Augusta National Golf Club

Antebellum and circa early 1930s

Some remnants of Fruitland Nurseries, one of the first commercial nurseries in the South, founded by Louis Edouard Mathieu Berckmans and P. J. A. Berckmans, remain. The allée of historic magnolias (now known as Magnolia Walk), the oval drive in front of the original house, other historic trees (including a Spanish cork oak and two Chinese firs), and a Chinese wisteria remain. The original antebellum house remains and now serves as the clubhouse for the Augusta National Golf Club. The golf course landscape (circa 1931), designed by Bobby Jones and Alister MacKenzie, is completely intact. The site is owned by the Augusta National Golf Club, a private organization. The site is listed in the National Register of Historic Places.

"The approach is by an avenue of magnolias grown from seed sent to Mr. Berckmans from two trees in Athens about 1858 or 1859. . . . Rare and lovely plants grow in the park-like grounds. Among those planted during the first twenty-five years after Fruitlands was developed, are a Darlington Oak, a Spanish cork oak, Japanese persimmons, Chinese pine, Chinese holly, Japanese trailing juniper, holly-leaved tea olive, a hardy lemon hedge (Citrus trifoliata) from Japan, an Amur privet hedge (Ligustrum Amurense), called the 'Mother Hedge' for from its ten original plants imported from France in 1860 have come all privet hedges in the South. There are many camellias from France, Germany, Japan and Belgium; azaleas, forty varieties of which were imported prior to 1861; an Elliottia racemosa, now practically extinct; and a Rhodophyllum Macropodon, a very rare broad-leaved evergreen imported from Japan about sixty years ago." (62)

Goshen Plantation, or the Mr. and Mr. Joseph McK. Speer Garden

House, circa 1906; garden, circa 1910s–1930s

Some facets of the historic garden remain. The main house and outbuildings remain. Historic garden features include the structure of two terraces, two pools, statuary (fountain, birdbath, and sundial), brick walls and walkways, concrete pathways, a central staircase to the first terrace, a double staircase to the second terrace, magnolias, hollies, and camellias. The original 1,100 acres were subdivided in the 1950s. The majority of the acreage now makes up the Goshen Plantation Golf Club and residential subdivisions. The five acres at the heart of the historic site, including the original house, outbuildings, and portions of the historic garden, is privately owned.

"The garden itself is arranged on two levels, reached by steps from the terrace. On the first level is the box garden. Here on either side of a sunken mill-stone, are two perfect roses, with blossom, foliage and stem embroidered on the turf in matched specimens of dwarf boxwood. The heart of each rose is planted with yellow pansies. Leading from this to the lower garden is a double set of steps, concealed by a white balustrade garlanded with pink Cherokee roses. This makes a background for the planting of tulips in shades of purple and lavender below. A high brick wall covered with climbing roses encloses this garden on three sides, while the wall to the south is low, affording another view of the far-away hills." (303, 305)

Green Court, or the Mr. H. P. Crowell Garden

House, circa 1823; garden, circa 1909–1910s

Substantial portions of the historic garden remain. Portions of the garden were restored around 2002 by a previous owner. The original house remains. The privately owned site is included in the National Register of Historic Places as part of the Summerville Historic District, which is also a locally designated district.

"Directly back of the house itself lies the sunken garden laid out in formal fashion. Four large divisions on different levels enclosed by high privet hedges and carpeted with winter grass are each centered by a pool, fountain or flower bed, and have corner plantings of roses, tulips and hyacinths. Dwarf flowering fruit trees form striking features here, growing in graceful fashion and lending a delicate lacework of shadow to the beds below. These secluded gardens are reached progressively through evergreen archways above steps of turf." (297)

Highgate, or the Mrs. Henry C. Cohen Garden

House, circa 1810, with updates circa 1860; garden, circa 1860s and 1930s

Little of the historic garden remains. The historic camellias, brick walls, iron gate, ironwork, and millstones remain. Contemporary garden rooms were added to the site between the 1980s and the present. The original house remains. The privately owned site is included in the National Register of Historic Places as part of the Summerville Historic District, which is also a locally designated district.

"Highgate's present owner came a decade ago,—came with appraising eye, skilled and tender hand. Choice shrubs and flowers from distant climes flourish side by side with native specimens. Camellias, Bamboos, azaleas, boxwood, tea olives, wild olive, dogwood, iris, lilies,—all are here. An interesting feature of the garden is the old summer-house, octagonal in form. Paved with brick, it has brick pillars supporting a tin roof, and is draped about with an ivy-vine as large in diameter as a ship's rope." (293)

Le Manoir Fleuri, or the Mrs. Robert G. Reese Garden

House, circa early 1920s; garden, circa 1930s

Substantial portions of the historic garden remain. The original house and garage remain. Louise Delaige Reese hired the landscape architect Ruth Bramley Dean of New York to design the garden around 1932. The garden was built by local unemployed men in Augusta during the Depression. The structure and most of the hardscape features of the Italian-influenced garden remain, including a wall fountain with Italian tiles, an Italian marble fountain, a rock-rimmed fountain, brick pathways, concrete and brick-lined pathways, a brick-and-concrete bench, a gate, and historic trees and shrubs. The privately owned site is included in the National

Register of Historic Places as part of the Summerville Historic District, which is also a locally designated district.

"Lying to the south side of the house is an oblong garden with fore-court and wide central path of flag stones, which leads to a fountain set in a high wall. This fountain, which stands between two unusually perfect specimens of boxwood, is of white and yellow marble, and is a copy of the fountain in the garden of the renowned Capuchin monastery in Amalfi. In the wall there are unusual panels of filagree [*sic*] tile brought from Italy. Opening from this garden is another one on a lower level, with formal beds outlined with boxwood and surrounded on all sides with tall evergreens and flowering shrubs. At the end of the main axis is a semi-circular seat made of brick." (306)

Morningside, or the Mrs. Alfred S. Bourne Garden

House, circa 1909; garden, circa 1910s–1920s

Portions of the historic garden remain. Of particular note are the form and water features of the upper formal garden and the sunken garden. The original main garden and a sunken garden date to around 1909. The formal layout of the garden, a series of garden rooms on a central axis, was primarily designed by the renowned American landscape architect Rose Nichols Standish of Boston, Massachusetts, in the 1920s for the second owners, Mr. and Mrs. Alfred Severin Bourne. Later additions to the garden were done by the Georgia landscape architect E. S. Draper around 1929. The original house, which remains, was designed for Mr. and Mrs. Francis Herron Denny by the Augusta architect Henry Ten Eyck Wendell and completed in 1909. The site is privately owned, and the current owners have been redeveloping the garden rooms over the past decade. The site is included in the National Register of Historic Places as part of the Summerville Historic District, which is also a locally designated district.

"In logical sequence, the rear sun-parlor opens upon a cement terrace comfortably furnished with easy chairs, tables and rugs, an inviting place to spend an idle morning. From this vantage point, there is a charming view of an adjoining garden framed in masses of greenery. Water rising from a buff marble basin upheld on a fluted tripod, overflows into a rectangular pool which marks the center of a grass plot. Biotas clipped into columns guard the pool and add dignity to the tranquil enclosure. Outside the square of turf the border is thick with azaleas bearing blossoms of white and rosy-lavender. From this intimate outdoor living-room a brick path, walled by privet hedges and heightened by rows of slender Italian cypresses, shortly leads to an old-fashioned wooden arbor overhung with purple wistaria. Below lies a small sunken garden, divided by walks of bluestone flagging into four grass panels, each enclosed by flower borders accented by Carolina cherry laurels clipped to resemble the little round-headed laurels so often seen in Italy, and rising above a carpet of pansies. The outside border of the entire rectangle is gay in spring with tulips of soft rosy-salmon and slaty-blue shades combining with lemon-yellow pansies. In the center of the garden a lead dolphin throws a spout of water above a circular pool set in a ring of tall cypresses which form a background for four eighteenth century English lead figures—Winter, Summer, Spring and Autumn—standing near the fountain." (284)

Old Medical College Garden

Old Medical College, circa 1835–37; gardens, circa 1930s

Some remnants of the historic garden remain, including the courtyard on the western side of the building, portions of the pierced brick walls, herringbone-patterned brick walkways, an ornamental gate, the grave of Dr. Milton Antony (the school's founder), a fountain, a statue, and historic trees, boxwood, and camellias. The Sand Hills Garden Club received a Founders Fund Award from the Garden Club of America in the 1960s for work on this project. The original building, altered in 1869 and again in 1897, remains. It was designed by the architect Charles B. Cluskey. The Sand Hills Garden Club owned the site from 1930 to 1987, installing gardens in the 1930s. In 1987, the Medical College of Georgia acquired the building from the Sand Hills Garden Club for the purpose of restoration. In 1988, Sartor Design Group, Landscape Architects, created plans for site improvements. In 2008, Lord Aeck Sargent was hired to investigate the building for possible restoration. The same year, Jim Cothran of Robert and Company was hired to examine the condition of the gardens. The site is owned by the Georgia Health Sciences University and is listed in the National Register of Historic Places.

"At present it is in the process of restoration by The Sand Hills Garden Club, who, with the Trustees of the [Richmond] Academy, have built a wall around the entire property—using brick from the old City Hospital which adjoined it, and which was condemned two years ago. The wall is an exact copy of the one section of the old wall left standing at the east end. Iron gates add beauty and protection, while on either side of the broad entrance walk, a memorial avenue of camellias leads to the front of the building.... On the west side, through an iron gate one enters a little walled-in boxwood garden where the initials S. H. G. C. and the date 1930 have been outlined in box. Here a sun-dial marks the hours." (423)

Rosemary Cottage

Antebellum

The historic garden and house no longer remain. The property was sold for commercial development in the 1950s.

"The central feature, a formal garden, was flanked by cultivated areas, one planted in small fruits and fruit trees, the other as a kitchen garden. Scuppernong arbors, each one hundred and twenty-five feet long, stretched from the house to the outer boundary of these units. In the middle of each arbor was a summer house. The other three sides of these sections were bordered by handsome euonymus bushes, the whole framed in oaks. In the center of the formal garden was a large oval bowling green bordered by handsome trees. Its character as such was marred by a central planting of euonymus. Surrounding it were beds in a variety of shapes, with strong magnolia and cedar plantings. At Rosemary Cottage is found a very interesting character of edging: bricks eighteen inches long have one end so molded that when two are set in the ground together they form a scallop.... Within this edging the lawn and four circular beds were bordered in dwarf arborvitae; all other beds in dwarf box." (60)

Salubrity Hall, or the Mr. and Mrs. John W. Herbert Garden

House, circa 1928; gardens, circa 1920s–1930s

Some remnants of the historic garden, designed by Olivia Herbert, remain. The original house, designed by the Augusta architectural firm of Scroggs and Ewing,

remains and has been restored. Original outbuildings remain on the site. The current owners have been working with the Atlanta landscape architect William T. Smith since 2006 to revive what remains of the original gardens and to design a series of new garden rooms that echo elements of the past while meeting twenty-first-century needs. The privately owned site is included in the National Register of Historic Places as part of the Summerville Historic District, which is also a locally designated district.

"On the west of the residence is the formal garden, with an ornamental fountain and a weeping willow drooping over a semi-circular marble seat. To the south is a terrace with a rose-covered pergola of antique columns. The back of the pergola is of weather-beaten brick, with a niche for a leaden figure of a boy holding a tray of flowers." (300)

Sandy Acres, or the Mr. and Mrs. Rodney S. Cohen Garden

House, circa early nineteenth century; gardens, circa late nineteenth century and 1920s

Substantial portions of the historic garden remain. Of particular note are the original sunken parterre garden and the water garden. The original house remains. The site is privately owned and is included in the National Register of Historic Places as part of the Summerville Historic District, which is also a locally designated district.

"The Loyless family made many improvements to the interior of the house as well as to the grounds. A vast amount of planting has been done in recent years, but the general plan of the garden and grounds, as developed by them, has not been altered. The present owners, Mr. and Mrs. Rodney Cohen, have added an outdoor living room with an open fireplace, which is a joy on cool days, as well as for picnics and barbecues. Leading off from this inviting spot is the path to the sunken garden. This was formerly an old clay tennis court; now thousands of specimens of dwarf boxwood—all rooted and grown by Mrs. Cohen—border the paths and march in and out among the flower beds, in formal and informal patterns. To the right, and screened by a wall of jasmine and honeysuckle, is the water garden, where five pools built on different levels present an ever-changing panorama. Both the water garden and the sunken garden open on to the rose garden." (294)

Twin Gables, or the Mrs. Harry Albright Garden

House, circa 1911; garden, circa 1910s, 1920s–1930s

Substantial portions of the historic garden remain. Of particular note are the parterre rose garden, the sunken water garden, and the bog garden. The garden was designed by the landscape architectural firm of Herbert, Pray and White of Boston, Massachusetts, and later developed by the Augusta landscape designer Julia Lester Dillon. The original house, which remains, was designed by the Augusta architect Henry Ten Eyck Wendell. The site is owned by Georgia Regents University and is included in the National Register of Historic Places as part of the Summerville Historic District, which is also a locally designated district.

"Entering the main garden from the terrace which opens out from the flower room of the house, one looks across a spacious lawn shaded with magnificent trees and ornamented with a lotus lily pool which mirrors slender willows, pink, blue and white hyacinths, and purple and yellow iris. Beyond is a high brick wall set after the fashion of English gardens, with a tea house at either end garlanded with climbing roses and star jasmine and canopied with purple wistaria." (282)

Mr. and Mrs. William B. White Garden

House, circa 1911; gardens, circa 1910s–1930s

Some remnants of the historic garden remain, including a large pool, an Italian pergola, double stairs, the front walkway, pavers on the side of the driveway, one circle of boxwood with a central birdbath, and a few historic trees and shrubs. The original house, which remains, was designed by the Augusta architect Henry Ten Eyck Wendall for Cornelia and William B. White in 1911. The outbuilding from around 1935 remains. The property was owned by the Augusta Women's Club from 1959 until the late 1990s and was used as the organization's clubhouse. In 2004, the site was sold, and is now a private residence. It is included in the National Register of Historic Places as part of the Summerville Historic District, which is also a locally designated district.

"At the front entrance of the grounds are stone steps leading to a walk bordered by pink camellias with broad-leaf evergreens as a background. It is an appropriate entrance to the house, the architecture of which is Italian Renaissance. To the right of the house is a large planting of Herme and Chandleri Elegans camellias. Near these are some fine specimens of Cedrus deodara, and a little further on is an old cedar, festooned with Cherokee roses. The formal box garden has as its special feature a fountain of old lead which is a copy of DeLagon's dancing girl and piping boy. Around the fountain is a bed bordered with boxwood, in which are planted Lady Derby, Enchantress hyacinths and Clara Butt tulips. Seven other box-edged beds are planted in daffodils, tulips and hyacinths. Behind the fountain is an Italian pergola covered with pink Cherokee roses." (308)

Thomas County

THOMASVILLE

Bay Tree Farms, or the Mr. and Mrs. M. L. Lively Garden

Circa 1920s–1930s

The historic garden no longer remains. Only a few pecan trees remain from the property's former role as a pecan plantation. The original Lively home and some outbuildings remain, but have been modified for use as administrative offices for the John D. Archbold Memorial Hospital. Numerous commercial and industrial buildings were subsequently built on other acreage of the original property.

"The plantings in the grounds surrounding the house include such sweet scented shrubs and trees as the tea olive, banana shrub, sweet shrub, mimosa, syringa, Cape jasmine, Christmas honeysuckle, magnolia, bay, mock orange, kumquat, and azalea. Various members of the lily family also thrive here in the semi-shade, among them Easter lilies, Madonna, butterfly, and several sorts of lemon lilies. Nearer the house are particularly fine specimens of the favorite ornamental shrubs of this region, azaleas and camellias. On the south porch of the house a trellis is covered with red and white roses, while the arbor on the west side presents a charming color harmony with the dainty yellow of the Lady Banksia roses and the lavender of wistaria. . . . Across the lawn and cutting it off from the pecan groves runs a broad, irregular bed of flowering shrubs and roses serving as a background for the annual and perennial borders. And beyond, the wide expanse of lawn slopes down to a meadow which is centered by a large, clear pool, a natural mirror, reflecting the tall, majestic pines in the distance." (399–400)

Elsoma, or the Mrs. Charles Merrill Chapin Garden

Antebellum; house, circa 1920s; gardens, circa late 1890s–1920s

Few remnants of the historic garden remain except for the allée of oaks. The circa 1925 house remains. The antebellum plantation was purchased by J. Wyman Jones and his wife, Salome Hanna Chapin Jones, in the early 1890s. Salome Hanna Chapin Jones's son, Charles Merrill Chapin, later acquired the property. The antebellum house was destroyed by fire in 1922, and a new residence, designed by the Thomasville architects Delano and Aldrich, was built in the 1920s. Over the years, the site has been divided numerous times. Some of the land holds the original 1920s-era house and a few remnants of the garden. It is privately owned. Another portion of the original land is now part of Longpine Plantation. And, another portion of the original land is now part of the modern Elsoma Plantation, which is privately owned by descendants of the Chapin family. It has a longleaf pine forest and serves as a quail-hunting plantation.

"From the open bricked terrace at the southern end of the living room, one gets a view of the old-fashioned flower garden enclosed by a tall hedge of arbor vitae, with its rose garden and formal beds of all the sweet old-timey flowers. Mrs. Chapin specializes in flowers that bloom during the winter months, and in these beds are found narcissi, jonquils, violets, primroses, thrift, verbena, daises, snowdrops, and literally millions of pansies; besides such shrubs as camellias, azaleas and tea olives. The central feature of the garden is a bronze statuette,—a small boy riding a dragon fly." (385, 387)

Greenwood Plantation, or the Mrs. Payne Whitney Garden*

House, antebellum; garden, circa 1899–early 1900s

Some remnants of the historic garden remain. The original antebellum house, completed in 1844, was designed by the English architect John Wind for Thomas P. Jones. In 1899, Greenwood was purchased by Colonel Oliver Hazard Payne of New York. He commissioned Stanford White, of the prominent American architectural firm McKim, Mead and White, to suggest improvements at Greenwood, which included designing wings and rear additions to the house, an iron gate, and sunken gardens. In 1916, Payne Whitney and his wife, Helen Hay Whitney, inherited Greenwood. In 1993, a fire destroyed the roof of the house, its staircase, and much of the house's interior. Restoration of the exterior and stabilization of the interior were completed before Helen Whitney's death in 1998. A complex of early twentieth-century outbuildings remains. The site has a longleaf pine forest and has served as a quail-hunting plantation since the early 1900s. The privately owned site is listed in the National Register of Historic Places.

"This fine home standing in a splendid grove of live oaks, palmettos and magnolias, demanded a garden just as fine. Squares of lawn now stretch where many flower beds once formed the fanciful patterns dear to the hearts of the 1830–40's." (91)

"An estate of twenty thousand acres it presents a finished and alluring picture from the driveway, set thickly with Cherokee roses and showing woodlands framed with azaleas, to the stately palm garden and classic garden of Italian type, planned and executed by the late Stanford White. . . . Camellias, magnolias and azaleas are proper color accents for a palm garden which includes all varieties that thrive in that locality and in the rectangular beds are carpet plantings of small and colorful flowers." (405)

* Greenwood Plantation was included in *Garden History of Georgia* twice: in part 1, "Georgia's Early Gardens," as Greenwood Plantation, and in part 2, "Modern Gardens," as Greenwood Plantation, or the Mrs. Payne Whitney Garden.

Inwood Plantation, or the Mr. and Mrs. J. Morse Ely Garden

Circa 1900s–1930s

The historic garden and house no longer remain. Some large trees and a few historic camellias remain. A few cottages remain, as do the ruins of the original boathouse. The property was subdivided and is now home to the Southwestern State Hospital and the Judge Thomas Jefferson Loftiss II Regional Juvenile Detention Center as well as the Georgia Bureau of Investigation Regional Office.

"At each of the entrance gates to the plantation there are massed plantings of native shrubbery such as wild azalea, Spanish bayonet, honeysuckle, yellow jessamine, as well as magnolia, dogwood, redbud, and crabapple trees. Beginning at the main gateway the winding drive is bordered with a clipped hedge, followed by a uniform line of dogwood trees and at all intersections of the plantation roads there are groups of native evergreens and flowering shrubs. . . . At the eastern end of the house are the rose gardens, heavily bordered with liriope. An entire section is devoted to yellow roses which are particularly fine in variety and color. The broad, open terrace across the south side of the house is banked with a planting of tea olive (Osmanthus fragrans), about ten feet in width. . . . Over against the right wing of the house is a planting of banana shrub (Michelia fuscata), which wafts its own subtle sweetness. The terrace looks out over the formal flower garden which is bordered with a clipped abelia hedge. Here are beds of various annuals and perennials, and a number of very handsome specimens of boxwood and camellia." (388)

Melrose Plantation, the Mr. and Mrs. Howard M. Hanna Garden, or the Melrose-South Eden Plantation

House, antebellum, and later expanded, circa 1896; garden, circa 1920s

Portions of the historic garden remain. Of particular note is the walled garden with greenhouse (circa 1930s), which was designed by the Cleveland architectural firm of Walker and Weeks. The firm also designed many brick outbuildings for the site in the 1920s. The Owl's Nest, circa late 1920s, designed as a guesthouse by Walker and Weeks, was later expanded extensively. The original house and an extensive complex of outbuildings remain. The site has a longleaf pine forest and has served as a quail-hunting plantation since the mid-1890s. The privately owned site is listed in the National Register of Historic Places as Melrose and Sinkola Plantations. The site is open to the public as South Eden Plantation, a luxury boutique resort.

"The approach to the house from the highway is by a broad grassed walk bordered with a luxuriant tea hedge. To right and left are spread many acres of velvety lawn with groups of ancient oaks and magnolias and such flowering trees as Japanese magnolia, flowering peach, redbud, dogwood, kumquat, crepe myrtle, and wild azalea. The fence bordering the estate is covered with Cherokee roses and native yellow jessamine vines, and just inside is a hedge of Madame Lombard roses. Clambering

over the house, fences and trees are lavender wistaria vines and on the grounds are many wistaria trees. East of the house and beyond the flower gardens is the riding field, a stretch of smooth turf at the edge of a forest of pines and dogwood trees. Indoors the deep bay of the living room, which is paneled in native pine tinted to the shade of the trunks of crepe myrtle trees, looks out over a white garden. This sunken garden is grass-carpeted and bordered with a hedge of pittosporum, and against the green background are masses of white azalea, white camellias, beds of snowdrops and white pansies. From the white garden, steps of snowy marble lead up to the pink garden with its pink camellias, azaleas and roses—a lovely contrast." (390, 393)

Millpond Plantation, or the J. H. Wade House and Garden

House, circa 1903–4; gardens, circa 1903–10

The majority of the historic garden remains. The garden was designed by the Boston landscape architect Warren H. Manning. The original house was designed by the Cleveland architectural firm of Hubbell and Benes. The site is privately owned by descendants of the Wade Family and is listed in the National Register of Historic Places. The descendants placed the land in a conversation easement to allow for consolidated oversight of the care of the land at Millpond Plantation, including the historic house and garden. The site has a longleaf pine forest and has served as a quail-hunting plantation since the early 1900s.

"The house is thickly hung with great ropes of purple wistaria and is shaded by magnificent live oaks. To the south is the Palm Garden with an infinite variety of palms grouped around a rectangular greensward, the whole bordered with liriope. At the extreme end is a lovely reflecting pool to mirror the fronds of the palms on its clear green surface. Toward the west is the Camellia Garden, containing a remarkably fine collection of these ever prized blossoms." (401)

❧ Pebble Hill Plantation, or the Mrs. Perry W. Harvey Garden

House, circa 1936; gardens, circa early twentieth century and 1930s

Portions of the historic garden remain. The original antebellum house, with additions from 1914, was destroyed by fire in 1934, although portions of the 1914

additions remain. The new main house was completed in 1936, designed by the Cleveland architect Abram Garfield for Kate Hanna Ireland Harvey. Garfield had also designed the 1914 addition. Portions of the gardens and grounds were designed by the Cleveland landscape architect V. Ethylwyn Harrison in collaboration with Abram Garfield in the 1930s. An extensive complex of outbuildings remains on the property, as do longleaf pine forests. The site is owned by the Pebble Hill Foundation and is operated as a museum and public event venue. The site is listed in the National Register of Historic Places. www.pebblehill.com

"At the extreme end of the east wing the drawing room opens on to a flower garden in all shades of blue, lavender and purple,—violets, violas, pansies, stocks, larkspur, and little tree wistarias. Around this garden is a hedge of Spiraea thunbergii. An opening in the hedge, flanked by tall Italian cypresses gives a view of the swimming pool which is enclosed by a low vine-covered wall, with stone seats and garden furniture at each of the four corners. From the pool to the east stretches a well kept lawn, with a wide view through the pine woods beyond. Another opening from the East Garden leads through a grassed crabapple walk to a tea house in the wood, the doorway framed by two enormous pine trees. Still another opening leads to the 'Maze,' planted in camphor wood, which is the delight of all children. The Maze and the Front Garden are connected by a path of abelia trained over an arched iron trellis, which makes a pleasant shady walk on hot summer days." (395)

Winnstead Plantation, or Pleasant Hill Plantation, or the Mrs. Coburn Haskell Garden, or Winnstead Plantation and Nature Preserve

House, circa 1833, renovated circa 1850s, and enlarged and renovated, circa 1902; gardens, circa early 1900s

The historic garden no longer remains. The original antebellum house was rebuilt and expanded in 1902 when the site was purchased by Mary Gertrude Hanna Haskell and Coburn Haskell. In the early 1900s, the Haskells re-created a formal garden using antebellum historic plants and also added a rose garden. They preserved the existing outbuildings and added barns, stables, and a racetrack. In 1947, Philip and Eleanor Rust purchased the house and surrounding garden and acquired more of the original plantation acreage. Until the 1980s, Winnstead and the Rust family were known

for raising Santa Gertrudis cattle on the site. Since 1990, the site has been managed as a nature preserve by a family descendant.

"Architecturally in keeping with the house is the white picket fence set inside a closely clipped hedge of privet. The gateway is between two huge magnolia trees and opens onto a broad brick walk which carries further the spacious feeling of the driveway, and leads directly to the doorway. On either side of the walkway is a border of handsome boxwood, clipped to uniform size, and beyond the border is an unusual planting, consisting of a line of alternating Arbor vitae, kumquat, and banana shrub, the latter about ten feet in height and clipped to a smooth, round ball. Against this line of evergreens are the rose beds, each containing a different variety. . . . In the main flower garden there are many beds of annuals of various kinds, as well as rose beds bordered with violets. . . . To the south of the flower garden is the tennis court, the wire fencing covered with roses at one end and sweet peas at the other, with a background planted of kumquats. . . . Across the western wing of the house a long glassed loggia with its great tubs of orange trees overlooks a court filled with masses of azaleas of every variety. The living room at the extreme end of this wing looks out over another rose garden which is Mrs. Haskell's particular pride. This is laid out in formal beds around a central sundial—each bed exhibiting a different kind of rose—and the whole garden bordered with a low clipped hedge of Louis Phillippe roses." (396, 398)

Troup County

LAGRANGE

﹛ Hills and Dales Estate, or Ferrell Gardens or the Mr. and Mrs. Fuller E. Callaway Sr. Garden*

House, circa 1916; gardens, circa 1840s and later

The historic garden is primarily intact, and large portions have been restored. The antebellum house no longer remains. The mansion (circa 1916), designed by the Atlanta architect Neel Reid for Ida Cason Callaway and Fuller E. Callaway Sr., remains and has been restored. After Fuller E. Callaway Jr. died in 1992 and Alice Callaway in 1998, the property was bequeathed to the Fuller E. Callaway Foundation, with the request that it be used for the instruction and enjoyment of the public. In 2004, the Hills and Dales Estate formally opened as a public house and garden museum. www .hillsanddales.org

"Proceeding along a high box hedge banded by spirea, the oldest of the gardens is reached. Situated immediately to the south of the house, it shares a wide level with fine trees. Completely walled in by box trees, in this parterre are found mottoes of close clipped dwarf box. On one side is Mrs. Ferrell's 'God is Love,' companioned by the Judge's 'Fiat Justitia;' opposite are the present owners' 'Ora Pro Mi,' and 'St. Callaway.' (94)

"Surrounded by the gardens and a vast area of natural woodland—the estate comprises three thousand acres—the mansion, which is Italo-Georgian in architecture, was erected in 1916 on the site of the old homestead. South of it lie the famous Ferrell gardens intact and almost exactly as their first mistress left them, only an occasional boxwood having, of necessity, been replaced by the present owner, Mrs. Fuller E. Callaway." (330)

* Hills and Dales Estate was included in *Garden History of Georgia* twice: in part 1, "Georgia's Early Gardens," as Ferrell Gardens, and in part 2, "Modern Gardens," as Hills and Dales, or the Mr. and Mrs. Fuller E. Callaway Garden.

Walker County

FLINTSTONE

Ashland Farm, or the Mr. and Mrs. Z. C. Patten Garden

House, circa 1906; gardens, circa 1906, 1910s–1930s

The historic garden is primarily intact. The original house and outbuildings, including Peeler Mill, the wagon pavilion, a barn, a gashouse, and guesthouses, remain. The Atlanta architect W. T. Downing designed the main house and several outbuildings. Biltmore Nurseries designed formal gardens and provided much of the nonnative plant material for the site. The privately owned site remains in the Patten family. It is listed in the National Register of Historic Places.

"All the natural beauty of the North Georgia woodland has been most carefully preserved and protected at Ashland Farm, picturesquely situated in the foothills of Lookout Mountain. . . . The woodland at Ashland Farm is never so entrancing as when spring contends with winter. Even under the snow the delicate hepatica blooms, wrapped in fuzzy furs against the cold and the pink blossom of trailing arbutus opens among withered leaves of oak and chestnut. Quaker Ladies, sometimes called 'Bluettes,' are among the first flowers to appear and in a few short weeks the woods are blue with bird's-foot violets. . . . At the water's edge near the old mill are great patches of the delicate blue and pink of mertensias (Virginia bluebells) and along the winding pathways wood anemones grow in accordance with the Greek tradition that Anemos, the wind, sends his fragile namesakes to herald his coming in early spring. Next are foam flower, blue and white-eyed grass, and pink wood sorrel. A step farther on one may discover wild geranium, true Solomon's seal, wild delphinium, and trillium. Then a mass of blue phlox, mountain columbine, and white vetch, combine with primroses, jonquils and narcissi, these last adding to the charm of the wildings." (144)

LOOKOUT MOUNTAIN

✣ Rock City Gardens, or the Mr. and Mrs. Garnet* Carter Garden

Circa 1928, 1930s, and 1940s

The historic garden is primarily intact. The original main house remains, as do the majority of the outbuildings, gnomes, pathways, and other features throughout the tourist attraction site. The garden and the tourist attraction were designed by Frieda and Garnet Carter. The site is owned by See Rock City, Inc., and is listed in the National Register of Historic Places. The tourist attraction is open to the public. www.seerockcity. com

"Though located on Lookout Mountain, in Tennessee, the gardens of Mr. and Mrs. Garnet Carter are on the side of the mountain that is part of Georgia. Hence Rock City is rightfully included in Georgia gardens, and is presented as a unique rock garden. A strange formation of lichen-covered sandstone, it is of interest to geologists, artists, horticulturists and others. . . . For countless years this great extent of rock had rested undisturbed, and, until Mr. and Mrs. Carter in 1932 built their Enchanted Trail, it was impossible to pass through the many narrow tunnels and devious windings. . . . The Trail, a path four feet wide, leads through tunnels and over bridges bordered with gray rocks and surfaced with pine needles and moss, and makes accessible every cranny and crevice in the entire ten acres. Stone stairways have been built to provide ease and comfort for the long trail. Pulpit Rock, Fat Man's Squeeze, the Needle's Eye and Grand Corridor, Shelter Rock, Lover's Leap, Tortoise Shell Rock, Pedestal Rock and the Lion's Den are some of the named features, each one a garden in itself. . . . Many little figures add to the charm, the mystery and the interest of the place." (354)

* Garnet Carter's first name was misspelled in the original *Garden History of Georgia* as "Garnett."

Walton County

HIGH SHOALS

Casulon Plantation

House, circa 1820s; garden, circa 1820s, 1860s, and early twentieth century

Few remnants of the historic garden remain aside from some of the boxwood and historic daffodils. Ruins of the original house remain. The site was restored between 1975 and 1995, but fire destroyed the antebellum house in 2002, and the gardens have been neglected since that time. The privately owned site is listed in the National Register of Historic Places.

"Approaching the house through pine woods and past broad cotton fields one comes on the hardwood grove which surrounds the house and the garden area. Across the front and enclosed in a white picket fence lies the main garden, re-made in 1865 just after the war, while to the east, connected by a rose arbor, is a modern informal garden with hedges of flowering shrubs, a sun dial in a stretch of open lawn, many beds of flowers, and a summer house;—an interesting contrast in form with the old garden. Box-edged paths and parterres carry out the formal pattern of the front garden. The verandah looks down over the interwoven masses of pungent boxwood, and on one side of the doorway stands a big elm, covered in vines, on the other a native cedar." (124, 126)

SANDERSVILLE

Sandersville Library Garden

Library, circa 1925; garden, circa 1929

The historic garden no longer remains. It was designed by Anne Louise Irwin of the Transylvania Garden Club in the late 1920s and installed by the club. The building, which no longer houses the library, remains. The site is owned by the Transylvania Club, Inc., and is listed in the National Register of Historic Places as part of the Sandersville Commercial and Industrial Historic District.

"The garden made for the Sandersville Library by the Transylvania Garden Club is consistent in character with the historic charm of the library building. . . . The picturesque library is situated in the business center of Sandersville, so the garden plot is practically enclosed on three sides by the walls of buildings. Ivy, ficus, and Virginia creeper clothe the walls with greenery and on the fourth side is a fence covered with Georgia's State flower, the Cherokee rose. The garden, of formal design, is developed in an informal way. Around an open lawn—a pleasant place for meetings and parties—are plantings of evergreen and flowering shrubs and there are thick borders of bulbs and seasonal flowers to furnish continuous color. . . . The magazine, Better Homes and Gardens, awarded first honorable mention in its 'More Beautiful America' contest to the Transylvania Garden Club for their Sandersville Library Garden work." (426)

Whitfield County

DALTON

Oneonta, or the Mrs. M. E. Judd Garden

House, circa 1921; garden, circa 1920s

Portions of the historic garden remain. The garden was designed by Mrs. M. E. Judd (Lenna Gertrude Clark Judd). The main house remains, as do many of the outbuildings, including the teahouse. The house, a textbook example of English Arts and Crafts design, was rehabilitated by the owner in 2000 and 2001. The owner also hired a landscape architect to document the layout of the original gardens in order to re-create the landscape in its 1920s appearance. The site received an Excellence in Rehabilitation Award from the Georgia Trust for Historic Preservation in 2002. The site is privately owned.

"On the gentle rise of a hill and surrounded by fine trees the house overlooks a series of gardens. Wide steps, at either side of a dry wall full of rock plants, descend towards the upper garden. A natural spring is at the base of the wall and benches are placed near by. The upper garden is a succession of terraces held by walls of field stone, and paths of the same material are laid between the flower beds. A formal use of evergreens brings out the structural lines of the plan. . . . From this level, one path leads to a playhouse with a miniature lily pool, another to the greenhouse where rare plants are propagated. The lower garden with its retaining wall of stone is girdled by a swift mountain stream which flows through the lower reaches of the property. The flower beds here are bordered with dwarf box while taller box is used for accents. Near by a picturesque tea house, in a setting of evergreens and crabapple trees, looks off to the pine woods across the stream." (322, 325)

NOTES

Abbreviations

ALHNSCDAGA   Andrew Low House National Society of the Colonial Dames of America in the State of Georgia, Savannah

Barnsley Papers, Duke   Godfrey Barnsley Papers, David M. Rubenstein Rare Book & Manuscript Library, Duke University

Barnsley Papers, Emory   Godfrey Barnsley Papers, Stuart A. Rose Manuscript, Archives, and Rare Book Library, Emory University

BNDR   Biltmore Nursery Department Records, Biltmore Estate Archives, Asheville, N.C.

Bulloch Archives   Bulloch Hall Library and Archives, Roswell, Ga.

Callaway Papers   Callaway Family Papers, Troup County Archives, LaGrange, Ga.

CGL   Cherokee Garden Library, Kenan Research Center, Atlanta History Center

Cothran Papers   James R. Cothran Papers, MSS 989, Cherokee Garden Library, Kenan Research Center, Atlanta History Center

Daugherty drawings   Edward L. Daugherty, landscape architectural drawings, Cherokee Garden Library, Kenan Research Center, Atlanta History Center

Daugherty Papers   Edward L. Daugherty Papers, Cherokee Garden Library, Kenan Research Center, Atlanta History Center

Frazer   Frazer Center Archives, Atlanta

GHLIR   Georgia Historic Landscape Initiative Records, Cherokee Garden Library, Kenan Research Center, Atlanta History Center

Hargrett   Hargrett Rare Book and Manuscript Library, University of Georgia Libraries

Manning Papers   Warren H. Manning Papers, MS 218, Special Collections Department, Iowa State University Library, Ames

MBDA   Martha Berry Digital Library, Berry College, Mount Berry, Ga.

NARA   National Archives and Records dministration, Washington, D.C.

NRHP   National Register of Historic Places, Washington, D.C.

Olmsted Archives   National Park Service, Frederick Law Olmsted National Historic Site Archives, Brookline, Mass.

Olmsted Papers   Olmsted Papers and Records, Manuscript Division, Library of Congress

Pauley Drawings   William C. Pauley
                   Architectural Drawings
                   Collection, 0082M, Georgia
                   Archives, Morrow
Pauley Papers   William C. Pauley Papers,
                   Stuart A. Rose Manuscript,
                   Archives, and Rare Book
                   Library, Emory University
RHS   Roswell Historical Society
                   / City of Roswell Research
                   Library and Archives,
                   Roswell, Ga.
RLGC   Records of the Lullwater
                   Garden Club, private
                   collection
Seiferle Papers   Norma K. and Edward J.
                   Seiferle Papers, Cherokee
                   Garden Library, Kenan
                   Research Center, Atlanta
                   History Center
SHC   Southern Historical
                   Collection, Louis Round
                   Wilson Special Collections
                   Library, University of North
                   Carolina at Chapel Hill
Smith drawings   William T. Smith, landscape
                   architectural drawings,
                   Cherokee Garden Library,
                   Kenan Research Center,
                   Atlanta History Center

Introduction

The epigraph is drawn from Cooney and Rainwater, *Garden History of Georgia*, foreword and dedication.

1. Quoted in Birnbaum, *Protecting Cultural Landscapes*, 1.

2. Cultural Landscape Foundation, "About Cultural Landscapes," accessed January 9, 2017, http://tclf.org /places/about-cultural-landscapes.

3. Birnbaum, *Protecting Cultural Landscapes*, 2.

4. Howett and Atlanta Historical Society, *Land of Our Own*, 11.

5. Ibid.

6. Ibid., 13.

7. William P. Flatt, "Agriculture in Georgia: Overview," *New Georgia Encyclopedia*, October 17, 2016, accessed January 8, 2017, www.georgiaencyclopedia.org/articles /agriculture-georgia-overview.

8. Ibid.

9. Howett and Atlanta Historical Society, *Land of Our Own*, 18.

10. Flatt, "Agriculture in Georgia."

11. Georgia Historic Preservation Division, *Georgia's Living Places*, III-7.

12. Howett and Atlanta Historical Society, *Land of Our Own*, 23.

13. Flatt, "Agriculture in Georgia."

14. Georgia Historic Preservation Division, *Georgia's Living Places*, III-9.

15. Ibid.

16. Flatt, "Agriculture in Georgia."

17. Georgia Historic Preservation Division, *Georgia's Living Places*, III-10.

18. Howett and Atlanta Historical Society, *Land of Our Own*, 26; Georgia Historic Preservation Division, *Georgia's Living Places*, III-10.

19. Cultural Landscape Foundation, "Colonial Revival," accessed September 10, 2016, http://tclf.org /category/designed-landscape-style/colonial-revival.

20. Griswold and Weller, *Golden Age of American Gardens*, 38.

21. Ibid.

22. Darke, *In Harmony with Nature*, 16–27.

23. Hood, "Renaissance of Southern Gardening," 130.

24. Cooney and Rainwater, *Garden History of Georgia*, "A Message from the Georgia Bicentennial Commission."

25. Graham, *American Eden*, xiv.

Andrew Low House and Garden

The epigraph is drawn from Shultz and Lawrence, *Lady from Savannah*, 178.

1. Ryan and Golson, *Andrew Low*, 95.

2. Myers, *Children of Pride*, 1599.

3. Robin Williams, "Evolution and Adaptation: The Savannah Plan and Its Impact on Architectural Development," in Gomez and Rossell, *Savannah and the Lowcountry*, 51.

4. Cooney and Rainwater, *Garden History of Georgia*, 27.

5. Lane, *Architecture of the Old South*, 150.

6. Linley, *Georgia Catalog*, 331–32.

7. Ibid., 332.

8. Bell, "Vanishing Gardens of Savannah," 197.

9. Stephen Bohlin, interview by Mary Ann Eaddy, Andrew Low House, Savannah, May 24, 2016.

10. Ibid.

11. Ryan and Golson, *Andrew Low*, 132–33.

12. Huddleston and Koehler, *Bulloch Letters*, 1:206.

13. Bohlin interview.

14. Myers, *Children of Pride*, 1599.

15. Ryan and Golson, *Andrew Low*, 279.

16. "The National Society," National Society of the Colonial Dames of America in the State of Georgia, accessed September 12, 2016, www.nscdaga.org /about-us/.

17. Cooney and Rainwater, *Garden History of Georgia*, 27.

18. Ibid.; Hitchcock, "Savannah Gardens."

19. Cooney and Rainwater, *Garden History of Georgia*, 27; Bohlin interview; images from the collection of the ALHNSCDAGA).

20. "Chronology of the Low House Gardens as Recorded in the History of the NSCDA, April 1893–1993," typescript, ALHNSCDAGA.

21. Dolder, "Clermont Lee," 3, 6.

22. Report of Garden Committee, November 14, 1996, ALHNSCDAGA.

23. Andrew Low House Garden Committee Annual Report, April 26, 2006, ALHNSCDAGA.

24. "Chronology of Low House Gardens," ALHNSCDAGA.

25. Ibid.

26. Hitchcock, "Savannah Gardens."

27. Robert and Company, *Historic Landscape Plan*, 7.

28. Ibid.

29. Cooney and Rainwater, *Garden History of Georgia*, 26.

30. To the Georgia Society of the Colonial Dames of America, November 14, 1929, Garden Committee Report, "Andrew Low House and Garden," 2003, MSS 1007, GHLIR.

31. "Chronology of Low House Gardens," ALHNSCDAGA; Georgia, Chatham County, July 6, 1939, Legal Boundary Confirmation, "Andrew Low House and Garden," 2003, MSS 1007, GHLIR.

32. "Chronology of Low House Gardens," ALHNSCDAGA.

33. Ibid.

34. "History of the Savannah Town Committee, 1930–1981," excerpted pages, 8. "Andrew Low House and Garden," 2003, MSS 1007, GHLIR.

35. Plaque in rear courtyard of Andrew Low House; "Landscape Construction Plan Showing Scheme of Rear Garden, Georgia Headquarters, Colonial Dames of America, June 1951; Rev. April 1989, Andrew Low House and Gardens," 2003, MSS 1007, GHLIR.

36. Dolder, "Clermont Lee," 1, 5.

37. Ibid., 4.

38. Robert and Company, *Historic Landscape Plan*, 5.

39. Hitchcock, "Savannah Gardens."

40. "Landscape Construction Plan," GHLIR.

41. Ibid.; "Chronology of Low House Gardens," ALHNSCDAGA.

42. Hitchcock, "Savannah Gardens."

43. "Chronology of Low House Gardens," ALHNSCDAGA.

44. Bohlin interview.

45. Ibid.

46. Ibid.

47. Ibid.

48. "A Mission Statement and Mandate," Andrew Low House, 2013, ALHNSCDAGA.

Ashland Farm

The epigraph is drawn from Cooney and Rainwater, *Garden History of Georgia*, 144.

1. Elizabeth B. Cooksey, "Walker County," *New Georgia Encyclopedia*, November 29, 2016, accessed December 16, 2016, www.georgiaencyclopedia.org /articles/counties-cities-neighborhoods/walker -county.

2. Ibid.

3. Ned L. Irwin, "Zeboim Cartter Patten," *Tennessee Encyclopedia of History and Culture*, University of Tennessee Press Online Edition, December 15, 2009, accessed December 16, 2016, http://tennesseeencyclopedia .net/entry.php?rec=1040.

4. Ibid.

5. Ibid.

6. Patten and Patten, *So Firm a Foundation*, 116.

7. Irwin, "Zeboim Cartter Patten."

8. Patten and Patten, *So Firm a Foundation*, 95.

9. Ibid., 100.

10. Ibid., 122.

11. The architect Walter T. Downing designed numerous structures in Chattanooga, including the Hotel Patten, the Chattanooga Golf and Country Club clubhouse, J. T. Lupton's Lyndhurst mansion in Riverview, and buildings at the Baylor School and the University of Tennessee at Chattanooga.

12. NRHP, "Ashland Farm," Flintstone, Walker County, Georgia, 1973, National Register #73000646, item 7, p. 2.

13. Patten and Patten, *So Firm a Foundation*, 122.

14. Ibid., 123.

15. NRHP, "Ashland Farm," item 7, p. 2.

16. Ibid.

17. Patten and Patten, *So Firm a Foundation*, 124.

18. Ibid.

19. Alexander, *Biltmore Nursery*, 11.

20. Ibid.

21. Biltmore Nursery to Mrs. Z. C. Patten,

Chattanooga, Tenn., November 1, 1906, BNDR. The drawings have not been located.

22. Biltmore Nursery to Mrs. Z. C. Patten, Chattanooga, Tenn., November 14, 1906, BNDR.

23. Biltmore Nursery to Mrs. Z. C. Patten, Chattanooga, Tenn., November 27, 1906, BNDR.

24. Patten and Patten, *So Firm a Foundation*, 125.

25. Biltmore Nursery to Mrs. Z. C. Patten, Chattanooga, Tenn., November 27, 1906, BNDR.

26. Biltmore Nursery to Mrs. Z. C. Patten, Chattanooga, Tenn., April 6, 1907, BNDR.

27. Biltmore Nursery to Mrs. Z. C. Patten, Chattanooga, Tenn., December 15, 1906; Biltmore Nursery to Mrs. Z. C. Patten, Chattanooga, Tenn., April 16, 1907, both in BNDR.

28. Cooney and Rainwater, *Garden History of Georgia*, 144.

29. Ibid.

30. Patten and Patten, *So Firm a Foundation*, 125.

31. Georgia Historic Landscape Initiative Survey form for Ashland Farm, completed by Nancy Gadberry, Cherokee Garden Library Fellow, 2009, MSS 1007, GHLIR.

32. Patten and Patten, *So Firm a Foundation*, 136.

33. Ibid., 149.

34. Ibid., 153.

35. Armstrong, *History of Hamilton County* 2:233.

36. Obituary of Elizabeth Bryan Patten, *New York Times*, February 10, 1990.

Barnsley Gardens

The epigraph is drawn from an April 23, 1871, letter of Godfrey Barnsley to unknown, B. F. A. Saylor Family Papers, MS 63, Hargrett.

1. Howett, "Barnsley Gardens," 174.

2. Coker, *Barnsley Gardens at Woodlands*, 13, 16.

3. Hoffman, "Godfrey Barnsley," 132.

4. Nestor, "Paradise Rediscovered," 57.

5. Vaux, *Villas and Cottages*, 220.

6. Nestor and Mann, "Archival Restoration," 107.

7. Ibid., 114.

8. Downing, *Treatise on Landscape Gardening*.

9. Ibid.

10. Downing, *Cottage Residences*, 128–29.

11. Nestor and Mann, "Archival Restoration," 116.

12. U.S. Census, Slave Schedule, 1850, index and images, FamilySearch, accessed November 14, 2015, http://FamilySearch.org, citing NARA microfilm publication M432 (Washington, D.C.: National Archives, n.d.); Correspondence, 1841–1860, Barnsley Papers, Emory.

13. Hoffman, "Godfrey Barnsley," 138; Nestor and Mann, "Archival Restoration," 108.

14. Hoffman, "Godfrey Barnsley," 138.

15. Nestor and Mann, "Archival Restoration," 108.

16. Downing, *Cottage Residences*, 160.

17. Photograph of visitors in the oval parterre garden at Barnsley Gardens, Floyd County, Georgia, ca. 1880s, Vanishing Georgia Collection, Georgia Archives, Morrow.

18. Cooney and Rainwater, *Garden History of Georgia*, 109.

19. Downing, *Treatise on Landscape Architecture*, 390–94.

20. Nestor, "Paradise Rediscovered," 74.

21. Nestor and Mann, "Archival Restoration," 111. It is important to note that contrary to popular myth, Prosper Jules Alphonse Berckmans, the owner of Fruitland Nurseries, was not involved in the garden design at Woodlands.

22. Ibid., 111.

23. Cooney and Rainwater, *Garden History of Georgia*, 108.

24. Ledger, 1841–1843, B. F. A. Saylor Family Papers, MS 63, Hargrett.

25. Julia Barnsley to Godfrey Barnsley, April 14, 1842, Papers, 1824–1846, Barnsley Papers, Duke.

26. Nestor and Mann, "Archival Restoration," 110.

27. Coker, *Barnsley Gardens*, 49.

28. Hoffman, "Godfrey Barnsley," 150–57.

29. John Connolly to Godfrey Barnsley, March 20, 1847, Papers, 1847–1852, Barnsley Papers, Duke.

30. Coker, *Barnsley Gardens*, 78–79.

31. Ibid., 98–99.

32. J. P. Baltzelle to Godfrey Barnsley, March 10, 1866, Correspondence, 1866, Barnsley Papers, Emory.

33. Hoffman, "Godfrey Barnsley," 270.

34. Ibid.

35. Coker, *Barnsley Gardens*, 144.

36. Ibid., 159–60.

37. "St. Elmo Born at Barnsley Gardens," *Atlanta Journal*, January 25, 1942.

38. Hoffman, "Godfrey Barnsley," 303.

39. Ibid., 304.

40. Cofer, *Barnsley Gardens Story*, 36.

41. Nestor, "Paradise Rediscovered," 83.

42. Ibid.

43. Cofer, *Barnsley Gardens Story*, 40–41.

44. Mark Stith, "Blooming Again: A Bavarian Prince Comes to the Aid of Long-Neglected Barnsley Gardens," *Atlanta Journal-Constitution*, September 22, 1991, R7; Barnsley Gardens, "Barnsley Gardens Map, Self-Guided Walking Tour," undated.

45. Nestor and Mann, "Archival Restoration," 107.

46. Patty Rasmussen, "The Flowering of Barnsley Gardens," *Georgia Trend*, February 2007.

47. Ibid.

Barrington Hall and Bulloch Hall

1. The City of Roswell also owns and operates Smith Plantation, the former home of Archibald and Ann Smith, one of the community's founding families. The site consists of a farmhouse and numerous outbuildings.

2. Clarke, *Dwelling Place*, 190–91.

3. Cooney and Rainwater, *Garden History of Georgia*, 112.

4. NRHP, Roswell Historic District, Roswell, Fulton County, Georgia, National Register #74000682, item 8, p. 4.

5. Martin, *History of Roswell Presbyterian Church*, 116.

6. Ibid., 27.

7. Bulloch Hall's exact construction date, now attributed to 1839, has been questioned.

8. Martin, *History of Roswell Presbyterian Church*, 31–32.

9. Ibid., 27.

10. Clarke, *Dwelling Place*, 194–95, 489–90. The epigraph is drawn from F. K. Pratt, "The Old Garden," lines 1–4, 1918, King, Baker, Simpson Families Papers, RHS. The poem was written at Barrington Hall for Frances Pratt's aunt, Eva Baker.

11. Robert Winebarger, e-mail message to Mary Ann Eaddy, June 21, 2016; "Barrington Hall and Mrs. Baker," photocopy [before 1923?], King, Baker, Simpson Families Photographs, RHS.

12. Jaeger Company and Robert and Company, *Barrington Hall*, 17.

13. Ibid.

14. Lockwood, *Gardens of Colony and State*, 321.

15. Ibid., 322.

16. Robert Winebarger, interview by Mary Ann Eaddy, Barrington Hall, Roswell, September 25, 2015.

17. Jaeger Company and Robert and Company, *Barrington Hall*, 25–26.

18. Robert Winebarger, e-mail message to Mary Ann Eaddy, June 21, 2016.

19. Roswell was originally located in Cobb County, which was created in 1832. County lines changed over the years, and the city is now in Fulton County.

20. Winebarger interview, September 25, 2015.

21. Lucretia Merrell Camp to Elisabeth Hitchcock Camp, August 16, 1843, in Cox and Walsh, *Providence*, 41.

22. Jaeger Company and Robert and Company, *Barrington Hall*, 23–31, 38–39.

23. Robert Winebarger, e-mail message to Mary Ann Eaddy, June 21, 2016.

24. George Hull Camp to Elisabeth Hitchcock Camp, July 26, 1846, in Cox and Walsh, *Providence*, 74. For years, Camp boarded with the King family while working for the Roswell Manufacturing Company. After the death of Barrington King, he briefly served as its president.

25. The Roswell Manufacturing Company was able to rebuild, and the mills eventually reopened.

26. Martin, *History of Roswell Presbyterian Church*, 53.

27. Lois Virginia King Simpson, typed notes, April 4, 1978, King, Baker, Simpson Families Papers, RHS.

28. Ibid.

29. Image of the Reverend William Elliott Baker and Catherine Evelyn King Baker at Barrington Hall, c. 1905, King, Baker, Simpson Families Photographs, RHS.

30. Jaeger Company and Robert and Company, *Barrington Hall*, 18. See photographic prints of Barrington Hall, VIS 2.31.009, ca. 1876, King, Baker, Simpson Families Photographs, RHS; Barrington Hall, VIS 2.31.012, 1909 or 1910, King, Baker, Simpson Families Photographs, RHS.

31. Simpson, typed notes, April 4, 1978.

32. Pratt, "The Old Garden," line 33.

33. Ibid., lines 2, 9, 19, 22, 25, 27.

34. Ibid., lines 31–32; Barrington Hall, Catherine Evelyn King Baker, VIS 2.31.039, [before 1923?], King, Baker, Simpson Families Photographs, RHS. Notation on the back of the photographic print: "She is standing by the Hydrangea bush that was her father's pride and joy."

35. Peggy Mitchell, "Bridesmaid of 87 Recalls Mittie Roosevelt's Wedding," *Atlanta Journal Magazine*, June 10, 1923.

36. Pratt and Pratt, *Early American Homes*, v.

37. Ibid., 108.

38. "Miss Katharine, 1895–1995, Is Fondly Remembered," *Roswell Historical Society Newsletter*, April 1995, King, Baker, Simpson Families Papers, RHS.

39. NRHP, Barrington Hall, Roswell, Fulton County, Georgia, National Register #71000275, item 8.

40. Jaeger Company and Robert and Company, *Barrington Hall*, 8, 35.

41. Julie Negley, "Past Times," *North Fulton above the River*, February 1988, 5–6, Barrington Hall, RHS.

42. See Jaeger Company and Robert and Company, *Barrington Hall*; see also *A Comprehensive Interpretive Plan for the Roswell Historic District including Barrington Hall, Bulloch Hall and Smith Plantation*, prepared by Avient Museum Services for the City of Roswell, Department of Historic and Cultural Affairs, March 4, 2008.

43. Robert Winebarger interview by Mary Ann Eaddy, Barrington Hall, Roswell, April 25, 2016.

44. Winebarger interview, September 25, 2015.

45. Ibid.

46. Ibid.; Lockwood, *Gardens of Colony and State*, 321.

47. Cooney and Rainwater, *Garden History of Georgia*, 112.

48. Winebarger interview, April 25, 2016.

49. Ibid.

50. Ibid.

51. Winebarger interview, September 25, 2015.

52. "Our Garden Urn," *Eva's Garden News: A Garden Newsletter for Barrington Hall, Roswell, GA*, September 2012, 1.

53. Janet Rigsby, conversation with Mary Ann Eaddy, Barrington Hall, Roswell, September 16, 2014; Winebarger interview, September 25, 2015.

54. "New Garden Benches," *Eva's Garden News*, Spring and Summer 2014.

55. Van Beck, *Daffodils in American Gardens*, 213–15.

56. Winebarger interview, September 25, 2015.

57. Cooney and Rainwater, *Garden History of Georgia*, 112.

58. Winebarger interview, September 25, 2015.

59. Winebarger interview, April 25, 2016.

60. The epigraph is drawn from Huddleston and Koehler, *Bulloch Letters*, 1:120.

61. McCullough, *Mornings on Horseback*, 46.

62. Sever, " Memory of the South," 21.

63. Cooney and Rainwater, *Garden History of Georgia*, 113.

64. Roswell Historic Preservation Commission, "Criteria for the Landscape Development of Bulloch Hall, Roswell, Georgia: A Master Plan for Restoration, Rehabilitation and Use," photocopy, 1984, n.p., RHS.

65. Sever, "Memory of the South," 18.

66. Martin, *A Glimpse of the Past, 18*; Griffin and Attaway to Mrs. Emily Cleland Howell, March 14, 1908, Bulloch Hall Site Files, Bulloch Archives.

67. McCullough, *Mornings on Horseback,* 46.

68. Ibid., 42.

69. Perkerson, *White Columns in Georgia*, 174.

70. Griffin and Attaway to Howell, March 14, 1908, Bulloch Archives.

71. "Order of Ownership of Bulloch Hall," n.d., and "Abstract of Title to 'Bulloch Home' in Town of Roswell," photocopy, 1908, Bulloch Archives.

72. Power, *Ginny's Chairs*, 80.

73. Mrs. George W. Power (Virginia) to Richard S. Myrick, November 2, 1971, 6, Bulloch Archives.

74. Power, *Ginny's Chairs*, 35, 147–48; see Margaret Shannon, "The High Cost of Nostalgia," *Atlanta Journal and Constitution Magazine*, December 22, 1974, 6.

75. NRHP, Bulloch Hall, Roswell, Fulton County, Georgia, National Register #71000276, item 8.

76. Shannon, "High Cost of Nostalgia," 5–7.

77. Pam Billingsley, interview by Mary Ann Eaddy, Bulloch Hall, Roswell, November 13, 2015.

78. Robert and Company, *Bulloch Hall Master Plan Update,* prepared for the City of Roswell, September 2009.

79. Billingsley interview.

80. Julie Negley Groce, conversation with Mary Ann Eaddy, Sapelo Island, Georgia, January 2016; Howett, "Criteria for Landscape Development," 13, 16. The cited pages are missing from the photocopied planning document found in the RHS. The authors were unable to locate the questionnaires footnoted in the article.

81. Billingsley interview.

82. Howett, "Criteria for Landscape Development," 9.

83. Ibid., 10.

84. *A Walk in the Splendor of the Past at Bulloch Hall,* photocopied brochure, [early 1980s?], RHS.

85. Virginia W. Power, June 1971, 7, unpublished paper, Bulloch Archives.

86. Roswell Historic Preservation Commission, "The Historic Trees of Bulloch Hall, Roswell, Georgia," [1996?], MSS 1007, GHLIR.

87. "2008 Preservation Awards: Excellence in Stewardship, City of Roswell," *Rambler*, Spring 2008, 12.

Battersby-Hartridge Garden

The epigraph is drawn from Mary Ann Eaddy's interview with Cornelia McIntire Hartridge in Savannah, March 19, 2015.

1. Bell, "Vanishing Gardens of Savannah," 197.

2. Sources differ on the spelling of "Battersby." Cooney and Rainwater, in *Garden History of Georgia*, use "Batersby," as do several other publications; however, that form is believed to be a simple misspelling.

3. Cooney and Rainwater, *Garden History of Georgia*, 24.

4. *The Cheshire*, 70 U.S. 231 (1865), accessed October 15, 2016, https://supreme.justia.com/cases/federal/us/70/231.

5. Linley, *Georgia Catalog*, 323–24.

6. Cornelia McIntire Hartridge, interview by Mary Ann Eaddy, Savannah, May 24, 2016.

7. Clermont H. Lee to Dr. David O. Percy, attachment, March 23, 1998, MSS 989, Cothran Papers.

8. Hartridge interview, May 24, 2016.

9. Bell, "Vanishing Gardens of Savannah," 198.

10. Cothran, *Gardens and Historic Plants of the Antebellum South*, 9.

11. Ibid., 123.

12. Ibid., 48, 54–55.

13. Cooney and Rainwater, *Garden History of Georgia*, 24; "Battersby-Hartridge House," 2011, no. 5, MSS 1007, GHLIR.

14. "Sites: Savannah Day Self-Guided Walking Tour," in Gomez and Russell, *Savannah and the Lowcountry*, 173.

15. Cooney and Rainwater, *Garden History of Georgia*, 24.

16. Ibid.

17. Ibid.

18. Ibid.

19. Ibid.

20. Ibid.

21. "Sites," in Gomez and Russell, *Savannah and the Lowcountry*, 173. By the early 1950s, the banker William Murphey owned the property. The businessman Brailsford T. Nightingale and his wife, Ruth Hogan Nightingale, who was active in the arts and local community groups, followed Murphey.

22. "Battersby-Hartridge House," 2011, no. 7, MSS 1007, GHLIR.

23. "Battersby-Hartridge House," no. 11, "Tree Planting Plan for Historic Residence of Mr. and Mrs. Donald Livingston, Savannah, March 1971" (photocopy).

24. "Battersby-Hartridge House," no. 7.

25. "Battersby-Hartridge House," no. 11, "Tree Planting Plan."

26. "Battersby-Hartridge House," no. 8.

27. Hartridge interview, May 24, 2016.

28. Hartridge interview, March 29, 2015.

29. Cornelia McIntire Hartridge, telephone conversation with Mary Ann Eaddy, November 15, 2016.

30. Hartridge interview, March 29, 2015.

31. Connie Hartridge, the current owner, believes that the 1850s landscape contained a knot garden. When she and her husband purchased the property, she adapted the boxwood in the garden to continue this concept. She called the pattern that she selected "hugs—and—kisses."

32. Hartridge interview, May 24, 2016.

33. Ibid.

34. An architectural firm occupies the basement level of the residence, and the carriage house, which once had apartments for family members, is now rented to tenants.

35. Hartridge interview, May 24, 2016.

36. Ibid.

Beech Haven

The epigraph is drawn from Cooney and Rainwater, *Garden History of Georgia*, 155.

1. Tankard, "Gardens of Earthly Delights."

2. Ibid.

3. Darke, *In Harmony with Nature*, 16–27.

4. U.S. Census, 1920, database with images, FamilySearch, accessed December 14, 2015, https://familysearch.org/ark:/61903/1:1:MJ8T-Y9N, C. A. Rowland, Athens Ward 4, Clarke, Georgia; citing sheet 21A, NARA microfilm publication T625; FHL microfilm 1,820,243.

5. NRHP, Nomination Draft, Beech Haven Historic District, Athens, Clarke County, Georgia, item 7, p. 7. Rebecca McManus (master of historic preservation, College of Environment and Design, University of Georgia) and Cari Goetcheus (associate professor, College of Environment and Design, and director of the Cultural Landscape Lab, University of Georgia) are in process of completing the nomination. Ms. McManus and Professor Goetcheus generously shared their draft nomination form with the authors.

6. NRHP, Nomination Draft, Beech Haven Historic District, item 7, p. 6.

7. Frances T. Thomas, "Athens," *New Georgia Encyclopedia*, August 5, 2015, accessed July 18, 2016, www.georgiaencyclopedia.org/articles/counties-cities-neighborhoods/athens.

8. NRHP, Nomination Draft, Beech Haven Historic District, item 7, p. 8

9. Ibid.

10. Carruthers, *Arts and Crafts Movement*, 12.

11. NRHP, Nomination Draft, Beech Haven Historic District, item 7, p. 9.

12. Ibid., 6.

13. Ibid., 7.

14. Ibid., 11.

15. Ibid., 13.

16. Ibid., 15–16.

17. Ibid., 18.

18. Ibid., 19.

19. Ibid., 25.

20. "Personal and Social News," *Athens Banner*, July 29, 1913, 8.

21. Katharine Rowland Crane, "My Memories of Beech Haven," unpublished paper, 101, Charles Alden Rowland family papers, MS3599, Hargrett.

22. NRHP, Nomination Draft, Beech Haven Historic District, item 7, p. 22.

23. Crane, "My Memories of Beech Haven," 102.

24. Ibid.

25. NRHP, Nomination Draft, Beech Haven Historic District, item 7, p. 22.

26. Cooney and Rainwater, *Garden History of Georgia*, 155.

27. Ibid.

28. NRHP, Nomination Draft, Beech Haven Historic District, Item 7, p. 24.

29. Cooney and Rainwater, *Garden History of Georgia*, 155.

30. Ibid.

31. NRHP, Nomination Draft, Beech Haven Historic District, item 7, p. 27.

32. Ibid.

33. Ibid., 39.

34. "Bible Conference to be Held at Beech Haven May 9th to May 13th," *Athens Banner*, May 7, 1913.

35. "The Week-End at Beech Haven," *Athens Banner*, November 9, 1915, 2.

36. NRHP, Nomination Draft, Beech Haven Historic District, item 7, p. 40.

37. Amy Kissane, "Beech Haven: Work on the Historic Property Moves Forward," *Heritage* (Spring 2015): 8.

38. Helen Kuykendall, "Beech Haven: A Historic Arts & Crafts Landscape," presentation given as part of the Athens–Clarke County Library Heritage Room program. Available on YouTube, https://www.youtube.com/watch?v=G_gxmHyuloo, uploaded March 12, 2015.

Berry College

The epigraph is drawn from Cooney and Rainwater, *Garden History of Georgia*, 447.

1. Coleman, *History of Georgia*, 329.

2. Dickey and Mathis, *Berry College*, 7.

3. Ibid., 6–7.

4. Ibid., 6.

5. *Berry Trails*, 7.

6. Jamil S. Zainaldin and John C. Inscoe, "Progressive Era," *New Georgia Encyclopedia*, September 22, 2015, accessed November 7, 2016, www.georgiaencyclopedia.org/articles/history-archaeology/progressive-era.

7. Ibid.

8. Ibid.

9. *Berry Trails*, 66.

10. Owens, *Personal History*, 43.

11. Ibid.

12. Ibid.

13. Martin and Mitchell, *Landmark Homes of Georgia*, 174.

14. Cultural Landscape Foundation, "Robert B. Cridland: Related Content," http://tclf.org/pioneer/robert-b-cridland, accessed December 18, 2016.

15. Cridland, *Practical Landscape Gardening*, 109.

16. Martha Berry, "Letter to Mr. J. B. Campbell from Martha Berry," MBDA, 2012), accessed January 7, 2017, https://mbda.berry.edu/items/show/9673.

17. Dickey and Mathis, *Berry College*, 57; *Berry Trails*, 10.

18. Cooney and Rainwater, *Garden History of Georgia*, 448.

19. Tim Brown, "A Glorious Restoration: Martha Berry's Gardens at Oak Hill," *Scatter Info as We Bloom and Grow* 2, no. 3 (March 2015): 3. This newsletter is published by the Garden Club of Georgia.

20. Cridland, *Practical Landscape Gardening*, 124.

21. Cooney and Rainwater, *Garden History of Georgia*, 448.

22. Ibid., 448.

23. Barron, "History of the Sunken Garden," 1.

24. Cooney and Rainwater, *Garden History of Georgia*, 448.

25. Barron, "History of the Sunken Garden," 1.

26. Ibid.

27. Ibid.

28. Brown, "Glorious Restoration," 4.

29. Cooney and Rainwater, *Garden History of Georgia*, 448.

30. Ibid.

31. Dickey and Mathis, *Berry College*, 146, 148.

32. Brown, "Glorious Restoration," 4.

33. Timothy D. Brown, e-mail message to Mary Ann Eaddy, December 13, 2016.

34. Cridland, *Practical Landscape Gardening*, 45.

35. Dickey and Mathis, *Berry College*, 46.

36. Cooney and Rainwater, *Garden History of Georgia*, 452.

37. Cridland, *Practical Landscape Gardening*, 133.

38. Cooney and Rainwater, *Garden History of Georgia*, 452.

39. Ibid.

40. Ibid.

41. *Berry Trails*, 64.

42. Cooney and Rainwater, *Garden History of Georgia*, 452.

43. Dickey and Mathis, *Berry College*, 158; *Berry Trails*, 64.

44. Timothy D. Brown, e-mail message to Mary Ann Eaddy, December 9, 2016.

45. Berry College Mission and Purpose, accessed October 25, 2016, www.berry.edu/mission/.

46. Ibid.

Bradley Olmsted Garden

The epigraph is drawn from Lawliss, "Residential Work," 24.

1. John S. Lupold, "Columbus," *New Georgia Encyclopedia*, August 26, 2013, accessed June 17, 2016, www.georgiaencyclopedia.org/articles/counties -cities-neighborhoods/columbus.

2. NRHP, Wynn's Hill–Overlook–Oak Circle Historic District, Columbus, Muscogee County, Georgia, 2005, National Register #05000403, item 7, p. 4.

3. NRHP, Wynn's Hill–Overlook–Oak Circle Historic District, Columbus, Muscogee County, Georgia, 2005, National Register #05000403.

4. Lawliss, Loughlin, and Meier, *Master List*, 151.

5. Ibid.

6. Ibid.

7. Ibid., 163.

8. Ibid.

9. Claude Scarborough and D. Abbott Turner were Bradley's sons-in-law, so most of the Olmsted Brothers firm's designs in Columbus had a connection to one family.

10. Lawliss, "Residential Work," 24.

11. The P. J. Berckmans Company owned and operated Fruitland Nurseries, the first large-scale horticultural nursery in the South. The company also did landscape design work. The trade name was sold to Bailie and Gwin in the early 1920s and continued to operate until the 1960s.

12. Mr. B. S. Miller Estate, Columbus, Ga., "Sketch of Layout," designed by W. B. Marquis for the P. J. Berckmans Co., Augusta, Ga., n.d., Columbus Museum Archives; the original drawings are in the Olmsted Archives.

13. Lawliss, "Residential Work," 22.

14. Ibid.; Cooney, and Rainwater, *Garden History of Georgia*, 313.

15. Mr. William C. Bradley, Columbus, Ga., "Sketch Plan Showing Arrangement of Rose Garden and Swimming Pool," designed by W. B. Marquis for Olmsted Brothers, Brookline, Mass., file no. 6797, plan no. 28, November 18, 1925, Columbus Museum Archives; the original drawings are in the Olmsted Archives.

16. "Brick Miller's Home Sold to W. C. Bradley, Whose Home Is in Deal," *Columbus Enquirer-Sun*, February 21, 1925.

17. NRHP, Wynn's Hill–Overlook–Oak Circle Historic District, item 7, p. 6.

18. Minnie Hall was the biological daughter of Sarah Hall Bradley's brother. After Sarah's brother's wife died,

he asked Sarah and her husband, W. C., to raise the child as their own.

19. W. C. Bradley, Eagle & Phenix Mills, Columbus, Ga., to Wm. B. Marquis, care of Olmstead [Olmsted] Brothers, Landscape Architects, Brookline, Mass., June 4, 1925, Olmsted Papers; photocopy included in Lawliss, "Bradley Residence."

20. Bush, "Bradley Olmsted Garden," 5.

21. W. C. Bradley, Eagle & Phenix Mills, Columbus, Ga., to W. B. Marquis, Olmsted Brothers, Brookline, Mass., November 9, 1925, Olmsted Papers.

22. William C. Bradley, Columbus, Ga., "Sketch Plan Showing Arrangement of Rose Garden and Swimming Pool," Olmsted Brothers, Landscape Architects, Brookline, Mass., file no. 6797, plan no. 28, November 18, 1925, Columbus Museum Archives; original drawings in Olmsted Archives.

23. Bush, "Bradley Olmsted Garden," 10. The racial politics of this site warrant further investigation.

24. Ibid., 9.

25. Cooney and Rainwater, *Garden History of Georgia*, 313.

26. Ibid.

27. Exhibition booklet for *Center for Culture: The Bradley Property and the Olmsted Garden*, April 7–August 11, 2013, Columbus Museum, Columbus, Georgia, 7.

28. Cooney and Rainwater, *Garden History of Georgia*, 313.

29. Lawliss, "Residential Work," 27, 30.

30. Lawliss et al., "Julia Orme Martin,," 3.

31. Exhibition booklet for *Center for Culture: The Bradley Property and the Olmsted Garden*, 6.

32. Lord Cultural Resources, "Columbus Museum: Strategic Plan 2015–2019" (Columbus, Ga.: Lord Cultural Resources, May 2014), 4.

Cator Woolford Gardens

The epigraph is drawn from Cridland, *Practical Landscape Gardening*, 9.

1. Cooney and Rainwater, *Garden History of Georgia*, 275. Unfortunately, the landscape architectural drawings of Robert B. Cridland for the Cator Woolford estate have not been located.

2. Cooney and Rainwater, *Garden History of Georgia*, 213–15, 232–34, 262–63, 447–52.

3. Cator Woolford served as head of the Retail Credit Company until his retirement in 1931; see "Cator Woolford," *Atlanta Constitution*, September 22 and 29, 1940, and Krista Reese, "Equifax," *New Georgia Encyclopedia*, August 19, 2013, accessed September 19,

2016, www.georgiaencyclopedia.org/articles/business
-economy/equifax.

4. "At Camp Woolford," *Atlanta Constitution*, July 15, 1917, C2.

5. "Boyd-Woolford Marriage Brilliant Griffin Event," *Atlanta Constitution*, January 2, 1920.

6. No extant correspondence or drawings from Robert B. Cridland for the Cator Woolford property have yet been located, but *Garden History of Georgia* names Cridland as the designer for the gardens at the estate.

7. "House of Cator Woolford, Esq., Atlanta, Ga.," *Southern Architect and Building News*, December 1930, 27–31.

8. "Cator Woolford Gardens Cultural Landscape Report," prepared for a course taught in cultural land-scape preservation at Georgia State University by Andrew D. Kohr, fall 2010, 12.

9. Cator Woolford Sparks, "History of the Woolford Estate," January 2014, Atlanta Hospital Hospitality House website, Accessed September 1, 2016, http ://atlhhh.org/history-of-woolford-estate.

10. Cooney and Rainwater, *Garden History of Georgia*, 277.

11. Ibid., 275, 277.

12. Ibid., 277.

13. Ibid., 275.

14. Aerial view of the Cator Woolford Estate, ca. 1930s, Frazer.

15. Cooney and Rainwater, *Garden History of Georgia*, 277.

16. Ibid.

17. Ibid.

18. Two photographs of a keyhole garden with a man-sion on the distant hill at the Cator Woolford Estate, ca. 1930s, Frazer.

19. Lucile Thomas Keyes, "700 Rock Gardens in Atlanta," *Atlanta Journal Magazine*, December 22, 1929, 10.

20. Cooney and Rainwater, *Garden History of Georgia*, 277.

21. Woolford also supported the Georgia Vegetable Growers' Association, the beautification of Georgia's roadsides, the preservation of scenic and historic monu-ments, and the state's garden clubs.

22. Edward L. Daugherty, interview with Staci L. Catron, Atlanta, December 14, 2016. *Azalea indica* was rare in Atlanta in the mid-1930s, so there was great interest by the public in seeing the specimens at the Cator Woolford estate.

23. The Lane Building was named in honor of Anne Lane (Mrs. Mills B. Lane). Anne Lane and Rebecca

Frazer (Mrs. James N. Frazer) founded the school in 1949.

24. Mitchell, *Gardens of Georgia*, 146; "Cator Woolford Gardens Cultural Landscape Report," 2.

25. Daugherty interview.

26. Eight photographs of the larger sunken garden, ca. early 1960s, Frazer.

27. Cerebral Palsy School Scrapbook, 1961–67, Frazer.

28. Indian Creek Garden Club, "Indian Creek Garden Club Project Scrapbook, 1961–1963," Frazer.

29. Daugherty/Anderson & Associates, Cator Woolford Gardens Master Plan, 1996, VIS 207, Daugherty drawings.

30. Ibid.

31. Laufer, "Rocking the Landscape," 3, 9, 10.

32. Ibid., 9.

33. "Friends of the Frazer Forest," Frazer Center, accessed on September 24, 2016, www.frazercenter.org /frazerforestfriends.

34. "Cator Woolford," *Atlanta Constitution*, September 22 and 29, 1940.

35. Ibid.

Coffin-Reynolds Mansion

The epigraph is drawn from Carlyle McKinley, "Sapelo," lines 21–24. See George Armstrong Wauchope, *The Writers of South Carolina* (Columbia, S.C.: State Co., 1910), 283, accessed June 4, 2016, https://catalog.hathitrust. org/Record/100390576. A Georgia native, McKinley (1847–1904) visited relatives on Sapelo Island. A writer of poetry and prose, he worked for the *News and Courier* in Charleston, South Carolina. An earlier version of his poem "Sapelo" differs slightly from the one cited here.

1. Seabrook, *World of the Salt Marsh*, 151–52.

2. Martin, *This Happy Isle*, 6–7.

3. Vanstory, *Georgia's Land*, 60.

4. Sullivan, *Early Days*, 99–101; Lane, *Architecture of the Old South*, 68.

5. Vanstory, *Georgia's Land*, 58.

6. Sullivan, *Early Days*, 134–37; McFeely, *Sapelo's People*, 62–67.

7. Sullivan, *Sapelo Island*, 16, 18.

8. Sullivan, *Sapelo Island*, 19; Sullivan, *Sapelo*, 26–27.

9. Marquis, *Book of Detroiters*, 116.

10. Sullivan, *Sapelo Island*, 22, 26–27.

11. McCash and McCash, *Jekyll Island Club*, 223–25.

12. Aslet, *American Country House*, v, vi, 20, 135; Ferree, *American Estates and Gardens*, 1–2.

13. Sullivan, *Early Days*, 611–12; Sullivan, *Sapelo Island*, 71.

14. Sullivan, *Early Days*, 611–14; Sullivan, *Sapelo Island*, 70.

15. Coffin had a general sketch of the plan for Spalding's antebellum garden and house, apparently drawn from memory by Spalding's grandson, Charles S. Wylly (1836–1923). A copy is reproduced in Cooney and Rainwater, *Garden History of Georgia*, and in Lockwood, *Gardens of Colony and State*. Coffin's formal garden alludes to Spalding's; however, the garden designs differ somewhat.

16. Cooney, and Rainwater, *Garden History of Georgia*, 365.

17. Ibid.

18. Jean Oliphant Rentz, "Howard Coffin's Georgia Retreat," *Macon Telegraph Sunday Magazine*, September 2, 1928, 1.

19. Vanstory, *Georgia's Land*, 65.

20. Cooney and Rainwater, *Garden History of Georgia*, 365.

21. Perkerson, *White Columns in Georgia*, 142.

22. Cooney and Rainwater, *Garden History of Georgia*, 365.

23. Rentz, "Howard Coffin's Georgia Retreat," 1.

24. James M. Smith, comp., Montgomery Smith Inc., "Needs Assessment and Evaluation of the R. J. Reynolds Estate Greenhouses, Sapelo Island, Georgia," prepared for the University of Georgia, University Architect for Facilities Planning Office, Athens, June 2004, 4.

25. Cooney and Rainwater, *Garden History of Georgia*, 365.

26. Ibid.

27. Smith, "Needs Assessment and Evaluation," 7.

28. W. Robert Moore, "The Golden Isles of Guale," *National Geographic Magazine*, February 1934, 248.

29. Sullivan, *Sapelo Island*, 41.

30. Rentz, "Howard Coffin's Georgia Retreat," 1.

31. Martin, *This Happy Isle*, 40.

32. Ibid., 22–23.

33. Sullivan, *Early Days*, 621, 624–25.

34. President Herbert Hoover and First Lady Lou Hoover came to Sapelo in 1932 after the death of Matilda Coffin. President Jimmy Carter visited the island in 1979 and 1980.

35. Sullivan, *Sapelo Island*, 96–97; Sullivan, *Early Days*, 643–47.

36. *Successful Men of Michigan*, 140.

37. Martin, *This Happy Isle*, 11, 40–41.

38. Ibid., xiii–xiv. *This Happy Isle* tells the story of the relationship between Coffin and Jones and their work in building Sea Island and the Cloister.

39. Ibid., 64–68.

40. Moore, "Golden Isles of Guale," 248.

41. Dowling, *American Classicist*, 200.

42. "Residences: 1940–1950," descriptive inventories of landscaping projects, residential, 1922–1969, MSS660, box 4, folder 7, 6, Pauley Papers; see "A Plan for the Development of the Grounds of the House of Sapeloe, Mr. R. J. Reynolds, Owner, Sapeloe, Georgia, July 1935," Pauley Drawings.

43. "Topographical Survey, Portion of the Grounds, Sapeloe Plantation, May 1935," Pauley Drawings.

44. Jaeger Company, *Coffin-Reynolds Mansion*, 8.

45. Sullivan, *Early Days*, 677–78.

46. Sullivan, "Historic Buildings of Sapelo," 14.

47. Andrew Sparks, "Sapeloe Opens Its Golden Door," *Atlanta Journal Magazine*, July 17, 1949, 8.

48. Bailey and Bledsoe, *God, Dr. Buzzard*, 115; Seabrook, *World of the Salt Marsh*, 154–55; McFeely, *Sapelo's People*, 28–29, 148–49.

49. Seabrook, *World of the Salt Marsh*, 156–59; Sullivan, *Early Days*, 681–83.

50. Seabrook, *World of the Salt Marsh*, 158.

51. Ibid., 160.

52. Ibid., 5, 41–42, 48–49, 168.

53. Hog Hammock was also listed in the National Register of Historic Places in 1996.

54. June Thomas, Odum Garden Club, telephone interview by Mary Ann Eaddy, August 2, 2015.

55. Martin, *This Happy Isle*, 5–6.

56. McKinley, "Sapelo," lines 105–8.

Dunaway Gardens

The epigraph is drawn from Mary Ann Eaddy's interview with Jennifer Rae Bigham, September 26, 2014.

1. Sources differ in the spelling of Hetty Jane Dunaway Sewell's name. Some sources list her as "Hetty," others as "Hettie." The former is used in this text.

2. "The Lady of the Decoration: Hettie Jane Dunaway," promotional flyer [1916], "Traveling Culture," http://digital.lib.uiowa.edu/cdm/ref/collection/tc/id/55553.

3. Ibid.

4. Stephen Holden, "Minnie Pearl, 'Grand Ole Opry' Star for 50 Years, Dies at 83," *New York Times*, March 5, 1996, http://www.nytimes.com/1996/03/05/nyregion/minnie-pearl-grand-ole-opry-star-for-50-years-dies-at-83.html.

5. Danny C. Flanders, "Diamond in the Rough," *Atlanta Journal Constitution*, June 8, 2003.

6. NRHP, Roscoe-Dunaway Gardens Historic District, Roscoe, Coweta/Fulton Counties, Georgia, National Register #96001414, sec. 8, p. 11, 14–15.

7. Linton Weeks, "When America Was Crazy about Rock Gardens," National Public Radio, History Department, April 20, 2015, accessed January 15, 2016, www.npr.org/sections/npr-history-dept/2015/04/20/398517359/when-america-was-crazy-about-rock-gardens.

8. Cridland, *Practical Landscape Gardening*, 223–30.

9. Cooney and Rainwater, *Garden History of Georgia*, 347.

10. Ibid.

11. NRHP, Roscoe-Dunaway Gardens Historic District, sec. 8, pp. 11, 14.

12. Ibid., sec. 8, p. 11, 14.

13. "Visit the Hetty Jane Dunaway Gardens," promotional flyer, private collection.

14. Ibid.

15. Cooney and Rainwater, *Garden History of Georgia*, 347.

16. Ibid.

17. *Hettie Jane Dunaway Gardens*, brochure, [1934–1940?], private collection.

18. Ibid.

19. Ibid.

20. Ibid.

21. Ibid.

22. NRHP, Roscoe-Dunaway Gardens Historic District, sec. 8, p. 11.

23. Holden, "Minnie Pearl."

24. Ida A. Thomasson, "Dunaway Gardens," unidentified article, [mid-1960s?], MSS 1007, GHLIR.

25. Doris Lockerman, unidentified article, 1961, Dunaway Gardens website, accessed January 15, 2017, www.dunawaygardens.com/dlockermanartcl.php.

26. NRHP, Roscoe-Dunaway Gardens Historic District, sec. 7, p. 8.

27. Flanders, "Diamond in the Rough."

28. Bigham and Fisher, "Tea in the Garden."

29. Flanders, "Diamond in the Rough."

30. Ibid.

31. Bigham and Fisher, "Tea in the Garden."

32. Ibid.

33. Ibid.

34. Ibid.

35. Dunaway Gardens, History, Photo Gallery, "Wetlands Rehabilitation," accessed January 16, 2017, www.dunawaygardens.com.

36. Bigham interview.

37. Bigham and Fisher, "Tea in the Garden."

38. Ibid.; Jennifer Bigham, e-mail to Mary Ann Eaddy, January 17, 2017.

39. Dunaway Gardens, brochure, n.d.

40. Lockerman, unidentified article, 1961.

Governor's Mansion

The epigraph is drawn from Moses, *Georgia Governor's Mansion*, back inset.

1. NRHP, Nomination Draft, Historic Resources of West Paces Ferry Road (partial inventory: architectural and historic resources), Atlanta, Fulton County, Georgia, 1988, item 7, p. 1.

2. Knight, *Standard History of Georgia*, 4:1864.

3. Mrs. Thaddeus Horton, "The Summer Home of a Georgian," *Country Life in America*, July 1908, 282.

4. A 1962 *Atlanta Journal and Constitution* article refers to the landscape engineers Thomas Meehan and Son of Philadelphia as having designed the landscape, but there is no evidence to confirm this singular reference.

5. Horton, "The Summer Home of a Georgian," 282.

6. Andrew Sparks, "Site of New Governor's Mansion Is an Atlanta Showplace," *Atlanta Journal and Constitution Magazine*, November 25, 1962, 9.

7. Cooney and Rainwater, *Garden History of Georgia*, 240.

8. Ibid., 243.

9. "World's First Citizen Dines with Atlanta's First Citizen," *Atlanta Constitution*, October 8, 1910.

10. Guest Book, Woodhaven, Maddox Residence, 1905–1913, MSS 143, Robert Foster Maddox Jr. Papers, Kenan Research Center, Atlanta History Center.

11. *Garden Club of America Annual Meeting, Atlanta, April 18th, 19th, and 20th, 1932*, MSS 681, Peachtree Garden Club Records, CGL; Sparks, "Site of New Governor's Mansion," 47.

12. Deal, Dickey, and Lewis, *Memories of the Mansion*, 23–24.

13. Robert M. Craig, "A. Thomas Bradbury (1902–1992)," *New Georgia Encyclopedia*, April 16, 2014, accessed May 26, 2016, www.georgiaencyclopedia.org/articles/arts-culture/thomas-bradbury-1902-1992.

14. Ibid.

15. Deal, Dickey, and Lewis, *Memories of the Mansion*, 25.

16. Ibid., 24.

17. Staci L. Catron and Jennifer E. Yankopolus, cocurators, in collaboration with Edward L. Daugherty, of the exhibition *Edward L. Daugherty: A Southern Landscape Architect, Exploring New Forms*, on display at the Atlanta History Center, October 17, 2008, to October 10, 2009.

18. VIS 207.182, Daugherty drawings.

19. Catron and Yankopolus, *Edward L. Daugherty*; VIS 207.182, Daugherty drawings.

20. VIS 207.182, Daugherty drawings.

21. "Executive Center, State of Georgia, Second Phase, Planting Plan, December 31, 1968, revised August 18, 1969," VIS 207.182, Daugherty drawings.

22. Edward L. Daugherty, interview by the Cultural Landscape Foundation, 2007, https://tclf.org/sites /default/files/atoms/files/Daugherty-Transcript.pdf.

23. MSS 997, Daugherty Papers.

24. Deal, Dickey, and Lewis, *Memories of the Mansion*, 77.

25. Ibid., 31.

26. Ibid., 74.

27. MSS 997, Daugherty Papers; VIS 207.182, Daugherty drawings.

28. MSS 1050, Seiferle Papers.

29. Deal, Dickey, and Lewis, *Memories of the Mansion*, 91.

30. "Garden of Terraces," *Atlanta Journal and Constitution*, November 3, 1974, 2-G.

31. Deal, Dickey, and Lewis, *Memories of the Mansion*, 105–7.

32. Ibid., 117.

33. Roy Wyatt, "Homage to Mansion's Gardens of Yesteryear," *Atlanta Constitution*, July 28, 1985, 24L.

34. Mitchell, *Gardens of Georgia*, 203.

35. Deal, Dickey, and Lewis, *Memories of the Mansion*, 133.

36. Ibid., 154, 156–57.

37. Ibid., 157.

38. Ibid., 160.

39. Ibid., 160–61.

40. Kirk Talgo, grounds manager, Georgia Governor's Mansion, on-site interview by Staci L. Catron, October 23, 2014.

41. Deal, Dickey, and Lewis, *Memories of the Mansion*, 174–75.

42. Elliot Brack, "Many Fernbank Rose Bushes Moved to Georgia Governor's Mansion," *Gwinnett (Ga.) Forum*, June 12, 2015.

43. One of the original four statues is now a replica.

44. MSS 1050, Seiferle Papers.

45. Talgo interview.

46. Trees Atlanta, "Assessing Urban Tree Canopy in the City of Atlanta: Why Urban Trees and Forests Are Important?," accessed July 15, 2016, https://treesatlanta .org/resources/urban-tree-canopy-study.

47. Ibid.

48. Ibid.

Hills and Dales Estate

The epigraph is drawn from Howett, "Southern Lady's Legacy," 350.

1. Cooney and Rainwater, *Garden History of Georgia*, 94.

2. Johnson, *Histories of LaGrange*, 5:55.

3. Smith, *History of Troup County*, 188.

4. Melton and Melton, *Fuller E. Callaway*, 129.

5. Ibid., 5–9.

6. Ibid., 130–38.

7. U.S., Selected Federal Census Non-Population Schedules, 1850–1880, for Blount Ferrell, Agricultural Schedule, accessed through Ancestry.

8. U.S. Census, 1850, "Blount C Ferrell," Troup County, Georgia, and U.S. Census, 1850, Slave Schedule, "Blount C Ferrell," Troup County, Georgia, both accessed through FamilySearch.

9. Sarah Ferrell to Blount Ferrell, July 25, 1860, transcribed letter, Callaway Papers, MS-009.

10. Howett, "Southern Lady's Legacy," 350.

11. Melton and Melton, *Fuller E. Callaway*, 128–29.

12. Howett, "Southern Lady's Legacy," 350.

13. Ibid., 351.

14. Melton and Melton, *Fuller E. Callaway*, 130.

15. Ibid.

16. The identity of the builder of this house is not known for sure, but likely was Robert M. Browning, a previous owner of the property; see Johnson, *Histories of LaGrange*, 5:40, and Troup County, Deed Book 11, Troup County Archives, LaGrange, Ga., 418.

17. Melton and Melton, *Fuller E. Callaway*, 130.

18. T.J., "Beautiful Homes of LaGrange: The Far Famed Terraces," *LaGrange (Ga.) Reporter*, May 28, 1888.

19. Howett, "Southern Lady's Legacy," 353.

20. Melton and Melton, *Fuller E. Callaway*, 133.

21. T.J., "Beautiful Homes of LaGrange."

22. Donhardt, "Ferrell Gardens" 49.

23. Fuller E. Callaway Foundation, "Hills and Dales Visitors Guide."

24. Donhardt, "Ferrell Gardens," 54; and Fuller E. Callaway Foundation, "Hills and Dales Visitors Guide."

25. Melton and Melton, *Fuller E. Callaway*, 135.

26. T.J., "Beautiful Homes of LaGrange"; Barbara Madison Tunnell, "The Garden of Memories," *Country Life*, August 1920, 44; Constance Knowles Draper, lecture notes for Ferrell Gardens, ca. 1927, Constance Knowles Draper Collection, MSS 968, CGL.

27. *LaGrange Reporter*, March 22, 1872.

28. *Descriptive LaGrange, Georgia*, 6.

29. *LaGrange Reporter*, May 14, 1888.

30. Troup County, Deed Book 11, Troup County Archives, LaGrange, Ga., 511–13.

31. Kaye L. Minchew, "Callaway Family," *New Georgia Encyclopedia*, December 29, 2014, accessed June 22, 2016, www.georgiaencyclopedia.org/articles/history-archaeology/callaway-family.

32. Melton and Melton, *Fuller E. Callaway*, 138.

33. Ibid., 138–39.

34. Ibid., 139.

35. Ibid.

36. The date of the Callaways' silver wedding anniversary was April 28, 1916, but the celebration occurred in June, since the house was not completed in time.

37. W. B. Marquis, P. J. Berckmans Co., Inc. Augusta, Ga., "Report on the Improvement and Maintenance of the Property of Mr. Fuller E. Callaway, LaGrange, Ga., 1916," series 2, subseries D, box 4, Callaway Papers, MS-009.

38. E. S. Draper, "The Gardens at Hills and Dales," *House Beautiful*, May 1932, 376.

39. Ibid.

40. Fuller E. Callaway Foundation, "Hills and Dales Visitors Guide"; Carleton B. Wood, "Who's on Third," *The Portico: News from Hills & Dales Estate* 21 (Fall 2016): 12–15. Evidence from a 1915 catalogue order suggests that the statues are actually of Aratus (located on the west end of path) and Sophocles (east end) rather than Plato and Socrates. Ida and Fuller E. Callaway Sr. always referred to the statues as Plato and Socrates.

41. Draper, "Gardens at Hills and Dales," 377.

42. Fuller E. Callaway Foundation, "Hills and Dales Visitors Guide."

43. Cooney and Rainwater, *Garden History of Georgia*, 332.

44. Tunnell, "Garden of Memories," 47.

45. Ida Cason Callaway, 1929, quoted in the Hills and Dales Estate brochure, 2014.

46. Minchew, "Callaway Family," *New Georgia Encyclopedia*.

47. Verey and Samuels, *American Woman's Garden*, 45.

48. Fuller E. Callaway Foundation, "Hills and Dales Visitors Guide."

49. Verey and Samuels, *American Woman's Garden*, 43.

50. Fuller E. Callaway Foundation, "Hills and Dales Visitors Guide."

51. Ibid., 2.

Lullwater Conservation Garden

1. Mrs. George Phillips, "The Lullwater Conservation Garden," [1930s?], 1, RLGC.

2. NRHP, Druid Hills Historic District, Atlanta, DeKalb County, Georgia, National Register #79000715, item 8.

3. "Information of Plans to Develop Lullwater Conservation Garden," *Atlanta Journal*, April 30, 1933, RLGC.

4. Cooney and Rainwater, *Garden History of Georgia*, 421.

5. "Atlanta's Champion Trees," Trees Atlanta, accessed October 1, 2016, https://treesatlanta.org/our-programs/atlantas-cha.

6. Coleman, *History of Georgia*, 323.

7. White, *Sixty-Year History*, 31.

8. "Forty Year Club History, State of Georgia Award #20," Lullwater Garden Club, [1970?], RLGC.

9. Lullwater Garden Club History, [1960s?], RLGC.

10. Ibid.

11. "Lullwater Garden Club Adds to Its Conservation Garden," 1938, unidentified newspaper clipping, 1937–38, scrapbook, RLGC.

12. Phillips, "Lullwater Conservation Garden," 1, RLGC.

13. Cooney and Rainwater, *Garden History of Georgia*, 421.

14. Lullwater Garden Club History, 1932–33 reference, RLGC.

15. Meeting minutes, February 1934, RLGC.

16. "Full Size Detail Sign for Lullwater Garden Club, 1935," FF 293, William C. Pauley, landscape architecture drawings, VIS 184.139, CGL.

17. Meeting minutes, February 1934; "October," Award #1, McHatton Trophy of the Garden Club of Georgia, Lullwater Garden Club, 1965–66, both in RLGC.

18. Club History, [1960s?], RLGC.

19. Ibid.

20. Ibid.

21. "Forty Year Club History, State of Georgia Award #20," RLGC.

22. "Project(s)," Lullwater Garden Club Yearbooks, [September] 1942–[June] 1943; 1943–44; 1944–45, RLGC; Mrs. Olin S. Cofer, president, "Annual Report 1942–1943," RLGC.

23. "Sixty Year History of the Lullwater Garden Club," State History Award #20-A5, Lullwater Garden Club, [1988?], 7, RLGC.

24. "Forty Year Club History," RLGC.

25. Ibid.

26. Ibid.; Mrs. R. T. Smith to Mrs. James T. King, May 13, 1953, RLGC.

27. Mrs. James T. King, "President's Report, 1952–1953," RLGC.

28. Ibid.

29. "Forty Year Club History"; Anne Perry to Garden Club Member, June 15, 1964, both in RLGC.

30. "Petition for Charter," *DeKalb (Ga.) New Era*, [August?] 1964, RLGC.

31. DeKalb County, Quitclaim Deed, October 14, 1964, Deed Book 1928, folio 238, copy, RLGC.

32. Ibid.

33. Conservation Project, Lullwater Garden Club, 1965–1966, 2, RLGC.

34. Accomplishments, 1966–1967, "The Conservation Garden, 1966," RLGC.

35. Award #1, McHatton Trophy, 1965–66, RLGC.

36. Mrs. Julian C. Cowan, historian, "Lullwater Garden Club History, 1968–1969," RLGC.

37. Award #1, McHatton Trophy, 1965–66, RLGC.

38. Cosigners of the covenant included representatives of the cities of Atlanta and Decatur; DeKalb County; Emory University; Fernbank, Inc.; the Children's Rehabilitation Center (Cator Woolford Estate); Druid Hills Golf Club; and Lullwater Garden Club.

39. Lullwater Garden Club History, January 1989–March 1990, RLGC.

40. Fay Brewer, Ivy Dougherty, and Chris Hauck, comps., "History of Lullwater Garden Club, March 1995–May 1996," RLGC.

41. "Inside Our Garden Gate," *Lullwater*, Spring 2002; "Inside Our Garden Gate," *Lullwater*, September 2002, RLGC.

42. Plaque in the Patriots' Bridge Commemorative Garden, Lullwater Conservation Garden.

43. Ibid.

44. "Lullwater Garden Club History," Lullwater Garden Club, 1999–2000, 15, RLGC. A charter flight carrying 106 of the city's major leaders and supporters of the arts crashed on takeoff at an airfield outside Paris, France. Only two crew members survived. The group was returning home after a museum tour sponsored by the Atlanta Arts Association. This organization evolved into the Atlanta Arts Alliance, which eventually came to administer the High Museum of Art, the Atlanta Symphony Orchestra, the Alliance Theatre, the 14th Street Playhouse, and the Atlanta College of Art.

45. "Scenes in Lullwater Conservation Garden," *Atlanta Journal*, April 30, 1933, RLGC.

46. Mrs. James H. Loftis to District Engineer, U.S. Army Corps of Engineers, March 28, 1966, RLGC.

47. Club History Award #20 A-6, Lullwater Garden Club History, 75 Years, 1928–2003, 7, RLGC.

48. See Spencer Tunnell, Tunnell and Tunnell, *A Masterplan for the Lullwater Conservation Garden: A Report Prepared for the Lullwater Garden Club* (draft), 2012, RLGC.

49. Lullwater Garden Club History, 1936–38 item, [1960s?], RLGC.

50. "Forty Year Club History," RLGC.

51. Lullwater Garden Club History, Lullwater Garden Club booklet, Atlanta, Ga., 1999–2000, 11, RLGC.

52. "Lullwater Conservation Garden and Bird Sanctuary Restoration Project," Georgia Native Plant Society, accessed October 8, 2016, http://gnps.org/restoration/lullwater_garden_club.phb.

Millpond Plantation

The epigraph is drawn from "The Ideal Place; What Winter Residents Say of Thomasville," *Thomasville (Ga.) Times-Enterprise*, August 26, 1904.

1. NRHP, Millpond Plantation, Thomasville, Thomas County, Georgia, 1976, National Register #76000651, item 7, p. 2; "Third Handsomest Place in the Entire South Is House of J. H. Wade, At Thomasville, Georgia," *Atlanta Constitution*, April 23, 1905.

2. Mitchell, *Thomasville*, 96–98.

3. *Atlanta Constitution*, "Third Handsomest Place."

4. Mitchell, *Thomasville*, 160; NRHP, Millpond Plantation, item 8, p. 1.

5. NRHP, Millpond Plantation, item 8, p. 1.

6. Cleveland Landmarks Commission, "Hubbell and Benes Building List," accessed March 28, 2015, http://planning.city.cleveland.oh.us/landmark/arch/pdf/archdetailPrint.php?afil=&archID=285.

7. Ibid.

8. *Atlanta Constitution*, "Third Handsomest Place."

9. Mitchell, *Thomasville*, 160.

10. Robin Karson, "Manning, Warren Henry (1860–1938)," in Birnbaum and Karson, *Pioneers of American Landscape Design*, 236–37.

11. Karson, *Genius for Place*, 31.

12. Karson, Brown, and Allaback, *Warren H. Manning*.

13. Karson, "Manning, Warren Henry (1860–1938)," 237.

14. Karson, *Genius for Place*, 31.

15. Karson, Brown, and Allaback, *Warren H. Manning*. A brief essay regarding Millpond Plantation (the J. H. Wade estate), written by Staci L. Catron, appears in Karson, Brown, and Allaback, *Warren H. Manning*.

16. *Atlanta Constitution*, "Third Handsomest Place."

17. NRHP, Millpond Plantation, item 7, p. 1.

18. "Survey of Mill Pond Plantation, Estate of J. H. Wade, Esq., Thomasville, Thomas County, Georgia, October 12, 1904," no. 602-20, Manning Papers.

19. Ibid.

20. "Plan for Arrangement and Planting, Mill Pond Plantation, Estate of J. H. Wade, Esq., Thomasville, Ga., September 21, 1904," no. 602-10, Manning Papers.

21. "Plan of Road System, Estate of J. H. Wade, Esq., Thomasville, Ga., June 1905," no. 602-61, Manning Papers.

22. Bartram, *Travels of William Bartram*, 110.

23. Georgia Department of Natural Resources, *Comprehensive Wildlife Strategy for Georgia*, 122.

24. Nature Conservancy, "Longleaf Pine: Restoring a National Treasure," *Nature Conservancy* (2015), 1, www.nature.org/ourinitiatives/regions/northamerica/unitedstates/longleaf-pine-forests-landing-page.xml.

25. Finch et al., *Longleaf*, 69.

26. Albert Way, "Longleaf Pine Ecosystem," *New Georgia Encyclopedia*, July 8, 2014, accessed December 9, 2015, www.georgiaencyclopedia.org/articles/geography-environment/longleaf-pine-ecosystem.

27. Ibid.

28. Nature Conservancy, "Longleaf Pine," 1.

29. Albert Way, *Conserving Southern Longleaf*, 94.

30. Albert Way, "Herbert L. Stoddard (1889–1970)," *New Georgia Encyclopedia*, August 17, 2015, accessed December 9, 2015, www.georgiaencyclopedia.org/articles/geography-environment/herbert-l-stoddard-1889-1970.

31. Quoted in Way, *Conserving Southern Longleaf*, 93–94.

32. Way, "Herbert L. Stoddard."

33. "Plan of Open Court, J. H. Wade, Esq., Thomasville, Ga., October 24, 1904," no. 602-22, Manning Papers.

34. Cooney and Rainwater, *Garden History of Georgia*, 401.

35. Ibid., 401.

36. "Plan for Arrangement and Planting," no. 602-10, Manning Papers.

37. Undated photograph of observation platform, Millpond Plantation, Wade Family collection (private).

38. "Plan for Arrangement and Planting," Manning Papers.

39. Cooney and Rainwater, *Garden History of Georgia*, 401.

40. NRHP, Millpond Plantation, item 8, p. 2.

41. Cooney and Rainwater, *Garden History of Georgia*, 401–404.

42. Tall Timbers Research Station and Land Conservancy, "The Wade Tract Preserve: A Window to the Past," accessed March 28, 2014, http://talltimbers.org/the-wade-tract-preserve-a-window-to-the-past.

Oakton

The epigraph is drawn from a letter to Georgia King Wilder from Anne Page Wilder, at Oakton, June 19, 1889, Wilder and Anderson Family Papers, 1837–1938, Collection No. 01255, Southern Historical Collection, Louis Round Wilson Special Collections Library, University of North Carolina at Chapel Hill.

1. Mildred Irwin White to Robert M. Goodman II, November 6, 1974, private papers of the Goodman Family. Mildred Irwin White was the niece of Mary Ann Irwin, who was the niece of Judge David Irwin, the original owner of Oakton and the first judge of the Blue Ridge Circuit in North Georgia.

2. U.S. Census, 1850, Slave Schedule, index and images, FamilySearch.org, accessed February 22, 2015, citing NARA microfilm publication M432.

3. Plat for the property of John R. Wilder, in the 11th Dist, 2n Sect. Cobb Co. Geo. near Marietta with the number of acres in each lot respectively, according to the former surveys furnished me and the additional ones made by myself for total content of 141.56 acres by surveyor Wm. R. Hunt, C.E., March 22, 1869; remainder of lots 1079 and 1082, also all of lots 1080, and 1081 were superimposed upon this map of March 22, 1869; necessary information was furnished by Mr. J. R. Anderson to surveyor J. A. Logan, M.E., June 28, 1934, photocopy, MSS 989, Cothran Papers.

4. U.S. Census, 1850, Slave Schedule.

5. Vlach, *Back of the Big House*, 33–34.

6. Cothran, *Gardens*, 8.

7. Frey, *Marietta*, 15.

8. Robert M. Goodman to Wilbur G. Kurtz, December 26, 1958, Wilbur G. Kurtz Sr. Visual Arts Collection, VIS 197, Kenan Research Center, the Atlanta History Center.

9. *Marietta (Ga.) Journal*, July 3, 1879, 3.

10. U.S. Census, 1880, index and images, FamilySearch, accessed January 24, 2015, https://familysearch.org/pal:/MM9.1.1/M8LK-CQP, William Annandale, Marietta, Cobb County, Georgia; citing enumeration district 37, sheet 219B, NARA microfilm publication T9, roll 0141; FHL microfilm 1,254,141.

11. Cooney and Rainwater, *Garden History of Georgia*, 116.

12. Ibid.

13. *Atlanta Constitution*, June 8, 1902, 28.

14. Ibid., November 4, 1879, 1.

15. Contract between Joseph J. Wilder and Wm. Annandale, November 28, 1885, photocopy, Cothran Papers.

16. Anne Page Wilder to John J. Wilder, Oakton, July 24, 1884; Anne Page Wilder to Georgia King Wilder, Oakton, June 19, 1889, both in Wilder and Anderson Family Papers, 1837–1938, Collection No. 01255, SHC.

17. Frey, *Marietta*, 21.

18. "Historic Oakton Sold to Goodman," *Atlanta Constitution*, December 30, 1939, 10K.

19. Robert M. Goodman Sr., original lots for Oakton subdivision, ca. 1950, photocopy, Cothran Papers.

20. Will Goodman, interview by Staci L. Catron, Marietta, May 16, 2014.

21. Ibid.

22. Ibid.

Rock City Gardens

The epigraph is drawn from the world-famous advertisement motto created by Garnet Carter in 1935.

1. Andy Peters, "Lookout Mountain," *New Georgia Encyclopedia*, July 1, 2014, accessed July 5, 2016, www.georgiaencyclopedia.org/articles/counties-cities-neighborhoods/lookout-mountain.

2. NRHP, "Rock City Gardens," Lookout Mountain, Walker County, Georgia, 2014, National Register #14000619, item 7, p. 3.

3. Hollis, *See Rock City*, 7.

4. Elizabeth B. Cooksey, "Walker County," *New Georgia Encyclopedia*, March 5, 2013, accessed July 5, 2016, www.georgiaencyclopedia.org/articles/counties-cities-neighborhoods/walker-county.

5. Morgan, "From Old South to New South," 18–19.

6. Hollis, *See Rock City*, 9–10.

7. Ibid., 11.

8. Ibid.

9. Ibid., 17.

10. Hollis, *Land of the Smokies*, 164–65.

11. Ibid., 167.

12. NRHP, "Rock City Gardens," item 7, pp. 3–4.

13. Ibid., 4–5.

14. Ibid., 10.

15. Cooney and Rainwater, *Garden History of Georgia*, 354.

16. Ibid., 354, 357.

17. Ibid., 357.

18. Ibid.

19. Ibid.

20. NRHP, "Rock City Gardens," item 7, p. 10.

21. Ibid., 24–25.

22. Ibid., 5.

23. Ibid.

24. Ibid., 6, 21.

25. Ibid., 8.

26. Ibid., 17.

27. Ibid., 17–18.

28. Ibid., 19.

29. Ibid., 20–21.

30. Ibid.

31. Ibid., 25.

32. McKechnie, *USA 101*.

Salubrity Hall

The epigraph is drawn from Mary C. Alexander, "Augusta—of Yesterday and Today—Welcomes You," *Garden Gateways* 6 (April 1940): 5.

1. Edward J. Cashin, "Augusta," *New Georgia Encyclopedia*, August 12, 2013, accessed August 18, 2016, www.georgiaencyclopedia.org/articles/counties-cities-neighborhoods/augusta.

2. Cooney and Rainwater, *Garden History of Georgia*, 281–310.

3. National Park Service, "Summerville Historic District," accessed August 15, 2016, https://www.nps.gov/nr/travel/Augusta/summervillehd.html.

4. Erick D. Montgomery and Kim Overstreet, "Augusta, Georgia: Discover Our Shared Heritage Travel Itinerary," U.S. Department of the Interior, National Park Service, accessed August 19, 2016, https://www.nps.gov/nr/travel/augusta/.

5. Cashin and Eskew, *Paternalism in a Southern City*, 56.

6. Cooney and Rainwater, *Garden History of Georgia*, 300.

7. Ibid.

8. Ibid.

9. Ibid.

10. Ibid., 302.

11. Ibid.

12. Ibid.

13. "Social Chat," *Augusta (Ga.) Chronicle*, March 26, 1935, A5.

14. Olivia showed her further love of Augusta in 1937 when she purchased the historic house called Ware's Folly (also known as the Ware-Sibley-Clark House) and saved it from demolition. She donated it to the Augusta Art Club and requested that the site be renamed in memory of her daughter, Gertrude Herbert Dunn, who died in 1933. The Gertrude Herbert Institute of Art in Augusta remains a nonprofit art school primarily serving

citizens of the central Savannah River region and show-casing the visual arts through exhibitions, classes, and other programs.

15. "For Sale: Salubrity Hall," *Augusta (Ga.) Chronicle*, April 11, 1946, A2.

16. Carole Hawkins, "History Lives at Tea House," *Augusta (Ga.) Chronicle*, November 13, 2010; Richmond County Property Records (online) for Elizabeth R. Anderson Property.

17. William T. Smith, landscape architect, interview by Staci L. Catron, Augusta, May 1, 2010.

18. William T. Smith and Associates, "Plan for Rose Arbor," for Dr. and Mrs. Don Williamson, Augusta, Ga., August 29, 2011; updated September 19, 2011, Smith drawings.

19. William T. Smith and Associates, "Plan for Fountain Garden with White Perennial Borders," for Dr. and Mrs. Don Williamson, Augusta, Ga., October 12, 2010, Smith drawings.

20. William T. Smith and Associates, "Plan for Herb Parterre Garden," for Dr. and Mrs. Don Williamson, Augusta, Ga., February 9, 2011; updated March 14, 2011, Smith drawings.

21. William T. Smith and Associates, "Rondel Garden Plan and Planting Plan for Woody Shrubs," for Dr. and Mrs. Don Williamson, Augusta, Ga., May 30, 2012; updated November 26, 2012, Smith drawings.

22. William T. Smith and Associates, "Motor Court / Lawn Area Site Plan," for Dr. and Mrs. Don Williamson, Augusta, Ga., February 15, 2011, Smith drawings.

23. "Our Mission Is to Preserve and Protect Historic Buildings in Augusta, Georgia," Historic Augusta, Inc., accessed August 25, 2016, www.historicaugusta.org/about-us.

Savannah Squares

The epigraph is drawn from Latrobe, *Rambler in North America*, 2:20.

1. Edward J. Cashin, "Trustee Georgia, 1732–1752," *New Georgia Encyclopedia*, September 2, 2015, accessed October 1, 2016, www.georgiaencyclopedia.org/articles/history-archaeology/trustee-georgia-1732-1752.

2. Edwin L. Jackson, "James Oglethorpe (1696–1785)," *New Georgia Encyclopedia*, August 16, 2016, accessed November 28, 2016, www.georgiaencyclopedia.org/articles/government-politics/james-oglethorpe-1696-1785.

3. Cashin, "Trustee Georgia, 1732–1752."

4. Buddy Sullivan, "Savannah," *New Georgia Encyclopedia*, August 4, 2016, accessed September 27, 2016, www.georgiaencyclopedia.org/articles/counties-cities-neighborhoods/savannah.

5. Ibid.

6. Buddy Sullivan, "Naval Stores Industry," *New Georgia Encyclopedia*, August 2, 2016, accessed October 1, 2016, www.georgiaencyclopedia.org/articles/business-economy/naval-stores-industry.

7. Sullivan, "Savannah."

8. Ibid.

9. Ibid.

10. Beth Reiter, "Historic Savannah Foundation," *New Georgia Encyclopedia*, February 16, 2015, accessed October 21, 2016, www.georgiaencyclopedia.org/articles/arts-culture/historic-savannah-foundation.

11. Beth Reiter, "Savannah City Plan," *New Georgia Encyclopedia*, March 10, 2016, accessed October 2, 2016, www.georgiaencyclopedia.org/articles/history-archaeology/savannah-city-plan.

12. Ibid.

13. Ibid.

14. Wilson, *Oglethorpe Plan*.

15. Ibid., 135.

16. Jordan and McCay, *Savannah Square by Square*, 9.

17. Sullivan, "Savannah."

18. Jordan and McCay, *Savannah Square by Square*, 9.

19. Ibid.

20. Reiter, "Savannah City Plan."

21. Jordan and McCay, *Savannah Square by Square*, 9.

22. Ibid.

23. Ibid.

24. Ibid., 106.

25. Ibid., 107.

26. Ibid., 13.

27. Sieg, *Squares*, 31.

28. Jordan and McCay, *Savannah Square by Square*, 17.

29. Sieg, *Squares*, 43–44.

30. Jordan and McCay, *Savannah Square by Square*, 17.

31. Julie A. Sweet, "Tomochichi (ca. 1644–1739)," *New Georgia Encyclopedia*, August 16, 2016, accessed October 21, 2016, www.georgiaencyclopedia.org/articles/history-archaeology/tomochichi-ca-1644-1739.

32. Jordan and McCay, *Savannah Square by Square*, 19.

33. Ibid., 33–35.

34. Ibid., 33.

35. Ibid.

36. Ibid., 38.

37. Ibid., 37.

38. Sieg, *Squares*, 185.

39. Ibid., 186–87.

40. Jordan and McCay, *Savannah Square by Square*, 41.

41. Ibid., 57.

42. Ibid., 57, 59.

43. Ibid., 77.

44. Barton Myers, "Sherman's Field Order No. 15," *New Georgia Encyclopedia*, August 3, 2016, accessed October 6, 2016, www.georgiaencyclopedia.org/articles /history-archaeology/shermans-field-order-no-15.

45. Ibid.

46. Jordan and McCay, *Savannah Square by Square*, 62–63.

47. Ibid., 63.

48. Ibid., 91.

49. Ibid.

50. Ibid., 21.

51. Clermont Huger Lee, architectural drawings and negatives, MS 1480, Georgia Historical Society, Savannah; "Clermont Huger Lee's Recollection of the Squares of Savannah," recorded by Winette Almon, Chatham County, Savannah (Squares/Parks) 2004, Georgia Historic Landscape Initiative records, MSS 1007, CGL.

52. Jordan and McCay, *Savannah Square by Square*, 95.

53. Ibid.

54. Ibid., 97.

55. Ibid., 99.

56. Ibid.

57. Ibid.

58. Ibid.

59. Ibid.

60. Ibid.

61. Savannah Tree Foundation. "Candler Oak / Conservation Easements," accessed October 7, 2016, www.savannahtree.com/programs/candler-oak -conservation-easements.

62. Wilson, *Oglethorpe Plan*, 187.

Stephenson-Adams-Land Garden

The epigraph is drawn from Mary Ann Eaddy's interview with Mary Young Land in Atlanta, October 26, 2015.

1. "Mr. Paullin, of Atlanta, Addresses Charter Circle," January 15, 1931, MSS660, box 1, folder 17, Pauley Papers. A clipping from an unidentified newspaper describes a talk that Pauley (his name is misspelled throughout the article) gave to a garden club in Columbus, Georgia.

2. Cooney and Rainwater, *Garden History of Georgia*, refers to both "H. W. Stephenson" and "W. H. Stephenson"; however, the 1957 *Atlanta Suburban Directory* lists H. Warren Stephenson and his wife as the property's residents. Pauley's early plans refer to "H. W. Stephenson," while his later ones read "W. H."

3. NRHP, Druid Hills Historic District, Atlanta, DeKalb County, Georgia, National Register #79000715, item 8.

4. Ibid.

5. Favretti and Favretti, *For Every House a Garden*, 34–36.

6. Favretti and Favretti, *Landscapes and Gardens*, 53.

7. "Residences: 1930–1940," descriptive inventories of landscaping projects, residential, 1922–1969, MSS660, box 4, folder 7, 6. Pauley Papers

8. Descriptive inventories of landscaping projects, residential, 1922–1969, MSS660, box 4, folder 7, Pauley Papers.

9. Ibid.

10. "Residences: 1930–1940," 3, Pauley Papers.

11. Spencer Tunnell, "Pauley, William C. (1893–1985)," in Birnbaum and Karson, Pioneers of American Landscape Design, 291.

12. Tunnell, "William C. Pauley, Landscape Architect," 258.

13. "Two Outstanding Residences Developed over a Period of Thirty or More Years," MSS660, box 4, folder 7, Pauley Papers.

14. Mitchell, *Gardens of Georgia*, 90–91.

15. "Two Outstanding Residences," Pauley Papers.

16. Tunnell, "Pauley, William C.," 293.

17. "Residences 1930–1940," 6, Pauley Papers.

18. NRHP, Druid Hills Historic District, item 8, p. 6.

19. Cooney and Rainwater, *Garden History of Georgia*, 266.

20. Ibid.

21. "Mr. Paullin, of Atlanta, Addresses Charter Circle," January 15, 1931, Pauley Papers.

22. Cooney and Rainwater, *Garden History of Georgia*, 266.

23. Ibid.

24. Tunnell, "William C. Pauley, Landscape Architect," 256.

25. "Mr. Paullin, of Atlanta, Addresses Charter Circle," January 15, 1931, Pauley Papers.

26. Tunnell, "William C. Pauley, Landscape Architect," 256.

27. Cooney and Rainwater, *Garden History of Georgia*, 266.

28. "Plant Survey for Mr. & Mrs. W. H. Stephenson" and "Planting Plan for Mr. & Mrs. W. H. Stephenson," Atlanta, December 18, 1953, H. W. Stephenson House, Pauley Drawings.

29. Land interview.

30. Ibid.

31. Ibid.

32. Ibid.

33. Ibid.

34. "Mr. and Mrs. W. H. Stephenson Garden," 2008, MSS 1007, GHLIR.

35. Land interview.

36. Ibid.

37. Ibid.

Swan House

The epigraph is drawn from Philip Trammell Shutze, "Inman description, 14 pages," 12, Shutze Collection, Kenan Research Center at the Atlanta History Center.

1. Atlanta History Center, *Swan House*.

2. Preston, *Automobile Age Atlanta*, 97.

3. Atlanta History Center, *Swan House*.

4. *Atlanta Journal*, June 12, 1901; Atlanta History Center, *Swan House*.

5. Atlanta History Center, *Swan House*.

6. Robert M. Craig, "Philip Trammell Shutze (1890–1982)," *New Georgia Encyclopedia*, November 4, 2013, accessed August 5, 2016, www.georgiaencyclopedia.org /articles/arts-culture/philip-trammell-shutze-1890-1982.

7. Ibid.

8. Marcus Binney, *Swan House, Atlanta, Georgia*, a booklet reproduced from two articles in *Country Life* (May 1983) and distributed by the Atlanta Historical Society.

9. Dowling, *American Classicist*, 33.

10. Tunnell, "Stylistic Progression," 43.

11. Atlanta History Center, *Swan House*.

12. Ibid.

13. Ibid.

14. Deirdre Digrande, "Swan House: A History of the Building and Its Occupants, 1928–1995," a docent manual prepared for the Atlanta History Center (1995), 43.

15. Dowling, *American Classicist*, 107.

16. Cooney and Rainwater, *Garden History of Georgia*, 230.

17. Ibid., 228.

18. Dowling, *American Classicist*, 107.

19. Cooney and Rainwater, *Garden History of Georgia*, 230.

20. Atlanta History Center, *Swan House*.

21. Hentz, Adler & Adler, Philip Trammell Shutze, Associate, Job No. 591, "Plan Showing Garden Layout for Mr. E. H. Inmans Residence, Atlanta, Ga., dated December 23, 1925," Kenan Research Center, Atlanta History Center.

22. Cooney and Rainwater, *Garden History of Georgia*, 230.

23. Atlanta History Center, *Swan House*.

24. *Garden Club of America Annual Meeting, Atlanta, April 18th, 19th, and 20th, 1932*, 23, MSS 681, Peachtree Garden Club Records, CGL.

25. Tunnell, "Restoration of the Boxwood Garden," 10–11.

26. Ibid., 10.

27. Ibid., 11.

28. Roberts, "Goizueta Gardens," 9.

29. In 2015, the Atlanta History Center's Goizueta Gardens staff began compiling a cultural landscape report for the entire site. It will trace the history, evolution, and significance of the property; facilitate stewardship of the landscape; and guide decisions about the preservation, restoration, rehabilitation, and reconstruction of elements in Swan House's landscape.

30. Ambrose, "Living Exhibits," 14.

University of Georgia

1. Larry B. Dendy, "University of Georgia," *New Georgia Encyclopedia*, August 4, 2016, accessed September 1, 2016, www.georgiaencyclopedia.org/articles/education /university-georgia.

2. *Augusta (Ga.) Chronicle*, July 25, 1801.

3. Frances T. Thomas, "Athens," *New Georgia Encyclopedia*, August 5, 2016, accessed September 1, 2016, www.georgiaencyclopedia.org/articles/ counties-cities-neighborhoods/athens.

4. The University System of Georgia Board of Regents, "The University of Georgia Master Plan," dated July 22, 1999, prepared by Ayers/Saint/Gross, University of Georgia Consultants, sec. 1, p. 2, https://www.archi-tects.uga.edu/planning/current-master-plan.

5. Dale M. Jaeger, "Campus Planning," *New Georgia Encyclopedia*, June 4, 2013, accessed September 2, 2016, www.georgiaencyclopedia.org/articles/arts-culture /campus-planning. The epigraph is drawn from the University of Georgia's motto on its 1785 seal. "To serve" was later added to the motto without changing the seal. The university motto in English now is "To teach, to serve, and to inquire into the nature of things."

6. Dendy, *Through the Arch*, 21.

7. Franklin College was also the name of the university in its early days.

8. Dendy, *Through the* Arch, 37–38..

9. This development over time can be seen in the University of Georgia's Historic Campus Maps, 1805 to 2006, University Architects for Facilities Planning,

University of Georgia, https://www.architects.uga.edu/maps/historic.

10. Dendy, *Through the Arch*, 21.

11. Ibid., 31.

12. Ibid., 24–25.

13. The Arch was originally referred to as the campus gate. The entrance became known as the Arch in the twentieth century. The university's botanical garden was closed in 1856 because of loss of funding. Funds from the sale of the land and the plants in the garden were allocated to purchase the iron fence for the North Campus. University of Georgia, Prudential Committee, "Minutes, 1834–1857," Hargrett, UA 97-104, box 37, p. 109, minutes from the meeting of August 29, 1856. The minutes of the Prudential Committee also indicate that "two small iron gates [were] to be put in the College enclosure" (minutes from the meeting of May 20, 1857, p. 113). There are no images of that area of the campus in the 1860s.

14. "Library, Old building (Academic building), 1875, Negative #701," Hargrett Library's Historic Images of Athens, Georgia, www.libs.uga.edu/hargrett/selections/athens/uga_rev.html. This image shows the Arch with iron gates, at street level, and the adjacent iron fence.

15. "Campus view, ca. 1850s, Negative #53," Hargrett Library's Historic Images of Athens, Georgia.

16. "Campus view, 1875, Negative #708," Hargrett Library's Historic Images of Athens, Georgia.

17. "Improvement of Campus Grounds," Chancellor's Report, July 1881, 265, "Minutes of the University of Georgia's Board of Trustees, 1878–1882," Hargrett, www.libs.uga.edu/hargrett/archives/trustees/1878-1882.html.

18. Ibid., 264.

19. "Campus Grounds," Chancellor's Report, August 1879, 115–16, "Minutes of the University of Georgia's Board of Trustees, 1878–1882," Hargrett.

20. Dendy, *Through the Arch*, 22.

21. Ibid.

22. "The Campus," Chancellor's Report, July 1882, 320, "Minutes of the University of Georgia's Board of Trustees, 1878–1882," Hargrett.

23. Janine Duncan, "Landscape Evolution (1801–1915): Historic North Campus, University of Georgia," paper prepared for Historic Landscape Management Course 6840, College of Environment and Design, University of Georgia, fall 2016, 15–17.

24. "Campus view, 1900, Negative #1365," Hargrett Library's Historic Images of Athens, Georgia.

25. Duncan, "Landscape Evolution," 30.

26. Dendy, *Through the Arch*, 43, 56–57.

27. Ibid., 21, 44.

28. Ibid., 41.

29. Hubert Owens, "Georgia to Commemorate Founding of First Garden Club," *Garden Gateways* 5 (January 1939): 1; Dendy, *Through the Arch*, 39.

30. University of Georgia Latin American Ethnobotanical Garden, "About the Garden," University of Georgia website, accessed September 9, 2016, http://ethnobot.uga.edu/Abt.html.

31. Jaeger, "Campus Planning."

32. University of Georgia, Campus Arboretum Committee, *Campus Arboretum Walking Tour*, 4.

33. University of Georgia, "UGA by the Numbers," accessed September 8, 2016, https://www.uga.edu/profile/facts.

34. Ibid.

35. The epigraph is drawn from Cooney and Rainwater, *Garden History of Georgia*, 78.

36. Linley, *Georgia Catalog*, 269.

37. Cothran, *Gardens*, 48.

38. Nichols, *Early Architecture of Georgia*, 117.

39. Cothran, *Gardens*, 103.

40. Owens, *Personal History*, 109.

41. Cothran, *Gardens*, 103.

42. Owens, *Personal History*, 108.

43. NRHP, Cobbham Historic District, Athens, Clarke County, Georgia, National Register #78000973, item 7.

44. Cooney and Rainwater, *Garden History of Georgia*, 78.

45. Ibid.

46. Ibid.

47. Ibid.

48. Ibid.

49. Ibid.

50. Marshall, *Historic Houses of Athens*, 42.

51. Owens, *Personal History*, 108.

52. Cooney and Rainwater, *Garden History of Georgia*, 78.

53. Hitchcock, "Colonial Revival Gardens," 39.

54. Owens, *Personal History*, 107–8.

55. Ibid., 109.

56. Ibid., 108.

57. Ibid.

58. According to the landscape historian Susan Hitchcock, Harry Baldwin (BLA, 1950) contributed to the design of the rose garden and terrace as part of his senior project.

59. Owens, *Personal History*, 108.

60. Ibid., 108–9.

61. "Grant-Hill-White-Bradshaw Place," miscellaneous papers cited from Dexter Adams, landscape architect,, 2–4, MSS 1007, GHLIR.

62. Janine L. Duncan, e-mail message to Mary Ann Eaddy, September 22, 2016.

63. Marshall, *Historic Houses of Athens*, 42.

64. NRHP, University President's House, Athens, Clarke County, Georgia, National Register #72000380, item 8.

65. Owens, "Georgia to Commemorate Founding." The epigraph is drawn from this source.

66. Today, the antebellum house is referred to as the Lumpkin House and sometimes the Founders House. There are two other historic Lumpkin Houses in Athens, both listed in the National Register of Historic Places. One is the Governor Wilson Lumpkin House (1844), also known as the Rock House, which is located on Cedar Street on the University of Georgia South Campus. The other is the Joseph Henry Lumpkin House, also known as the Athens Womans Club House, which is located on Prince Avenue.

67. NRHP, "Garden Club of Georgia Museum—Headquarters House, Founder's Memorial Garden," Athens, Clarke County, Georgia, 1972, National Register #72000376.

68. Cultural Landscape Foundation, Styles of Designed Landscapes, "Colonial Revival," accessed September 10, 2016, http://tclf.org/category /designed-landscape-style/colonial-revival.

69. Griswold and Weller, *Golden Age of American Gardens*, 38.

70. Cultural Landscape Foundation, "Colonial Revival."

71. Ibid.

72. Owens, *Personal History*, 46.

73. Hitchcock, "Colonial Revival Gardens," 38.

74. Minutes from the UGA Board of Trustees indicate that this antebellum structure was approved for construction as a boardinghouse at the August 4, 1859, meeting. Minutes from the August 1, 1860, meeting report that the boardinghouse would soon be finished. University of Georgia, Board of Trustees, Minutes, vol. 4, part 1, November 6, 1858–July 1877, Hargrett, UA 97-104, box 15 (typed transcript). The National Register of Historic Places form indicates that the antebellum structure was constructed in 1857. NRHP, "Garden Club of Georgia Museum—Headquarters House, Founder's Memorial Garden," Athens, Clarke County, Georgia, 1972, National Register #72000376.

75. Dexter Adams, "Founders Memorial Garden, Athens, Georgia: A Site History with an Overview of Existing Conditions," report prepared for the University of Georgia, 7.

76. Ibid., 6–7.

77. Ibid., 7–8.

78. Ibid., 8.

79. "Georgia's Tribute to Founders," *Garden Gateways* 5 (March 1939): 3.

80. Ibid; Grace Arrington Kempton, "Georgia's Garden Club Memorial Garden in Athens," *Garden Gateways* 6 (May 1940): 3, 25.

81. Adams, "Founders Memorial Garden," 11.

82. Kempton, "Georgia's Garden Club Memorial Garden in Athens,"3.

83. Ibid., 3.

84. Ibid., 25.

85. Ibid., 25.

86. "Founder's Memorial, Terrace and Perennial Gardens Completed," *Garden Gateways* 7 (October 1941): 9.

87. Ibid.

88. Ibid.

89. "Future Plans for Memorial Garden: Two New Units Added to Horticultural Shrine on Campus of State University," *Atlanta Journal*, August 3, 1941.

90. Ibid.

91. Ibid.

92. Tracy D. Cohen, "Living Memorial," *Garden Gateways* 12 (June 1946): 13.

93. Mrs. Ralph Black, "Founders Memorial Garden," *Garden Gateways* 8 (May 1942): 12.

94. Hitchcock, "Colonial Revival Gardens," 40–41.

95. Ibid., 41; Adams, "Founders Memorial Garden," 19.

96. Tracy D. Cohen, "In Memory," *Garden Gateways* 11 (April 1945): 1.

97. Adams, "Founders Memorial Garden," 25.

98. Bessie Fray Kirven, "Memories and Trees," *Garden Gateways* 11 (October 1945): 5.

99. Hitchcock, "Colonial Revival Gardens," 47.

100. Ibid.

101. Kirven, "Memories and Trees," 5.

102. Adams, "Founders Memorial Garden," 30.

103. Ibid., 32.

104. "Memorial Garden Advisory Committee Meeting Report," May 26, 1988, Cothran Papers. The committee chairman was the landscape architect, garden historian, and author James R. Cothran.

105. Adams, "Founders Memorial Garden," 33.

106. Ibid.

107. Founders Memorial Garden Mission Statement, University of Georgia College of Environment and Design, March 2009, Founders Memorial Garden Office Archives, University of Georgia.

108. Jaeger Company, "Founders Memorial Garden Management Plan."

Valley View

The epigraph is drawn from Cooney and Rainwater, *Garden History of Georgia*, 110.

1. James R. Cothran, vice president, Planning and Landscape Architecture, Robert and Company, to David Lamm, state conservationist, February 22, 2007, in support of the "Bartow County–Valley View Farm Conservation Easement Project: A Farm and Ranch Lands Protection Program Proposal," submitted to the USDA–Natural Resource Conservation Service by the Bartow County Government, April 27, 2007.

2. Chantal Parker, "Bartow County," *New Georgia Encyclopedia*, November 30, 2016, accessed December 1, 2016, www.georgiaencyclopedia.org/articles/counties-cities-neighborhoods/bartow-county.

3. Ibid.

4. Family descendants state that Sproull acquired the acreage from his brother-in-law, Wade Cothran, an early settler in Rome, Georgia, and that the original deed was lost when the Cass County Courthouse, in Cassville, was burned during the Civil War.

5. Cothran, *Gardens*, 118.

6. Rebecca Sproull Fouché, "Our Mother's Memories of That Other Beautiful World We Used to Live in before the War," September 1912, typescript, original at Valley View, Cartersville, Georgia.

7. "Valley View Farm Main House, Cartersville, Georgia Historic Structure Report," prepared by students in the Conservation of Historic Building Materials course, Heritage Preservation Graduate Program, Georgia State University, fall 2011, 12, from MSS 1007, GHLIR.

8. NRHP, "Valley View," Cartersville vicinity, Bartow County, Georgia, 1974, National Register #74000657, item 7, p. 2.

9. Ibid.

10. "Valley View Farm Main House, Cartersville," 23.

11. Atlanta Historical Society, *Neat Pieces*, 47.

12. Fouché, "Our Mother's Memories."

13. "Valley View Farm Main House, Cartersville," 59–60.

14. Vlach, *Back of the Big House*, 33–34.

15. Georgia Historic Landscape Initiative Survey Form for Valley View, completed by Robert Fouché Norton, MSS 1007, GHLIR.

16. "Valley View Farm Main House, Cartersville," 16.

17. Ibid., 15; copies of the 1860 Cass County Census and Slave Schedule in the appendix to the report, MSS 1007, GHLIR. The slave schedule indicates that James Sproull owned four enslaved people and that his mother, Rebecca Walkup Caldwell Sproull, owned thirty-three enslaved people.

18. Vlach, *Back of the Big House*, 33–34.

19. Georgia Historic Landscape Initiative Survey Form for Valley View; Cooney and Rainwater, *Garden History of Georgia*, 111.

20. Cooney and Rainwater, *Garden History of* Georgia, 111; Cothran, *Gardens*, 116–17.

21. Cooney and Rainwater, *Garden History of Georgia*, 110; Cothran, *Gardens*, 117.

22. Fouché, "Our Mother's Memories."

23. Ibid.

24. Ibid.

25. NRHP, "Valley View," Cartersville vicinity, Bartow County, Georgia, 1974, National Register #74000657, item 8, p. 3.

26. Georgia Historic Landscape Initiative Survey Form for Valley View. According to Rebecca's memoirs and family oral history, Union troops brought the horses into the parlor because Confederate snipers were shooting at them. The names of two Union soldiers are still visible in an upstairs closet.

27. Fouché, "Our Mother's Memories."

28. "Obituary of Charles William Sproull," *Cartersville (Ga.) Free Press*, March 29, 1883.

29. "Georgia, County Marriages, 1785–1950," database with images, FamilySearch, accessed July 18, 2016, https://familysearch.org/ark:/61903/1:1:KXJT-WZL, Robert T. Fouché and Rebecca C. Sproull, February 20, 1868; citing marriage record, Bartow, Ga., county courthouse; FHL microfilm 283,520.

30. U.S. Census, 1880, database with images, FamilySearch, accessed July 15, 2016, https://familysearch.org/ark:/61903/1:1:M8LY-9T2, Robert T. Fouché, Rome, Floyd County, Ga.; citing enumeration district ED 64, sheet 156D, NARA microfilm publication T9, roll 0146; FHL microfilm 1,254,146. Robert Turnbull Fouché died in 1908, and his wife, Rebecca, died in 1918.

31. Mary Norton, ed., "Life at Valley View," Norton Family Archives, Cartersville, Ga.

32. "Valley View Farm Main House, Cartersville," 17.

33. Ibid.

34. Ibid.

35. Valley View photographs, ca. late 1800s and early 1900s, Norton Family Archives, Cartersville, Ga.

36. Cooney and Rainwater, *Garden History of Georgia*, 110.

37. Ibid.

38. Ibid.

39. Ibid.

40. Georgia Historic Landscape Initiative Survey Form for Valley View.

41. Valley View photographs, ca. late 1800s and early 1900s, Norton Family Archives, Cartersville, Ga.

42. "Valley View Farm Main House, Cartersville," 18.

43. Chris Hastings, master arborist, to David Lamm, state conservationist February 12, 2007, in support of the "Bartow County–Valley View Farm Conservation Easement Project."

44. Gregory B. Paxton, president and CEO of the Georgia Trust for Historic Preservation, to David Lamm, state conservationist, March 26, 2007, in support of the "Bartow County–Valley View Farm Conservation Easement Project."

45. "Preservation Plan," "Bartow County–Valley View Farm Conservation Easement Project," appendix S, 1.

46. Mountain Conservation Trust, "Valley View Farm," 6–7.

47. Georgia Trust for Historic Preservation, "2015 Preservation Awards."

Wormsloe and Wormsloe State Historic Site

1. Coulter, *Wormsloe*, 15.

2. Noble Jones originally called his estate "Wormslow." The spelling was changed to "Wormsloe" by his descendant George Wymberley Jones De Renne.

3. Coulter, *Wormsloe*, x. The epigraph is drawn from p. 255 of the same source.

4. Swanson, *Remaking Wormsloe Plantation*, 41–43.

5. Ibid., 44–46.

6. Coulter, *Wormsloe*, 173.

7. Swanson, *Remaking Wormsloe Plantation*, 57.

8. Coulter, *Wormsloe*, 213, 215–16; Bragg, *De Renne*, 56–58.

9. Coulter, *Wormsloe*, 214–16.

10. Ibid., 214; Cooney and Rainwater, *Garden History of Georgia*, 20.

11. Swanson, *Remaking Wormsloe Plantation*, 77, 88.

12. Ibid., 66.

13. Ibid., 76–77.

14. Bragg, *De Renne*, 144.

15. Coulter, *Wormsloe*, 252.

16. Bragg, *De Renne*, 223; Swanson, *Remaking Wormsloe Plantation*, 123–28.

17. Swanson, *Remaking Wormsloe Plantation*, 134.

18. Bragg, *De Renne*, 229.

19. Ibid., 230.

20. See "Photograph of Landscaped Grounds with Gazebo, 1899" in Swanson, *Remaking Wormsloe Plantation*, image insert.

21. Bragg, *De Renne*, 231.

22. Ibid.

23. Ibid., 316.

24. Swanson, *Remaking Wormsloe Plantation*, 148.

25. Bragg, *De Renne*, 327.

26. Cultural Landscape Foundation, Styles of Designed Landscapes, "Colonial Revival," accessed November 28, 2016, http://tclf.org/category/designed-landscape-style/colonial-revival.

27. Ibid.

28. Cooney and Rainwater, *Garden History of Georgia*, 370, 372.

29. See "Wormsloe Garden, 1928 Additions by Augusta Floyd De Renne," in Swanson, *Remaking Wormsloe Plantation*, image insert; Cooney and Rainwater, *Garden History of Georgia*, 370.

30. Cooney and Rainwater, *Garden History of Georgia*, 370.

31. Ibid., 372–73.

32. See "Wormsloe Garden, 1928 Additions by Augusta Floyd De Renne," in Swanson, *Remaking Wormsloe Plantation*.

33. Ibid.

34. Cooney and Rainwater, *Garden History of Georgia*, 372.

35. Ibid., 20.

36. Bragg, *De Renne*, 354, 357.

37. Ibid., 388.

38. Writers' Program of the Work Projects Administration in the State of Georgia, *Georgia*, 268.

39. Paul Cady and Cari Goetcheus, "Wormsloe Cultural Landscape Report: History, Existing Conditions, Analysis, and Evaluation," draft, 99, Cultural Landscape Laboratory, University of Georgia, 2015.

40. Ibid.

41. Joe D. Tanner to Mr. and Mrs. Craig Barrow Jr., September 22, 1978, Georgia Archives, RCB 15870.

42. Cady and Goetcheus, "Wormsloe Cultural Landscape Report," 108.

43. Diana D. Barrow, e-mail message to Mary Ann Eaddy, August 26, 2016.

44. Ibid.

45. Ibid.

46. Ibid.

47. Cady and Goetcheus, "Wormsloe Cultural Landscape Report," 113.

48. Barrow, e-mail message to Eaddy.

49. Ibid.

50. Ibid.

51. Ibid.

52. Ibid.

53. Craig Barrow III, conversation with Mary Ann Eaddy, Wormsloe, June 25, 2014.

54. Barrow, e-mail message to Eaddy.

55. Carter, *Addresses of Jimmy Carter*, 176. The epigraph is also drawn from this source.

56. Swanson, *Remaking Wormsloe Plantation*, 174–77.

57. Wormsloe State Historic Site Visitor Pass, May 2014.

58. Governor Zell Miller, executive order, November 6, 1998, Georgia Archives, RCB 51225, RG-SG-S, 1-1-3.

59. Seabrook, *World of the Salt Marsh*, 245; Wormsloe State Historic Site Visitor Pass, May 2014.

60. Wormsloe State Historic Visitor Pass, May 2014.

Zahner-Slick Garden

The epigraph is drawn from Loyer Lawton Zahner, "Design in the Garden," ca. 1930, 14, from the private collection of Edward L. Daugherty, Atlanta, Georgia.

1. Hewitt et al., *Carrère & Hastings Architects*.

2. "Plan for Subdivision of the Property of Peachtree Heights Park Co., Atlanta, Georgia," designed by Carrère and Hastings, 1910–11, Neighborhood Plat Maps, Land District 17, Land Lots 111, 112, 113, Kenan Research Center, Atlanta History Center.

3. Buckhead Heritage Society, "Peachtree Heights Park Historic District," accessed June 18, 2016, www.buckheadheritage.com/content/history/ historic-neighborhoods/peachtree-heights-park.

4. NRHP, Peachtree Heights Park Historic District, Atlanta, Fulton County, Georgia, 1980, National Register #80004457, pp. 1–2.

5. Handwritten record of the search and acquisition of the property at 45 Peachtree Battle Avenue, written by Kenyon B. Zahner, April 1924, private collection of Edward L. Daugherty.

6. Robert Zahner Personality File, Kenan Research Center, Atlanta History Center.

7. "Lawton-Zahner; Lawton-Daugherty," *Atlanta Constitution*, June 28, 1921, 6.

8. Obituary of Loyer Lawton Zahner, *Franklin (N.C.) Press*, July 3, 1987.

9. Edward L. Daugherty, interview by Staci L. Catron, Atlanta, November 3, 2016.

10. Primrose Garden Club scrapbook, MSS 656, Primrose Garden Club Records, CGL.

11. Ibid.

12. Zahner, "Design in the Garden," 3.

13. Ibid.

14. Flores, "Early Works of Burge & Stevens", 103.

15. Cooney and Rainwater, *Garden History of Georgia*, 278.

16. Zahner, "Design in the Garden," 7.

17. Cooney and Rainwater, *Garden History of Georgia*, 278.

18. Loyer Lawton Zahner, pencil drawing, ca. 1930, private collection of Edward L. Daugherty, Atlanta.

19. Mary Will McCall Cauthorn, "Mrs. Zahner's Garden," *Atlanta Journal*, June 15, 1930; Cooney and Rainwater, *Garden History of Georgia*, 280.

20. Cauthorn, "Mrs. Zahner's Garden."

21. Ibid.; Cooney and Rainwater, *Garden History of Georgia*, 280.

22. Cauthorn, "Mrs. Zahner's Garden."

23. *Garden Club of America Annual Meeting, Atlanta, April 18th, 19th, and 20th, 1932*, MSS 681, Peachtree Garden Club Records, CGL.

24. Mitchell, *Gardens of Georgia*, 173.

25. Zahner, "Design in the Garden," 14.

BIBLIOGRAPHY

Books, Articles, and Scholarly Works

Adams, Dexter. "Founders Memorial Garden, Athens, Georgia: A Site History with an Overview of Existing Conditions." Report prepared for the University of Georgia, 2000.

Alexander, Bill. *The Biltmore Nursery: A Botanical Legacy.* Charleston, S.C.: Natural History Press, 2007.

Ambrose, Andy. "Living Exhibits: Glimpses of Atlanta's Past in the Structures, Historic Houses, Gardens and Topography at the Atlanta History Center." *Atlanta History: A Journal of Georgia and the South* 37, no. 3 (Fall 1993): 6–15.

Armstrong, Zella. *The History of Hamilton County and Chattanooga, Tennessee.* Vol. 2. 1940. Reprint, Johnson City, Tenn.: Overmountain Press, 1993.

Aslet, Clive. *The American Country House.* New Haven, Conn.: Yale University Press, 1990.

Atlanta Historical Society. *Neat Pieces: The Plain-Style Furniture of Nineteenth-Century Georgia.* Athens: University of Georgia Press in conjunction with the Atlanta History Center and the Madison Morgan Cultural Center, 2006.

Atlanta History Center. *Swan House at the Atlanta History Center.* Atlanta: Atlanta History Center, 2015.

Bailey, Cornelia, and Christena Bledsoe. *God, Dr. Buzzard, and the Bolito Man: A Saltwater Geechee Talks about Life on Sapelo Island.* New York: Doubleday, 2000.

Bartram, William. *The Travels of William Bartram: Naturalist's Edition.* Edited by Francis Harper. Athens: University of Georgia Press, 1998.

Beck, Lewis H. *Historic Gardens of Georgia.* Griffin, Ga.: Southern States Printing, 1942.

Bell, Laura Palmer. "The Vanishing Gardens of Savannah." *Georgia Historical Quarterly* 28, no.3 (September 1944): 196–208.

Bell, Malcolm, Jr. *Savannah.* Savannah, Ga.: Historic Savannah Foundation, 1977.

Berry Trails: An Historic and Contemporary Guide to Berry College. 3rd ed. Mount Berry, Ga.: Berry College, 2001.

Bigham, Jennifer and Josh Fisher. "Tea in the Garden." Program presentation and tour, annual meeting of the Redbud District of the Garden Club of Georgia, Dunaway Gardens, October 15, 2015.

Birnbaum, Charles A. *Protecting Cultural Landscapes: Planning, Treatment, and Management of Historic Landscapes.* Washington, D.C.: U.S. Department of the Interior, National Park Service, 1994.

Birnbaum, Charles A., and Mary V. Hughes, eds. *Design with Culture: Claiming America's Landscape Heritage.* Charlottesville: University of Virginia Press, 2005.

Birnbaum, Charles A., and Robin Karson, eds. *Pioneers of American Landscape Design.* New York: McGraw-Hill, 2000.

Bishop, W. Jeff, *Newnan.* Images of America. Charleston, S.C.: Arcadia, 2014.

Bragg, William Harris. *De Renne: Three Generations of a Georgia Family.* Athens: University of Georgia Press, 1999.

Bush, Rebecca. "The Bradley Olmsted Garden." *Muscogiana* 24, no. 2: (Fall 2013): 1–15.

Carruthers, Annette. *The Arts and Crafts Movement in Scotland: A History.* New Haven, Conn.: Yale University Press, 2013.

Carter, Jimmy. *Addresses of Jimmy Carter (James Earl Carter), Governor of Georgia, 1971–1975.* Edited by Frank Daniel. Atlanta: Georgia Department of Archives and History, 1975.

Cashin, Edward F., and Glenn T. Eskew, eds. *Paternalism in a Southern City: Race, Religion, and Gender in Augusta, Georgia.* Athens: University of Georgia Press, 2001.

Chirhart, Ann Short, and Betty Wood, eds. *Georgia Women: Their Lives and Times.* Vol. 1. Athens: University of Georgia Press, 2009.

Clarke, Erskine. *Dwelling Place: A Plantation Epic.* New Haven, Conn.: Yale University Press, 2005.

Cofer, Carl H. *The Barnsley Gardens Story.* Adairsville, Ga.: Barnsley Gardens, 1992.

Coker, Clent. *Barnsley Gardens at Woodlands: The Illustrious Dream.* Atlanta, Ga.: Julia, 2000.

Coleman, Kenneth, ed. *A History of Georgia.* 2nd ed. Athens: University of Georgia Press, 1991.

Cooney, Loraine M., comp., and Hattie C. Rainwater, ed. *Garden History of Georgia, 1733–1933.* Atlanta: Peachtree Garden Club, 1933.

Cooper, Polly Wylly. *Isle of Hope: Wormsloe and Bethesda.* Images of America. Reprint ed. Charleston, S.C.: Arcadia, 2002.

Cordery, Stacy A. *Juliette Gordon Low: The Remarkable Founder of the Girl Scouts.* New York: Viking, 2012.

Cothran, James R. *Gardens and Historic Plants of the Antebellum South.* Columbia: University of South Carolina Press, 2003.

Coulter, E. Merton. *Wormsloe: Two Centuries of a Georgia Family.* Athens: University of Georgia Press, 1955.

Cox, Connie M., and Darlene M. Walsh, eds. *Providence: Selected Correspondence of George Hull Camp, 1837–1907; Son of the North, Citizen of the South.* Macon, Ga.: Indigo, 2008.

Cox, James A. D. *Savannah: Secret and Public Gardens.* Savannah, Ga.: Historic Savannah Foundation, 2000.

Cridland, Robert B. *Practical Landscape Gardening.* 2nd ed. New York: De La Mare, 1918.

Darke, Rick. *In Harmony with Nature: Lessons from the Arts and Crafts Garden.* New York: MetroBooks, 2000.

Deal, Sandra D., Jennifer W. Dickey, and Catherine M. Lewis. *Memories of the Mansion: The Story of Georgia's Governor's Mansion.* Athens: University of Georgia Press, 2015.

Dendy, Larry B. *Through the Arch: An Illustrated Guide to the University of Georgia Campus.* Athens: University of Georgia Press, 2013.

Descriptive LaGrange, Georgia. LaGrange, Ga.: Reporter Job Office, 1881.

Dick, Susan E., and Mandi D. Johnson. *Savannah, 1733–2000: Photographs from the Collection of the Georgia Historical Society.* Images of America. Charleston, S.C.: Arcadia, 2001.

Dickey, Jennifer W. *A History of the Berry Schools on the Mountain Campus.* Charleston, S.C.: History Press, 2013.

Dickey, Ouida, and Doyle Mathis. *Berry College: A History.* Athens: University of Georgia Press, 2005.

Dolder, Ced. "Clermont Lee, (1914–2006): Pioneering Savannah Landscape Architect." *Magnolia* 27, no. 2 (Spring 2014): 1, 3–6.

Donhardt, Christine. "Ferrell Gardens: A Designed Landscape of the 19th Century." Master's thesis, University of Georgia, 2007.

Dowling, Elizabeth Meredith. *American Classicist: The Architecture of Philip Trammell Shutze.* New York: Rizzoli, 1989.

Downing, A. J. *Cottage Residences; or, A Series of Designs for Rural Cottages and Cottage Villas, and Their Gardens and Grounds, Adapted to North America.* 2nd ed. New York and London: Wiley and Putnam, 1842.

———. *Treatise on the Theory and Practice of Landscape Gardening, Adapted to North America.* New York and London: Wiley and Putnam, 1841.

Favretti, Rudy J., and Joy P. Favretti. *For Every House a Garden: A Guide for Reproducing Period Gardens.* Hanover, N.H.: University Press of New England, 1990.

———. *Landscapes and Gardens for Historic Buildings.* 2nd ed. Nashville, Tenn.: American Association for State and Local History, 1991.

Ferree, Barr. *American Estates and Gardens.* New York: Munn, 1904. Biodiversity Heritage Library, http://www.biodiversitylibrary.org.

Finch, Bill, Beth Maynor Young, Rhett Johnson, and John C. Hall, *Longleaf, Far as the Eye Can See: A New Vision of North America's Richest Forest.* Chapel Hill: University of North Carolina Press, 2012.

Flores, Carol A. "The Early Works of Burge & Stevens, Stevens & Wilkinson, 1919–1949." Master's thesis, Georgia Institute of Technology, 1991.

Frey, Douglas M. *Marietta: The Gem City of Georgia.* Marietta: Cobb Landmarks and Historical Society, 2010.

Fuller E. Callaway Foundation. "Hills and Dales Visitors Guide and Map." LaGrange, Ga.: Fuller E. Callaway Foundation, 2004.

Garden Club of America Annual Meeting, Atlanta, April 18th, 19th, and 20th, 1932. Atlanta: Peachtree Garden Club, 1932.

Garrett, Franklin M. *Atlanta and Environs: A Chronicle of Its People and Events.* Vol. 1. 1954. Reprint, Athens: University of Georgia Press, 1969.

Georgia Department of Natural Resources. Wildlife Resources Division. *A Comprehensive Wildlife Conservation Strategy for Georgia.* Social Circle:

Georgia Department of Natural Resources, Wildlife Resources Division, 2005.

Georgia Historic Preservation Division. *Georgia's Living Places: Historic Houses in Their Landscaped Settings.* Atlanta: Georgia Department of Natural Resources, Division of Parks, Recreation & Historic Sites, Historic Preservation Section, 1991.

Georgia Trust for Historic Preservation. "2015 Preservation Awards." *Rambler* 42, no. 2 (Summer 2015): 12.

Gillespie, Michele. *Katherine and R. J. Reynolds: Partners of Fortune in the Making of the New South.* Athens: University of Georgia Press, 2012.

Gomez, Marisa C., and E. G. Daves Rossell, eds. *Savannah and the Lowcountry: Vernacular Architecture Forum 2007; Field Guide for the 28th Annual Meeting, Savannah, Georgia, March 28–31, 2007.* Savannah: Savannah College of Art and Design, 2007.

Graham, Wade. *American Eden: From Monticello to Central Park to Our Backyards: What Our Gardens Tell Us about Who We Are.* New York: HarperCollins, 2011.

Griswold, Mac K., Eleanor Weller, Helen E. Rollins, and the Garden Club of America. *The Golden Age of American Gardens: Proud Owners, Private Estates, 1890–1940.* New York: Abrams, in association with the Garden Club of America, 1991.

Haltom, Susan, and Jane Roy Brown. *One Writer's Garden: Eudora Welty's Home Place.* Jackson: University Press of Mississippi, 2011.

Hamlin, Talbot. *Greek Revival Architecture in America: Being an Account of Important Trends in American Architecture and American Life prior to the War between the States.* 1944. Reprint, New York: Dover, 1964.

Hartle, Robert, Jr. *Atlanta's Druid Hills: A Brief History.* Charleston, S.C.: History Press, 2008.

Heeb, Mark William. "Sapelo Island, Georgia: Analysis of a Multiple Period Landscape Using National Park Service Landscape Preservation Methodology." Master's thesis, University of Georgia, 1997.

Hewitt, Mark Alan, Kate Lemos, William Morrison, and Charles D. Warren. *Carrère & Hastings Architects.* New York: Acanthus, 2006.

Hitchcock, Susan L. "Savannah Gardens: Past and Present." February 28, 2001. Unpublished paper, in author's possession.

———. "The Colonial Revival Gardens of Hubert Bond Owens." Master's thesis, University of Georgia, 1997.

Hoffman, Nelson Miles. "Godfrey Barnsley, 1805–1873: British Cotton Factor in the South." Master's thesis, University of Kansas, 1964.

Hollis, Tim. *The Land of the Smokies: Great Mountain Memories.* Jackson: University Press of Mississippi, 2007.

———. *See Rock City: The History of Rock City Gardens.* Charleston, S.C.: History Press, 2009.

Hood, Davyd Foard. "The Renaissance of Southern Gardening in the Early Twentieth Century." *Journal of Garden History* 16, no. 2 (Summer 1996): 129–152.

Howett, Catherine M. "Barnsley Gardens: The Facts behind the Fables." *Georgia Historical Quarterly* 64, no. 2 (1980): 172–189.

———. "Criteria for the Landscape Development of Bulloch Hall, Roswell, Georgia," 1984. This typed essay is an attachment to a student paper by Marty Goldsmith in MSS 989, Cothran Papers. It is also included in Roswell Historic Preservation Commission, "Bulloch Hall," in which Catherine M. Howett is listed as the plan's landscape historian.

———. "A Southern Lady's Legacy: The Italian 'Terraces' of La Grange, Georgia." *Journal of Garden History* 2 (1982): 343–360.

Howett, Catherine M., and Atlanta Historical Society. *Land of Our Own: 250 Years of Landscape and Gardening Tradition in Georgia, 1733–1983.* Atlanta: Atlanta Historical Society, 1983.

Huddleston, Connie M., and Gwendolyn I. Koehler, eds. *The Bulloch Letters.* Vol. 1, *Mittie and Thee: An 1853 Roosevelt Romance.* Roswell, Ga.: Friends of Bulloch, 2015.

Jaeger Company. *Coffin-Reynolds Mansion, Sapelo Island, Georgia: Landscape Analysis and Recommendations; Final Report.* Prepared for the Georgia Department of Natural Resources, July 1998.

———. "Founders Memorial Garden Management Plan for the University of Georgia—College of Environment and Design, October 6, 2014."

Jaeger Company and Robert and Company. *Barrington Hall: Master Plan Report.* Prepared for the City of Roswell, Ga., August 25, 2006.

Jansma, Harriet H., and C. Allan Brown. "Landscape Gardening in the South: Changes in Residential Site Design in a Nineteenth-Century Southern Town." *Journal of Garden History* 16, no. 2 (Summer 1996): 111–128.

Johnson, Forrest Clark, III. *Histories of LaGrange and Troup County, Georgia.* Vol. 5. LaGrange, Ga.: Sutherland–St. Dunston, 1993.

Jordan, Michael, and Mick McCay. *Savannah Square by Square.* Savannah, Ga.: Historic Savannah Foundation, 2015.

Kane, Harnett T., and Inez Henry. *Miracle in the Mountains*. Garden City, N.Y.: Doubleday, 1956.

Karson, Robin. *A Genius for Place: American Landscapes of the Country Place Era*. Amherst: University of Massachusetts Press in association with the Library of American Landscape History, 2007.

Karson, Robin, Jane Roy Brown, and Sarah Allaback, eds., *Warren H. Manning: Landscape Architect and Environmental Planner*. Critical Studies in the History of Environmental Design. Athens: University of Georgia Press in association with the Library of American Landscape History, 2017.

Kelso, William M. *Captain Jones's Wormslow: A Historical, Archaeological, and Architectural Study of an Eighteenth-Century Plantation Site near Savannah, Georgia*. Athens: University of Georgia Press, 1979.

Knight, Lucian Lamar. *A Standard History of Georgia and Georgians*. Vol. 4. Chicago: Lewis, 1917.

Lane, Mills. *Architecture of the Old South: Georgia*. Savannah, Ga.: Beehive, 1986.

Latrobe, Charles Joseph. *The Rambler in North America*. Vol. 2. New York: Harper and Brothers, 1835.

Laufer, Geraldine Admich. "Rocking the Landscape: Atlanta Artist and Gardener Is Renovating a Historic Rock Garden." *Magnolia* 27 (Summer 2014): 3, 8–10.

Lawliss, Lucy A. "The Bradley Residence, 1920–1937, Columbus, Georgia: Documentation of a Landscape (Compiled from research at the Library of Congress Manuscript Division, Frederick Law Olmsted Collection and The Frederick Law Olmsted National Historic Site Archives)." Report prepared for the Columbus Museum, 1988.

———. "Residential Work of the Olmsted Firm in Georgia, 1893–1937." *Magnolia Essays: Occasional Papers of the Southern Garden History Society* 1 (Spring 1993): 24–35.

Lawliss, Lucy, Daniel Eberly, Melissa Tufts, Maudie Martin Huff, and Julie Martin McClelland. "Julia Orme Martin: Atlanta Landscape Designer." *Garden Citings: Cherokee Garden Library Newsletter of the Atlanta History Center* (Fall 2012), 2–3.

Lawliss, Lucy, Caroline Loughlin, and Lauren Meier. *The Master List of Design Projects of the Olmsted Firm, 1857–1979*. Washington, D.C.: National Association for Olmsted Parks, 2008.

Linley, John. *The Georgia Catalog: Historic American Buildings Survey; A Guide to the Architecture of the State*. Athens: University of Georgia Press, 1982.

Lockwood, Alice G. B., ed. *Gardens of Colony and State: Gardens and Gardeners of the American Colonies and of the Republic before 1840*. New York: Published for the Garden Club of America by C. Scribner's Sons, 1931–34.

Lovell, Caroline Couper. *The Golden Isles of Georgia*. Boston: Little, Brown, 1933.

Marquis, Albert Nelson, ed. *The Book of Detroiters: A Biographical Dictionary of Leading Living Men of the City of Detroit*. 2nd ed. Chicago: Marquis, 1914. Available at the Hathi Trust Digital Library, www.haithitrust.org.

Marshall, Charlotte Thomas. *Historic Houses of Athens*. Athens, Ga.: Athens Historical Society, 1987.

Martin, Clarece. *A Glimpse of the Past: The History of Bulloch Hall and Roswell, Georgia*. Roswell, Ga.: Historic Roswell, 1973.

———. *A History of Roswell Presbyterian Church*. Dallas: Taylor, 1984.

Martin, Harold H. *This Happy Isle: The Story of Sea Island and the Cloister*. Sea Island, Ga.: Sea Island, 1981.

Martin, Van Jones, and William R. Mitchell. *Landmark Homes of Georgia, 1733–1983: Two Hundred and Fifty Years of Architecture, Interiors, and Gardens*. Savannah, Ga.: Golden Coast, 1982.

McAlester, Virginia, and Lee McAlester. *A Field Guide to American Houses*. New York: Knopf, 1984.

McCash, William Barton, and June Hall McCash. *The Jekyll Island Club: Southern Haven for America's Millionaires*. Athens: University of Georgia Press, 1989.

McCullough, David. *Mornings on Horseback*. 1981. New York: Simon & Schuster Paperbacks, 2013.

McFeely, William S. *Sapelo's People: A Long Walk into Freedom*. New York: Norton, 1994.

McKechnie, Gary. *USA 101: A Guide to America's Iconic Places, Events, and Festivals*. Washington, D.C.: National Geographic, 2009.

Melton, Buckner F., and Carol Willcox Melton. *Fuller E. Callaway: Portrait of a New South Citizen*. Winston-Salem, N.C.: Looking Glass Books in association with the Georgia Humanities Council and the Fuller E. Callaway Foundation, 2015.

Mitchell, William R. *Classic Savannah: History, Homes, and Gardens*. Savannah, Ga.: Golden Coast, 1987.

———. *Gardens of Georgia*. Atlanta: Peachtree for the Garden Club of Georgia, 1989.

———. *Thomasville: History, Homes, and Southern Hospitality*. Savannah, Ga.: Golden Coast, 2014.

Morgan, Danielle. "From Old South to New South: Seeds of Industrialization for Chattanooga, Tennessee, 1863–1877." *Journal of East Tennessee History* 86 (2014): 18–40.

Morine, David E. *Good Dirt: Confessions of a Conservationist*. New York: Globe Pequot, 1990.

Moses, Elsie Crutchfield. *The Georgia Governor's Mansion, Atlanta, Georgia*. Atlanta: Georgia Building Authority, 1973.

Mountain Conservation Trust. "Valley View Farm . . . 160 Years of History Preserved." *Mountain Conservation Trust Newsletter* 12, no. 1 (Winter 2009–2010): 6–7.

Myers, Robert Manson, ed. *The Children of Pride: A True Story of Georgia and the Civil War*. New Haven, Conn.: Yale University Press, 1973.

Nestor, Bradley A. "Paradise Rediscovered: An Archival Restoration of the Horticultural and Design Elements of Barnsley Gardens, Georgia." Master's thesis, University of Georgia, 1995.

Nestor, Bradley A., and William A. Mann. "An Archival Restoration of the Horticultural and Design Elements of Barnsley Gardens, Georgia." *Landscape and Urban Planning* 42 (1998): 107–22.

Nichols, Frederick Doveton. *The Early Architecture of Georgia*. Chapel Hill: University of North Carolina Press, 1957.

Owens, Hubert B. *Personal History of Landscape Architecture in the Last Sixty Years, 1922–1982*. Edited by Gail Karwoski. Athens: University of Georgia Alumni Society, 1983.

Paden, Rebecca Nash, and Joe McTyre. *Historic Roswell, Georgia*. Images of America. Charleston, S.C.: Arcadia, 2001.

Patten, Z. C., and Cartter Patten. *So Firm a Foundation*. [Chattanooga, Tenn.?]: Cartter Patten, 1968.

Perkerson, Medora Field. *White Columns in Georgia*. New York: Rinehart, 1952.

Power, Virginia Wing. *Ginny's Chairs*. Chattanooga, Tenn.: BookTree, 1998.

Pratt, Dorothy, and Richard Pratt. *A Guide to Early American Homes: South*. New York: Bonanza, 1956.

Preston, Howard I. *Automobile Age Atlanta: The Making of a Southern Metropolis, 1900–1935*. Athens: University of Georgia Press, 1979.

Robert and Company. *Historic Landscape Plan, Andrew Low House, Savannah, Georgia*. Atlanta: Prepared for Andrew Low House, December 2009.

Roberts, Sarah. "Goizueta Gardens at the Atlanta History Center." *Garden Citings: Cherokee Garden Library Newsletter of the Atlanta History Center* (Spring 2015), 8–9.

Roswell Historic Preservation Commission. "Bulloch Hall, Roswell, Georgia: A Master Plan for Restoration, Rehabilitation and Use." Report prepared by the Roswell Historic Preservation Commission, 1984.

Ryan, Jennifer Guthrie, and Hugh Stiles Golson. *Andrew Low and the Sign of the Buck: Trade, Triumph, Tragedy at the House of Low*. Savannah, Ga.: Biel, 2011.

Seabrook, Charles. *The World of the Salt Marsh: Appreciating and Protecting the Tidal Marshes of the Southeastern Atlantic Coast*. Athens: University of Georgia Press, 2013.

Sever, Catherine Elliott. "A Memory of the South." *Atlanta Historical Bulletin* 14, no. 1 (March 1969): 7–22.

Shultz, Gladys Denny, and Daisy Gordon Lawrence. *Lady from Savannah: The Life of Juliette Low*. 1958. Reprint, New York: Girl Scouts of the U.S.A., 1988.

Sieg, Chan. *The Squares: An Introduction to Savannah*. Norfolk, Va.: Donning, 1984.

Smith, Clifford L. *History of Troup County*. Atlanta: Foote and Davies, 1933.

Successful Men of Michigan: A Compilation of Useful Biographical Sketches of Prominent Men. Detroit: Collins, 1914. Available at https://www.hathitrust.org.

Sullivan, Buddy. *Early Days on the Georgia Tidewater: The Story of McIntosh County and Sapelo*. 6th ed. Darien, Ga.: McIntosh County Board of Commissioners, 2001.

———. "The Historic Buildings of Sapelo: A 200-Year Architectural Legacy." *Occasional Papers of the Sapelo Island National Estuarine Research Reserve* 2 (2010): 1–15. Available at www.sapelonerr.org.

———. *Sapelo: A History*. 2nd ed. Darien, Ga.: Sapelo Island Restoration Foundation, 1989.

———. *Sapelo Island*. Images of America. Charleston, S.C.: Arcadia, 2000.

Swanson, Drew A. *Remaking Wormsloe Plantation: The Environmental History of a Lowcountry Landscape*. Athens: University of Georgia Press, 2012.

Tankard, Judith B. "Gardens of Earthly Delights: The Arts & Crafts Garden," *Old-House Journal* (July 2008). Accessed September 1, 2016. www.oldhousejournal.com/gardens_of_earthly_delights/magazine/1523.

———. *Gardens of the Arts and Crafts Movement: Reality and Imagination*. New York: Abrams, 2004.

Toledano, Roulhac. *The National Trust Guide to Savannah*. New York: Wiley and Sons, 1997.

Tunnell, Spencer. "The Restoration of the Boxwood Garden at Swan House." *Land and History* 6, no. 2 (Fall 1996): 10–11.

———. "Stylistic Progression versus Site Planning Methodology: An Analysis of the Residential Architecture of Philip Trammell Shutze." Master's thesis, University of Virginia, 1989.

———. "William C. Pauley, Landscape Architect."

Annual Meeting Proceedings of the American Society of Landscape Architects, 1997, 256–59. Washington, D.C.: American Society of Landscape Architect, 1997.

University of Georgia. Campus Arboretum Committee. *The University of Georgia Campus Arboretum Walking Tour of Trees*. Athens: University of Georgia, ca. 2000.

Van Beck, Sara L., *Daffodils in American Gardens, 1733–1940*. Columbia: University of South Carolina Press, 2015.

Vanstory, Burnette. *Georgia's Land of the Golden Isles*. New ed. Athens: University of Georgia Press, 1981.

Vaux, Calvert, A. J. Downing, Frederick Clarke Withers, and Alexander Anderson. *Villas and Cottages: A Series of Designs Prepared for Execution in the United States*. New York: Harper and Brothers, 1857.

Verey, Rosemary, and Ellen Samuels. *The American Woman's Garden*. Boston: Little, Brown, 1984.

Vlach, John Michael. *Back of the Big House: The Architecture of Plantation Slavery*. Chapel Hill: University of North Carolina Press, 1993.

Way, Albert G. *Conserving Southern Longleaf: Herbert Stoddard and the Rise of Ecological Land Management*. Athens: University of Georgia Press, 2011.

White, Mrs. E. Carl, ed. *Sixty-Year History of the Garden Club of Georgia, Inc*. Athens: Garden Club of Georgia, 1988.

Williams, Robin B., David Gobel, Patrick Haughey, Daves Rossell, and Karl Schuler. *Buildings of Savannah*. Charlottesville: University of Virginia Press, 2016.

Wilson, Thomas D. *The Oglethorpe Plan: Enlightenment Design in Savannah and Beyond*. Charlottesville: University of Virginia Press, 2012.

Wood, Louisa Farrand. *Behind Those Garden Walls in Historic Savannah*. Savannah, Ga.: Historic Savannah Foundation, 1982.

Writers' Program of the Work Projects Administration in the State of Georgia. *Georgia: A Guide to Its Towns and Countryside*. American Guide Series. Athens: University of Georgia Press, 1940.

Manuscript and Visual Arts Collections

Barnsley, Godfrey. Papers. David M. Rubenstein Rare Book and Manuscript Library. Duke University, Durham, N.C.

———. Manuscript collection no. 13. Stuart A. Rose Manuscript, Archives, and Rare Book Library. Emory University, Atlanta.

B. F. A. Saylor Family Papers. MS 63. Hargrett Rare Book and Manuscript Library. University of Georgia Libraries, Athens.

Biltmore Nursery Department Records. Biltmore Estate Archives, Asheville, N.C.

Biodiversity Heritage Library. www.biodiversitylibrary.org.

Bradley, W. C., and B. S. Miller. Plan and drawings, job no. 06797, Olmsted Archives Collection. Frederick Law Olmsted National Historic Site Archives, Brookline, Mass. Digital copies held at the Columbus Museum Archives, Columbus Museum, Columbus, Ga.

Bulloch Hall Site Files. Bulloch Hall Library and Archives, Roswell, Ga.

Callaway Family Papers. MS-009. Troup County Archives, LaGrange, Ga.

Charles Alden Rowland Family Papers. MS 3599. Hargrett Rare Book and Manuscript Library. University of Georgia Libraries, Athens.

Collection of Andrew Low House National Society of the Colonial Dames of America in the State of Georgia. Savannah.

Cothran, James R. Papers. MSS 989. Cherokee Garden Library. Kenan Research Center, Atlanta History Center, Atlanta.

Daugherty, Edward L. Landscape architectural drawings, VIS 207. Cherokee Garden Library. Kenan Research Center, Atlanta History Center, Atlanta.

Daugherty, Edward L. Papers. MSS 997. Cherokee Garden Library. Kenan Research Center, Atlanta History Center, Atlanta.

Draper, Constance Knowles. Papers. MSS 968. Cherokee Garden Library. Kenan Research Center, Atlanta History Center, Atlanta.

Equifax Archives. Equifax, Atlanta.

Frazer Center Archives. Frazer Center, Atlanta.

Georgia Historic Landscape Initiative Records. MSS 1007. Cherokee Garden Library. Kenan Research Center, Atlanta History Center, Atlanta.

Goodman Family Papers. Private collection, Marietta, Ga.

Hentz, Reid and Adler. Architectural drawings. Kenan Research Center, Atlanta History Center, Atlanta.

Historic Images of Athens. Georgia collection, Hargrett Rare Book and Manuscript Library. University of Georgia Libraries, Athens.

Historic Preservation Division. Georgia Department of Natural Resources, Atlanta.

King, Baker, Simpson Families Papers. Roswell Historical Society / City of Roswell Research Library and Archives, Roswell, Ga.

King, Baker, Simpson Families Photographs. Roswell Historical Society / City of Roswell Research Library and Archives, Roswell, Ga.

Kurtz, Wilbur G., Sr. Visual Arts Collection. VIS 197. Kenan Research Center, Atlanta History Center, Atlanta.

Lullwater Garden Club Records. Lullwater Garden Club. Private collection, Atlanta.

Maddox, Robert Foster, Jr. Papers. MSS 143. Kenan Research Center, Atlanta History Center, Atlanta.

Manning, Warren H. Papers. MS 218. Special Collections Department. Iowa State University Library, Ames.

Marietta Museum of History Archives. Marietta Museum of History, Marietta, Ga.

Martha Berry Digital Archive. Berry College, Mount Berry, Ga. http://marthaberry.org.

Minutes of the University of Georgia's Board of Trustees, 1878–1882. Hargrett Rare Book and Manuscript Library. University of Georgia Libraries, Athens.

Norton Family Archives. Private collection, Cartersville, Ga.

Parks and Historic Sites. Historic Preservation Section. Information and Awareness Subject Files. Sapelo Island Collection RG30/4/36. Georgia Archives, Morrow.

Pauley, William C. Architectural Drawings Collection, 0082M. Georgia Archives, Morrow.

Pauley, William C. Landscape architecture drawings. VIS 184. Cherokee Garden Library. Kenan Research Center, Atlanta History Center, Atlanta.

Pauley, William C. Papers. Manuscript collection no. 660. Stuart A. Rose Manuscript, Archives, and Rare Book Library. Emory University, Atlanta.

Peachtree Garden Club Records. MSS 681. Cherokee Garden Library. Kenan Research Center, Atlanta History Center, Atlanta.

Primrose Garden Club Records. MSS 656. Cherokee Garden Library. Kenan Research Center, Atlanta History Center, Atlanta.

Seiferle, Norma K., and Edward J. Papers. MSS 1050. Cherokee Garden Library. Kenan Research Center, Atlanta History Center, Atlanta.

Shutze, Philip Trammell. Papers. MSS 498. Kenan Research Center, Atlanta History Center, Atlanta.

Smith, William T. Landscape architectural drawings. VIS uncatalogued. Cherokee Garden Library. Kenan Research Center, Atlanta History Center, Atlanta.

"Traveling Culture: Circuit Chautauqua in the Twentieth Century." Digital Collection, University of Iowa Libraries, Iowa City. http://digital.lib.uiowa.edu/tc.

Vanishing Georgia Collection. Georgia Archives, Morrow.

Wilder and Anderson Family Papers. Collection no. 01255. Southern Historical Collection. Louis Round Wilson Special Collections Library. University of North Carolina at Chapel Hill.

Zahner, Loyer Lawton. Papers. Edward L. Daugherty private collection, Atlanta.

INDEX